MW01123617

Gender and Allegory in Transamerican Fiction and Performance

Gender and Allegory in Transamerican Fiction and Performance

Katherine Sugg

GENDER AND ALLEGORY IN TRANSAMERICAN FICTION AND PERFORMANCE
Copyright © Katherine Sugg, 2008.

All rights reserved.

First published in 2008 by PALGRAVE MACMILLAN® in the United States -
a division of St. Martin's Press LLC, 175 Fifth Avenue, New York, NY 10010.

Where this book is distributed in the UK, Europe and the rest of the world,
this is by Palgrave Macmillan, a division of Macmillan Publishers Limited,
registered in England, company number 785998, of Houndmills,
Basingstoke, Hampshire RG21 6XS.

Palgrave Macmillan is the global academic imprint of the above companies
and has companies and representatives throughout the world.

Palgrave® and Macmillan® are registered trademarks in the United States,
the United Kingdom, Europe and other countries.

ISBN-13: 978-0-230-60476-6
ISBN-10: 0-230-60476-5

Library of Congress Cataloging-in-Publication Data

Sugg, Katherine.
    Gender and allegory in transamerican fiction and performance / by
Katherine Sugg.
        p. cm.
    Includes bibliographical references and index.
    ISBN 0-230-60476-5 (alk. paper)
    1. American fiction—Minority authors—History and criticism.
    2. American fiction—Hispanic American authors—History and criticism.
    3. American fiction—Women authors—History and criticism.   4. Mexican
literature—Women authors—History and criticism.   5. Caribbean
literature (Spanish)—History and criticism.   6. Minorities in literature.
    7. Group identity in literature.   8. Feminism in literature.   I. Title.

PS153.M56S85 2008
809'.897—dc22   2008007165

A catalogue record of the book is available from the British Library.

Design by Macmillan India Ltd.

First edition: November 2008

10 9 8 7 6 5 4 3 2 1

Printed in the United States of America.

Contents

Preface: Gender and Allegorical Pedagogies in the Americas   vii

Acknowledgments   xvii

1   Cultural Politics in Transamerica: Identity, Narrativity, and
Allegory   1

2   "The Ultimate Rebellion": Political Fictions of Chicana
Sexuality and Community   39

3   Apocalyptic Modernities: Transamerican Allegory,
Revolution, and Indigeneity in *Almanac of the Dead*   67

4   Allegory and Transcultural Ethics: Narrating Difference in
Rosario Castellanos's *Oficio de tinieblas*   101

5   Encrypted Diasporas: Writing, Affect, and the Nation in
Zoé Valdés's *Café Nostalgia*   135

6   Performing Suspended Migrations: Novels and Solo
Performance Art by U.S. Latinas   163

Notes   195

Bibliography   217

Index   229

Preface: Gender and Allegorical Pedagogies in the Americas

The snakes say this: From out of the south the people are coming, like a great river flowing restless with the spirits of the dead who have been reborn again and again all over Africa and the Americas, reborn each generation more fierce and more numerous. Millions will move instinctively; unarmed and unguarded, they begin walking steadily north.

(Almanac of the Dead)

Leslie Marmon Silko's *Almanac of the Dead* imagines a hemispheric revolution that begins in "the South" and moves inexorably northward. Taking a cue from Silko's prophetic remapping of the Americas, *Gender and Allegory in Transamerican Fiction and Performance* works to trace a few key circuits of political desire and vocabulary that traverse the Americas. For example, a vehement critique of neoliberal social formations and political norms has emerged in contemporary Latin America. At more or less the same time, indigenous social movements across the Americas increasingly adopt the rhetoric and human rights paradigms of ethnic identity.[1] These exchanges of social and political languages, ideas, and activism illustrate the "trans" in transamerica. *Gender and Allegory* explores such manifestations of cultural exchange and influence as they appear in aesthetic cultural production, particularly in narrative forms—in the stories that people tell about themselves and to which audiences. As Silko also proclaims, particular stories and images have the power to generate "an immense energy that arouse(s) the living with a fierce passion and determination for justice" (520). *Gender and Allegory* is especially interested in what such stories can teach us, both about local contexts and about the role and status of artistic and political endeavors in transamerica at the beginning of the twenty-first century.

Understanding how narratives travel through the Americas requires a methodology that is able to articulate their pathways across temporal and geocultural borders—preferably without doing too much violence to locally specific narratives, scenarios, and vocabulary in the process. Like many interdisciplinary and transnationally oriented scholars, I often discover my own way into these pathways by tracing common hauntings that link practices, peoples, and regions and suggest patterns of contestation and intensity. Sara Ahmed has said that she likes to "follow words around," and some of what I do here echoes that Foucauldian cultural studies approach. I find remarkable, for instance, the words a woman in the Texas borderlands chooses to express her outrage and exhaustion in dealing with the U.S. Department of Homeland Security, exclaiming, "Ya basta! Enough is enough!"

In January 2008, this protest by Rosie Molano Blount ("Ya basta" roughly translates as "enough already") consciously "cites" the popular slogan from the 1994 Zapatista uprising in Chiapas, Mexico (Norrell). That Blount, an Apache tribal member and U.S. citizen in Del Rio, Texas, has so viscerally absorbed both the revolutionary rhetoric and political lessons of a remote indigenous underclass at the outskirts of southern Mexico suggests circuits and affective links that profoundly intrigue me, and preoccupy this book. Though the protest perhaps says as much about the globalization of media and the commodification of social movements discourse, Blount's outburst also denotes a transnational affiliation in collective resistance to state practices of control and totalitarianism, like those of the U.S. government at the U.S.-Mexico border. In marking the extension of these forms of injustice and state power in U.S. society, as well as the transnational networking of modes of collective resistance, Blount articulates the kind of hemispheric connections that are already being made "on the ground" in the Americas and that I hope to highlight and contextualize for my readers.

I place special importance on the ways that gender operates in such circuits, particularly because the figure of "woman" has so often functioned as an *index* of collective desires and anxieties at any given historical and geocultural site—as the paradigmatic discourse of "La Malinche" so clearly teaches.[2] The figuring of gender in politics, art, and ideology tends to offer a material as well as an epistemological tracking of the flows and recombinations of discourses and ideologies of collectivity and history, both hegemonic and contestatory (Mirzoeff). What can be most illuminating about this tracking are its unexpected flashes of insight and uncomfortable connections. Performance art and theorizations of performativity have further helped shift discussions away from the ruts of positivist identity theories in order to enable alternative modes of thinking about, experiencing, and challenging the status quo of contemporary sociality. Sometimes these challenges require their own optic, or at least a suspended frame of reference, to fully comprehend the multiplicity of ideas, affects, and representations being deployed.

Cultural theorist and performance artist Coco Fusco illustrates how art can provide these new optics in her 2006 performance work, "A Room of One's Own: Women and Power in the New America." In this piece, Fusco fashions a small and succinct artistic grenade that she throws out into liberal politics, exploding customary discussions of identity, technology, the female body, and its cultural work. This performance exemplifies Diana Taylor's notion of a "scenario" that disrupts narrative's linear modes of understanding and historicizing social information and illustrates the radical potential of performance art. "A Room of One's Own" elaborates a harrowing yet sadly plausible occasion in which a female U.S. military personnel (Fusco) appears alone on stage to offer the audience an inspirational speech about the empowering opportunities available to women in "today's military." As her character "The Interrogator" explains to the audience, "The War on Terror offers an unprecedented opportunity to the women of this great country. Our nation is putting its trust in our talents, and is providing the support we need to show the world that American women are the linchpin in the worldwide struggle for democracy" (Fusco 2006).

Among other things, Fusco spotlights the language of feminism, the status of language more generally, and the vulnerability of both to being co-opted into an authoritarian nation-state project of policing and terrorizing certain populations and persons. Staying in character throughout the "lecture-performance," Fusco's Interrogator is a graduate of a military intelligence school and advocate of both the "fight against terrorism" and the use of female military personnel in "de-patterning" detainees through the use of sexual innuendo and threat during interrogations. She explains, "The struggle for democracy is being waged by women plying their trade in rooms just as Woolf imagined. These are simple rooms, furnished with nothing more than a desk and a couple of chairs. And in these sanctorum of liberty, American women are using their minds and their charms to save American lives" (Fusco 2006). Yoking the genealogy of modern feminism to the liberalist discourses of "liberty" and "choice," "A Room of One's Own" simultaneously implicates the uses of gender and sexuality and the language of "American freedom" in projects of interrogation, policing, and torture.

The Interrogator appears on stage along with a video monitor that shows a detainee being prepared for interrogation. Every now and then Fusco interrupts her speech and disappears from the stage, reappearing on the monitor in the cell of the male detainee (actor Eliyas Qureshi). Since questions of sexuality, power, and gender politics are being ironically posed behind the foregrounded language of Western feminism, these scenes are both counterpoint and illustration to the Interrogator's motivational speech. "A Room of One's Own" thus generates a profound discomfort, and confusion, in U.S. audiences who struggle to keep up with the iterations and disjunctions that preoccupy Fusco's project. Simultaneously a critique of Western feminist discourse and of U.S. global hegemony and warmongering, Fusco offers an uncannily appalling, if hilarious, re-presentation of the militarization of public discourse, U.S. global power, and feminism itself.

In its staging of iconic (and ironic) images of gender, of military uniforms, and of surveillance technologies, Fusco's piece signals the complexity of contemporary allegorical modes. As a whole, "A Room of One's Own" combines profoundly unassimilable images and rhetorics to create an allegorical composition that "organizes multiple interpretations regarding collective experience" (Hariman 267). That is, Fusco's performance piece exemplifies the allegorical encoding of an array of visual technologies and emblematic scenarios, such as a podium and a cell and an "infomercial," that saturate a widely shared cultural imaginary. In eschewing narrative explanation and development, "A Room of One's Own" works through an alternative logics that I affiliate with this allegorical mode in writing and performance. Robert Hariman has claimed that we are witnessing a rise in, or return to, allegory "in no small part because it activates a mode of consciousness that is ideally suited to managing contemporary paradoxes of cultural transformation" (289). Of course, this understanding of allegory as paradoxical and affecting consciousness in new ways runs counter to its reputation as a "dogmatic" mode of representation that is often "aligned easily with reactionary rhetoric or ideological hegemony" (Hariman 282).

I suggest that this oscillation in allegory between being a hegemonic or recuperative dogma and a mode conveying the emblematic complexity of juxtaposed scenarios and discourses fulfills an important but underexamined function in aesthetic projects that narrativize identities, particularly gender. And as Bill Brown notes in his seminal essay on allegory, the problem of theory is facing "the unsymbolizable real of history, the global historical process—which we can only approach in its narrativization" (743). To explore how performers and writers have used such narrativizations to challenge audiences and readers and to induce new, or unexpected, affective states, I turn to a variety of textual and performance archives from across the Americas. Chapter 2, for example, examines the cultural production of lesbian Chicanas in the 1980s and 90s, such as Cherríe Moraga, who worked to reclaim the political rhetorics of Chicano cultural nationalism from the jaws of the dominant sexual and racial allegory of *La Malinche*. Other chapters interrogate the function of identity narratives and discourses of "origin" in the performance work of the Def Poets and, in Chapter 6, Carmelita Tropicana. These performers, like several of the writers discussed, tend to bring a distinct (sometimes kitschy or postmodern) sensibility to their emblems and images of race and sex in the Americas—a sensibility that is more likely to disrupt "official" stories than uphold and reiterate them.

One of my underlying claims is that at some undecidable moment in the late twentieth century, "the North," specifically the United States, experienced a paradigm shift—at least at the level of public critical understanding—that political theorists such as Wendy Brown have described as an evacuation of the public spheres of democratic culture. This growing awareness of a fractal break that dislodges the concerted mechanisms of state power and capital from the idealized scripts of our political national imaginary has been experienced as cataclysmic by U.S. intellectuals, particularly since 9/11. However, in Latin America such perceptions and critical awareness took root in intellectual circles and political and aesthetic critiques many decades ago—signaling both an inversion of the standard U.S. version of American temporalities of "North" and "South" and a profound opportunity. Artistic and theoretical insights emerging from actors operating at the supposedly "object" end of processes of globalization manifest a critical pedagogy and narrativity that are perhaps the product of "the South" having fuller access to more explicit and intensified experiences of what Achille Mbembe calls "necropower"—a biopolitics of capital and state control that has long been fully operational in the United States, though only intermittently perceived.[3]

This recently perceived paradigm shift, though, isn't the only catalyst for the comparative archive and methodology of *Gender and Allegory*. Both in its faith in aesthetic projects and in the specific work of key multigeneric artists such as the Chilean Diamela Eltit, Latin American literary and artistic practices offer productive and enabling models for the comprehension and consumption of cultural production in literature and performance. In a review essay, "Comparative Literary Studies of the Americas," Claire Fox calls for more "Latin American material to be incorporated into . . . comparative studies, for it might shed light on how the American Dream and its political realities interact with Latin American national imaginaries that also exert pressure on U.S.–based Latina (o) populations" (880). I agree with Fox but think that these interactions and pressures extend deep into U.S. national imaginaries in ways that cannot be limited to Latina/o contexts, though these contexts are certainly an important circuit of both political and aesthetic transamerican transmissions. *Gender and Allegory* addresses the imperative to consider the interrelationships and intersections of national imaginaries in the Americas and the consensus that transnational archives and methodologies are needed to broaden the scope, and critique the foundations, of concepts of "America" and "American studies." "Look to the South," Silko admonishes, and I have tried to comply.

One place I have looked and found much to inform and support this project has been the distinct character of Latin American discussions of aesthetics, particularly in the work of Chilean critic and editor Nelly Richard, who founded the influential journal *Revista de crítica cultural* [Journal of Cultural Critique]. For over 30 years, Richard and a cohort of artists, critics, and philosophers have used that platform to insist on the power of aesthetic cultural production to challenge, and even remake, social formations at the popular level. These projects mobilize against "the linguistic tyranny of the simple, direct, and transparent discourse characterizing today's social communications" that reflects a bankrupting of narrative and of language in the interests of a transparent economy of commodification (Richard, quoted in Nelson and Tandeciarz, xv). As Richard notes elsewhere, this critique resonates powerfully with the fraught musings of Walter Benjamin in the face of fascism's rise in the Europe of the 1920s and indicates one of the links between allegory, melancholy, and periods of social transformation and upheaval *(The Insubordination of Signs)*.

Reading aesthetic and political projects together demands a precise attention to narrative and to the role of the aesthetic in discursive disruptions of political and public spheres, as well as their upholding. *Gender and Allegory* joins these critical efforts to comprehend the dynamics of these spheres and resonates in particular with concepts such as the "New World Baroque." Reinvigorated recently by scholars such as Mabel Moraña, Monika Kaup, and Lois Parkinson Zamora, the Baroque has long been considered a hemispheric rubric of aesthetic and cultural analysis. As Moraña explains, the notion of a baroque tradition in the Americas overcomes "restrictive models such as those of identity, culture, or the *national* literary canon (. . . that is, as a migrant, totalizing, and transnationalized model of symbolic representation)" (246). My focus on allegorical aesthetic strategies that rely on excess, iconic imagery, and nonmimetic thematics and plotlines in works by artists such as Silko (Chapter 3) and the Cuban writer Zoé Valdés (Chapter 5) are likely to resonate with those interested in these reappropriations of the Baroque to contemporary uses. And indeed the shared genealogies that bind the historical period of the Baroque and the allegorical mode are a central focus of Benjamin's own discussions in his classic work on allegory, *The Origins of Tragic German Drama*.

The coincidence of allegory's aesthetic form and its impact in various publics, what I call its *narrativity*, has been productively analyzed by Latin Americanists, including Richard and Idelbar Avelar, and others working on relations of affect and narrative. Vilashini Coopan notes the importance of fiction that works against the conventions of the novel, particularly "the notion of a mimetic compact between the nation and the novel form" in order to achieve a kind of "emblematization of national loss" (255). Such a description of an antinovelistic aesthetics—an aesthetics that is uncannily baroque and allegorical in its emphasis on the emblem—further underlines analogous similarities between allegory and postmodern cultural production. As Deborah Madsen also observes, "allegory engages in a dialectic, moving between contradictory desires for stability and disruption" and this "necessary balance between oppression and liberation [is what] Benjamin prescribes as demystification" (125). Like Benjamin and his many admirers, I too turn to allegory for its "dialectical" abilities to articulate, though often in unfamiliar pictures and scenarios, the political and historical meanings embedded in aesthetic modes.

Recalling Gayatri Spivak's "Can the Subaltern Speak?" Mexican cultural theorist Marisa Belausteguigoitia describes this knot of simultaneously political and aesthetic questions, the need "for *the right story.*" Following on Belausteguigoitia's work on the representational tactics of indigenous and disenfranchised women at the borders of the Mexican nation, one of the implicit questions *Gender and Allegory* asks is how this "right" story is recognizable, and to whom?

A key element of allegory is its explicit attention to the question of audiences and their multiple and indeterminate character. Like irony, which I also explore in detail, allegory is a communicative mode that necessarily produces an array of "insiders" and "outsiders"—of those who recognize and understand the allegorical encoding and those for whom that code and its referents are not intelligible. This element of differentiation and its emphasis on local knowledge is another aspect that makes the allegorical mode particularly useful politically and comparatively: allegories travel across time and place, but are only decipherable to those who know or have taken the trouble to learn the histories and traditions that inform them.

Because I argue for a particular and uneasy relationship to the concept and use of "identity" as it has been handed down in a liberal Euro-American tradition, the question of what to do and how to do it emerges as pressing for both artists and their audiences interested in significant changes in the social orders of the Americas. *Gender and Allegory* suggests that politically motivated cultural production has proven itself to be a mixed endeavor, but one that remains deeply meaningful and effective in various ways. My attention to performance as a genre and medium that operates easily at this crossroads of public cultures and aesthetic practices follows the contributions of theorists such as Diana Taylor and José Muñoz.

Taylor's influential work on performance across the Americas has asserted that the performative mode works against the predetermined expectations (for discrete and nameable identities, for example) that are generated in narrative, thus allowing for the "transmission" of cultural memory rather than the representation of identity through the logics of Western epistemology *(The Archive and the Repertoire)*. Likewise, theorists of performance and affect such as Amy Villarejo have also announced a transition away from writing and the identitarian logics of representation to what has called she, and others, call a "politics of affect."

However, although *Gender and Allegory* shares this interest in an "epochal" transition in public cultures toward the alternative logics of affect and away from the politics of identity and its logics of naming and recognition, I also suggest that some of these announcements are in some senses premature. That is, I want to both acknowledge and caution that this study is focused on a particular archive that involves a distinct temporality and articulation of public processes. Much of this book attends to the (increasingly archaic) logics of writing and reading. The "texts" I discuss, including literature and other cultural production such as solo performance art, often occupy a territory somewhere between the familiar, even clichéd, and the new. I argue that this mix of temporalities, as well as logics, is in fact necessary and constitutive to their cultural work and their impact. Rather than insisting on the radicality of "new" identity formations or, conversely, on the bankruptcy of "identity" itself as a lived experience and category, *Gender and Allegory* explores specific manifestations of the rhetorics of identity and difference in contemporary cultural production from around the Americas. Given that the figuring of gender is among the most intransigent rhetorics in public cultures, I attend in particular to projects that deploy the allegories of gender and "the nation," as well as those that try to dislodge such stultifying scripts in order to pressure the links between gender and collectivity, and narrative and allegory, in other directions, and toward other futures.

In Chapter 1, "Cultural Politics in Transamerica: Identity, Narrativity, and Allegory," I establish the theoretical and disciplinary framework of the book by exploring the possible relations between aesthetic forms and public spheres, especially as they relate to the disciplines of U.S. ethnic studies and Latin American cultural criticism. This chapter takes the genre of spoken-word poetry and the cross-media phenomena of HBO's *Def Poetry Jam* as its starting point and then traces the links between stereotype, allegory, irony, and the politics and performativity of minority cultural production in the contemporary United States. Exploring the debates on the uses of allegory in literary representation in the contexts of minority literature in the late twentieth century, I show how allegory uncannily reenacts the dynamic of oscillation between normative prescription and a liberatory agency found embedded in the terms of minority identity itself. Allegory, therefore, becomes a key site for negotiating competing interpretations of both specific minority texts and the status of minority expressions, political and aesthetic.

Chapter 2, "'The Ultimate Rebellion': Political Fictions of Chicana Sexuality and Community," turns to the play of cultural, racial, and sexual identities and various genealogies of belonging in Chicana feminist discourses and considers the retrenchments of their appeals to "blood" and "territory" as the basis of political and affective definitions of identity in texts such as Cherríe Moraga's "Queer Aztlán" and Terri de la Peña's *Margins*. In close readings of Chicana literature, memoir, and cultural theory from the 1980s and 1990s that trace the allegories of identity persisting within Chicana/o activist narratives, I ask why the heteropatriarchal foundations of collective identifications so often remained intact after decades of feminist, queer, and poststructuralist critique. The answer involves both the legacies of liberalism lodged in particular minority political fictions and the structures of narrative itself when negotiating a complexity of appeals to identity scripts and "national allegories."

Chapter 3, "Apocalyptic Modernities: Transamerican Allegory, Revolution, and Indigeneity in Leslie Marmon Silko's *Almanac of the Dead*," theorizes an allegorical mode in transamerican poetics that is distinct from the allegories of gender and nation that bind the Chicana poetics and politics of Chapter 2. *Almanac of the Dead* is a work whose generic instability has become central to the criticism surrounding it; as Silko says, "It's not quite realism." I argue that the overlapping of modes in *Almanac of the Dead* requires alternative reading practices that are explicitly antimimetic and nonidentitarian. In its break with representational logic, allegory emerges as a particularly apt mode for the expression of a "perceived world structure" (Bill Brown) that is impossible to narrate or signify in the sequential logic of modernist narrative realism, but makes sense as allegory. Understanding this paradoxical turn to allegory as both a narrative pedagogy and a reflection of emerging technologies of selfhood, this chapter emphasizes the relation between Silko's narrative modes and the necropolitical landscape she re-presents.

Chapter 4, "Allegory and Transcultural Ethics: Narrating Difference in Rosario Castellanos's *Oficio de tinieblas* (*The Book of Lamentations*)," continues this exploration of allegorical epic writing by considering Castellanos's midcentury revision of *indigenismo*, the foundational Latin American genre of cultural reconciliation in which a mestizo or European-identified writer defends indigenous culture. Recalling *Almanac*, *Oficio's* epic tale of Mexican national culture and conflict offers an allegory of the function and history of indigenous peoples and cultural differences in the Americas to explicate an apocalyptic vision of transamerican pasts and futures. And yet both texts also deploy key scenarios of allegorical storytelling to signal the leap out of the apocalypse narrative, or at least the possibility of another story, and another, less bleak, future—this leap being the quintessential allegorical move according to Benjamin. In *Oficio*, the minute attention to storytelling as an expression of cross-cultural intimacies makes narrative a technology of both transcultural hybridity and dangerous power hierarchies, paradoxically suggesting literature's ethical possibilities without glossing over the violence of these translations.

Chapter 5, "Encrypted Diasporas: Writing, Affect, and the Nation in Zoé Valdés's *Café Nostalgia*," continues this emphasis on writing and its complexities in a reading of Paris-based Cuban writer Zoé Valdés. Valdés's Spanish-language Caribbean oeuvre offers a distinct perspective on the flow of both political discourses and aesthetic strategies across and within diasporic formations of the Hispanic Caribbean. Reading Valdés's narrative "encryption" of a personal melancholy and narcissism as the remains of national loss, I underline the slippery politics of irony in suspended narrative modes and explore the function of the "nostalgia" that preoccupies Valdés's figuring of the Cuban condition.

Chapter 6, "Performing Suspended Migrations: Novels and Solo Performance Art by U.S. Latinas," continues with these questions of genre and geopolitics by looking at the transamerican narrative pedagogies at work in U.S.-based texts by the novelists Achy Obejas and Julia Alvarez and the performance artist Carmelita Tropicana. In reading allegorically these women's narrativizations of personal, familial, and national migrations, this chapter simultaneously emphasizes several forms of comparative geopoetics. These works by Obejas, Alvarez, and Tropicana all interrogate the uses of memory in hyperbolically gendered projects of collective cohesion, which prove both seductive and dangerous to these female "daughter" figures in distinct but comparable ways. Comparing popular novels and the parodic register of Tropicana's performance, this final chapter works to illuminate the intersections of aesthetics and geocultural contexts in the production of public spheres and audiences. In particular, these comparisons highlight the distinct logics at work in Tropicana's appropriation of both the images of "Cubana dyke camp" and the melodramatic plotlines of return and reconciliation. Through these comparisons across genres, languages, and political discourses, *Gender and Allegory* explores the differential effects of specific geopoetics and offers a comparative perspective on transamerican aesthetic practices.

Acknowledgments

I wish to express my gratitude to my early mentors, especially Michael Palencia-Roth for the vision and training that led me to comparative studies of the Americas and to Norma Alarcón for the rigorous intellectual generosity and passion with which she has shaped an entire generation of activist-scholars, including me. Others whose work and example have provided the models and intellectual foundations that led to this project, in direct and indirect ways, are Inderpal Grewal, Caren Kaplan, Elizabeth Freeman, Nancy Blake, May Joseph, Minoo Moallem, Rey Chow, María Josefina Saldaña-Portillo, James Phelan, Silvia Spitta, Larry La Fountain-Stokes, José Muñoz, Juana María Rodriguez, Janet Smarr, Carmelita Tropicana, Ricardo Ortiz, Neil Larsen, Djelal Kadir, Román de la Campa, Lois Parkinson Zamora, Doris Sommer, and Mary Louise Pratt.

Central Connecticut State University has provided generous support, particularly from Dean Susan Pease and the School of Arts and Sciences and the English Department. I feel fortunate to have landed in this warm and enriching environment and among colleagues and friends such as Candace Barrington, Burlin Barr, David Cappella, Steve Cohen, Robert Dowling, Gil Gigliotti, Beverly Johnson, Jason Jones, Eric Leonidas, Laurence Petit, Mary Anne Nunn, Aimee Pozorski, and Ravi Shankar, and for the interdisciplinary community offered by my Latin American Studies colleagues, including Antonio García-Lozada, Mary Ann Mahony, Cynthia Pope, and Robert Wolff. I am also grateful for the welcome and intellectual community I have found at the Humanities Institute Faculty Seminar on the Transmission of Cultures at Stony Brook University. I owe particular thanks to Ann Kaplan for her leadership at the Institute and her generosity as a colleague and collaborator. And thanks to the many other colleagues and friends I've found at Stony Brook, including Adrián Pérez-Melgosa, Shirley Lim, Daniela Flesler, Celia Marshik, David Anshen, Matt Christensen, Troy Rasbury, Bill Holt, and, most especially, Peter Manning.

I also want to thank my students at Central Connecticut State and before that at Stony Brook University, the University of California, Davis, and San Francisco State University; their generative and enthusiastic engagement with this material was one of its key foundations. In presentations at the

Universidad nacional autónoma de México (UNAM) in Mexico City, I was encouraged to think critically about both "transamerican studies" and to appreciate more fully the possibilities offered by allegory. For these experiences, I am grateful to Marisa Belausteguigoitia, Director of the Programa universitaria de género (PUEG), as well as Julia Constantino, Nattie Golubuv, Lucía Melgar, Irene Artigas, and Claudia Lucotti. Any weaknesses of argument or clarity found here occur in spite of the efforts of many generous and insightful readers: Celia Marshik, Pramila Ventakawaran, Riché Richardson, Elizabeth Freeman, Carine Mardorossian, Jasbir Puar, Susan Scheckel—and most especially Jane Elliott and Adrián Pérez-Melgosa. Heartfelt thanks as well to Heather Gilligan for expert and timely editorial work and to John Beule for the index.

I am grateful to the editors at Palgrave Macmillan who found the project interesting and helped push it to conclusion, as well as to Indiana University Press and Pion Publishing for allowing me to use material from earlier versions of chapters 2 and 6 that appeared in *Meridians: Feminism, Race, Transnationalism* 3.2 (2003): 139–70, and *Environment and Planning-D: Society and Space* 21 (2003): 461–77. I would also like to thank the Patricia Correa Gallery of Santa Monica, CA, for the use of Delilah Montoya's wonderful photograph, "*La Malinche*," as the book's cover image.

I have been sustained, personally and intellectually, by several individuals. My friendship with Marisa Belausteguigoitia has been a profound resource, particularly her innumerable insights into the practice of life, politics, and intellectual work. I am also indebted to Jasbir Puar—our winding excursions through urban and emotional landscapes and her critical contributions to cultural theory have all fed this project at key junctures. I hold especially dear the support and illumination provided by Jane Elliott; it's a long road we've traveled together and this book is only one of many testaments to what I've gained from it. I've also learned a lot about life and books from Brad Hebel. Closer to home, I treasure the friendship of Susan Scheckel whose feedback on the manuscript urged it forward and whose companionship, along with Peter's and Elizabeth's, have enriched my life in innumerable ways.

My parents, Donna and Calvin Sugg, and my brother Ike have influenced this project in more ways than they know and I thank them for their love and support through the many years of hard-to-explain endeavors. I am also deeply grateful for the intelligence, clarity, and generosity Terry Weiland brings to her care for my children. Finally, I offer humble thanks to Brian Phillips, whose love and commitment to our life together have expanded in amazing ways. And in the end, I find I really do have to dedicate the whole book to our three children, Thomas, Sarah, and Patrick, because they continue to teach me the meaning, and importance, of joy.

I

Cultural Politics in Transamerica: Identity, Narrativity, and Allegory

I. Performing Identities with *Def Poetry Jam*

During performances on HBO and in the Broadway production *Russell Simmons Def Poetry Jam,* the Oklahoma-born-and-bred poet Beau Sia warns audiences, "You're not shutting me up until the egg roll is recognized as an American food" (100). Sia gets a good laugh at this line, which appeals through both an aggressive insistence and a kind of wry charm. This rather soft-core challenge implicates not only the audience, but also Sia himself in *Def Poetry Jam's* mainstreaming of poetry slams. While promoting the predominantly youth-of-color artists of the poetry slam circuit has provided a crucial venue of expression for this community, *Def Poetry Jam* might also be said to participate in the reshaping of minority identities as market commodities.

I call this a paradox of "suspended selves," meaning that while many minority artistic and cultural productions continue to build on and deploy identities, these cultural productions often push back, critique, and question specific identities, as well as the category of identity itself. Increasingly, the political and social formations that generated the explosion of politicized identities at the end of the twentieth century are understood as defunct, archaic, and bankrupt in cultural and political theory. Therefore, the invocation of identity politics conjures a bygone era of a totalized and coherent civil rights politics based on notions such as cultural and racial origin, tradition, authenticity, opposition, and purity and also signals a discursive, political, and affective entrapment in this modernist myth of group coherence. In his own criticism of the uses of identity and the racialized body, Mark Hansen notes that "the raced image can no longer broker processes of identity formation and struggles for social recognition, and in effect, remains in force solely as an instrument of social techniques for identification and exclusion" (126).

Cutting to the heart of key questions concerning the relations between identity, representation, and politics, Hansen's quote highlights the difficulties faced by efforts to devise more productive, as opposed to reductive, ways of reading minority representation, and especially self-representation, in writing and performance. And although this harsh judgment echoes several of the political and cultural critiques I will quote below (Wendy Brown, Rey Chow, Jasbir Puar, etc.), *Gender and Allegory* takes as its focus the very persistence of these discourses of identity, self, and collectivity within artistic production. In analyzing and tracing this persistence, my book works to theorize more precisely relations between the aesthetics and cultural politics inscribed within this "profound paradox of our contemporary moment" (Hansen 126). For example, even as the Def Poets continue to build on and deploy identity scripts that emerged between 1965 and the late 1990s, the show itself and the poets' individual performances reflect an awareness of the deeply compromised status of the "raced" (as well as "gendered," "national," "ethnic," etc.) image. While utilizing the persistent power and perceived validity of identity logics, these performative texts suggest an ironic distance that *suspends* those logics and images as objects of critique, even within their deployment.

That is, while staging the persistence of certain categories of identity in U.S. progressive cultural politics, *Def Poetry Jam* also exemplifies a particular and productive oscillation in such performances. This oscillation repeatedly swings from a rather predictable display of a multicultural celebratory politics of minority identities to the undoing of precisely those politics through ironic performative citations. These citations puncture and interrogate racial and ethnic stereotypes even as the individual poet is deploying them through her body and words. In this oscillation, *Def Poetry Jam* marks a suspension between the "politics of identity" (increasingly the scourge of critical cultural studies) and the hope for a radical political and social transformation that is effected through aesthetics or culture.

This turn in discussions of identity politics aimed at liberal audiences signals important changes in the logic of identity thinking, particularly in this contemporary era of the transnationalization of the Americas. Examining the complex cultural work done by *Def Poetry Jam* and several other key narrative and performance projects of the late twentieth century, *Gender and Allegory* considers such ironic stereotypes as part of an allegorical turn in minority cultural production. While my goal is to understand more critically the relations between aesthetics and politics, the question of what, or even whether, aesthetics and politics intersect at all in contemporary society has emerged as a central concern among activists and academics of all stripes, as well as among artists and critics working inside and outside the academy. Because allegory is often considered a "reductive" and even "regressive" narrative mode, it is particularly interesting to note its growing role in cultural production, especially in minority expression, across the Americas.[1]

Most current discussions of allegorical writing and reading draw upon the controversies generated by Fredric Jameson's 1986 essay "Third World Literature in the Era of Multinational Capitalism" and his reverberating assertion that all Third World narratives are "necessarily . . . national allegories" (69). As Shu-Mei Shih suggests, Jameson's statement became "its own prophecy" as academic critics and other readers found it applicable (or not) and as ethnic and Third World writers and artists fit their work into, or even produced work for, whichever rubric of "national allegory" that gained currency in their community and in the marketplace. This aspect of allegorical reading signals its complicity with the forces of both global capitalism and colonial and neocolonial discourse, particularly because here, allegory functions as a reductive, reifying mode of signification: "In other words, allegory works and sells because it makes the non-Western text manageable, decipherable, and thus answerable to Western sensibilities and expectations (sometimes even by way of the non-Western text's inscrutability)" (Shih 21). Other theorists of allegory such as James Clifford and Doris Sommer concur that narrative production, which responds to and feeds the liberal desires of Euro-American modernity, often works through allegories that help an "us" to resolve or cover over conflicts of power and interest with a "them".[2] In this characterization, allegory produces a manageable and commodifiable narrative whose appeal to, and participation in, powerful structures of feeling makes it easily consumed and disseminated for a variety of audiences and markets, both mainstream and minority.

Here, allegory and "the raced image" join with the stereotype to occupy a paradoxical space of signification in which their complicity in particular (liberalist and surreptitiously dominant) "structures of feeling" meets with other possibilities opened by re-reading the work of media, narrative, and performativity. Raymond Williams introduces the notion of "structures of feeling" in *Marxism and Literature* in order to analyze and consider seriously "the experiences to which the fixed forms [of social analysis and categorization] do not speak at all, which indeed they do not recognize" (130). One reason this concept has been so influential in cultural theory is Williams' insistence on the historical and contextual specificity of any given "structure of feeling" as it arises, particularly in art and literature: "what we are defining is a particular quality of social experience and relationship, distinct from other particular qualities, which gives the sense of a generation or a period" (131). The question that drives *Gender and Allegory* returns to this foundational interpenetration of the social and the historical in Williams's concept of "affect" to ask whether narrativizations must always reproduce and confirm the structures of feeling of a particular context and historical moment—which in the context of this investigation would be to reproduce the liberalist scripts of Euro-American modernity and identity? One possible response raised in these readings is that the re-eruption of allegorical modes of narrative and image representation express and push readers, spectators, and audiences toward alternative understandings and experiences of the social.[3] The process of "reading" a figure that offers itself for a multiplicity of significations within intersecting cognitive maps of the social illustrates the paradoxical operations of allegory through narrativitiy. In Leslie Marmon Silko's *Almanac of the Dead*, for example, it is the very extremity of her Manichean vision of a transamerican apocalypse that pushes readers into revised understandings of narrative—of plot, character, causality, and chronology—as well as of history, race, capitalism, and violence. In either pushing or slipping through the "predetermined signifieds" (Shih) that readers bring to these texts, allegory can demonstrate the power of narrative tactics to "suspend" such categories and schemas—through irony, but also through hyperbole. However, such slippery genres and aesthetic forms run the risk of also passing unnoticed through the public sphere, in which literature and aesthetics are generally seen as increasingly irrelevant and anachronistic. I argue that the recent turn to allegory reflects artistic and critical efforts to both play on and work through a recognizable politics of identity and its logics of representation—discourses that are more able to "stick" in the public sphere, to use Sara Ahmed's phrase—while deploying ironic performativities and baroque narrative manipulations to induce a critical shift in perceptions, emotions, and reading practices.[4]

In this interrogation of reading habits and the meanings they produce, I am particularly interested in the role of genre, as well as media, in generating specific narrativities at specific geohistorical junctures. The Foucauldian concept of "technologies of the self" has been linked to notions of narrativity, for example, in considerations of the novel as the literary form that best reflects, and helped to shape, the bourgeois, modern subject during the eighteenth and nineteenth centuries.[5] Likewise, contemporary forms of media as well as the distinctions between writing genres (theory, novel, autobiography, poetry, and play, among others) can all be analyzed for their capacities to simultaneously mirror and produce the forms of selfhood adequate to a particular epoch and social context. For similar reasons, Walter Benjamin emphasized the crises of faith and worldview in seventeenth-century Europe that fed and sustained the Baroque preference for emblem-books and other allegorical genres over the classical artistic forms of the Renaissance. In exploring and explaining the seventeenth-century Baroque turn to allegory, Benjamin notes its distinction from the symbol, which became the eighteenth- and nineteenth-century Romantics' aesthetic mode of choice. In contrast to the momentary illumination of the symbol, allegory relies on a distinct temporal and dialectical logics that roots allegory in specific slices of history (what often seems to "date" allegorical cultural production from other eras). That is, Benjamin insists that allegory is its own "form of expression, just as speech is expression, and indeed, just as writing is"; which is why, he explains, critics of allegory miss its significance if they do not consider its native media, "the literary and visual emblem-books of the baroque" (162). As Jameson notes and my later discussions will demonstrate, a distinct mode of allegorical expression can be said to have emerged toward the end of the twentieth century that appears in narrative form and is deployed to respond to and account for aspects of our own historical crisis moment. I suggest that these late modern "crises" include identity differentiation and conflict, popularly known as multiculturalism. The surprisingly reifying impact of identity discourses in public spheres have nevertheless generated narratives that—even in this so-called post-identitarian moment—benefit from a sustained attention to their specific logics and effects.

The reemergence of allegory at the end of the twentieth century and beginning of the twenty-first century and its deployment to explore minority identity positions have been noted by a number of Latin American cultural critics, artists, and writers. These critics, such as Nelly Richard and Idelbar Avelar, consider allegory to be especially useful in writing against the commodifying operations of late capitalism and globalization. Drawing upon the work of Benjamin, this influential school of Latin American cultural critique has developed its theory of allegory as a mode of representation that can manifest the relationship between history and writing in ways that are especially pertinent to the contemporary moment in the Americas.[6] This Latin American understanding of allegory almost directly contradicts its reputation in the United States as facile and reductive, thus indicating an important intersection, and divergence, in how genres and narratives operate and circulate around the Americas and the globe. Following these critical signposts, I argue that a hemispheric entity that can be called "Transamerica" is linked by circuits of cultural production (such as a turn toward allegory and performance). However, significant differences in transmission, circulation, and interpretation of this cultural production point to the need to consider comparative and distinct approaches to "reading allegorically" in the Americas.[7]

In considering allegorical narrativities of identity on a transnational scale, my analysis allows a more sustained investigation into specific minority narratives and the various reading practices we bring to them. For example, certain works aimed at radical social transformation, such as *Almanac of the Dead,* inscribe a narrative pedagogy of allegory. Silko provides a powerful vehicle for learning to think, that is, to *read,* outside the binaries of identity, even as those binaries are pushed to their extremes. As I argue below, these moments of ironic or excessive exaggeration implicate allegorical representations in critical discussions of the stereotype by Chow, and by Jameson too. The poets of *Def Poetry Jam* are known to perform their own ethnic stereotypes in ways that are simultaneously *against* and *in the grain* of their predetermined signifieds. In season five of the HBO series, for example, Willie Perdomo performs his poem "Nigger-Reecan Blues" as a scenario that conveys an almost impossible embodiment of Puerto Rican racial and cultural contradictions and negotiations. Through a litany of multiple voices, languages, and accents, the "I" in this poem articulates the self's questioning of his own body's racial-national-ethnic ontologies while also being the voice of uncomprehending by-standers, all of whom are figured as "types" in Perdomo's performance of distinct accents and tonal modulations. The African American elderly man ("I tell you that boy is colored") confronts the street slang of Spanish-speaking youth until all meld into a litany of "spicspicspicspic" that is explicitly framed as an assault on the poet-speaker's confusedly "black" body. Until finally who, as the previously uncomprehending African American southern gentlemen notes, "Y'all let that boy alone. Can't you see he's got the nigger-reecan blues?"

I suggest that by pushing Manichean allegories of identity to an extreme—to the moment of linguistic and symbolic rupture—contemporary minority allegories of race, ethnicity, and gender can produce an excess that moves the reader into another kind of logic, one that subverts those binaries while still reiterating the persistent traces of the colonial, racist, and violent histories that make them possible. In a sense, one can say that just as allegory is foundationally linked to the development of myth, identity constitutes the mythos of contemporary social formations in the Americas. As a narrative mode, identity allegories draw upon the embedded character of myth and cultural differences. Allegory thus presupposes, or posits, a collectivity to which such myths refer, that is, a collectivity constituted through its embrace of particular allegories. Shih explicates this understanding of allegory's logic in her analysis of the contemporary international literary market in Third World allegory. Understanding identity as collective binding emphasizes its tendency to cohere around dominant ideologies of difference, which in turn resonates with Chow's critique of "culturalism." In contrast with Shih's negative reading of allegory as complicit in the commodification of minority literatures and minority selves, the Latin American school of "cultural critique" tends to read allegory as a testament to the fragmentations and discontinuities of modernity (and postmodernity). Avelar and Richard, for example, claim that allegory actually challenges the totalizing work of official mythic narratives. These contradictions indicate the troubled status of allegory in contemporary literary and cultural criticism, but they also suggest allegory's productive capacity as a wedge in deciphering the way certain writers attempt to resuture the "lost" relations between individuals, collectivities, and the violent histories of modernity, especially the colonial, neoimperial, and necropolitical modernities of the Americas.

II. Ironic Distancing and the Stereotype

As I mention above, contemporary allegorical figuring owes much to the operations of the stereotype and its centrality to our understanding of the politics of representation in minority cultural production. *Def Poetry Jam* offers a key example of an emergent form of performativity that simultaneously deploys the stereotype while also performing an ironic distancing that moves the narrative(s) of racialized and gendered identities into other, less scripted and less predictable, directions. Its repackaging as a book, *Russell Simmons Def Poetry Jam on Broadway . . . and More* (2003), highlights the tension between what I am calling ironic performance in *Def Poetry Jam* and its pedagogical intentions and thematic repertoire, which are largely based on liberal notions of multiculturalism as "ethnic diversity." Discussing the Broadway production, producer Stan Lathan comments in his notes that "I tried to pick the best writers and performers from varied backgrounds" (xii). In seeking out a scripted array of "varied backgrounds," Lathan indicates the pedagogical goal of *Def Poetry Jam* to be an expression and illustration of a predetermined understanding of what constitutes minority persons and representations. *Gender and Allegory* interrogates the slippery cultural work of, and collective ideas about, such "minority" collectivities and cultural productions—particularly those marked by discourses of racialization, sexual difference, and national otherness. Minority texts in writing, performance, film, and visual art have been celebrated over the last 20 years or so for their potential intervention in discourses and narratives of nation formation and collective identity. But the production and consumption of *Def Poetry Jam* as a cable television and DVD series, publishing enterprise, and Broadway show illustrate the complexity of these moves to both represent and reshape collectivities and particular discourses of identity in the Americas.

In their very effort to be transformative, these various media enterprises and their different audiences articulate key paradoxes of performance and identity.

Gender and Allegory thus signals the resilience of a politics of identity that persists within narrative practices aimed at the transformation of social formations. I question, however, to what extent can we say that shifts in such practices operate through a "new" transformative poetics and politics. Do performances or texts that eschew the archaic modalities (usually binary and identitarian) of a long-gone civil rights world and move toward new political modalities better reflect and shape the social formations of the twenty-first century? In relation to such questions, *Def Poetry Jam* illustrates—particularly as a multimedia phenomenon—the ongoing performative function of identity discourses within the paradoxical work of contemporary minority cultural production.[8] Like the Def Poets themselves, *Gender and Allegory* revisits this space of contradiction and paradox—of suspension—that has persistently haunted efforts to theorize an aesthetics of social change that can slip the binaries, and therefore the totalizing system, of identity-based thinking. I also seek to challenge the tenacious drag exerted by binary paradigms of ideological complicity versus liberatory agency within the efforts to understand minority cultural production as doing something else, something transformative and resistant to the operations of identity discourses in late capitalist social formations.

That both artists and critics alike seem unable to elude this insistent haunting by the trap of identities as grounded in a complicit liberal cultural logic actually signals an important function of identity in contemporary cultural and aesthetic logics. These logics emerge as we attend more closely to processes of suspension and the aesthetic operations of irony, performance, narrativity, and allegory that articulate them. For instance, in his poem "Love" Sia mocks his adolescent narcissism as well as the racialized, sexual scripts that cling to him. Beginning with the plea, "Women who hear this / Fall in love with me!" (Simmons 70), he wryly moves toward a conclusion: "But you don't want to / understand me / you just want to hear the part about / my small dick again" (72). Sia's autobiographical meditations on Asian American manhood meld ironic dissonance into expressions of longing and outrage, which he offers as both uniquely personal and insistently collective. Sia uses the affective registers of autobiographical self-representation to both resonate with and represent against the racialized stereotypes of Asian masculinity that he simultaneously critiques and sardonically embodies, wearing a very fuzzy pink sweater when performing on the television show. Communicating the intersection of race and gender through his embodied performance of both, Sia invites the audience to laugh at him—and with him, at themselves.

Such ironic invocations of identity narratives signal a binding function for identity scripts, or what Diana Taylor might call "scenarios," even as particular performances work against the very logic of identity.[9] *Def Poetry Jam*—particularly its production and consumption as a cable TV and Broadway product—succinctly manifests the constraints on marketed aesthetic forms that rely on an identificatory effect/affect relation with their audience. At the same time, the traces of its circulation indicate new possibilities and shifts in collective affect, such as those that the Def Poets often produce in their audiences, which have the potential to generate new publics and new politics.[10] *Def Poetry Jam* has carved out a multimedia space for minority artists and opinions, particularly the worldviews and expressions of both artists and audiences of color. Intentionally or not, *Def Poetry Jam* also demonstrates the instrumentality of identity discourses by showcasing the performance of a racialized celebrity that cuts both ways. However, one can also interpret this multimedia phenomenon as exemplifying the cultural work of media as a producer of "affect" that operates through an "assemblage" of collectivities and technologies, rather than discrete minority identities and images.[11] In highlighting the tension between pandering to audiences saturated in a dominant celebrity-media rich environment and generating alternative publics through the technologies of television and Broadway, the show underscores the complexity of its negotiation of contradictory genres, subcultures, and aesthetic and media logics.

Like the other "texts" analyzed in this book, *Def Poetry Jam* is explicitly and self-consciously engaged with political and cultural questions surrounding minority identities and experience, especially in regard to issues of social justice, stereotyping, and the discourses of racialization and sexual normativities. When Simmons's book jacket announces that the cultural work of *Def Poetry Jam* allows its audiences to take a "fresh, exuberant, sometimes insightful, sometimes comedic look at who we are and where we are today," it is announcing its pedagogical goals, grounded in the representation, dissemination, and marketing of a multiculturally progressive America. And yet the Def Poets themselves also perform the crucial pauses, incommensurability, and incoherence of such collective narratives of "who we are," destabilizing and questioning those narratives from within. Sia's tongue-in-cheek caution when he addresses the audience as "other," as an oppositional and vaguely hostile "you," exemplifies the importance of irony in his performance of ethnicity. It also suggests the key function of the gaps of meaning and understanding that emerge in the performative moment of each poet's embodied mediation and translation of identity scripts and audience expectations. Such contingent dialogues generate unpredictable and unsettling representations of the "perplexity of living" in late modernity and new understandings that both support and suspend the identity narratives that *Def Poetry Jam* itself puts into play.

In avant-garde literary and artistic circles, progressive artists have also worked to generate and transform contemporary public spheres. Performance artist collectives across the Americas, such as Think Again! or the Chilean poets and performance art collective *Colectivo Acciones de Arte* (CADA) of the 1970s, have been celebrated by critics for "trying to forge a multi-front response to [the] conditions of permanent war and right-wing attacks" that characterized the early twenty-first century in the United States, as well as the postdicatatorships of the Southern Cone of Latin America (Villarejo 134).[12] *Def Poetry Jam* can be read as such a response to contemporary politics, but with key differences from these more marginalized and avant-garde artist groups. For example, Villarejo praises the group Think Again! for the way their "[r]efusing to identify themselves independently of the context of that struggle is a key element of their project: anonymity and solidarity reign over individual, industrial, or aesthetic forms of identity" (134).[13] But that refusal is nowhere to be found on *Def Poetry Jam,* in which an ironic awareness of the value-added function of celebrity dominates, as at the end of each episode when Mos Def exclaims in shrill pseudo-excitement, "Oh my god, it's Russell Simmons . . ." So, on the one hand, both the program of celebrities-of-color on *Def Poetry Jam* and the resultant generation of energy and excitement help to highlight a political agency for this television-world by and for people of color and progressive ideals. On the other hand, the television series may ultimately only underline its participation in a contemporary *biopolitics* that deploys discourses of identity in venues that are organized by the interests of capital with the goal and effect of "capturing" these collectivities. Such technologies co-opt for corporate capital these very moments of intensified public feeling and solidarity generated in the studio audience and broadcast to and through the wider, dispersed TV audience at home.

The problem has been, of course, in the seemingly endless capacity of capitalism to reinscribe any resistant or political impulses back into its own operations. So that the "raced image" like the stereotype is now the vehicle of a regime of the visible in which advertising is the paradigmatic example of the political vacuity of racialized images and emblems. Thus Mark Hansen, following Giorgio Agamben, asserts the bankrupcy of "the image as a basis for any representational or performative politics of identity that would function by linking agency to transgression via the category of visibility and the visibly marked body" (109). Agamben notes that "individual existence . . . has become . . . so senseless that it has lost all pathos and been transformed, brought out into the open, into an everyday exhibition," underlining the saturation of media and advertising "from which every trace of the advertised product has been wiped out '(Agamben, *The Coming Community* 64)' (109)." This claimed absence, or loss, of "pathos" calls into question the repeated emphasis in *Def Poetry Jam* on its efforts to make audiences "feel and think" and "be moved." Likewise, the identitarian logics of the cultural politics of identity are all-too-easily rein-scribed into that capitalist regime, rendering efforts to deploy "identities" complicit in their own commodification. According to Hansen, and others, the status and impact of the "raced image" exemplifies this paradox of racial visibility as inescapably significant in predictable and already co-opted ways.

The studio audience for the HBO series is most often shown as dominated by people of color, particularly African Americans who geographically and culturally coincide with the New York City hip-hop context and mode of address of the show. The camera focuses the television audience's gaze using one of two basic strategies: it is either aimed at the poet-performer on stage in varying degrees of close and distant focalization or it scans the faces of a visibly multiracial audience, highlighting their reactions (usually of laughter or energized approval). This camera work generates a visual link for the TV spectator that purports to correspond to the experiences of studio audience members and also suggests a process of community formation through these affective and bodily connections—connections that the TV spectator experiences solely as images and through her own body's reactions to those images. This mode of visual representation and TV spectatorship participates simultaneously in the codes, albeit compromised and commodified, of racial images, but also suggests the possibility—or rather the *potentiality*—for new connections and community formations that, at the very least, cross racial lines of identification and address.[14] Although its reliance on racial images, and raced bodies, undercuts any claims to a radical new aesthetics or politics of racial signification for *Def Poetry Jam*, the accrued effect of the audience, the racial codes invoked by both *hearing* the poems and *seeing* the poets combine with the performers' often ironic citations of those codes to produce what Hansen calls a "complexity of address" that pushes *all* spectators away from dominant paths of racial, ethnic, national, and geographic identifications (urban or rural, East Coast or West Coast, Midwestern U.S. or Trinidadian immigrant, etc.) into other relations and potential communities.

Following Hansen and other cultural critics, I suggest that affectivity can be a key vehicle for the potentiality unleashed in the TV show and its images, an affectivity that I will suggest can also be unleashed in allegory. As Puar explains, affect moves us from the question, "What does this body mean? To what and who does this body affect?" Puar notes that in the "shift from origin to affect, bodies can be thought of as contagious, or mired in contagions: bodies infecting other bodies with sensations, vibration, irregularity, chaos, lines of flight that betray the expectation of loyalty, linearity, the demarcation of who's in and who's not" (Queer Assemblages 172). The productive uses of such betrayals are highlighted in a number of discussions of the cultural work of affect, particularly those influenced by the philosophies of Gilles Deleuze and Brian Massumi. Patricia Clough, for example, helpfully explicates contemporary affect as a mechanism of Deleuze's concept of "societies of control."[15] Whereas the modernity analyzed in Foucault's notion of "disciplinary societies" depends on structures of interpellation, Clough notes how "the target of control is not the population of subjects whose behaviors internalized social norms" but rather aims at bodies (of population, data, and information) and their "moods, capacities, affects and potentialities" (19). Clough emphasizes that understanding control as an extension of Foucault's biopolitics and its concern with the control of populations rather than individuals "also involves the investment in and regulation of a market-driven circulation of affect and attention" (19).

For *Def Poetry Jam* this discussion underlines possible mechanisms at work in the show: rather than reiterating a politics of identity, the television series and DVD sets can be understood as operating according to an affective logic of "capture" aimed at the attention and capital of a swath of the consuming public. This audience can be understood as a provisional and ever-changing "assemblage" whose various incarnations (in the studio, at the time of broadcast, or later in the HBO sponsored fan blogs) may momentarily respond to the affective call of liberal identity politics or race pride or other familiar discourses and images, but where the real work is done elsewhere through the effects of its "market-driven circulation of affect and attention." However, I maintain that these effects and operations preserve a place for the operations of "identity," language, and representation whose "hold" on populations, in the bodies of U.S. citizens at least, still functions quite effectively and efficiently. In fact, the problem may turn out to be the very efficiency with which irony can wedge itself between a performance and an audience, generating outsiders and insiders all over again. Its very legibility in any given context implies that irony itself is an effect of those identitarian representational logics. However, the productivity of affect as an ontological category is that it offers the possibility that ironic performances are able to set into motion affective circulations that "teach" us things we don't yet know we know. This mix and suspension of modalities and logics (old and new, regressive and emergent) signal how the contemporary moment is one of tectonic shifting and transition that requires astute reading practices that can acknowledge and analyze the instrumental function of identity, and even identity politics, in order to recognize the potential for transformative cultural practices lodged within those aesthetics. This intransigent lodging of identity discourses within emerging expressions of collectivity and politics signals the contemporary moment as manifesting a mixed temporality: one that paradoxically suspends the modes, languages, political logics, and "technologies of selfhood" of several times or epochs, we might say. The assemblages of a TV public that nods with understanding and shared outrage, as well as humor, at the jokes and critiques of the Def Poets thus operate *through* the representational logics of identity politics, showing how civil rights–era discourses are now married to the postsubject technologies of television and Broadway.[16] In fact, the legacies of representational politics are exactly what many of the Def Poets enthusiastically embrace, albeit with varying degrees of irony and equivocation.

The Def Poets strongly emphasize that element of irony in their invocations of identity narratives, thus simultaneously incorporating and critiquing a U.S. history of struggle by peoples of color for social and political recognition. The performances of these "citations" of political discourse of social recognition are manifestly inflected by what feminist philosopher and poet Denise Riley calls "the hesitancy, the qualifications, the awkwardness, and the degrees of secret reserve which will often shadow a self-description" (9). Most of the Def Poets explicitly echo this discomfort with the categories of naming, especially those of race and ethnicity. Nonetheless, the categories enable a legibility, even the irony itself, so that an iterative or citational practice that depends on the categories of "identity politics" is necessary to simultaneously articulate and critique the available language for both politics and personal and collective experiences of belonging and affinity. By foregrounding their discomfort ironically— as in the Puerto Rican poet Lemon's ode to Brooklyn as the domicile of New York's "scariest teenage mothers"—these performances demonstrate how the cumulative effect of expressing identity by highlighting its contradictions, agonies, and falsehoods works to shift the direction of their aesthetic expressions toward new affective affinities, intensities, and political critiques.

III. Ironic Narrativities

A central lesson of these performances and of much of the narrative cultural production studied in the subsequent chapters of *Gender and Allegory* is that irony sustains such paradoxes and contradictions of linguistic self-description. As Riley puts it, "Irony possesses [the] skill of making mention of something by displaying it, holding it aloft to view in a pair of tongs" (126). Suspension thus emerges as a crucial trope of critical understanding at that moment of encountering the most deeply and painfully held politico-linguistic representations of self and community. The act described by Riley of suspending "something by displaying it, holding it aloft" further marks the key roles played by both language and the political and social "real" of the world of social formations in these performative acts of critical understanding. The audience is presumed to represent a specific array of identities and to reflect shared feelings about politics, the social, and race, sex, and other identity categories. The audience therefore functions as the crucial interlocutor to the Def Poets' critical interrogation of ethnic and racial stereotypes: it is only together, with an audience in the communicative moment, that any transformation or interrogation of the narratives of racialized identity can occur.

The collaboration inherent in ironic performance echoes the double-edged function of the stereotype as a linguistic and social norm—a norm that we are used to understanding negatively, particularly in the context of minority identity formations and disseminations. While customary indictments of stereotyping reflect the liberal ideologies of difference as a universal human attribute to be benevolently tolerated, critics such as Jameson and Chow have delved more deeply into the repercussions of understanding the stereotype as an inescapable cross-cultural communicative mode.[17] In suggesting that "collective abstractions" always articulate and mediate relations between groups, Jameson and Chow implicitly question the nature of self-representation in a contemporary political landscape of competing ethnic surfaces and labels.[18] In their acknowledgment of the communicative as well as political function of the stereotype, we find a key question for *Gender and Allegory*: what kind of cultural political work (of representation and/or of affect) is done by stereotyping, particularly when deployed through the "liberalist alibi" of embracing one's *own* stereotype/image/identity?

I have suggested that irony works on the same linguistic ground as stereotyping in that its political meaning is generated by interpreting a specific linguistic act as "good" or "bad" by (and for) a particular public. In her book *Irony's Edge: The Theory and Politics of Irony*, Linda Hutcheon emphasizes the paradoxical operations of irony as a political and aesthetic tool that works by generating an intensity of feeling in its targets and its interpreters, doing affective work based in positive or negative emotional responses to the ironic communication (37).[19] Likewise, irony both creates communities and is created by communities, signaling its dependence on audience and ideology—on dialogic communicative act that presupposes division and categories. "Irony clearly differentiates and thus potentially excludes . . . Some theorists have felt that the implied superiority/inferiority dualism is implied in any ironic distancing" (de Man [1969] in Hutcheon 195).[20]

Thus, the affective charge shared by various *Def Poetry Jam* audiences— when the entire audience laughs loudly or gives a standing ovation to particular poets, for example—is grounded in the ability to draw distinctions and in the identity differences that are being invoked and insisted upon, as in Sia's mock-angry utterance, "You're not shutting me up." Recalling classical theories of irony, the work done by ironic performance is largely dependent on a shared comprehension of the norms and the deviations being invoked. By merging and dissipating multiple audiences (in the studio, at home, or on Broadway), the poets often risk a certain amount of productive confusion. Interestingly, this risk also undergirds the paradox of allegory: how to make the audience understand the prophetic message being communicated in code? In ironic performance, the codes and affective excess or surplus generated in the disjunctions of both irony and the raced image work in concert, but toward ends that are often hard to assess.[21]

The disjunction between the raced body on stage, the expectations it generates, and the audiences' reactions speaks to the particular performative effects of *Def Poetry Jam* and the question of whether or not its "affective logics" operate in ways that resist the commodification and reification of racial identities. Because the HBO series announces itself as both a progressive and explicitly "raced" media enterprise, *Def Poetry Jam* exemplifies the paradox of raced images and the stereotypes they ontologically carry. While showcasing a predominantly African American line-up of performers, celebrities, and audience members, *Def Poetry Jam* also deploys the raced image to mark itself as a "liberal" space that tolerantly includes like-minded whites and other "others" who are bound by the hip-hop context and mode of address the series claims. Mos Def announces this hip-hop aesthetic and politics in the opening credit scenes. As both a well-known celebrity and one of the creative producers of *Def Poetry Jam*, Mos Def's initial appearance is remarkable in several ways. His head and voice are the first images shown, appearing in this opening scene before the title credits and music and with his face dramatically up-lit against an abstract background as he reads excerpts from a wide range of published poetry.

These solemn invocations of the genre of written poetry (whose audience is usually not considered a mass or celebrity-saturated public) generate an interesting and initial disjuncture that sets each episode in motion. Not only do Mos Def's physical image and his use of voice and light underline the value of these words, he also generates a certain excitement and suspense by radically varying his poetic sources: Langston Hughes, Amira Baraka, Ezra Pound, and William Shakespeare have all had lines read by the well-known hip-hop and movie star. After each brief recitation, Mos Def pauses, names the author of the lines, followed by the assertive tag, "Def Poet." This prefatory moment sutures *Def Poetry Jam* to a revisioning of canonical literary history (and dominant culture) as feeding into and participating in poetry slams and spoken word performance. It also works to re-animate and offer its own pop caché to what is usually considered one of the more moribund and high-brow contemporary art forms: poetry.

Like poetry, irony works to call attention to the very fact of language itself, articulating the ways in which ironic expressions and performances contest the operations of language, as well as those of identity politics. As Denise Riley notes about the fusing of political and social content within the sharpness and unforgiving rigidity of linguistic assertions and definitions, even or especially self-definitions, irony can be understood as "language presenting itself to itself" (14) and suggests it can be best understood as "the rhetorical form of self-reflexiveness" (20). Riley insists that ironic hesitations and ambivalence "aren't manifestations of an individual weakness, a failure of solidarity"; rather these hesitancies are lodged within "self-categorisation's peculiarly fused linguistic-political nature" (9). Thus, irony and ambivalence do not necessarily signal failures of sincerity, political identity, or collective "solidarity," but rather reflect the inevitable gaps that undermine the perceived coherence and wholeness of identity itself and haunt its representation in language. And like irony, allegory relies on and deploys the "mythic" identity narratives of late modernity. Irony and allegory thus share an opaque and deceptive expressive mode that relies on the logic of enunciations that, fundamentally, do not mean what they say.

Ultimately, the slippery dance with an audience that is seduced, confronted, and "moved" by the poet-performer in *Def Poetry Jam* demonstrates two things that are emblematic of the contemporary performance of minority selfhoods, or rather minoritarian, explored in *Gender and Allegory*. First, such performances illustrate the ironic register of recent minority cultural production and its engagement with the norms and antagonisms of contemporary identity and collectivity in the Americas, particularly but not exclusively in the United States. The supplemental significance of irony occurs in its social operations and effects: not only presenting "language itself to itself" but also ethnic categories themselves to both performer and audience to consider critically. Such identity categories are held up with the tongs, as it were, and often presented with pleasure as well as outrage in order to be "considered" rather than reflexively occupied. Second, what I call a new *narrativity* of political identities and their "plots" emerges in this interaction of representation and reception and affect, suggesting the possibilities and alternative narratives being opened and explored in contemporary cultural production. Calling these dialogues with the audience "narrativity" emphasizes the triangulation and transformation that spoken word performance aims for and its status as a historically situated narrative genre.

In her influential work on narrativity, *Alice Doesn't: Feminism, Semiotics, Cinema,* Teresa de Lauretis called for a clearer acknowledgment of "the relation of narrative, meaning, and desire; so that the very work of narrativity is the engagement of the subject in certain positionalities of meaning and desire" (106). What de Lauretis marked at this key juncture in feminist and psychoanalytic narrative theory is precisely how narrative operates as its own technology of selfhood. For her, theorizing narrativity placed a much-needed emphasis on "a materially, historically, and experientially constituted subject, a subject engendered, we might say, precisely by the process of its engagement in the narrative genres" (106). The question of genre further underlines the role of expectation, at a linguistic as well as subjective level (which is a point made clearly by Derrida in "The Law of Genre"). Such expectations illustrate how the narrativity of spoken word and the Def Poets is constrained by the simultaneously generic and ideological conditions of specific media and performative contexts, as well as by the generic, ideological, and affective expectations that readers and spectators bring to those texts and events at any historical moment.

Thus, stereotypes join other allegorical representations of minority selfhood in the category of identity narratives that function paradoxically and with a double effect, if not purpose. On the one hand, many of this book's main examples (such as the political narratives of community in queer Chicana writing in Chapter 2) demonstrate how such narratives of self and community can generate powerful affects through the representational logics of identity; that is, through familiar liberal scripts of selfhood, collectivity, and modernity's "others." However, as the Def Poets show us, contemporary artists often work through identity narratives in ways that are critical and disruptive of—not just oppositional to or complicit with—predictable reified meanings.[22] Because discourses of self-identification (Riley's "banners of reforming collectivity") and their metonymic representation of ethnic communities are the result of both political and generic pressures, contemporary cultural production indicates much about the shifting sands of the simultaneously political and representational strategies that create and reflect emergent and partial identities and collectivities. For instance, Def Poet Mayda Del Valle's piece "In the Cocina" illustrates again the cultural work done by spoken-word performance when she ironically refigures the gendered, ethnic, and sexual components of the "hot Latina" stereotype. Del Valle takes the "image repertoire" of sexuality, spicy food, exoticism, mambo, and femininity and overruns the stereotype in a performance that incorporates shouting, cursing, singing, and dancing.[23] What emerges is not the expected script about the oppression or exploitation of Latina sexuality or the ethnic woman's entrapment in culturally prescribed gender roles, but rather a tribute to the memory of del Valle's mother and to specifically gendered and "ethnicized" articulations of power. Del Valle's way of "blendin' my hip hop and mambo like a piña-colada" (25) uses her voice and her body to convey pleasure in the very cultural markers that otherwise threaten to pin her within racialized gender stereotypes.[24]

It is in the slippage between an anticipated identity politics and "In the Cocina" that *Def Poetry Jam* most effectively enacts its transformative work on audiences. This cultural production proposes another kind of performance pedagogy in which the performance's own "suspended" narrativity engages new understandings and ways of seeing that cannot be named, categorized, or catalogued in the more authoritarian pedagogies of national narration.[25] In a sense, what these poets perform is a constitutive ambivalence about race and identity and about the personal and collective histories that brought them to this "stage." And in embracing a suspended consciousness between and among prepackaged narratives of minority identity, these artists demonstrate the potential of aesthetic work to transform the narrativity of ethnic allegories of race and gender in the United States and in the Americas in ways that address or confuse our generic, as well as our political, expectations.

IV. Liberalism and Racial Melancholia as Technologies of Selfhood

The role of the audience in this discussion of ironic performance and narrativity highlights how the linkages between affect and desire to aesthetics are fundamentally embroiled in questions of language, as well as politics. And the history of theories of narrative and the social in the twentieth century further reveals a persistent concern with the linguistic as well as political grounds of a seemingly inescapable epistemological and psychological reliance on generic and linguistic norms for the very experience of selfhood. As Riley says, "The imperative to be *something* in this expansive world is a hard directive" (50). Thus the questions raised by identity and its "borrowed diction" bring together the inquiries of linguistic and literary philosophers such as Mikhail Bakhtin, Benjamin, and Ludwig Wittgenstein and the concerns of contemporary cultural critics such as Chow and Jameson. In addition to its struggles with the prison house of language, our understanding and conceptualization of minority identities are thus deeply imbricated in what Chow calls the "culturalism" of racial categorizations in late modernity—and particularly "ethnicity," which has emerged as the "borrowed diction" par excellence in the late twentieth and early twenty-first centuries. Even if critical theory is shifting to postsubject and postethnic terrain, the dominant public discourses of identity in the United States (and increasingly in Latin America) are based on an ethnic and racial culturalism that connects histories of colonial exploitation and violence, anthropological discourses of cultural difference and preservation, and liberal notions of "multiculturalism." Yet critics in both the north and the south of the Americas have wondered whether the language of ethnic and other culturalized identities and the politics they generate don't ultimately leave intact the economic, linguistic, and political hierarchies of a liberal social order that feeds the interests of white, imperial, and capital power.[26]

In her book, *The Protestant Ethnic and the Spirit of Capitalism,* Chow names the implicit hierarchies feeding this social order the "liberalist alibi" of twentieth century identity politics, in which the ethnic identities (and their affects) emerge as *effects* of "the well-intentioned, liberalist telos of anthropological culturalism itself inherent to the expansionist logic of biopower" (14).[27] Chow explores the complicity of our most commonly held ideas about identity and cross-cultural relations (such as stereotypes are bad and tolerance is good) using Michel Foucault's concept of "technologies of the self." By understanding all public spheres as necessarily participating in a social totality that is dominated by the logics and operations of late capitalism, Chow follows Foucault in highlighting that discourses as well as institutions are themselves "technologies" that are complicit with those operations, even when individuals appear, or believe themselves, to be in opposition to power. Chow's critique of how the culturalism of liberal discourse has generated the "liberalist alibi" of identity differences as "tolerance" emphasizes the impersonality and ubiquity of dominant logics of race, capital, and the "selves" that live within those logics. That is, stereotypes operate like "machines" in social spheres and are not special cases or even "crises." Rather, like scapegoating and other instances of discursive and material violence, these discourses emerge as "manifestations of preserved possibilities, the expression of an underlying discourse of permanent social war, nurtured by ... biopolitical technologies" (Stoler 69). Thus, the modern liberal self emerges as an effect and participant in the flow of "power" and its interests (mostly capital but also the state and other "disciplinary" bodies, institutions, and forces). And along with its ideals and "reality sense" of the world, this self remains imbricated in the matrix of dominant social formations that generate both selves and discourses.

To see how literary genres also "feed" this machine, one can turn to Bakhtin's theory of the novel and his descriptions. "To a greater or lesser extent, every novel is a dialogized system made up of 'languages,' styles and consciousnesses that are concrete and inseparable from language. Language in the novel not only represents, but itself serves as the object of representation. Novelistic discourse is always criticizing itself" (*The Dialogic Imagination* 49).[28] When fully elaborated, Bakhtin's theory demonstrates that in making consciousness an object in itself, languages and the ideas they shuttle (such as ideas about sovereignty or justice) are at some level always a product of their historical moment and its dialogic condensation of various worlds. In collapsing the border between the private and the public, Bakhtin's dialogism speaks to that status of language as a given of experience and of history; all enunciations are thus "borrowed" from that totality of languages available to a particular individual born into a particular world.[29]

Chow's work critiques of the modern self as necessarily implicated in what we can call "dominant liberal ideology," so that one will experience and reiterate that ideology through the "feelings of certainty" that emerge in encounters with identity and its claims. Likewise, Riley observes that the "borrowed diction" of identity generates a relationship between selfhood and the affective residue of collective identification and its language that she characterizes as an effect of desire and "self-fascination":

> Not that it's regrettable that being caught up in a political movement so often entails a surge to historicise the self and its dramatic scenarios, to fish up and to refurbish half-lost histories and identifications and loyalties—in any event, to not be so damned alone. Just that, once you have realised that some inescapable leaven of self-fascination is busily at work under the banner of reinterpreting oneself as a sliver of the history of the present, then you are forced to speculate about exactly what it's up to there. (29–30)

This speculation about the self and its surreptitious agendas challenges the reality effect of identity. What Riley calls the "leaven of self fascination" harbors within it a self that is welded to what psychoanalysis would call narcissistic fantasies (such as the self's ideal image) *and*—given the dialogics of language and society as described by Bakhtin—ensconced within the impossibility of any "authentic" language or experience of identity.

This "self-fascination"—like the "protest" in Chow's theory of ethnicity and the "wounded attachment" in Brown's critiques of identity politics—demonstrates the crucial overlap between identity and the "structures of feeling" that drives collective affect forward (in politics, culture, and ideology) in late modernity. Sexuality, nationality, ethnicity, race, and even class all prove to be categorical effects of, rather than agents against, the dominant social formations of capitalism and the modern nation-state. But such critiques only raise further questions about the uses of identity and why, as a category of thought, it may or may not be necessary. These critiques also convey the intransigence of identity plots and the penetrating impact of their affective work at both individual and collective levels. In narratives of the self—both in the autobiographical confessions of minority cultural theory and in the fictional and staged representations of such confessions in literature and performance—we often see the teleological plot of ethnicity as protest and victimization. Such plots offer a fundamental insight into the ways that ethnicity's status as a narrative genre operates prescriptively to shape its own representation and intelligibility; that is, how the narrativity of ethnic identities is a contemporary technology of selfhood.

Chow shows that ethnicity operates as a "protest" as well as a liberal alibi, suggesting that the prevalence of anger and denunciation as dominant emotions or public feelings associated with the performance of ethnicity is itself complicit in biopower and identity narratives as contemporary technologies of selfhood. The examples of Sia's performance and *Def Poetry Jam* more generally illustrate the operations of such emerging technologies of ethnic subjects and their publics in new genres of cultural production such as spoken word and the media of television. The protest lodged within this ethnic identity is intimately linked to theories of identity grounded in the identitarian logics of trauma and injury, as well as recognition. Thus, the archive of *Gender and Allegory* moves from *Def Poetry Jam* and the wounded attachments of Chicana narratives of the 1980s and 1990s to later chapters' discussions of "diasporic selfhood" as articulated in Cuban and other Caribbean Latina narrativizations of exile and diaspora. In her novel *Café Nostalgia* and its postnostalgic and ironic investigations of exilic subjectivity as fundamentally melancholic, Cuban writer Zoé Valdés stages an interrogation of exile as a technology of pathological affects and explores the repercussions of embracing those affects.

Likewise, the framing of memory and identity as themselves "screens" for the intentions and desires of others pushes Juani, the Cuban American protagonist of *Memory Mambo* in Chapter 6, to read her experience as allegorical and yet phantasmatic: an illusion of past traumas that nevertheless wreak real violence in contemporary lives. These allegorical narrativizations of identity thus simultaneously reiterate the "protest" narrative of ethnicity discussed by Chow, but also critique that identity narrative and its "predetermined signified" of traumatized and melancholic selfhoods. These are texts that signal to the reader their own reconsideration of the foundational supports that identity as an allegory or as a stereotype offers the self and the collective. These pathologies of wounding and melancholia discussed by critics such as Brown, Chow, and Anne Anlin Cheng are succinctly articulated in Chow's summary of Slavoj Žižek's reading of the notoriously troubled tale of Althusserian subjectification as a "place" and a "trap" set by powerful histories and dominant discourses.[30] Likewise,

Chow argues, ethnic identity illustrates the double bind of desire and biopower: "Only by more or less allowing one's self to be articulated in advance by this other, symbolic realm, can one avoid and postpone the terror of a radically open field of significatory possibilities. If one must speak of resistance, Zizek's argument implies, what the subject always resists is this *terror of complete freedom*" (110).

This recasting of the scene of identificatory processes strikes at the heart of two conundrums simultaneously. First, it underlines the impossibility of "disidentification" as this term is most commonly used in cultural criticism. Even when a subject may be choosing against one identity or stereotype, she (or he) is constrained by fundamental psycholinguistic structures that she relies upon to orient herself through the pathways of language, which of course are always socially marked and constructed. Thus, minority counteridentifications and even perhaps their ironic redeployments remain within this matrix of sociolinguistic intelligibility, which is the engine of social recognition. Second, identity is a "structure of feeling" in the classic sense in that it is not only the result of imposed norms and borrowed languages, but also that the available identities are generated simultaneously through the desires and subjective experiences of selves and collectivities. The self engages in what Chow calls "a kind of unconscious automatization, impersonation, or mimicking, in behavior as much as in psychology." And it is this "automatic," that is, depersonalized and post-subject, impulse to particular kinds of selfhood that "give[s] identity its sense of legitimacy and security—and, ultimately, its sense of potentiality and empowerment" (110).[31] The unwilled and automatic character of both behavior and self-identifications further emphasizes the role of unconscious mediations of the social within processes of subjectification so that any collective "structure of feeling" must be acknowledged as participating in specific social formations (such as racism or totalitarianism) in unpredictable and implicated operations.[32] While this participation is not necessarily always "complicit" with dominant ideologies, cultural producers and critics alike remain wisely skeptical of any exact formulas for resistance to and transgression of hegemonic social formations.[33]

The question of opposition, or resistance, within a context that acknowledges the mutual implication of representational logics and dominant social formations has been a main focus of interrogation for cultural theorists, especially those interested in one of the most prominent "structures of feeling" at the turn of the twenty-first century: racial melancholy as a response to collective trauma. As objects of inquiry, the affective formations associated with trauma articulate a knot of historical and interpretive questions that have come to dominate a wide array of discussions in social theory and cultural studies—questions about representation, memory, and grasping the "real" of history precisely through its affective work at individual and communitarian levels. In both transnational models of selfhood and materialist considerations of racialization, for example, concepts of "racial melancholy" and cultural trauma highlight the corpses that literally and figuratively litter contemporary narratives of political selfhood: community identity; social agency; the notion of historical traumas such as racialization, displacement, and the expropriation of territory and populations; and the practices of torture and incarceration in the totalitarian regimes of Latin America (and increasingly in the United States). Identity categories enable cultural and literary representations to both explore and memorialize the repercussions of racialization as a psychic and affective dynamic in the public sphere of community formations and political discourse. Drawing from the insights of trauma theories emerging from late twentieth-century Holocaust studies and psychoanalytic practice, critical race and postcolonial studies have likewise turned to collective articulations of identificatory processes in which the terminology of "mourning and melancholia" has gained considerable purchase. For example, Cheng's *The Melancholy of Race* (2001) combines insights from trauma studies and psychoanalysis with a rigorous analysis of the social and political contexts of U.S. ethnic identities to analyze both the production and reception of narratives of racial grief. Cheng characterizes this U.S. public sphere by its "transformation from grief to grievance"—by which she means the phenomenon known as "identity politics" (3).

The relevance of melancholia to politics emerges through various adaptive readings of Freud's seminal essay "Mourning and Melancholia," in which the dynamics of unconscious identification generate a profound ambivalence in the subject for the lost object. These readings of Freud have produced at least two distinct understandings of the uses and significance of melancholia as a collective affect, or structure of feeling. For Cheng, racial melancholia marks the primary symptom of the dynamics of racialization in the United States that produce a minority subject constituted through its relation to racist imaginaries. As Cheng puts it: "The melancholic is not melancholic because he or she has lost something but because he or she has introjected that which he or she now reviles. Thus the melancholic is stuck in more ways that just temporally: he or she is stuck—almost choking on—the hateful and loved thing he or she just devoured" (9). The "thing" that the melancholic ethnic in the United States introjects is precisely the language and social significance of ethnic and racialized identities within the dominant social formations of whiteness, or what used to be called "Eurocentrism."

Cheng and other critics have also noted the deepest paradox of understanding collective mourning as the successful work of grieving the injuries of history (e.g., U.S. imperial and racist violence): if successfully achieved, such grieving erases history. That is, Cheng describes Freud's characterization of successful mourning as a process that "goes beyond mere forgetting to complete eradication" (53). In reading Freud's melancholia through the lens of processes of racialization as they are represented in minority and ethnic writing in the United States (e.g., particularly in works that focus on ethnic childhoods and family dramas), Cheng asserts, "'Getting over' the pathologies of . . . childhood and origin means, in a sense, never getting over those memories so that health and idealization turn out to be nothing more than continual escape, and nothing less than the denial and pathologization of what one is" (50). From this perspective, the melancholic's refusal to "get over" the past through a process of narrative remembering and repetition takes on deeper significance. The suspensions of ambivalence become a strategy of resistance to the demand for forgetting, whether in the name of national unity, political practicality, or personal health. Thus getting over "identity" becomes a capitulation to the demands of a social regime that is based on repression and on revisionist rewritings over the violations of racism and other histories. The language of trauma studies and the concept of racial melancholy are able to address the subjective experiences and collective processes that the juridical sphere of "politics" has often repressed, ignored, and perpetuated, however unwittingly. In this sense, notions of collective affect generally, and the concept of racial melancholy in particular, mark an intersection of psychic and historical "interpretation" that is profoundly important to fuller comprehension of the dialectics that generate both individual selves and public spheres.

And it is because of this crucial contribution to cultural theory that so many scholars and critics focus on racial melancholia as a key analytic, and also perhaps why such work has taken a particular and familiar turn. For example, in their influential introduction to their edited collection *Loss* (2001), David Eng and David Kazanjian downplay the symptomatically pathological reading of racial melancholy as a collective affect—the elements Cheng emphasizes—in order to underline its productive capacities as a structure of feeling that signals resistance to the nation's demand for grief, that is, for forgetting race and identity. This movement against conventional models that portray melancholia as neurotic stagnation and mourning as a productive "letting go" has the benefit of recognizing the historical and psychically constitutive function of melancholy at both individual and collective levels. In a global context of racism and other very real traumas of displacement and the expropriations of land, culture, language, and value, Eng and Kazanjian articulate the productive aspects of minority *affect* and especially its ability to resist the commodification and erasure of experiences that disassemble dominant ideologies and narratives (e.g., of American identity and exceptionalism).[34]

However, again we see how a particular interpretation of subject formation slips toward a celebratory reading of the very constitution of the subject. Such a reading runs the risk of repressing the deeply pathological character of the social formations that have produced this seemingly "resistant" melancholic subject.[35] And in this journey toward the celebratory registers of cultural studies and the emphasis on the "productive" capacities of cultural trauma and melancholy, we can also identify a familiar pattern of idealizing particular subjects within those social formations. Even when we might more generally acknowledge their impossibility, a forgetting, a disavowal even, of the constitutive dynamics of identification within language and social formations enables the elevation of particular "outsider" subjects as the potential source for radical social transformation. But one thing that psychoanalytic theories of narcissism and identification teach us is that subject formation remains a foundationally ambivalent process—and product. Thus even the usefully and productively melancholic identity assumed by racialized subjects necessarily participates in the regimes of identity, presence, protest, and wounding as critiqued by Chow, Brown, and Žižek.

Nonetheless, it is extremely interesting that this impulse to lionize a resistant melancholic subject so closely mirrors preceding theories of transgressive identities, such as disidentification and queering. Such mirroring indicates that recent debates about the significance of racial melancholy as a structure of feeling reflect ongoing and fundamental questions about identity itself. In its uncanny parallel to the cultural and critical work performed in the 1990s by terms such as "hybridity," "*mestizaje,*" "border," and "diaspora," racial melancholia threatens to emerge as a liberatory ethos stripped of the melancholic's suffering and its constitutive and bodily relation to neurotic repetition—demonstrating again the overwhelming power of modernist binary thinking that presumes an either/or option between ideological complicity and revolutionary transformation. Thus there remains a need for cultural critiques and theorizations of the social sphere that engage all the facets of "psychic citizenship" in late modernity, which, it must be allowed, is at least partially *coerced* even when working to stall or suspend hegemonic social formations—that is, to read suspended identities without glossing over the *maladaptive* realities of melancholic suffering, stagnation, and neurotic repetition.

If using melancholy as an analytic has not fully solved the problem of identity, it nevertheless remains a key field of inquiry—and an archive that offers a significant analogy to aesthetic representation, and especially narrative, in its ability to articulate the dialectic of social and psychic processes. This alternative path into the meaning and uses of collective trauma and melancholia has been clearly marked by Latin American literary and cultural critics such as Avelar and Richard. Their contrarian perspectives on expressions of melancholia in the public sphere delineate a dynamics of public memory and collective forgetting in the midst of traumatic histories. In the context of the current "postdictatorial" era in Latin America, for example, Avelar notes that neoliberal political and economic reforms at the end of the twentieth century—which followed violent dictatorships in several countries—have also seen the rise of prominent artists and critics who use an "aesthetics of mourning" to sustain the memory of threatened (and threatening) histories. Writing and other forms of artistic production express a collective melancholia that ultimately works to resist what Avelar calls the "market dynamic of commodification" that operates through the logic of substitution inherent to late transnational capitalism, one in which "the erasure of the past *as past* is the cornerstone of all commodification" (1999, 204).

Interestingly, Avelar blurs the distinction between mourning as "grief work" and melancholia as persistent, if neurotic, remembering by collapsing both as "mourning"—an aesthetic and psychic process that signals significant resistance to dominant cultural logics. "Today the transnational capitalism imposed in Latin America over the corpses of so many has taken this logic [of substitution] to the point where the relation between past and present is entirely circumscribed within that substitutive, metaphoric operation. The past is to be forgotten because the market demands that the new replace the old without leaving a remainder" (1999, 204).[36] Here again, the critique is aimed at a dominant public discourse that demands forgetting and getting over history; a discourse that works as a catalyst to melancholic resistance—clinging tenaciously to histories, identities, and collective organizations that preserve and memorialize a traumatic past.

V. Suspension as Oscillation: A New Reading of Ambivalence

While the "suspension" in *Gender and Allegory* derives some of its dynamics from psychoanalytic models of collective affect and particularly melancholia, it also seeks to mark and analyze the relation between pathological social orders and the psychic suspensions they engender. To access this relation, I turn to close and comparative readings of narrative texts and performance genres, which, as Bakhtin suggests, do double duty because they operate simultaneously as "borrowed" and as normative structures of communication and expression. Narrative practices thus function as an *index* of suspension, as well as signal an array of possible relations between subjects and social orders in various public spheres. My readings are necessarily complicated by the understanding that subject-centered "suspension" has not proven to be wholly positive for the selves who find their own subjectivities oversaturated by discourses and narratives of identity—discourses and identifications that remain caught up in the mechanisms of *ressentiment,* historical wounding, and the violations of racism, sexism, and other inequitable social systems. To attend simultaneously to the negative impact as well as the productive function of these personal and collective experiences of violence and violation, *Gender and Allegory* analyzes their narrativization. As Avelar notes, "Mourning and storytelling are even at the most superficial level, coextensive with one another: the accomplishment of mourning presupposes above all the telling of a tale about the past" (20).[37]

The double edge of processes of melancholic subjectivation and their mixed relation to dominant social formations are painfully exposed, for example, in the theory and cultural work of Cherrié Moraga, who protests notions of a transgressive "hybridity" even as she works to account for the ambivalent operations of a historically "real" and collective wounding of Chicanos and Chicanas.[38] Moraga's writing encapsulates the paradoxes of minority self-representation at the end of the twentieth century, particularly in her outraged response (in 1986) to the accusation that she could "choose" to pass for white, thereby socially and economically enjoying her ambiguously racialized body and family history: "You call this a choice? . . . to fall away nameless into the mainstream of this country, running with our common blood?" (*Loving* 97). In her emphatic interpretation of cultural assimilation as an individual and collective abjection, as social erasure, Moraga pinpoints a key moment in U.S. ethnic identity formation and conflict. The slippery opposition in her protest between "our common blood" and "the mainstream of this country" suggests the affective and political constraints and paradoxes working on transamerican minority subjects in the late twentieth century. Though the "our" Moraga invokes purports to connect her to an extended "Mexican" family and to indigenous "tribal" Americans, it performs the paradigmatic disavowal of *mestizaje* as the "ground" of Chicano identity. Chicanos and Chicanas, Moraga argues, are by blood and history already mixed into the U.S. Anglo mainstream.[39] Moraga's temporality of contamination has a belated and fantastic quality that signals its relations to that quintessential nostalgia of modernity for the imagined purity of "before" in a precolonial (or in this instance, preassimilationist) past. And yet, Chicanos and Chicanas have undeniably loomed in the dominant U.S. national imaginary as a stereotype, the placeholder for an equally fantasmatic racial-cultural-national "other," the gringo's "doppelganger," as Gloria Anzaldúa put it.[40]

In later writings, Moraga again bemoans the tragedy of a general Chicana/o cultural assimilation as a loss whose "ghost haunts me daily in the blonde hair of my sisters' children" ("Queer Aztlán" 148). This grief, horror even, and its uncannily intimate context offer an alternative perspective on the dynamics of racialization narratives; such narratives can be used to retrench racial difference as the index of community boundaries, though from an inverted perspective. Moraga's cautionary tale of Chicano racial assimilation into the U.S. mainstream proposes that a racial difference between Chicana/o bodies and white ones can carry the weight of Chicano community identity and survival. That racialized body difference, however, is also the very one that marks the boundaries between "American" selves and the discourses of an ethnic "other"; that is, between citizen and expelled outsider in conventional discourses and familiar allegories of a racist national imaginary in the United States. To transmute the historical significance of racialization, Moraga moves from the narrative figuring of race as the mark of exclusion from the body politic to positing race as the boundary marker of inclusion in a minority collective, thereby manifesting the boundaries—and very existence—of that negated "outside." This inversion of racialization narratives points to an important question asked by Brown: "In the context of contemporary liberal and bureaucratic disciplinary discourse, what kind of political recognition can identity-based claims seek—and what kind can they be counted on to want—that will not resubordinate a subject itself historically subjugated through identity, through categories such as race or gender that emerged and circulated as terms of power to enact subordination?" (55).[41]

Throughout *Gender and Allegory,* I am implicitly focused on this question and the paradoxical meanings generated by the dissemination as well as the writing of narratives that depend on the figuring of identity as central to the social and political histories and structures of the Americas. Both of these acts of interpretation (of the circulation as well as the writing of these narratives) entail a "reading" of texts of fiction and criticism that are understood as manifestations of social processes. How these narratives spread, as a contagion of modernity one might say, and the uses to which they are put in specific contexts—such as in women's studies or ethnic literature classrooms—actually *index* the emergence of affective and linguistic collectivities of selfhood across the Americas. Toni Morrison's melancholic tale of the "suspended, racialized 'ghosts'" of African Americans and the history of slavery lodged in the U.S. national imaginary can be identified as a narrative that arises in other literatures and contexts across the Americas, though with other ghosts and stories to tell. Such shared grounds for comparison have to do with the confluence of literary studies in Anglo-European modernity and its mechanisms of publication, criticism, and popular reception; shared histories of slavery, colonialism, and migration; and the racialized fictions of nation formation across the Americas.[42] My readings explore how such narratives can simultaneously reflect and determine contemporary understandings of the subjective and political realities of transamerica even as they analyze the dynamic oscillations between retrenchment and transformation that mark this body of cultural production. I argue that this oscillation, or suspension, operates on and through the interdependence of psychic and political structures in narrative and that these oscillations embedded within narrativizations constitute a significant result, or remainder, of histories of colonialism, slavery, expropriation, displacement, market commodification, and other traumas of the Americas. Significantly, the ability of narrative to represent, reflect, and even embody history is a key question in the debates and theories surrounding the genre of allegory, offering a central conceptual frame for this discussion and the book as a whole.

VI. Allegory and the Reading of Identities and Narratives

As noted above, the narrative inscription of minority selfhood is often forced (by the laws of genre, biopolitics, modernity, etc.) to deal in stereotypes and allegories, communicative modes that underline the crises of language and representation inherent to contemporary social formations. The double speak of allegory becomes especially meaningful when its "subversion" of language and its break with transparent meanings are analyzed in terms of the aporias of self-representation and collective identities in the late twentieth and early twenty-first centuries. In his classic study of allegory, Angus Fletcher notes: "In the simplest terms, allegory says one thing and means another. It destroys the normal expectation we have about language, that our words 'mean what they say.' . . . allegory would turn Y into something other (*allos*) than what the open and direct statement tells the reader" (2). This predicament of language—and the analogous predicaments of the categories of both identity and literature—hints toward powerful rationales behind the proliferation of identity allegories in popular ethnic writing and performance of the 1980s and 1990s and also leads to a more nuanced grasp of the different kinds of allegorical narratives and readings that are emerging in the twenty-first century's transition from identity to "postidentity."

Allegory foregrounds the question of genre in literary and cultural criticism, which I have linked to fundamental questions of language and identity in discussions of norms and social hegemony. The slippage between the vernacular uses of the term "genre" and various attempts to systematize narrative theory also reflects the undecidable status of genre and genre theory in contemporary literary and cultural studies.[43] Such undecidability can be read as an analogy that illustrates the way the normative function of genres and categories (and identities) remains linguistically tenuous, fragile, and incomplete. Much recent narrative criticism of minority literatures has focused on these gaps and the possible transformations of the real that they enable. However, as allegory emerges as an increasingly prominent narrative mode in the production and reception of minority narratives of identity, the fact that allegory is customarily read (at least in the late twentieth century) as a particularly rigid and reductive genre reflects a general tendency in the reading practices being brought to minority cultural politics. Here, the intersection of generic expectations and the "culturalism" that upholds discourses of ethnicity and race demonstrate a confluence of ideologies and expectations regarding minority writing—for example, that like allegory itself, this writing tends to be reductive and rigid. In fact, theorists of allegory such as Deborah Madsen (and earlier, Benjamin) have argued that the history of allegory criticism demonstrates its own oscillation between competing, even opposing, understandings of allegory, particularly the opposition between metaphor and metonymy. *Gender and Allegory* argues that the issues raised by various understandings of allegory within narrative theory and its uses in minority cultural production enact exactly the dynamic of oscillation between normative prescription and a liberatory agency found embedded in the terms of identity itself. Allegory therefore actually manifests the oscillating dynamics of contestation and recuperation that mark competing interpretations of specific minority texts as well as the very status of minority aesthetic projects themselves, particularly their value in the social spheres of politics, education, and academia.

One way that contemporary U.S. ethnic literature functions has been to allegorize social formations and their histories by establishing correspondences between the narrative histories of a protagonist, her family, and the community or nation. Thus the popularity of novels that tell the story of migration to the United States, such as Esmeralda Santiago's *When I Was Puerto Rican* and Junot Díaz's *Drown*, is supported by reading them as allegories, as plots that stand in for the entire diaspora and the struggle of Caribbean Latinos in the United States. Gloria Anzaldúa's *Borderlands/La Frontera* offers a foundational example of a work that functions allegorically with a protagonist-narrator who literally *embodies* the history and collective subjectivity of the community. Such allegories have come to be embraced by both insiders and outsiders to these communities, showing that the consumption, if not the writing, of much U.S. ethnic and minority literature remains largely framed by an expectation of repeatable patterns that signify this story-as-community history equation. Shih describes this dynamic as the effect of a "predetermined signified" that makes allegory a preferred mode of representation for both artists and consumers: "A predetermined signified is produced by a consensus between the audience in the West and the Third World writer or director. It is a contractual relation of mutual benefit and favor that works first to confirm the stereotyped knowledge of the audience and second to bring financial rewards to the makers of those cultural products" (21).

To an extent, I agree with Shih that the question of allegory thus proves to be as much about interpretation and marketing as about genre and narrative practices, especially when we note that the question of whether we understand these plots as calcified into a "predetermined signified" depends deeply on the patterns of consumption that constitute the work's status in a particular public. Shih calls this "the time lag of allegory" in which "the temporal gap between the literal and the allegorical meaning of a text is then the designated field of interpretive labor." She adds, "In the end, it is in the politics of allegorical interpretation as value-producing labor—who has the privilege of doing it, who is forced to do it, who has the luxury of not doing it—that the nostalgia of the First World theorist becomes legible and can be fruitfully critiqued" (21). Clifford's analysis of "ethnographic allegories" offers an influential and instructive model of the First World nostalgia that operates in this kind of interpretive labor.[44] Such habits of reading collude with and produce the demands of a market for exactly such narratives of power relations and "predictable signifieds," confirming the long history of the commodifying function of ethnicity in a global and hegemonic Western culture.[45]

However, critics have recently begun to protest that Jameson, in particular, actually wrote a very different theory of allegory from the one attributed to his essay by Shih, and most famously by Aijaz Ahmad.[46] Jameson's writing on allegory emphasizes the work of Benjamin and posits an alternative understanding of allegorical interpretation, one that works against the logic of metaphor and commodification that critics of both Jameson and allegory have presumed.[47] This alternative understanding of allegory is also woven through the work of many important contemporary Latin American writers and critics who see allegory as the aesthetic mode that best accounts for the intertwining of history with politics and strategies of representation and emphatically not as the commodifiable "predictable signified" that Shih claims for allegorical reading. Allegory's *dialectic* ability to express "the truth of history" is key to this specifically Latin American understanding of cultural critique and its engagement with aesthetic production in the public sphere.[48] Avelar's book *The Untimely Present,* for example, marks how contemporary Latin American literature deploys allegorical narrativizations in order to slip exactly the predictability and commodified substitutions of *official* national narratives and histories. In this

Latin American allegorical writing, the collective and the identificatory functions of literature are confounded, deflected from pregiven paths of signification and plotting. Richard describes such writing as often working aside from the representational logic of naming in order to sidestep narrative's "cathartic" effect on liberal cosmopolitan readers, who expect and desire certain kinds of self-confirming knowledge and affect from their minority and Third World texts.[49]

Another tactic is adopted by Silko, whose *Almanac of the Dead* ironically sidesteps readerly desires precisely through its hyperbolic invocation of identity categories and names. *Almanac*'s litany of abuses constructs its explicitly allegorical correspondence between the violence of its story of various Native American, indigenous, African American, and Anglo characters in transnational Americas and the violence of the socioeconomic past and present of the Americas. The narrativity of this litany pushes the reader toward unscripted reactions and affective zones, representing main characters who often generate responses of disgust and repulsion rather than identification and desire.[50] Because Silko writes so clearly against the expectations and comfort zones of all its readers—both minority identified and cosmopolitan, white, U.S.-oriented—*Almanac* illustrates the ability of particular narratives to use allegory "with a vengeance." Chapter 3 will discuss in detail the narrative pedagogy of *Almanac of the Dead*, which works by pushing readers into these uncomfortable, even new, readerly positions. Silko thus uses the representational logic of narrative against itself—against the realist novel, actually—to generate a text that works pedagogically on other intersecting planes, demonstrating the *something else* that emerges at this intersection of allegory and affect.[51]

Silko thus both warns of and enacts allegory as "the petrification of history" (Avelar) in that a discourse of failure and violence is transmuted into narrative, and from that material ground—that is, the reading experience—allegory as the history of violence and defeat proves to have a very different effect and purpose from the rigid schemas ascribed to it. As Avelar puts it,

> Allegory is thus shown to have nothing to do with a mere encoding of self-identical content that masks itself in order to escape censorship (the notion of allegory hitherto hegemonic in the criticism of the literature produced under dictatorships). In contrast to such instrumentalist view, I contend that the turn toward allegory spelled an epochal transmutation, parallel to and coextensive with a fundamental impossibility to represent the ultimate ground. (15)

With the term "ultimate ground," Avelar signals a key and often camouflaged element embedded in controversies over allegory and allegorical reading: its relation to totalizing systems of interpretation and the question of historical crisis. As Jameson has pointed out, critique is itself an allegorical operation "in which a text is systematically *rewritten* in terms of some fundamental master code or 'ultimately determining instance.'" Like allegory, then, interpretation demands the distortion and transformation "of a given text into an allegory of its particular master code or 'transcendental signified'; the discredit into which interpretation has fallen is thus at one with the disrepute visited on allegory itself" (*The Political Unconscious*, 58). Even more recently, Bill Brown addressed this question in terms of allegory and of Jameson's own work, in which the desire for that master code (i.e., the transcendental signified of some interpretive system, which for Jameson is Marxism) expresses the desire for a kind of bird's-eye view of a social totality: "This longing might indeed be translated into the desire for a kind of cognitive mapping, into the desire that cognitive mapping *is*" (737).[52]

Like Benjamin, Brown underlines the important cultural work that only allegory or allegorical thinking can accomplish when language, politics, and other familiar epistemological systems are in crisis. The "allegorical mind" is generated by the confluence of faith (meaning here the commitment to some kind of totality) and an apocalyptic challenge to that faith. As noted above, Benjamin draws on the parallels between the epistemological and religious cataclysms of the Counter-Reformation in seventeenth-century Europe and the rise of fascism in the 1920s, while Jameson's crises (like those described by Avelar in Latin America) are produced by late capitalism and its overwhelming of politics as a viable public sphere. Silko, too, uses allegory as the means to address an apocalyptic crisis that she represents as the fruition of the Americas' long history of colonial violence and racism and the exploitative and brutal operations of capitalist commodification and biopower. Brown further highlights the contemporary moment as one that one sees itself through the lens of "when it all changed," be that in postmodernity or post-9/11— signaling how one thing allegorical readings of the long history of the recent past in the Americas can emphasize is the historical distortion and foreshortening encapsulated by a "post-9/11" schema of nation-state crisis. Along with patriarchy and heteronormativity, the totalizing systems of twentieth-century critical thought (racism, capitalism, and colonialism, in particular) mark the hermeneutics most often employed by contemporary minority cultural politics.[53] The key or master code in allegorical interpretation is thus always apprehended before the fact—of writing, reading, or criticizing—of the text itself; this a priori schema for social formations and processes (of wrongdoing and wrongdoers) has been considered one of the significant weaknesses of both allegory and minority identity politics. However, the ontological orientation and predetermined rubrics of allegory may prove to be precisely the engine of its productivity in the dialectics of aesthetics and politics.

The commitment to rendering a totalizing theory concrete is precisely what binds Jameson's use of allegory to the aesthetic projects of minority artists in the Americas, including those read in *Gender and Allegory*. In the United States, allegorical narratives are often read—at least surreptitiously— as always already failed attempts reflecting their "wounded attachments" to a compromised logic of identity. However, reading these texts allegorically not only allows an analysis of this representational logic but also opens the possibility that we can understand the impulse to totalization in minority cultural production through its allegorical inscription of its faith, its apprehension of social formations. Reading for the affective work of allegory tracks its work as the expression of a perception, of a "perceived world structure" that is impossible to narrate using liberal rationalism or to signify in the sequential logic of representation (i.e., of narrative modernism), but which makes sense as allegory. Here, the notion of "reading allegorically" gains its useful complexity: we can choose to read allegorical totalizations solely for their complicity in a debunked cosmology of identity categories and their failed logics or we can explore what emerges through such failures and the persistent attachment to them. This attention to detail in the close analysis of text and context ultimately allows a clearer and more precise understanding of what is expressed through contemporary allegorical narrativizations of identity and social totality.[54]

On the one hand, then, allegorical identity narratives can be said to appeal to and perform a belated or suspended selfhood. This selfhood can manifest a nostalgic phantasm produced for the benefit and pleasure of a colonially trained, liberal reading public and simultaneously may also reflect the "duped" desires of a minority public that misrecognizes itself in visibility-oriented ethnic identity narratives, which are in fact technologies operating in the service of biopower. But what else is inscribed in those allegories besides this appeal to preexisting structures of feeling? I have used examples from *Def Poetry Jam*, Cherríe Moraga, and *Almanac of the Dead* to suggest that the logic of representation in identity politics—particularly when represented in the ritual codes of allegory and stereotype—generates an aesthetic excess or supplement. Sometimes through an ironic performance of the stereotype but other times through the very citationality of narrative plots themselves, these counter-aesthetics do not explicitly challenge the ground of identity and yet they often ultimately concede the fantastic and arbitrary nature of that foundational ground. Such implicit acknowledgments lodged within the ironic narrativities of performance and written texts thus necessarily undermine the rationalist truth value of identity's boundaries and constitutional exclusions, even as they affirm the necessary usefulness of identity categories. In its constructedness, aesthetic cultural production, and especially literature, offers a stage, or canvas, for the reworking of these categories and paradigms of thought and politics. As Avelar says, "The painful dissociation between literature and experience is countered with a strategy made possible by the machine: the recombination of stories allows for the appropriation, dissemination, and desubjectivation of proper names. Narrative becomes a way of producing apocryphal experience" (16).

Sharing Avelar's sense of the contemporary moment as one of epochal transition throughout the Americas, I have embarked on a comparative consideration of the allegorical mode in contemporary cultural production. Benjamin's defense of allegory and its particular and peculiar resonance in periods of historical crisis insists on allegory's unique ability to preserve the image or emblem of an epoch: "In allegory the observer is confronted with the *facies hippocratica* [the Hippocratic face] of history as a petrified, primordial landscape. Everything about history that, from the very beginning, has been untimely, sorrowful, unsuccessful, is expressed in a face—or rather in a death's head" (166).[55] Its debated status shows that our definitions of allegory depend on how we use it, especially as a reading strategy, for as Shih notes, "Clever readers can, I would suggest, interpret any text as an allegory" (21). In contrast to Shih, though, *Gender and Allegory* suggests that the paradoxes of allegory indicate the ways that we can shift contemporary strategies of reading and interpretation of minority "genres" to allow readers and critics a fuller apprehension of the ironic performance of plots, feelings, and memories. Such performances generate a mix of scripts and affects that are often presanctioned by familiar cultural narratives of identity and yet reiterate such narratives in tandem with their parodic hesitations and negation—the implied refusals that insist there is something else, something *more* going on. So in the *Def Poetry Jam* performances by del Valle and Sia, we see how such narrativities reveal new directions and audiences for minority cultural production, often directions that contemporary interpretations of both narrative and politics have not fully appreciated or theorized.

In minority and anticolonial cultural critique, the figure of the woman retains a crucial instrumentality in narrative, an instrumentality and allegorical function that was most explicitly theorized in the 1990s by critics such as Norma Alarcón, Gayatri Spivak, Mary Louise Pratt, Inderpal Grewal, and Chow, among others. The texts taken up by *Gender and Allegory* revisit this terrain "between woman and nation" to explore the repercussions and permutations of representations of gender difference in recent narratives of social formations and conflicts of community across the Americas. While not always explicitly theorized as such, transnational feminism and its interrogation of nation formation in relation to the racialized female figure have always implied a discourse of collective affect. Including the exploration of "Political Fictions of Chicana Feminism" in Chapter 2 and focus on the baroque narrative pyrotechnics of Cuban French writer Valdés's "encryption" of diaspora and exile in Chapter 5, this book analyzes narrativizations of female relations to identity and history—narrativizations that have consistently foregrounded their own allegorical function—as emblematic encapsulations, or indexes, of general processes of collective history and affect.

Gender and Allegory deals with many texts that belong to different epochs: historically, politically, and geoculturally. Comparing these instances of narrativization in writing and performance suggests that the affective work of identification and collectivity continues to generate contemporary confusions of identity, injury, and futurity within political narratives in the Americas. Yet, I argue that this confusion may ultimately be productive rather than a sign of "weakness" or failure to transform oneself or the social. Thus, while heeding critics such as Peter Hallward and Frederick Luis Aldama who have sounded wake-up calls to the "disastrous confusion" of politics and aesthetics in "cultural politics," I join those who are exploring the "how" and the "why" of that collusion as it emerges in politics, in aesthetic production, and in collective affectivities.[56] That these more diagnostic explorations occur at the edge of feminist theory and other interdisciplinary inquiries is not surprising, particularly because when any question of collective affect and social formations arises, feminists are particularly attuned to the possibly dire consequences of the rushes of feeling that propel and cohere collective responses. Gender and Allegory thus considers questions of politics and aesthetics in minority cultural production through an optic that eschews the a priori rejection of either politics or aesthetics.

My discussions often turn to the influential school of Latin American cultural critique promoted by thinkers such as Richard, which holds—as I do—that aesthetic materiality can in fact "critically transform the real." Not coincidentally, this is also the faith that upholds and promotes minority writing and performance across the Americas. The argument that the affective registers and structures of feeling generated in this cultural politics only work to reify complicit public spheres and do not promote political transformation has become increasingly de rigueur in literary studies. At the same time, however, in the rush to the aesthetic as a counter to the real of a failed identity politics, the causes, residues, and logics of these powerful discourses of identity have been somewhat understudied in the precise context of the works themselves. Gender and Allegory therefore explores that residue in contemporary cultural production in order to better understand the persistent "structures of feeling" attached to minority identities and what both together can tell us. Articulating the equally persistent ironic acknowledgment of identity's failures, performance and written narratives that deploy identities in this "suspended" fashion effectively promote a practice of cultural critique and reading that illuminates the recent pasts and incipient futures of the Americas. That is, they offer a vision of our contemporary moment as one suspended between late modernity and a "something else" that aesthetic practices themselves can forcefully teach us to recognize, once we come to appreciate their shifts in codes and logics; that is when we learn to read their distinct allegories.

2

"The Ultimate Rebellion": Political Fictions of Chicana Sexuality and Community

For the lesbian of color, the ultimate rebellion she can make against her native culture is through her sexual behavior.

(*Gloria Anzaldúa*)

I. Malinche and Chicana Allegory

In highlighting the paradoxical intertwining of sexual practices, political resistance, and cultural ideologies, the above epigraph by Gloria Anzaldúa flags the complex relations among women of color, their communities, and their sexualities. Such analyses of the gendered and racialized nature of community identity—and its inherent linking of the dynamics of belonging and betrayal—emerge as central tropes in the writings of many Chicanas, particularly those who identify as lesbian or as otherwise sexually transgressive. Writers such as Anzaldúa, Ana Castillo, Sandra Cisneros, Cherríe Moraga, Terri de la Peña, and Emma Pérez have persisted in demonstrating the deep relationship between racial-ethnic identities and disciplinary ideologies of sexuality and gender. This chapter explores the critical links between personal histories, cultural and ethnic communities, and political identities as a way of accounting for the tendency of sexuality narratives to interrupt and even shape individual and collective politics. In Chicana feminist writings from the 1980s and 1990s, we see how specifically sexual identities and sexual practices do not just interact or intersect with other forms of identity, but are often used to negotiate through them.

As highlighted in Chapter 1, an array of practices and experiences can be marshaled into stories that stand in for ideological orientations and trajectories. The fictional and autobiographical writing of queer Chicanas signals the intersections of sexual practices and desires with other kinds of desire, such as investments in political and social transformation and emancipation. One significant upshot of the specific histories of Chicana feminism and Chicano cultural nationalism has been a sustained critical attention to the uses of female sexuality in community formations, particularly cultural nationalism. For example, many Chicana writers have analyzed explicitly or in fictional form the Chicano Movement's discourse of *La Malinche* as both a sexist tool and a powerful structure of feeling. A cultural icon of Mexican identity that refers to the historical figure of Hernán Cortés's indigenous mistress and translator, *La Malinche* (also known as "*Doña Marina*" and "*Malintzin*") emerges in surreptitious ways in contemporary writing by Chicanas and has been discussed, critiqued, and celebrated by turn. Among several important analyses of this figure and the narratives that have become attached to her, the most influential is probably the seminal essay by Norma Alarcón "*Traddutora, Traditora: A Paradigmatic Figure of Chicana Feminism.*"[1] As Alarcón notes, *La Malinche* first emerges into contemporary cultural theories of Mexican identity in the work of Octavio Paz, who wrote that all Mexicans carry the traumatic scar of being "*Hijos de la Chingada*" (children of the fucked one). Feminist writers and artists have turned this ideological and discursive "wounding" back onto concepts of Chicana/o identity in order to claim a specifically feminine agency and genealogy of cultural belonging for Chicana feminists. As the indigenous "mother" who betrayed the nation of Mexico by sleeping and aligning herself with the European conqueror, *La Malinche* has signified female capacities for self-invention and political agency, as well as encapsulated the facts of racial *mestizaje* that constitute Chicana/o identity.

As Paz illustrates, *La Malinche* figures a transborder patriarchal Chicano and Mexicano ideology of treacherous womanhood—of the female traitor whose sexual actions have dire political repercussions, if not intentions. For queer Chicanas, this icon of female sexuality holds specific lessons and dangers about the inscription of Chicanas as inevitable and inherent traitors according to masculinist definitions of the collectivity and its historical foundations. Chicana artists and theorists have thoroughly critiqued the masculinism inherent to Chicano cultural nationalisms of the 1970s. Nevertheless, the allegory of *Malinche* continues to work its way into even recent Chicana narratives of cultural belonging and betrayal and demonstrates their persistent preoccupation with questions of sexual (mis)alliance. During the 1990s, it seemed at times that a new *Malinche* was threatening Chicanas and their *raza* belonging: the specter of the Chicana feminist's sexual and political turn to the white woman, that is, to the work of white feminist critics and activists. In the writings discussed below—primarily drawn from 1987 to 1999—the figuring of cross-racial feminist coalition often becomes a sexual and political misaffiliation that must be deflected, deflated, or defended. To understand more fully the pressures that bear on such negotiations of race, sexuality, and community, my readings focus on the mutually constitutive relation between collective politics and narratives that highlight individual experiences that appear primarily affective and intimate, rather than political and public. Such stories are especially apt barometers of the tensions between communal belonging and selfhood. During this period, much ethnic and minority writing in the United States underlined these constitutive tensions as they crosscut racialized selfhood, often though in ways that attracted critiques like Shu-Mei Shih's of the "predetermined signified" of ethnic and Third World literature. In autobiographical writings and realist novels during what we might call the "high multicultural" period at the end of the twentieth century, emotional and political desires for affiliation and belonging take center stage in fictions that feature the various negotiations that Chicana feminists, and especially Chicana lesbian feminists, were making between their cultural and racial identities and their feminism and transgressive sexuality. Influential works, particularly by Moraga and Anzaldúa, have represented personal stories as embedded in cultural histories, situating the Chicana lesbian's seemingly "resistant" sexuality as an effect, or function, of specific ethnic histories and of particular families and communities. As a consequence of this intersection of ethnic pride and sexual identity, these narratives can occasionally enact a retrenchment of exclusionary discourses of race and ethnicity that is paradoxically couched in terms of an intraethnic sexual pluralism and tolerance. Here the palimpsestic character of the *Malinche* allegory of female belonging or nonbelonging emerges in the identity logics of Chicana/o politics in which the masculinism of certain civil rights–era definitions of Chicano collectivities remains intact but camouflaged underneath revisions of these identity narratives.[2]

Controversies over identity narratives often involve tensions between existing political discourses that are complicit in masculinist ideologies of community coherence and the understanding that narrative itself is a cultural and political enterprise, a technology of selfhood that can transform society. I show how some of these controversies are played out in Chicana political fictions of community and identity, which in spite of their apparent contestation of the patriarchal ideologies of cultural nationalism still show a tendency to retreat into enclaves of cultural integrity and a liberal, managed diversity. Interestingly, these narratives of retrenching community boundaries are most apparent in late twentieth-century fictional and political narratives that introduce and neutralize the specter of white feminist co-optation and hegemony. In revising narratives of Chicana belonging around "new" allegories of home and *familia*, Chicana writings from the 1990s suggest the pull of neat narrative resolutions to perceived conflicts between ethnic identification and sexuality. I argue that the representational logics of these particular incarnations of identity allegories of belonging can help account for the force of this narrative pull toward resolution and stability in community formations and definitions.

In contrast to the Anglo-modernist tendency to posit "home" as a place of alienation and disidentification, Chicana lesbians have written familial homes and ethnic traditions into the center of their stories of sexual awakening, desire, and activity.[3] Nevertheless, the politics of queer Chicana sexualities often remain in conflict with the masculinist ideologies of the patriarchal *familia* and its role in Chicano cultural-nationalist narratives of identity. This chapter traces the ways that queer Chicana feminists deflect accusations of *"pocho"* or cultural traitor (as documented by Anzaldúa) by generating "new" narratives of "queer" Chicana belonging that nevertheless rely in part on established allegories of culture, community, and gender. These allegorical narrativizations also illustrate that the logics of identity itself, as well as the logics of community formation as necessarily exclusionary, work to constitute a deep structure for these feminist revisions of identity narratives, which find themselves conscripted into discourses of home and family and their patriarchal underpinnings.

Therefore, while these novels and essays attest to their own creative engagement with desire, sexuality, politics, and history, they also show the persistence of masculinist models of certain forms of cultural nationalism. The way such discourses have survived extended critical interrogations by both Chicana and other feminists speaks to the difficult dynamics of transethnic feminist coalitions in the Americas under conditions shaped by the continued impact of colonial histories and contemporary social and economic inequities. These writings illustrate important information about the infamous "double bind" U.S. women of color face: a given structure of racial identity politics and histories in the United States and options further constrained both by the participation and ambivalent relations of that history to most forms of feminism and, importantly, by the dynamics of narrative itself.

II. Terri de la Peña's Margins and New Narratives of Chicana Sexuality and Community

In the fictional and autobiographical works I discuss below, a tendency to conflate sexual (mis)alliances and political ones (à la *Malinche*) emerges as a narrative mechanism that negotiates among the various and contradictory plots of identity and belonging available to Chicanas. Because the creation and survival of Chicana/o communities is a primary focus of Chicana politics and narrative practices, the logic of community formation is pertinent, especially given that notions of a cultural-political "Chicano community" often rely heavily on the discourse of *familia* and home.[4] Nevertheless, if, as I suggest, the new disposable subject in the reworked narratives of Chicana feminism is often a white woman, that scapegoating has deep and difficult historical underpinnings.

The structural complicities of Anglo women with a white-dominant— classist and racist—society make them uneasy allies, even, or especially, in interethnic feminist coalitional politics. Since the 1980s, feminists of color have definitively shown that the social, political, and economic interests of Anglo feminists often result in their perpetuation, at times unconscious, of the class and race status quos that benefit them (Quintana 1996). And yet the history of coalitional feminist politics, and particularly of queer feminist communities, suggests a variety of complex political and libidinal links among Chicana and Anglo women. It remains true, however, that the persistently racialized political economies that account for a large percentage of Anglo and Chicano relations in the contemporary Americas (especially in domestic, service, agricultural, and other labor sectors) undermine positive interpretations of that history.[5]

The reliance on cultural authenticity in some forms of oppositional politics often emerges surreptitiously in queer Chicana writings, which find themselves in these minefields of economic, political, cultural, and sexual allegiances. Chicana texts have long contested the either/or assumptions behind conventional, masculinist notions of cultural identity and authenticity, and this contestation occurs most forcefully in two specific narrative genres: the autobiographical essay and the novel. De la Peña's novel *Margins* (1992), for example, reflects the convergence of political, personal, and community interests in contemporary Chicana literature, interests that include gender issues internal to Chicano families and communities as well as a critical representation of Chicana relations to a dominant white culture. De la Peña's novel also offers an exemplary illustration of how the conflicting relations between Chicana and Anglo feminists are worked out through allegorical narratives of cross-racial sexual desire. *Margins* follows the story of Veronica, a Chicana lesbian, whose longtime girlfriend has recently been killed in an auto accident. Veronica's experience of loss and trauma precipitates a transformation of her life during which she must choose between her previous, mostly closeted, existence and options for a new visibility that embraces both her sexual and ethnic identifications.

Because the dominant strains of Chicana/o cultural nationalism have understood gender issues as distracting and "white" concerns, both lesbian and feminist identifications are often viewed as the result of decadent and corrupting Anglo discourses. In part as a response to this masculinist ideology, Chicana writers have emphasized issues of ethnic and racial identity within their narratives of female sexuality and "rebellion"—both acknowledging and critiquing the ways that "sex remains the bottom line on which she proves her commitment to her race" (Moraga 1983, 104). In some instances, however, these revisions of ethnic identity recuperate notions of cultural authenticity and coherence at the expense of their implicit feminist critique of patriarchal community structures and dynamics. Moraga and other Chicana feminists have emphasized the disruptive significance of queer sexual identities and politics for conventional, patriarchal definitions of Chicano political "unity" and community (Trujillo 1991). However, this fundamental insight of queer Chicana feminist critique has at times been glossed over and evaded in the interests of a different kind of story: one that works to evade the communal expulsion that is demanded by masculinist paradigms of cultural identity and transgressive female sexualities.

Likewise, *Margins* offers a seemingly new plot for Chicana lesbians: one that shows how the lesbian protagonist's relation to her family and community can become public and affirmative in ways that allow her to maintain both her ethnic integrity and her lesbian sexuality. Thus, the Chicana queer's inside/outside relation to traditional Chicano nationalist discourses of cultural identity is rewritten and relocated to a secure center by de la Peña's narrative of Chicana/o lovers and families and the politics of community in Los Angeles. *Margins* incorporates numerous social and political themes into its story of a young Chicana lesbian writer and her decision to "come out" publicly, especially to her family: a strategic mixture of themes and issues that characterize de la Peña's other novels as well (*Latin Satins* [1994] and *Faults* [1997]). All three novels have been widely and positively reviewed in both niche and mainstream publications, including *Lambda Book Report, The Advocate,* and *Publishers Weekly.* In *Margins,* the story follows Veronica, a University of California, Los Angeles (UCLA) graduate student whose long-time lover was recently killed in a car accident, as she renegotiates her relations to her feminist, lesbian, and Chicana/o communities. The narrative becomes, then, a combination of coming-out-novel and a specifically Chicana story of political awakening.

However, the portrayal of overlapping ethnic and sexual communities involves a definition and containment of Veronica's world(s), so that her allegorical trajectory toward political agency and cultural identity occurs within and reifies established boundaries. This containment of possible identity narratives illustrates what Rafael Pérez-Torres calls "the self-enclosure of ethnic identification" (Pérez-Torres 542). *Margins* particularly emphasizes and valorizes the mutual support and unified consciousness achieved by lesbians of color in an oppositional collective identity that separates itself most emphatically from white queers and white culture in general. Thus, the novel's affirmation of Veronica's newly embraced identity as a "dyke" and queer of color entails a simultaneously reinvigorated sense of herself as Chicana, and combined the two progress narratives bring her to a reconciled and more harmonious relationship with her family of origin. It is not coincidental that the narrative movement toward growth and increased connection with and involvement in "the" Chicana/o world coincides with Veronica's political and ethical decision to go public about her lesbianism.

This progress narrative offers a kind of bildungsroman of political consciousness in its emphasis on the triumph of the "out" Chicana lesbian couple over the forces of homophobia and ignorance in their families and communities, thus redrawing the rules of participation and inclusion in that community. For example, by the novel's end both Veronica and her new Chicana girlfriend, René, are working in conjunction with their mothers for the improvement of the community as literacy activists. Simultaneously, however, the novel also produces an insistently negative portrayal of white women, and particularly white lesbians and would-be lesbians. This apparently necessary logic of exclusion, of the inside/outside dynamics of community formations that pertain to both feminist queers of colors and nationalists, illustrates how this "new" allegory of "la Chicanada" (Moraga) borrows from established narrative models of cultural authenticity and exclusionary community identity. The rather linear direction of this progress narrative and its reliance on ontologies of presence presume the sort of predetermined signified that is often associated with Third World allegory in the critiques of Shih and Sara Ahmed. But what *Margins* also illustrates is that a particular revision of an allegorical genre can have a wide impact on how the story proceeds and is read. De la Peña ultimately leaves little room for the oscillations of becoming that mark other Chicana writers' efforts to revise and reappropriate the logics of *La Malinche* in Chicana/o identity and its narratives.

The story begins with Veronica's recuperation after the car accident that injured her and killed her girlfriend Joanna. The two women had been close since childhood and had used that friendship as a cover for their love affair, with the result that they lived a fairly closeted and isolated life as a lesbian couple while maintaining close, if delicate, ties with their respective families. This balance of half-truths is shattered after the accident when Joanna's mother discovers explicit love letters among her daughter's belongings and a local boy begins spreading rumors about both Veronica and Joanna. Meanwhile, after moving in with her brother, Veronica meets and begins a sexual relationship with a white "straight" woman, Siena, who has moved into the apartment complex. Though sexually exciting and satisfying, the relationship with Siena is portrayed as problematic, at best; as Veronica's friend Michi Yamada puts it, "Siena's white and straight—I'm not sure which is the bigger hang-up" (de la Peña 1992, 85–86).

Siena's whiteness is highlighted from the beginning of their mutual seduction, in which Veronica oscillates between identifying Siena with her dead girlfriend Joanna and marveling at the contrast of light and dark skin whenever they are together (even though the name Siena, or "brown," complicates this whiteness). This initial representation of an attraction grounded in a bodily play of familiarity and difference quickly morphs into an emphasis on Siena's alien cultural background and discomfort with queer L.A. culture. The first murmurings of disapproval toward Siena come from Michi, who observes dryly, "She's so—white, a regular Aphrodite" (81). Though increasingly exaggerated, Michi's hostility is seemingly justified by her own negative romantic experiences with a German sociologist, a white lesbian who had "a thing about Asians" (76). And once a more appropriate partner for Veronica enters the scene, "that long-legged, smoky-voiced Tejana dyke," René Talamantes (107), this racialized rhetoric escalates. Veronica does voice a more ambivalent and fluid attitude toward Siena's racial and sexual identities, but those oscillations are ultimately stabilized by plot turns that make Veronica's "choice" crystal clear. Therefore, the novel hints at a complexity of perspectives on sexual identities and cross-racial desires that it rather arbitrarily flattens through clichéd plot devices, such as when Siena finally sleeps with a man and confirms her unreliability as white and straight. As Veronica moves inexorably toward a predestined sexual, cultural, and artistic partnership with René, the novel overloads the scales in favor of ethnic solidarity and lesbian visibility: an insistence that emerges most emphatically through the differences between what Siena and René can offer Veronica as potential lovers.

Thus, in the novel Siena mainly functions as a romantic obstacle and presents an opportunity for other characters to voice their concerns about Chicana lesbian solidarity and community, concerns that find their impetus in the possibilities, and potential threats, created by Veronica and Siena's sexual relationship. Such articulations play an especially important role in the courtship between René and Veronica. In her relentless and "*macha*" pursuit of Veronica, René never misses an opportunity to point out the advantages she has over Siena, such as when she tosses off an apt Judy Grahn line and asks: "Can Siena quote lesbian poetry?" (168). Siena cannot compete with such insider knowledge of queer cultural codes, of the way that "with René life as an 'out' lesbian beckoned" (217), nor with René's superior bicultural and bilingual skills. Ultimately, these skills and the promise of "sharing visions of Chicana creativity" with René render the two Chicanas' coupling inevitable. What adds to this inevitability is the way that René's clearly articulated Chicana and queer identities empower and encourage Veronica's own political and personal self-awareness. Their mutually confirming self-identities as Chicanas, artists, and dykes ostensibly explain how Veronica "had found a soulmate" in René (196).

Issues of race and ethnicity are repeatedly emphasized as fundamental to Veronica's choice between the two women, as when René taunts her: "Don't you stick your brown fingers inside *esa gabacha?*" (168). Even though Veronica protests, "I'm not with Siena because she's white" (168), this protest underlines the anxieties raised by cross-racial lesbian sex that the novel engages. One of the advantages that a relationship with René offers Veronica is a kind of cultural education that will allow her to bridge her new queers of color community and her Chicano family and community. Because Veronica is initially represented as fairly assimilated, and even as someone who has been accused of being "too white" on campus, the association with the very "brown" and "Indian"-looking René proves useful. As Veronica says to her dubious mother when she finally announces that she is a lesbian, "Mama, you'll never believe this, but I speak Spanish a lot with René. Remember all the times you've scolded me for not being bilingual? All of a sudden, I'm finding it easier to communicate in Spanish. You can give her credit for that" (285). Here, the exclusionary identity codes or logics of community formation are revealed and elaborated: speaking Spanish well, or more, is equated with a "more" Chicana/o formation, even within a narrative context that acknowledges the heterogeneity of *mestizaje*. Veronica herself does not speak Spanish so well, but that acknowledgment becomes instead the mark of her marginal status in the family and the community and her need for more cultural authentication, which René can provide.

The question of Veronica's family also highlights how cultural and ethnic belonging intersect with sexual and affective relationships, and this intersection permeates the representation of sexual desire and satisfaction in *Margins*. After she finally acquiesces to René's surefooted pursuit of her affections, Veronica marvels that "their desire was identical. She's like me, she thought—so brown, so Chicana" (267–68). Interestingly, Veronica's libidinal investment in René often seems to turn on such representations of raced bodies and their sameness: how they are both quite dark and "brown" and how sexually important this shared racialization becomes. Ethnic similarities—cultural background and Spanish fluency—now gain weight through a "body narrative" of desire and fulfillment. In one sex scene, an identification based on race is what makes Veronica climax: "She opened her eyes briefly and became even more excited at seeing that dark head between her legs, that passionate brown woman making love to her. Dizzy with ecstasy, Veronica came over and over" (268).

The foundational role of brownness in this scenario can be linked to what Pérez-Torres calls an "epistemological understanding of ethnic difference": "Culture as epistemology ostensibly moves one toward a totality—of self, of culture, of tradition, of oppositional praxis, and of identity politics" (Pérez-Torres 2000, 543). When René observes with satisfaction after making love, "You spoke only Spanish—before. *Sin duda,* I bring out your Chicana nature" (de la Peña 1992, 269), the positive value of Veronica's newly, and libidinally, enhanced cultural and linguistic belonging and selfhood is presupposed. Veronica and her lesbian friends invoke such racialized ethnic identifications as a kind of hermenuetical shorthand, with given meanings and predictable functions. As Michi says early in the novel, "We gotta support each other to the max from now on" (78). The "we" here explicitly encompasses the two women of color and their newfound solidarity in being both lesbians and nonwhite, forming an extended communal network based on shared racial and cultural identifications that rely on their oppositionality to dominant white and heterosexist culture. By underlining the libidinal aspects of racialized thinking—not necessarily a negative thing—the novel links the predictability of identity monikers to issues of cultural belonging and ethnic politics in the United States. Chicana/o scholars consistently emphasize the importance of Chicana/o cultural opposition to mainstream Anglo culture as a key element in their politics; the defining differences of language, history, food, religion, class, and family models constitute the ground of political mobilization. *Margins* affirms the political and personal benefits of solidarity and oppositionality for Chicana lesbians and other queers of color, but the novel also illustrates the tendency toward a statically racialized logic of inclusion and expulsion, a logic that in fact can exclude Chicanas as well.[6]

These questions of community formation and representation emerge as central to both queer and ethnic literary practices and politics. Moraga writes in her blurb on the back cover of *Margins,* "The world of *Margins* is not new to those of us who inhabit it, but it is seldom reflected in the mirror of literature. These are the recognizable Chicana *lesbianas de Aztlán* from San Antonio to Santa Mónica . . . with lesbian desires that cross race and culture, but fundamentally find home *entre los brazos de la hermana chicana.*" With her uncanny eye for the intersections of affect and politics, Moraga captures both the emotional and political import of de la Peña's novel and pinpoints a number of my own preoccupations. This statement links the cultural work of the "mirror of literature" to the novel's main theme that Chicana lesbians "fundamentally find home *entre los brazos de la hermana chicana.*" Moraga's endorsement precisely indicates the intersection of discourses and assumptions about "home" and appropriate lovers and the cultural work of the "mirror of literature" that had continued reverberations for both Chicana cultural politics and Chicana literary practices up through the 1990s.

That is to say, the problem with *Margins'* neat narrative of communal, cultural, and familial harmony is exactly its neatness. De la Peña flirts with a cross-racial lesbian coupling, only to dismiss it summarily from the novel's plot of cultural, emotional, and political awakening. Here, finding "home" comes to have a very specific and contained meaning, one that confirms the patriarchal logic of community formation and even the commodified role of female sexuality in that formation. In reference to this logic, Rosemary George comments that home turns out to be "the place where one is *in* because an Other(s) is kept out" (George 1996, 27). The logic of this narrative indicates that a "we" that involves lesbians of color must stick together in order to strengthen their ties with their families and communities of origin, in a sort of panethnic unity. But as Biddy Martin and Chandra Mohanty suggest, the problem with the notion of a political (or even affective) home based on the ideals of unity, safety, and coherence is that it is "an illusion . . . based on the exclusion of specific histories . . . [and] the repression of differences even within oneself" (Martin and Mohanty 1986, 196). Such differences within the family most obviously entail issues of gender and sexuality, but as *Margins* demonstrates, the anxiety generated by sexual difference can be shifted onto other differences, particularly race.

Although the novel's explicit feminist critique of homophobia and patriarchal privilege is apparent in its foregrounding of issues of gender and sexual liberation, this critique is simultaneously soft-pedaled and ultimately effaced. For example, Veronica's teenage nephew is thrust into the drama by walking in on Veronica and Siena making love (and by a friend who taunts him about Veronica being a "dyke"), but he is quickly won back to Veronica's side. Veronica's family generally reacts with relative equanimity to the news of her lesbianism, particularly her older brother (who "already knew") and her sister (a nun). The ease with which "the community," including the patriarchal family, incorporates the new couple of René and Veronica indicates that Veronica's newfound agency, grounded in a Chicana lesbian identity, is not necessarily threatening or impossible in the given context of Chicana/o families and social networks. In this sense, the valences of affect and identification work in ways that might serve ultimately to reify exclusionary matrixes of belonging, even when working to transform those matrixes from within. *Margins* suggests, hopefully, that Chicana/o communities are ready to embrace queer sexual identities as one more identity product on a shelf of expanded Chicana/o community options. However, the gaps in this progressive understanding of the relations between sexual and cultural identities are revealed in the familiar logic of the novel's dramatic structure: Veronica does not become a *"Malinche"* with Siena. Instead, she chooses correctly and remains an accepted member of both her family and the larger Chicana lesbian community.

This camouflaged allegory of belonging suggests that the logic of Chicano cultural nationalism and the masculinist pedagogy of *La Malinche* remain intact. Notions of family, refuge, home, and community unity inform de la Peña's carefully scripted representations of which differences are admissible and which must be managed, or expelled. And although many Chicana feminist writers, and especially Chicana lesbians, have deconstructed this logic, the 1990s saw a renewed sense of political urgency that revived it. The sense of political crisis for many artists and activists emerged from perceptions of both an increasingly apathetic and mainstreamed younger generation and the persistent competitions and conflicts over political primacy among identity-based movements (especially those concerned with race and ethnicity and those preoccupied by gender politics and sexual identities). Because they are often caught— suspended, as it were—among the interstices of these political identities and movements, queers of color have been important cultural and political actors, intervening in the mainstream white and middle-class assumptions of queer politics and academic theorizing as well as the heterosexist biases of ethnic "traditions." However, novels such as *Margins* show that in resolving these conflicts between racial and cultural belonging and transgressive sexualities, certain seductive narratives of home, cultural identity, and authenticity persist in organizing both political practice and the stories that are told.

III. An Identity Logics of Sex and Blood

De la Peña obviously does not intend her celebratory narrative of the unity and empowerment of lesbians of color and the inclusive tolerance of Chicano communities as a reification of patriarchal allegories of belonging. Still, both in form and in content, the novel valorizes the lesbian characters' incorporation into a *familia* that leaves the masculinist underpinnings of community formation intact and in fact affirms a heteronormatively self-reproducing community organized around cultural tradition and racial identity. The logic of scapegoating implied in the novel's deployment of Siena relies on a trajectory of "progress" in the move to René: from closeted to out, from politically and socially passive to connected and active in both the lesbian-of-color community and the Chicana/o community in a way that erases any contention between the two. This narrative reflects and maintains an ideology of *familia,* as well as the preservation of the Chicano (and lesbian-of-color) communities, against the incursions of white out-siders. Hence, the difference of race between Anglo and Chicana is under-lined in a way that naturalizes the sameness, the incorporability, of Chicana lesbian sexuality within the family-based rhetoric and values of both Chicana/o and lesbian-of-color communities. Literary critic Susan Sulieman calls such novels *"romans à thèse"* (ideological novels): "Novels with a clear ideological message—novels that seek, through the vehicle of fiction, to persuade their readers of the 'correctness' of a particular way of interpreting the world" (1). In her more recent work on sexuality and nar-rative, Judith Roof criticizes similar narrative trajectories as symptomatic of a discourse of knowledge and mastery, "the narrative logic by which visibil-ity and identity stand as the masterful rejoinders to conflict and disequilib-rium" (144–45).

Hence, the rhetoric of race and of "going public" about one's sexuality in de la Peña's novel indicates how a politics of visibility and unity becomes the perceived resolution to a crisis, a state of confusion. Both in the "ideo-logical novel" and in the politics of community, this confusion is seen as undermining political effectiveness and coherence, suggesting why Etienne Balibar characterizes all contemporary crises of community as "crises of equilibrium" (Balibar 1994). The threatened co-optation of Veronica by the apolitical outsider Siena creates a state of disequilibrium in Veronica's world, one that has its roots in the uncanny mechanics of sexual desire and the open-ended flux of social life in postmodernity. The alliance with Sienna blurs the boundaries between us and them and inside and outside in a way that the novel understands to be counterproductive, politically and emotionally, for Veronica. Sexuality and desire are thus marshaled in de la Peña's novel to contain their disruptive potential resulting in an "authori-tarian" fiction that espouses a doctrine of sameness and unity.

The predictable ending point of *Margins* clarifies the novel's values and message and leaves little room for alternative interpretations or multiple meanings. As Sulieman notes, these are characteristics of the *roman à thèse* genre: "The story told by a *roman à thèse* is essentially teleological—it is determined by a specific end, which exists 'before' and 'above' the story. The story calls for an unambiguous interpretation, which in turn implies a rule of action applicable (at least virtually) to the real life of the reader" (Sulieman 1983, 54). In calling such stories "authoritarian," Sulieman sug-gests that their unambiguous moral logic appeals to human needs for sta-bility, certainty, and unity. Such appeals bring us back to the function of affect and literary representation in the public sphere, particularly in the sphere of politics, which is precisely the target of de la Peña's narrative lesson. The ontologies of identity that are understood as central to this discursive tradition of a logic of representation for Chicana/o selves are not necessarily themselves the problem. Rather, *Margins* illustrates the regressive pull of particular *narrative* logics that arrange these ontologies into narrative totality based on "predetermined signifieds."

Balibar asserts that postmodernity is experienced as a crisis of community in which "the affirmation of difference(s) as a political force becomes the most sensitive point of the crisis of the community (or of the communal identity crisis)" (Balibar 1994, 58). Here, questions of disequilibrium and epistemological certainty intersect with processes of community formation and reformation in postmodernity. And, as Balibar notes, when it comes to community formation, the affirmation (and management) of "differences" assumes a central role in the adjustments and struggles of communities in crisis.

Balibar's characterization of the crises of late modernity are useful in the context of Chicana feminist politics and narratives of sexuality because female sexualities and questions of community formation constitute the central underlying problem in both de la Peña's novel and other queer Chicana writings. As the discourse of *La Malinche* illustrates, Chicana feminists contend with the residue of colonial histories as it is embedded in the logic of community formation. Rey Chow describes this logic in *Ethics After Idealism* (1998), where her analysis of Frantz Fanon on "the black woman" leads to the question, "Could female sexuality and sexual difference ever be reconciled with community? Are these mutually exclusive events?" (63). Chow's ultimate question demonstrates a cross-cultural current in understandings of female sexuality's disruption of cultural identity and the feminine disruption of communal unity. Like Chow, I consider such representations of the tensions between female sexual and gender difference and articulations of community to be crucial to any accounting of both subject and community in postcolonial contexts. Chow continues, "What Fanon accomplishes is a representation—representation both in the sense of portraying and in the sense of speaking for—of the woman of color as potentially if not always a whore, a sell-out, and hence a traitor to her own ethnic community. Women of color are, in other words, shameless people who forsake their own origins . . . for something more 'universally' desirable and profitable—association with the white world" (64).

The work of Chicana feminists further interrogates and exemplifies this impossible position that women occupy in relation to discourses of "community," "tradition," and "modernity." Since the 1970s, Chicana feminists have insisted on the need to transform the Chicano Movement's discourse of "tradition," which relies on patriarchal regimes of family and masculinist gender roles. These Chicano "traditions" maintain the difference of Chicana/o communities and exemplify a resistance to the political and cultural hegemony of Anglos. The complexity of this appeal is illustrated by its persistence in the work of Chicana feminists. Moraga, for example, worries in 1983 that "we are losing ourselves to the *gavacho*," referring simultaneously to "the white man" and the Anglo dominance of society in general (Moraga 1983, Preface). In later works, this fear persists through a rhetoric of haunting and the specter of a Chicana/o cultural disappearance (Moraga, "Queer Aztlán", 1993, 148).[7]

Moraga's fear of assimilation articulates a central concern of anticolonial nationalisms, such as those of the Chicano Movement. Still, various postcolonial theorists, including Fanon, have pointed out that binary oppositions between an "authentic" national culture and the violence introduced by the imposition of the colonizing culture often rely on mystifications and mythologies of what can never be recovered: the "pure," precontact culture that preceded conquest and colonization.[8] And yet Moraga makes clear in her own seminal essay "A Long Line of *Vendidas*" the ambivalent relationship that Chicana feminists have had to the certainties of Chicano "tradition" and to Chicano cultural nationalism (Moraga 1983). This ambivalence can be understood again as an effect of the position of women in relationship to narratives of nationalism and their patriarchal and heteronormative underpinnings.[9] In particular, nationalist discourses of tradition insistently rely on a figuring of "woman" as the bearer of that tradition via her reproductive and supporting roles in the family, community, and nation. Nationalism thus makes good use of women but without necessarily accounting for or including their highly gendered and sexualized difference from the masculine norm of the communal "we." The *"vendida"* (sell-out) in Moraga's title reflects the flip side of this nationalist use of women, who are perpetually under suspicion for sexual, and hence cultural and national, betrayal.

In asking why cultural-nationalist discourses of community identity continue to wield such consolidating power in Chicana writing even after extensive and internal contact with feminist critique, I am following the lead of Moraga and other Chicana feminists. The history of these debates and their narrativization in autobiography, novels, poetry, and critical theory indicates as well an area of intransigent attachment to certain dominant narratives of ethnic identity politics and female sexuality. This attachment is particularly clear in Moraga's 1993 collection of essays, stories, and poetry, *The Last Generation,* in which she claims, "I write for a much larger *familia* now" (Moraga 1993, 2). Although the figure of *"familia"* had been central to her critique of Chicano nationalism's deployment of patriarchal Chicano "tradition," Moraga now appropriates the term for herself. Lora Romero analyzes this simultaneous critique and deployment of the cultural nationalists' pervasive use of "family as a metaphor for the Chicano community" as Moraga's central strategy in refiguring the role of queer community intellectual (Romero 1993, 122). In other words, Moraga recasts her experiences of expulsion from the community as a critical positionality both inside and outside of it.

This liminal self-placement also indicates how Moraga resignifies her "outsiderhood" through narratives that oscillate between sexual and racial trajectories, or histories. On the one hand, in her earlier work *Loving in the War Years,* sexual outsiderhood works as "a kind of revelation," a "foreshadowing of the marginal place, within my culture and in society at large, my sexuality was eventually to take me" (Moraga 1983, 124). On the other hand, that critical "marginal place" depends to some extent on a simultaneous reworking of both lesbianism and Moraga's personal experiences to disallow a dreaded affiliation with whiteness and all the cultural betrayals such whiteness signifies. Moraga's avowed desires for community belonging and affiliation thus create a tension in her experiences of outsiderhood, which seem to follow a parallel trajectory along lines of sexual versus racial identifications. In some places, Moraga discusses the racialized dynamics of her liminal position in her family and Chicana/o community as a *"güera"* (light-skinned woman), and in other places she concentrates on how her lesbian sexuality has pushed her to the edges of her community, family, and home.

However, this split itself is problematic for Moraga, who has interrogated in detail the ways that lesbian sexuality is often coded as "white" and that lesbianism, like feminism, carries with it various cultural connotations that taint it with the *"gavacho."* This discourse of corruption and tainting echoes the uses of *La Malinche* in consolidating Mexican and Chicano nationalisms, though it also seems especially preoccupied with the intimate relations of Chicanas to other women, both Anglo and Chicana. Such discourses of corruption prove that even, or especially, when refigured through feminist critique, lesbian sexuality threatens Chicanas with communal expulsion due to their flirtations with the boundaries of cultural identity. Because she too despises the cultural dynamics of assimilation and refuses to "lose" herself to the *gavacho,* Moraga's negotiations with racial and sexual discourses of betrayal have become increasingly urgent and paradoxical in their oscillation between the scripts of cultural nationalism and a feminist queer critique of these very same scripts.

Morage often articulates such paradoxes of suspension as oscillations among given positions that offer more or less predetermined options for identification. This narrative practice of oscillation emerges most forcefully in her autobiographical and critical essays from the 1990s. I want to examine two in particular: "Breakdown of the Bi-Cultural Mind" and "Queer Aztlán," both from the collection *The Last Generation* (1993).

In "Breakdown," Moraga addresses her "mixed" racialization as a light-skinned mestiza in the context of her natal family—Anglo father and Mexican American mother—and in the process narrates her sexual history as being fundamentally about race. "If my thoughts could color my flesh, how dark I would turn. But people can't read your mind, they read your color, they read your womanhood, they read the women you're with" (Moraga 1993, 126). In contrast, in "Queer Aztlán" issues of sexuality and queerness emerge in the context of a larger history of anticolonial nationalisms. Hence, it is her "Native blood" in "Queer Aztlán" that ties her to the territory of Aztlán and to the Chicano community through a genealogical logic of "national" origins that evades the ambiguities of her family history and effaces the impact of multiple sexual histories and (mis)alliances. In this way, the proliferation of links and connections that sexual desires and feminist politics may generate is contained in such discourses of racial identity and allegiance. However, Moraga at times attempts to account for the complexities of her own liminal positionality and to acknowledge the logic behind her choices of affect and affiliation: "I am that raging breed of mixed-blood person who writes to defend a culture that I know is being killed. I am of that endangered culture and of that murderous race, but I am loyal only to one" (129).

The added weight placed here on blood and genealogies of origin suggests an important intersection of desires and ideologies that Moraga is trying to navigate while simultaneously acknowledging her own ambiguous mestiza background. Moraga's racial *mestizaje* as a Chicana and as a member of a particular family (being both Anglo and Mexican, of European and Native American extract) dominates her discussions of politics, family, and culture in ways that attest to the suffering indicated by the "breakdown" in the title. And in the process of this discussion of race and family history, sexuality keeps emerging as a central, joining figure. For example, when Moraga laments that people "read your color . . . they read the women you're with," she is following from an explicit discussion of the intersections of race and sexual politics that reveals the personal and political facets of her own libidinal investments and impulses. On remembering a Mexican lover, in Mexico, she says, "I remember again throwing up all that bitterness, all that self-hatred, all that disgust at my whiteness, my hunger to be part of that memory, that México" (121).[10]

In describing herself as "always hungry and always shamed by my hunger for the Mexican woman I miss in myself," Moraga engages discourses of racialization and sexual desire that combine to interrogate the links between a body narrative of her identities as a *güera* Chicana and as a lesbian of color. In this body narrative, the driving experience of her whitish body and all its cultural and personal significance is one of shame.

Moraga herself has identified that shame as a primary political catalyst in her activism:

> Only my sister understands. She tells me, "Nobody I know talks about this, Ceci, about being mixed." Nobody else has to—prove who they are, prove who they aren't. Of our 100-plus cousins, she and I are the only ones working with la Raza, working to maintain that conexión under the constant threat of denial. I know full well that my *mestizaje*—my breed blood—is the catalyst of my activism and my art. I have tasted assimilation and it is bitter on my tongue. Had I been born a full-blood Mexican, I sometimes wonder whether I would have struggled so hard to stay a part of la raza. (127)

In raising this question of political desire in the context of her ambivalent racial, cultural, and national identity, Moraga touches on a defining element of Chicana cultural politics: the fact of *mestizaje*. However, in Moraga's body narrative, the ambivalence and shame she feels about her "mixed blood" is ironically experienced as politically mobilizing.

Therefore, the fundamental sense of displacement and instability that Moraga describes as a function of both her familial and sexual histories is actually productive—both of her politics and her erotics. In his work on transgender autobiography, Jay Prosser describes shame as "a profound grappling with the self's location in the world—the feeling of being out of place, of not being at home in a given situation, combined with the desire to be at home" (Prosser 1998, 179). Moraga's narrative of sexual and bicultural histories invites a similar understanding of racial and cultural shame as the "crucible" of her identity, and her politics, in ways that draw an interesting analogy between gender liminality and racial liminality. Like Jess in *Stone Butch Blues*, Moraga experiences her own body—in its whiteness, rather than its femaleness—to be that "which is most *unheimlich* (not-of-the-home, uncanny) in herself" (178). This characterization of a subject split, and alienated, from a body that remains unfamiliar and unwelcoming to a chosen cultural identity clearly coincides with much of Moraga's autobiographical account of being "bicultural." And as the shame of the "stone butch" has its own lesbian folklore (regarding the butch's desire to remain partially clothed to cover her female parts), the mestiza's shame has its own storied past: "We are *Malinche*'s children and the new *Malinche*s of the 21st century" (Moraga 1993, 128).

The key to both the politics and the erotics of this Chicana lesbian feminist *mestizaje*, then, is what to do with the contradictions and discontinuities between the mixed-race body and the cultural politics of belonging to one "race" or the other—as in Moraga's insistence that "I am loyal only to one." Such statements affirm Chicana (and "transgender" in Prosser) contestations of the celebratory rhetoric that often surrounds postmodern theorizations of "crossing" and mobile subjects. As Prosser and Chicana feminist critics such as Dionne Espinoza have noted, these appropriations of "other" bodies—usually by a relatively privileged (white, middle-class, gendered) academic theorist—work to efface the specific histories, experiences, and challenges of distinct contexts.[11] Often poststructuralist and postmodern theorizations efface as well the persistent libidinal and even epistemological need for place, for "home" and identity, that such "border" subjects continue to articulate. For example, Moraga claims, "I can write, without reservation, that I have found a sense of place among la Chicanada. It is not always a safe place, but is unequivocally the original familial place from which I am compelled to write" (147).

This assertion, which opens "Queer Aztlán," indicates the direction of Moraga's navigations among queer and Chicana and feminist political communities. I argue that Moraga's turns to both "la Chicanada" and "Aztlán" are to an extent shaped by her uncanny experience of how her body is "raced" in various contexts, and especially in her Chicana/o family and community. These experiences exert a heavy pressure to "choose" a side (i.e., an identifiable race or "color") that will become a culturally decipherable and politically coherent location from which to speak and write, and desire. And yet "Breakdown" also documents the unruly paths that racialized sexual desires and histories have already taken; as Moraga asks, "What happened to all those women I laid and made history with?" (118). From that question's gesture toward half-hidden, half-remembered, and perhaps unspeakable pasts, "Queer Aztlán" restabilizes the potential lines of sexual and cultural affiliation and history-making, bringing them back into place—a specifically national and territorialized place.

To describe her understanding of the mythical Chicano homeland of Aztlán, Moraga tells a story of how "I remember once driving through Anza Borrego desert, just east of San Diego, my VW van whipping around corners, climbing. The tape deck set at full blast, every window open, bandana around my forehead. And I think, this is México, Raza territory" (151). The identificatory and libidinal gap between herself and "México"—the longing to "feel myself so much a *Mexican*" (121)—that Moraga describes in "Breakdown" is gone here, and in its place is a scenario of a simultaneously cultural and mystical Chicana/o belonging. The story culminates in finding that someone had carved "A-Z-T-L-A-N" in huge letters on the mountain, which tells her that "some other Chicano came this way, too, saw what I saw, felt what I felt" (151). It is this shared perception and experience of belonging that translates into a claim to *"tierra sagrada"* (the land) that emerges as the libidinal engine of the politics of "Queer Aztlán," marking a dramatic shift in Moraga's approach to these knots of desire and politics.

In other words, when Moraga comments that "regardless of verifiable genealogy, many Chicanos have recently begun to experience a kind of collective longing to return to our culture's traditional Indigenous beliefs and ways of constructing community" (166), she surreptitiously—and single-handedly—defines both "our culture" and its "ways of constructing community." La Chicanada is thus characterized by an experience of "collective longing" and the portion of "Indian blood" that necessarily runs in all Chicanas' and Chicanos' veins, bringing with it rights to both a cultural history and property title. However, the introductory clause "regardless of verifiable genealogy" reveals the paradoxes generated by Moraga's cultural-nationalist politics of genealogy. Recalling the influential work of Anzaldúa, Moraga deploys a discourse of revalorization of that which has long been a source of *desprecio* (contempt) in Mexican, and Chicana/o, culture: their Indian ancestry. However, as the above readings indicate, Moraga's sense of shame is actually located in her whiteness, not in her brownness.

Resonating with Moraga's locating of shame in her whiteness, "Queer Aztlán" re-appropriates a liberal U.S. allegory of Native American cultural authenticity and rootedness in order to redraw the boundaries of Chicana/o culture and community. These new cultural borders are simultaneously more exclusive and rigid (in their appeal to a specific premodern "Indianness" that may or may not be shared by all "Chicanos") and more inclusive (because this time around the vision is both "feminist" and "queer"). Moraga insists that the benefits of this revamped cultural nationalism can be found in its specificity: "I cling to the word 'nation' because without the specific naming of the nation, the nation will be lost (as when feminism is reduced to humanism, the woman is subsumed)" (150). This analogy demonstrates the shifting ground of Moraga's political treatise and suggests the fissures out of which she attempts to create a coherent political agenda. As in her earlier work, Moraga's central preoccupation is the assimilating power of the *"gavacho"* in Anglo America, who reflects (and succumbs to) the dominant nation's cultural, economic, and political structures. In searching for an effective subversion and transformation of those structures, "Queer Aztlán" relies on a politics of opposition to that Anglo modernity, which Moraga represents through her turn to "our culture's traditional Indigenous beliefs and ways of constructing community." The historical and experiential basis of this "our" is particularly shaky; Moraga herself grew up in urban California in a family that successfully mixed both Anglo and traditional Mexican ways of making family and coping with the class and racial hegemonies aligned against them. For example, it is the "white trash" Anglo side of the family that proves to be most difficult to acknowledge, for reasons having much to do with the higher class and social stability of her Mexican relatives.

Hence, blood and *tierra* stand in for social, political, and economic histories that have a much foggier provenance.[12] "Queer Aztlán"'s appeal to the transamerican ideology of *"indigenismo"* allows Moraga to unilaterally claim certain coalitional allegiances (with "'the traditions . . . of native peoples the world over'" [Moraga 1993, 165]) and ignore the possibilities of others (e.g., Asian and South Asian Americans).[13] However, in spite of these appeals to an indigenous genealogy and its oppositional difference from "Amerika," the essay opens with Moraga's fear that "were immigration from Mexico to stop . . . Chicanos could be virtually indistinguishable from the rest of the population within a few generations" (148). And it is exactly through this ghost that "haunts me daily in the blonde hair of my sister's children" that the uncanny politics of race reveal their cultural and political significance for Moraga and for *mestizaje* in general. The slippage from "the integrity of the Chicano people" to the color of the skin and hair of the next generation demonstrates how racialized bodies become the primary markers of community borders, which must be maintained so that the community itself does not "disappear." These issues of presence and visibility as the grounding for definitions of collectivity reappear in my later discussions of diasporic collectivities and the concept of "exile communities" that preoccupy Chapters 5 and 6.

Many have argued that a politics defined by such nostalgic reterritorializations flattens and reduces, even erases, the ambiguities of belonging of the intersections and shifts in subject, culture, and place in transamerican postmodernity. And even more importantly, these retrenchments of rigid and exclusionary identity politics may not ultimately serve their intended purpose. Wendy Brown critiques these politics of resistance, or opposition, for their inadvertent tendency to reiterate and confirm the very political, economic, and state structures that are their target. Brown emphasizes, through Foucault, "the extent to which resistance is by no means inherently subversive of power," nor exterior to it (Brown 1995, 22). Because oppositional politics involves a rhetoric of outside and inside and a binary logic, the interdependent relationship between dominant institutions and a politics based in resistance to them often slips from view. Therefore, by forgetting (or repudiating) the overlap and interdependencies between a dominant Anglo culture and a resistant Chicano one, Moraga produces a *"rebeldia"* (rebellion) that depends on what Brown would call a "wounded attachment" to Indianness. And yet these are exclusionary lines of identity that, by Moraga's own account, could be turned against Moraga and other Chicana mestizas. For example, Moraga documents how she "reads" as "gringa" or white in Mexico and how she is both "explorer" and *"indígena"* in terms of American history (Moraga 1993, 122).

The political and cultural turn to a "tribal" community structure represents to Moraga a "real hope for halting the quickly accelerating level of destruction affecting all life on this continent" (167). In addition to the genealogical gymnastics necessary to claim the culturally specific concept of "tribe," such statements resonate with questions raised in postcolonial studies, which has a long-held concern with the violence of modernity and the survival of "minor" cultures. Nevertheless, the obsession with "the native" and their oppositional purity vis-à-vis Euro-American modernity has been linked to a vein of cultural nostalgia that has itself been critiqued as symptomatic of colonial remorse and Euro-American culture (Kaplan 1996). Chow notes that "the problem of the native is also the problem of modernity and modernity's relation to 'endangered authenticities.' The question to ask is not whether we can return the native to her authentic origin, but what our fascination with the native means in terms of the irreversibility of modernity" (Chow 1993, 36). Chow's emphasis on the losses wrought by modernity and represented by "the native" is further reflected in Moraga's fear of a threatened disappearance that carries both cultural and political significance.

If "A Long Line of *Vendidas*" brings sexuality and gender politics into a direct confrontation with Chicano Movement discourse, by the time "Queer Aztlán" is written Moraga's focus has shifted to a rhetoric of incorporation, not confrontation, between Chicana queer feminism and Chicano cultural nationalism. What is lost in that shift is the sustained attention to the double bind of the *Malinche* allegory, which translates as "nothing the woman does is perceived as choice" and none of her choices are understood as authentically "Chicano" (Alarcón 1989). Moraga enlists the discourses of an inclusive cultural nationalism much in the same way that de la Peña envisions an inclusive Chicana/o family and community. In both narratives of belonging, however, the logic of allegorical exclusion remains particularly operative between women; as long as one's cultural identity is dependent on "the women you are with," the specter of betrayal and misalliance will continue to haunt the search for place and "home" in Chicana feminist politics. The woman (and the queer) remains under suspicion in ways that normative heterosexual and male members of the community do not. In fact, in their repudiation of white women as lovers and political allies, these narratives of Chicana queer politics and erotics ultimately conform to a binary logic of racial identification as well as masculinist community formations.

In characterizing community (and nation) as family, Chicana/o political discourse reveals an understandable yearning for "a clear central principle, identity, commitment, or disposition upon which a singular subjectivity can be grounded and secured" (Honig 1994, 16). However, the insistence on Chicana multiplicity and fragmentation in some of Moraga's writing and works such as Anzaldúa's *Borderlands/La Frontera: The New Mestiza* (1987) works to controvert the implicitly heterosexist political fantasy of integrity and refuge signified by narratives of home and community. Like Moraga, Anzaldúa turns to a genealogy of origins and the rhetoric of reterritorialization, where the very fact of the mestiza's rebellion against the sexist and heterosexist constraints of her culture is grounded "in the Indian woman's history of resistance" (Anzaldúa 1987, 21). In her appeal to *indigenismo*, however, Anzaldúa attempts to rewrite the meaning of femininity and female sexual practices and recenter them in Chicana/o cultural narratives of identity and history while simultaneously foregrounding the enormous sexual, racial, cultural, and historical complexity and multiplicity of mestizas (Alarcón 1989 and Yarbro-Bejarano).

Borderlands also plays on the tensions between "home" and the *Malinche* narrative by foregrounding sexuality as a general "queerness" shared by all outcasts, including women, gays, Indians, and mulattos. By linking sexual ideologies to blatantly racist exclusions (against those who are more "brown" and Indian-looking), Anzaldúa challenges the accusations of *"pocho"* (cultural traitor) on the very ground of "community" and history (Anzaldúa 1987, 55). In this way, *Borderlands* deploys queerness, as well as femaleness, as a disruption of cultural-nationalist exclusions of racialized and sexualized bodies. The proliferation of outsider women (the *mojada* [wetback], the mestiza, and the narrator) further indicates Anzaldúa's subversion of conventional relations between a given community's outcasts and "home." She insists that "as a mestiza I have no country, my homeland cast me out; yet all countries are mine because I am every woman's sister or potential lover. (As a lesbian I have no race, my own people disclaim me; but I am all races because there is the queer of me in all races)" (80).

However, by figuring alternative female sexualities as "the ultimate rebellion," Anzaldúa also enters into a debate precisely about the uses of sexuality in political narratives of self and community (19). Reading narratives of transgressive sexuality as allegories for social or political protest has deep roots in Euro-American modernity's emphasis on opposition and rebellion, an opposition that often proves complicit with Euro-American narratives of individualist selfhood.[14] Like Moraga, Anzaldúa attempts to circumvent the binaries of opposition, particularly through notions of the queer as liminal, as productively inside and outside the terms of belonging dictated by cultural nationalism ("People, listen to your *joteria*" [queer folk] [81]). Nevertheless, *Borderlands* threatens to elide these moments of scattered belonging through invocations of national territory and genealogical belonging that echo the incorporations of "Queer Aztlán" and *Margins* ("This land was Mexican once, was Indian always, and is. And will be again" [91]). In this way, queer narratives of Chicana belonging and identity can be seen to return to notions of community and origin that, as Brown puts it, "converge . . . with a regime's own legitimacy in masking the power of that regime" (Brown 1995, 23). The regimes in question, I assert, are the heterosexist foundations of cultural nationalism's claims to political coherence and agency.

IV. Queer Chicana Writing and the Erotic-Political Interrogation of Home

Moraga's fear of falling away "nameless into the mainstream of this country, running with our common blood" (Moraga 1983, 97) suggests the deeper dynamics in the narrative search for "home" and place in the context of Chicana/o cultural identities. Moraga and Anzaldúa, among others, enact a queering of Chicana identity that often acknowledges their personal and political imbrication in uncomfortably ambiguous networks of sexual histories, desires, and politics. And yet, "Queer Aztlán" illustrates how tempting, and how resolving, it can be to subsume the unruly logics of sexualities into a binary logic of race and to get rid of the "others" that threaten elsewhere: "the white women I love" and "the white woman I am" (Moraga 1993, 125). But then, ultimately, all narratives of self and community can come under fire as enacting their own particular reductions, exclusions, and erasures. Martin thus explicates the intimate relations between autobiographical writings and political formations of community and identity: "Self-worth, identity, and a sense of community have fundamentally depended on the production of a shared narrative and on the assimilation of individuals' life histories into the history of the group" (Martin 1988, 83). Martin signals how the cultural work of autobiography operates in this field of affectivity and collective identity formation and coherence, even when the coherence of both self and collectivity is acknowledged as partial or distorted.

Hence, the power of assimilation works in several directions, as indicated by the continued discourse of "home" and by its feminist interrogation across a range of disciplines, including sociology, political philosophy, cultural studies, queer theory, and literary criticism. For example, the political theorist Bonnie Honig deconstructs the discourse of home and its political uses, particularly the desire for political movements and coalitions to offer a "homelike refuge" (Honig 1994, 12). Anzaldúa asserts that home, like feminism, has always been riven with differences and has never been much of a refuge. Likewise, Honig warns that nationalist discourse signals "an unwillingness . . . to settle for anything less than the phantasmic imagery of home" (15). Anzaldúa's metaphor of "homophobia" (fear of going home, of not being taken in) illustrates both the desire for home— that is, the "mother, culture, and race"—and the difficulty, if not impossibility, of realizing that dream of return (Anzaldúa 1987, 20).

However, narratives of self and community, as well as return, are not necessarily so easily categorized into assimilation stories, or otherwise "authoritarian" fictions. One recent example of a narrative that slips through several of the identity allegories that I have described is Emma Pérez's novel *Gulf Dreams* (1996). Although Pérez's novel begins in a way that recalls Moraga's autobiographical stories (featuring a first-person narrator who speaks of her childhood as a light-skinned queer girl growing up in a bleak and often brutal working-class Chicano community), it challenges various readerly expectations. These expectations are embedded in the themes of the growing-up novel, the rhetoric of Chicana cultural identities, and a narrative practice that is both realist and impressionistic. Such structural characteristics bolster *Gulf Dreams*' evasions of the demand for narrative and political coherence, for a life story that can be contained and commodified via specific identity plots. However, the novel also disrupts other elements of ideological or authoritarian fictions. *Gulf Dreams* resists the thematic conventions and maneuvers of numerous standard plots; it weaves a romance, a bildungsroman, a courtroom drama, and a confessional novel into a loosely gathered whole. And though some of its narrative pyrotechnics obscure the reader's focus on the elements of racial and cultural oppression and sexual transgression, these themes nevertheless comprise the novel's main storyline(s).[15]

Growing up in a Texas town on the Gulf of Mexico (called "El Pueblo" in the novel), the narrator describes adolescent and childhood experiences that touch on her family's poverty and the town's racism, a town where "I memorized hate." Here, again, the protagonist-narrator is too light-skinned to belong in her Chicano community, and she consciously envies her siblings' darker skin, eyes, and hair: "I grew to resent the colors that set me apart from my family" (Pérez 1996, 15). In particular, she describes her initially close relationship with her brother who later rejects her: "Maybe I reminded him too much of the white world outside our home" (20). These inaugurating moments in the text underline the narrator's sense of herself as an "outcast," and they also set the stage for her various, often unpredictable, social negotiations with that town and that family. Pérez delineates the differences and conflicts within the family in a way that refuses a narrative allegory of cultural authenticity and betrayal. For example, when she chooses a white, Jewish friend in grammar school and then a popular white boyfriend in high school, the issues of belonging and betrayal are acknowledged even as she explicitly negates the conventional readings of those choices as "false" and wrong-headed. The interplay of short passages about her sexual molestation as a baby ("This is the betrayal I've been speaking about" [74]) and the present-day trial of five men who raped a young woman also emphasize the text's engagement with the narratives of *Malinche*.

However, in contrast, to the appropriation and refiguring of the *Malinche* narrative within an allegorical narrative of personal and communal development or growth, Pérez scrambles the coherence of the allegorical plots in ways that stymie or stall the reader's impulse to read her novel's "I" as representative. This disruption also occurs through the figuring of female sexual desire, but in ways that further derail familiar trajectories. The primary preoccupation of *Gulf Dreams* is "her," "the woman from El Pueblo," the unnamed and ever-present object of the narrator's obsessive desire and sexual interest. And although this other woman's persistent return to male boyfriends and husbands, her "betrayals," play a central role in their romance, the narrator blurs the lines between victim and manipulator. Such evasions and disruptions generate a story that is hard to grasp and that challenges conventional plots for both Chicana/o coming-of-age and lesbian coming-out stories, as well as stories about feminist or ethnic justice. The narrator's emphasis on her sexual obsession and romantic attachment to "her" both obfuscates and hints at the lurking agency of other issues: family dynamics and gender inequity, racial injustice and economic exploitation, and the distance the narrator has put between herself and "El Pueblo." And yet, these questions of class climbing, gender, and survival are subsumed in the story of the narrator's desire, such as when leaving home is portrayed as a function of her self-destructive desire for the other woman, a Chicana: "Even in sleep, voices gave me orders. They told me to leave, to leave her, to save myself" (Pérez 1996, 46) and the return is at least in part a search for "her kiss." The narrator also describes emotional and sexual relations with men and emphasizes her own fluid sexual desires, "the different ways I loved men from women" (69), as a further negation of progress plots for her identity or her sexuality.

If a faint outline of a plot trajectory emerges in *Gulf Dreams*, it centers on its many scenes of return. The narrator establishes her exit into another life of "many women, many lovers" but concentrates on this story of coming back to El Pueblo, where "a closed door, opened. Excavating, digging deeper, like an archaeologist uncovering remnants, piecing together what she has only imagined for years" (70). But that return is also multiple and contradictory; its destination shifts from El Pueblo to the woman, to her desire for the woman, and to the telling of the story. Leaving much of the novel's dramas open to various interpretations (sexual, political, and narratogological), Pérez evades discourses of "truth" and refuses to offer an end product of satisfactory knowledge and understanding about what we have just read. Instead, she ends the story thus: "This part of the story has to be over, even though I don't believe in endings. I believe in the imagination, its pleasures indelible, transgressive, a dream" (157). *Gulf Dreams'* refusals of naming and closure, of the narrative of visibility, demonstrate some of the ways that, as Jasbir Puar notes, "not every invisibility is an assimilation" (Puar 2002). In fact, Pérez's narrator seems to choose her invisibility, her faint political and social outline as a strategy of confusion and subversion, both in the narrative and in the political and sexual scenarios it describes. In a sense, these openings also signal the limits of an epistemology of undecidability and illegibility. One aspect that the works of de la Peña, Anzaldúa, and Moraga share is a narrative practice that operates allegorically to figure the conditions of possibility for social transformation. The precisely individualist cast of *Gulf Dreams,* as well as its emphasis on sexual violence and trauma, brings it closer toward the noncommodifiable narrativizations of postdictatorial Latin American aesthetics of Idelbar Avelar and Nelly Richard, which are discussed further in Chapters 3 and 5.

It now seems easy to say that texts such as de la Peña's *Margins* reflect the desire for, and the pleasures of, home while perhaps also succumbing to the temptations of what Bernice Johnson Reagon has called "little barred rooms" where differences "are held at bay" (Reagon 1983, 357). Alarcón too cautions against the seductive pull of "the autonomous self-making liberal subject" who organizes identity and community too neatly (Alarcón 1989, 86). And yet the epistemological nature of these debates—in particular, whether it is possible to account for differences of gender, culture, and community (hence of access, power, and freedom in the United States) without identifiable boundaries and coherent political agents—suggests the difficult negotiations of Chicana queer and feminist writers. Furthermore, the immense political productivity and influence of the work produced between 1983 and the 1990s indicate that such allegorics of identity circulated widely and with a huge public impact, which may (yet) not be the case with the slippery narrativizations of Pérez. The negotiations with identity narratives and their logic—particularly in Moraga and Anzaldúa—underline the contradictory pull of narratives, identities, and collectivities. However, both political theorists and literary critics of identity narratives acknowledge that narrative itself demands the structure and stability of identities, categories, and names—what I discussed in Chapter 1 as the linguistic prerequisite of norms, as well as genres.

The "problem" may not be, then, in the particularities of ethnic identity politics or coming-out narratives, but rather in the presumed correspondences between politics and narrative more generally. As my examples demonstrate, Chicana lesbian feminists map an uncomfortable territory where narrators and protagonists variously reinscribe and refuse the seductions of dominant political myths. In the process, they represent and make legible the complex matrices of relations between "home" and Chicana/o identities and sexualities that give the lie to those myths. Such narratives not only undermine appeals to purity and desires for separate spheres, but also reiterate the political, aesthetic, and cultural power of narrative practices.

Apocalyptic Modernities: Transamerican Allegory, Revolution, and Indigeneity in *Almanac of the Dead*

That might which is wielded by men rules over them. The human soul never ceases to be modified by its encounter with might. Might is that which makes a thing of anybody who comes under its sway. When exercised to the full, it makes a thing of man in the most literal sense, for it makes him a corpse.

(*Simone Weil*)

I. Apocalyptic Allegory: *Almanac* as Prophecy

In an interview in 1998, Leslie Marmon Silko describes her sense of the cultural work done by her 1991 epic *Almanac of the Dead*. When the interviewer, Ellen Arnold, explains that she had trouble reading *Almanac* the first time because she read it during the Los Angeles riots of 1992 and the novel seemed to be "coming to life all around me" (7), Silko responds, "The book seemed to know that . . . And of course the ultimate thing that it did—January 1, 1994, I pick up a Sunday paper, and it says that the Zapatistas in the mountains outside Tuxtla Gutierrez . . . Then the hair on my neck stood up" (7–8). She adds, "It's like *Almanac of the Dead* did everything that it wanted, that's how it's been" (8). Silko's suggestion that *Almanac* "did" the Zapatista uprising in Chiapas, Mexico, further underlines the trope of prophecy that runs through the work even as it also implicates her in an *"estadounidense"* (U.S.) habit of proprietary feeling toward "our" neighbors to the south.[1] However, although they seem to participate in a long history of North American hegemony in the

Americas, Silko's comments are actually complexly grounded in *Almanac's* formal and thematic structure, as well as in its explicitly "tribal epistemology" (Cherniavsky).

The project of *Almanac of the Dead* participates in the ethnic identity politics of the 1980s and 1990s, but it also recasts those politics and identity logics into a different kind of narrative: one with different trajectories, contents, and outcomes. The individual female protagonists discussed in Chapter 2 stand in for collective experience, both past and future, and their narratives invoke the solidifying function of distinct and stable (ontological) codes of racialization and belonging that constrain and confound the plots of Chicana feminist politics. Such codes are again in operation in Silko's specifically "Native" epic narrative of the contemporary Americas, but in Silko, the embrace of the "tribal" works to undo identitarian categories, even as the text reiterates—or cites—the ontological status of race (as well as culture and geography). Like Chicana feminist fictions, *Almanac* works to counter and oppose a contemporary U.S. society that offers "no choice," but its articulation of racial ontologies explicitly and hyperbolically insists on the totalized intertwining of race, political economies, and affective affiliations and belongings within the logic of late capitalism. The novel represents this logic as profoundly identitarian and Manichean, and yet also makes room for "something else" that might interfere or does not operate according to available political rhetoric. Ultimately, these Manichean epistemologies and the text's apocalyptic prophecies combine to articulate her insistence that both narrative, in the form of stories, and indigeneity do radical cultural work in the Americas.

The notion of apocalypse is closely tied to the allegorical mode in *Almanac,* as it is in traditional discourse studies of apocalyptic fictions and classical allegory. This connection between imagining new social formations and revolutionary violence is made clear even in the Bible where the prophesied apocalypse signals the desire for a radical cleansing, a sweeping away, of the old, corrupt social order. The cultural work of such narrativizations, prophetic and apocalyptic, is manifested in *Almanac's* complex structure and its reflection of a totalized vision of the Americas within the structure of the text itself: 6 parts, 20 books, and 215 chapters "map" the Americas both spatially and temporally. Silko has in fact suggested that the sheer difficulty of her notoriously confrontational and unwieldy 763-page epic is quite intentional, warning, "If you make it all the way through *Almanac,* it makes you strong" (Arnold 7). This textual pedagogy—reading to make oneself "strong"—underlines the purpose behind *Almanac's* narrativizations of the multiple and intersecting histories of the Americas. In its emphasis on indigeneity and the impact of stories and storytelling, *Almanac* draws on an image and discourse repertoire of indigenous revolution as a radical critique of European modernity in the Americas.[2] And in figuring a relationship between the given social order of the Americas and apocalyptic narrative, *Almanac* successfully teaches readers that the modernity brought by the Europeans is generated by, and structured through, the ongoing violence and terror of the colonial occupation of the Americas.

Sidestepping the allegory of individual identity as a figure for the collective that characterizes Terri de la Peña's novel *Margins* and even much of the work of the Def Poets, *Almanac* appropriates the form of allegory in a very particular fashion that recalls allegory's medieval roots in the prophetic traditions of Christianity while drawing on indigenous forms of storytelling and signification. For Silko's project, contemporary sociality demands allegory's rigorous impersonality, its refusal of the romanticized bourgeois individual as described by Walter Benjamin as a reliance on "emblems," images, and "ruins" that stand in for history. Benjamin notes that though the allegorical mode of figuring "lacks all 'symbolic' freedom of expression, all classical proportion, all humanity," it is nevertheless the form that best exposes "history as the Passion of the world" (166). Inventing a form that I call "apocalyptic epic allegory" to tell her story about an indigenous apocalypse, a hemispheric "War against the United States," Silko offers narrative itself—in the form of allegories of transamerican history—as the counter to what the anthropologist Rosalind Morris calls "the most significant loss of our age . . . namely, the loss of a commitment to revolutionary historical transformation" (30).[3]

In spite of differences of scale and emphasis, *Almanac* shares with the other texts discussed in *Gender and Allegory* a narrativity aimed at contesting and transforming dominant social formations and their pathologies of racism and other forms of violence. To different degrees, these are also texts whose narrative structures and mechanisms enable a critique of the normative plots that are the machines of those social formations. For its part, the narrative of indigenous revolution and large-scale social breakdown in *Almanac* operates at various levels—using prophecy as a narrative pedagogy—to narrate the social present as both "deadened" and "dead-end." The novel posits a present that holds no future without the cleansing of an apocalyptic revolution. *Almanac* eschews the registers of autobiographical self-disclosure (ironic or otherwise) and instead deploys archaic modes such as parable and mythic allegory to generate an apocalyptic rush toward the radical revolution that will transform society once the Indians can "take back the land."[4] That is, its complex plot does not elucidate a story of personal growth or pathos around its characters; indeed, individual characters are frequently repugnant, and the lack of characters to identify with is one of the elements that makes this novel so difficult for readers accustomed to realist conventions that help propel them through lengthy narratives.[5]

Rather than unfolding a personal story of growth or transformation, the majority of *Almanac* issues a warning. In shaping this cautionary allegory to her own ends, Silko deploys a mix of genres, both realistic and fantastic. It is these elements of realism that sharpen the apocalyptic plot of *Almanac*, even as the plot itself announces the epic, even mythic, character of the text and its narrative. Set primarily in Tucson, Arizona, the novel unfolds in a clearly fictional near future that is nevertheless quite recognizable—a future that in and of itself manifests the consequences of current social problems. Silko's hyperrealistic mode takes the negative aspects of the present—drugs, violence, abusive or exploitive sexual acts, torture, boredom, racism, and greed—and makes them the norm of all social life in the Americas. Accenting the real conditions of a contemporary transamerican moment, the realistic scenes in *Almanac* take on a fantastic, repulsive quality further emphasized by the blunt, cold, and flat affect of the characters' personas. These nightmarish emotional characterizations seem to reject the drive toward resolution and redemption that the characters of *Margins* and other U.S. ethnic novels often claim. In *Almanac,* methods of effecting change turn away from notions of a nostalgically rendered "home" in culture or collectivity—a refuge or utopia that has been lost to the forces of dominant society. Instead, the novel wants to tear down the bridge between past and present and offers its call to revolutionary violence as the only way to establish a break in social patterns; hence, its apocalyptic and epic character promises a different, even "new," future that is currently impossible.

Almanac's uncanny mix of familiar and strange allows Silko to reflect for the reader the dire consequences of a contemporary social world saturated by the neocolonial, and neoliberal, politics of rationalist instrumentality. In his consideration of a similar vision of contemporary Euro-American global society, Achille Mbembe coins the term "necropolitics" to describe this sociality and its ties to the linked genealogies of terror, late capitalism, and colonialism. Mbembe writes in his own rather prophetic and apocalyptic critical mode, describing "our contemporary world" as marked by "the creation of *death-worlds,* new and unique forms of social existence upon which vast populations are subjected to conditions of life conferring upon them the status of the *living dead*" (40, Mbembe's emphasis).

The necropolitical underpinnings of the story-world in *Almanac* emerges in its characterizations of a cast of difficult, often ugly, personages, some of whom are the apparent protagonists of the novel. Readers must wade through *Almanac* with few, if any, emotional connections to sustain them. Lecha and Zeta are Mexican Indian (Yaqui) twin sisters who at the opening of the book have reunited on their ranch outside Tucson on the eve of their sixtieth birthday. Zeta lives on the ranch with Lecha's son Ferro, who was raised by Zeta (after a fashion); Ferro hates Lecha, the mother who abandoned him, with a ferocious, animal-like intensity. The ranch is Zeta's base for smuggling drugs and weapons back and forth across the U.S.-Mexico border. Its other residents at the novel's opening include Ferro's strange, violent, and mutely adoring employee, Paulie, as well as Lecha's "nurse," the white and blond Seese, who is there to administer Demerol and Percodan to the drug-addicted, psychic Lecha; finally, there is the hapless gardener Sterling, a Laguna Pueblo Indian, who has wandered into Tucson after being expelled by his Laguna tribal community in New Mexico for allowing Hollywood filmmakers to "discover" a sacred tribal site.

This scattershot opening chapter highlights Silko's narrative technique of juxtaposing multiple character filters at hyperspeed, a technique that expands vertiginously to include a cast of over 60 names and four continents. And in this opening scene, we find a refiguring of family relations and "Indian" lifestyles that challenges conceptions of both "home" and domesticity, as well as Indianness: "No food anywhere. Pistols, shotguns, and cartridges scattered on the kitchen counters, and needles and pills all over the table. The Devil's kitchen doesn't look this good" (*Almanac* 20). Silko makes sure the reader understands that neither kitchens nor families nor Indians act like they are "supposed to" in this text.[6] Calling attention to its own ironic tactics, *Almanac*'s narrative pedagogy also refigures the very content of human subjectivity in this "death-world" of the near future in the Americas. In particular, nearly all of the characters are marked linguistically and affectively by death and violence and have developed an apparent numbness to both.

The existence of multiple "death-worlds" confronts Silko's readers in visceral detail as *Almanac* documents the subjectivity of both the perpetrators and the victims of necropolitics: a subjectivity characterized in the novel by the characters' generalized lack of affective energy and psychological nuance. Relying on the depersonalizing operations of allegory and on other narrative techniques that underline the deadening of internal experience and emotional life, *Almanac* in fact refigures the role of *affect* in the contemporary novel and in contemporary society. Silko's emphasis on characters that are not quite fully "realized" in the modern realist mode signals the coincidence between her narrative and allegorical modes. I argue that it is this allegorical mode that allows *Almanac* to articulate a critical representation of the contemporary cultural predicaments of "the Americas": through prophecy and allegory, the text offers a narrative "fix" to a broken society. This proffered narrative solution emerges structurally as well as thematically through a multiplying of intradiegetic and extradiegetic allegories that together gesture toward the prophetic totality of *Almanac*'s vision. This multiplication of allegorical tales told by an array of characters along with the Manichean allegorical reading that the text seems to require combine to push that narrative totality in a new or unexpected direction, away from the "predetermined signified" of its own apocalyptic scenario of a total race war.

II. Allegory as a New Temporality for the Americas

With its transnational focus, *Almanac* suggests a literary solution to problems articulated elsewhere by Latin American critics and artists, such as Nelly Richard and Ricardo Muñoz, who call for a new aesthetics that can more effectively intervene in contemporary sociality. As discussed in Chapter 1, these Latin American artists and critics form a group loosely identified with the Chilean "cultural critique" movement ("*la crítica cultural*") that insists that aesthetic strategies be developed to better acknowledge, account for, and ultimately interrupt human suffering in societies operating under neoliberal (official and state-mandated) regimes of "control." Such "democratic" and "free-market" national and global ideologies disavow their own implication in the overweening power regimes that "manage" sociality, such as the state, the interests of capital, and discourses of common sense and "security," all of which affectively and discursively saturate public and private social life. The concerns raised by these Latin American cultural theorists and producers (particularly in the "postdictatorial era") coincide with the diagnosis of Mbembe and other critiques of contemporary globalized and neocolonial social and political regimes. In *Almanac*, Silko extends the chronotopes and characters of its multiple plots deep into Mexico, Colombia, Brazil, and also into Alaska and the Arctic, explicitly generating a textual representation of a transamerican social, geographical, and cultural totality.

Interestingly, the text also articulates a very similar knot of questions and concerns in the context of this transnational Americas linked by its participation in the death-worlds of state violence, rapacious capitalism, and the violent exploitation and expropriation of human life. Echoing Richard and Avelar, Silko makes an implicit connection between the terror-driven dictatorships of Latin America in the 1960s–80s and the various forms of sociality that persist today as surreptitious legacies of both those specific dictatorships and the logic of late capitalist modernity more generally. The language of bureaucratic control and management threads through *Almanac*, almost always voiced by one or another criminal and often violently sadistic player in the various economic and power schemes that crisscross the plot. These schemes include illegal water rights and real estate development in Tucson, organ and plasma "donors" along the U.S.-Mexico border, pornographic torture tapes produced in South America and sold everywhere, private mercenary armies that "insure" wealthy persons and corporations in Mexico and the United States. These plots highlight *Almanac*'s focus on the "disposable" populations of various communities and nations: the poor in shantytowns outside Mexico City, the homeless in the United States, women, drug addicts, racial minorities, Vietnam vets, handicapped persons, and others. In tracing out various scenarios involving the torture, killing, exploitation, or other violence wrought on these bodies, as well as the "thoughts" of the perpetrators of such violence, Silko stages acts of murder and torture as politically performative scenarios within the narrative.

In geographically specifying the main action of the novel along the U.S.-Mexico border and at the "edges" (desert, jungle, urban underworld) of various nation-states, *Almanac* literalizes the notion of a "threshold" area in which, as Hannah Arendt and Giorgio Agamben have noted, the belief that "everything is possible" denotes a zone which marks the margins of the community, where those who are included are contrasted to those who inhabit the realm of "bare life" or "sacred life." Agamben's influential philosophical treatise on the constitutive exclusion of some incarnation of *"homo sacer"* from every modern society informs Mbembe's "necropolitics" and its production of the "living dead." Agamben writes that this foundational division of "the life of *homo sacer* (sacred man), who may be killed and yet not sacrificed" from the realm of the human or "good life" marks the margins of Western notions of sovereignty and society: "In the 'politicization' of bare life . . . the humanity of living man is decided" (8).[7] These theorizations of the fundamental boundaries of social community in Western modernity also suggest why Silko so often returns in the pages of *Almanac* to narrations of murder, torture, and other forms of bodily violence done not out of anger but with a calmly reasoned out exploitive purpose and goal. This instrumentalization of "life" is further impressed upon the reader when such scenes are presented as "emblems" in an allegorical mode that refuses the reader's efforts to involve herself as an identificatory model for the text.

In this refusal, Silko enacts what Richard calls an aesthetics of "disidentity," which operates in *Almanac* as part of its own particular and allegorical response to the proposition of a transamerican social totality. By allegorizing Western modernity precisely through its production of "death zones" where the rule of law and civility have been erased and public space has become a realm of violent performance, *Almanac* generates a narrative performance that shifts and challenges the reader's accustomed responses and positions in relation to a narrative text. Véronica Zebadúa-Yañez argues that in the context of the last decade's epidemic of femicides in

Ciudad Juárez, acts of violence should be understood performatively as marking the boundaries of the livable community and indicating (pedagogically, as it were) which lives count as valuable, "grieveable" human lives and which are to be considered "bare life" (and therefore occupying the inhuman zone of Mbembe's "living dead").[8] Unlike its uncannily similar real-life incarnation in Ciudad Juárez, Silko's representations of violent acts and the boundaries they produce remain literary and thus encode allegorically her arguments regarding the very foundations of Western sociality and its production of such uninhabitable zones and populations.

The emphasis on both the logic and the affective technologies of this sociality occurs particularly in the narrative sections that are focalized through the perpetrators of acts of terror and violation, such as Beaufrey and Serlo who are figures in one of the central plotlines that involves the white girl Seese's missing baby (she has come to Lecha for help in locating him). About mid-way through the text, the reader learns for certain that the baby was taken by his biological father, an artist named David who is involved with Beaufrey, the South American "aristocrat" who organizes the child's kidnapping and transfer to Cartagena by chartered jet. Once in Cartagena, David and the "blue blood" Latin Americans return to their preferred leisure activities:

> David had begun leaving the baby with the nurse in the suite to join Beaufrey and Serlo upstairs in the penthouse for drinks and dinner followed by cocaine and videos of police torture, autopsies, or other new acquisitions . . . Beaufrey had enjoyed watching the expressions on David's face as the torture had progressed conveniently into the 'autopsy' of the victim. (538)

This discussion of pornographic torture tapes and David's reluctant pleasure in them is followed by Serlo's meditations on his *finca* (ranch) as a needed refuge for "those of *sangre pura* as unrest and revolutions continued to sweep through" (541). Serlo's theory of "proper genetic balance" crudely exemplifies the convergence in *Almanac* of a specular logics of pornographic objectification, masculine privilege, racist ideologies, and the production of scientific and technological knowledge. Serlo segues from his obsessions with *sangre pura* (pure blood) to the "Alternative Earth module" plan for a colony of "self-sufficient, closed systems capable of remaining cut off from earth for years if necessary while the upheaval and violence" spread below (542–43). Thus, Silko emphasizes how the lines between the "home sacer" of the vast majority of humanity and the "select few" who are included in some future elite human community are literalized as distinctions in access to wealth and technology.

These allegorical scenarios expose the sociality of this specifically Euro-American modernity as a technology of selfhood; that is, as a social structure that produces certain horrific types of humanity exemplified by Serlo, Beaufrey, and David. Such scenarios in the text also stage narrative performances of that sociality: scenes, images, and uses of language that confront the reader with the deep structure of the affects and ideologies that enable such dead zones, or "zones of morbidity" as Jamie Skye Bianco has called them. Skye's piercing essay on *Almanac* and the contemporary conditions of globalized necropower claims that "above all the text [*Almanac*] is an affective machine for an emergent politics" (33). While concurring, I want to emphasize that *Almanac* is an "affective machine" that operates precisely through narrative writing, which also makes it a particular kind of anachronism. That is, it is not accidental that *Almanac*'s indictment of, and response to, the states of emergency of the late twentieth century occur as *writing* and through a deployment of familiar literary genres, such as the novel, the detective story, allegory and history.

That Silko's magisterial text only accrues more prophetic power in the twenty-first century—as the state and capital mechanisms of a global necropolitics gain traction in the United States and elsewhere—speaks of its profound capacity as a veritable "almanac" of transamerican sociality. In the first quotation from the intradiegetic "almanac" within the text, Silko warns the reader about what is to come.

What I have to tell you now is that
this world is about to end. (135)

The "almanac" continues, "Those were the last words of the giant serpent. The days that were to come had been foretold. The people scattered. Killers came from all directions. And more killers followed, to kill them" (135). Characterizing, in fact, all of modernity in the Americas as an era of "killers," Silko counters the dominant temporality of the inevitability and desirability of global capitalism and the Euro-American modern state with an apocalyptic epic that contests both capitalism and the Western democratic nation-state.

As I discuss below, the characters in *Almanac* appear to be fully, even ontologically, marked by identities such as Indian, white, Mexican, black, male, female, and queer.[9] So how, then, do these recurrent identity markers work in *Almanac*, a text that produces readings that oscillate between its clearly implied ontologies of transamerican racist social formations and its insistence on a fluidity and poststructural undecidability that understands identity as a "simulated regime" (Cherniavsky)? Apocalyptic temporality *in Almanac*, like the geographies that yoke it to history, is notoriously indigenous or "Indian" and encapsulates what Eva Cherniavsky calls Silko's "tribal epistemology": an epistemology oppositional to, but not outside, the specular logics of Western rationalism and capitalism, that is, the logics of identity thinking. By insisting that Silko's use of "tribal" is distinct from the specular logics of identity and its calcification into essential foundational categories, Cherniavsky emphasizes that neither Silko nor *Almanac* participates in the colonial nostalgia for indigeneity as the untouched "Other," or precedent, to modernity.[10] In fact, she argues that *Almanac* works against identity as part of "the specular difference engine and its production of an always accessible alterity" (Cherniavsky 124n3) and resists the "incorporative logic of identification" that is the engine of "the territorializing operations of specular thought" (118).[11] In reading the tribal epistemology of *Almanac* as an articulation of how identity and identification function as commodities in capitalist regimes of value production and control, Cherniavsky signals the crucial but underanalyzed function of how identity is actually represented and deployed in Silko's text.

This chapter focuses on the ambiguous status of ontologies of identity in *Almanac of the Dead* and traces how the text works through these impasse of identity and history using the narrative operations of allegory. The plot of indigenous revolution is structured as an allegory, and a specifically apocalyptic one, for the futurity that is scripted in transamerican historical pasts. Allegory depends, at least to some extent, on stable or agreed-upon systems of interpretation and a mythic register that is normally absent in the contemporary ethnic bildungsroman. Thus as a narrative technology, allegory requires some familiarity with the "simulated regime" of identity, which then allows the mechanisms of the text to underline that regime's operations, its constructedness. The text explicitly poses its identitarian surface structure as the inverse of the colonial ontologies of the racialized thinking of the Manichean allegory. As famously described by Abdul JanMohammed, Manichean allegory transforms "racial difference into moral and even metaphysical difference" so that "the function of racial difference, of the fixation on and fetishization of native savagery and evil" can be explained in terms of colonial economic, administrative, and affective regimes (80, 82).[12] That is, Silko enlists the colonial regime of racial difference and inverts it to pose an allegory of good and evil grounded in geocultural ontologies (white vs. Indian, torturer vs. victim). But in the text, these binaries do not hold for long and the identitarian logics of the Manichean allegory are soon turned against themselves. Therefore, reading Silko's allegory of the Americas ironically—as a text suspended between narrative modes that foreground both the literary conventions of realism and exaggerated racialized and sexualized stereotypes—allows us to follow the shifts in the text as it, too, oscillates between a regime of identity logics and a narrativization of the "something else" that might lead to the social transformation of those logics—a narrativization that occurs, somewhat ironically, through allegory.

One apparent connection between classical allegory and *Almanac* is the pedagogical intention behind both.[13] Such pedagogical modes of expression rely upon the key role of the reader-audience in producing narratives of revolutionary change. The narrative pedagogy of allegory in *Almanac* uses the prophetic mode of apocalyptic writing and marks the limits—conceptual and historical—of the world the text represents to the reader. Benjamin underlines how such narrative pedagogies of allegory also signal the specific and constraining work of history in narrative production—the precise historical moment of the text's enunciation and reception. In their shared preoccupation with writing and interpreting history, both the allegorical and apocalyptic modes articulate an ancient dilemma regarding the question of audience and narrative performativity. In *The Veil of Allegory*, Michael Murrin calls this "the prophetic dilemma" that faces biblical and other ancient prophets intent on warning their people of an impending catastrophe. The inevitable failure of any attempt at prophecy is in fact constitutive of the prophetic mode and generates its dilemma, which centers on the problem of how to communicate a divinely revealed truth that is difficult to accept, or even impossible to decipher. As Murrin notes, "Jerusalem was a tomb for more prophets than Christ. All of them provoked such hostility by their words that they feared death. Their rhetoric alienated rather than convinced. The prophetic movement is a record of constant failure" (26).[14] *Almanac*'s prophecies likewise must confront the reluctance to hear its message along with a lengthy march of failure—past, present, and future—in efforts to move transamerican publics toward critical awareness and sweeping social change, particularly regarding the conditions of indigenous collectivities.

In understanding allegory as "rhetoric," Murrin prefigures the current critical concern with performative enunciations and writing as a technology of selfhood. The shared roots of allegory and prophecy underline the central role of audience and what Murrin calls "the multitude." Murrin explains the prophetic dilemma and the role of the multitude, or "the many," in allegory in ways that resonate even more explicitly with what I defined as "ironic performativities" in Chapter 1:

The allegorist decided ahead of time the principles which would divide the few from the many; he presupposed such a division, which automatically occurred whenever he spoke. He tried to exclude the many from the understanding of truth, though not from its proclamation. He discovered the appropriate vehicle for truth in myth, parable, and apocalyptic vision, which the many could follow as a story but never interpret properly. (22)

Either the audience is divided by the truth (once the prophet makes the pronouncement) or else the way in which that truth is proclaimed (by the allegorist) divides the audience into a group of elite listeners who "get it" and the masses who cannot understand or refuse to accept the truth offered. Like irony, allegory divides the audience into insiders and outsiders, or in the language of prophetic and religious tradition, into "the initiate elite and the ignorant masses." Silko's recourse to allegory in *Almanac of the Dead* recognizes the role of different audiences and signals her determination to communicate a difficult truth. The choice to eschew conventional modes of novelistic realism in favor of a montage of realism and allegory stems from *Almanac*'s proffered solution to a contemporary and specifically indigenous and transamerican incarnation of the prophetic dilemma.

Because allegory necessarily encodes a specific historical moment in its cryptic communications, it also incorporates and communicates the philosophy of history inherent to its epoch's dominant discourses, events, and modes of signification. As Fredric Jameson suggests in his defense of allegory and interpretation in *The Political Unconscious,* the totalizing project of allegory maintains a dialectic engagement with history, politics, and specific collectivities in ways that conventional postmodernism's literary deferrals and negations seem to bypass (58). *Almanac of the Dead* articulates the specific dominance of necropolitics in the late twentieth-century modernity of the Americas and in so doing works to contest the loss of a revolutionary future. The plots that occupy the narrative of how that future comes into being, however, rely on the figures—the stereotypes and themes—that populate the contemporary transamerican imaginary; the violence and dehumanization of a racist and rapaciously capitalist late modernity is thus figured through an array of "stick figures" who act in a variety of scripts—some pretty well worn and some seemingly brand new.[15] Furthermore, if prophets are always necessarily failed prophets, and the mode of prophecy—like allegory—is constituted by failure and loss, the failure and loss that feeds the prophetic allegories in *Almanac of the Dead* is the very history of indigeneity in the Americas.

Almanac thus offers a series of replies to one of the central questions of the twentieth century: What can be learned from a people's relentless history of disaster and death—what the revolutionary Mayan character Angelita calls "the Native American holocaust" (530)—and what can be done about it? By figuring "the epoch of Death-Eye Dog," as Silko terms this history, as both an allegory and a critique of the colonial modernity of the entire hemisphere of the Americas, *Almanac* suggests that one important response is to make stories about it.[16] In the very narrativization of an apocalyptic race war in the Americas, *Almanac* offers narrative itself, particularly cathartic allegories of a struggle between good and evil, as a means of articulating and transforming social formations in the real.[17] This narrative pedagogy ultimately argues that the allegorization of both the apocalypse of the past and the one that is to come can become the rewriting that makes other futures possible.[18]

III. Allegory as Pedagogy

Looking to literary texts to "reactivate . . . hope," as Idelbar Avelar puts it, simultaneously speaks to literature's affective and political levels of signification and suggests the particular ways in which we tend to read narrative cultural production symptomatically and metaphorically, that is, allegorically. *Almanac of the Dead* directly encourages this impulse to allegorical thinking and reading through a variety of narrative techniques, such as the central plot function of the "old notebooks" of the ancient almanac and the particular diegetic ability of the notebooks to "carry" Native American history in the form of important allegorical stories and myths of the tribal collective. Above, I discuss that one of the functions these stories perform is to communicate the horror of the Manichean structure of contemporary colonial modernity and its racist capitalist sociality. But in her inversions of the Manichean colonial allegory of racial differences, Silko's narrativizations of cultural myth and her montage of generic iterations (modernist realist novel, postmodern montage, detective genre fiction) resonate at multiple levels for readers, particularly those conditioned to expect a "mythical" and non-linear mode as the mark of an "indigenous" perspective. That is, because it deploys the very cultural myths and racial ontologies that constitute Manichean, as well as cosmopolitan, Western perspectives, *Almanac*'s allegories operate *through* presignified understandings of culturalist ethnic identity.[19]

But if we understand Silko's narrative techniques as precisely literary, and therefore embedded within the Euro-American narrative tradition of the novel, *Almanac*'s allegorical mode can be seen working toward its own particular ends—ends that may not be as transparently or merely ideological as the figures deployed in the text. By threading a number of mythical stories handed down in encrypted form into its narrative, *Almanac*'s inclusion of these explicitly intradiegetic allegories reiterates the norms of identity logics but then pushes them to an allegorical extreme, recalling the mode's genesis in medieval and early modern society and literature.

As noted in Benjamin's classic studies (and more recently in Avelar's work), allegory specifically captures the Baroque aesthetics formed in its genesis in seventeenth-century Europe, particularly by explaining how allegory can operate along a very different logic from that of the "symbol" and its linguistic chains of signification. Benjamin posits a specifically Baroque relation to the past that elicits a distinct aesthetics that works through imagery than signification. His theoretical musings on seventeenth-century Baroque German drama offer descriptions that often uncannily illuminate the excessive, qualities of Silko's narrative: "With every idea the moment of expression coincides with a veritable eruption of images, which gives rise to a chaotic mass of metaphors. This is how the sublime is present in this style" (173). The emblematic function of the cacophony of images put forth in Silko's barrage of chapters, scenes, and locations encompasses a totalized vision of the Americas in which the land, as well as geography, manifests the violence of colonial and capitalist history.

Almanac thus reinvigorates allegorical modes of representation from within the epic novel form by challenging accustomed practices of reading for character and the identificatory pleasures of bourgeois subjectivity. Avant-garde writing has worked to dislodge and disparage this readerly bias in twentieth-century narrative, but it remains a dominant feature of popular textual practices, often existing alongside a desire for the "predetermined signified" of minority fiction's culturalist plots.[20] Silko confronts the reader with these desires for identificatory options within the text and undercuts the teleologies of narrative structures as well as presumptions to particular kinds of selfhood that are embedded in neoliberal fantasies of individuality. By thus generating her own reversal of the Manichean allegory out of a vast neobaroque tableau of transamerican geographies, cultures, and discourses, Silko highlights a kind of grim, repetitive, and antihumanist deadness to contemporary social totality.

Even the title, *Almanac of the Dead*, announces the text's preoccupation with violence and defeat, which is developed over the course of the novel via its hybrid of realist and experimental narrative forms: offering itself simultaneously as a science fiction of the near future and a prophetic "first text"—a bible as well as an almanac—of the repressed counterhistory of indigenous peoples in the Americas. Because the title is clearly intended to be simultaneously literal and figurative, it signals how Silko's *Almanac* and the almanac that occupies a key place in the narrative are both books that offer "forecasts" for (or from) "the dead." Or as the text defines itself, an almanac "predicts or foretells the auspicious days, the ecclesiastical and other anniversaries" (Silko 136). This notion of a book of forecasts and prophecies underlines Silko's emphasis on time and on recovering repressed or lost knowledge for future use. "The Dead" and its place in the doubled title thus refer to both the wisdom and stories of "the ancients," as well as the contemporary implosion of the temporal and geographical apocalypse portrayed in the narrative. This simultaneity of "scale" allows indigenous ancestors, tribal revolutionaries, and the disposable "living dead" of a corrupt Euro-American late modernity to speak together in one text. The resulting baroque cacophony of stories coheres in a non-linear logic that prophesizes the present and functions as a kind of prophylactic intervention against possible horrific futures.[21]

Confirming its apocalyptic narrative pedagogy, Silko has compared *Almanac of the Dead* to "an ogre Kachina to scare bad kids. It's like, read this and be horrified, and then don't let it be this scenario" (Niemann interview 10)—a statement that further highlights the relation Silko sees between herself and her ideal reader, who is chided here like a recalcitrant child. A close reading of both *Almanac's* Table of Contents and its many metacritical moments reveals to what a great extent Silko has translated this pedagogical impulse into a text that constantly interrogates and theorizes itself, emphatically signaling its own allegorical reading. The very notion of an "almanac of the dead," for example, is turned into a narrative aside about prophetic allegories and their uses. As a drugged-up Lecha tells her sister, "Those old almanacs don't just tell you when to plant or harvest, they tell you about the days yet to come—drought or flood, plague, civil war or invasion" (137). But in spite of such overt messages to the reader (who might need this information rather more than Zeta, who does not appear to need instruction on how to "read" or interpret anything), the term "almanac" also gets its postmodern twist, both thematically and structurally.[22] Before the exchange between the twins, the reader has waded through a series of poems, sayings, and admonitions, all that presumably fall under the heading "Pages from the Snakes' Notebook" (135). This juxtaposition of forms illustrates Silko's narrative tactics and highlights how the novel relies simultaneously on the power of the text's metacritical postmodern montage and on an almost soap-operatic (or *telenovela*) exaggeration of *incident* that suggests the novel's ties to popular genre forms. Such exaggeration also recalls Benjamin's own defense of Baroque allegory: "That awkward heavy-handedness, which has been attributed to either lack of talent on the part of the artist or lack of insight on the part of the patron, is essential to allegory" (187).[23]

Silko, then, does not shy from utilizing the appeal of popular modes and their generic conventions of plot, character, and ideology, but she deploys them in ways that ultimately challenge dominant imaginaries. One clear success of *Almanac* has been its critique of nation-state borders and thus implicitly of garden-variety nationalisms. But on the infamous map of the Americas that appears in its front pages, the dominance of the word

"MEXICO" indicates a number of key questions and ambiguities that the text also develops, particularly the suggestion of a specific double function for its border tropology and its implied ontologies. The map, like the narrative, seems to combine opposing impulses: on one hand, we find an alliance with the contemporary emphasis in cultural theory on border crossing and emerging transgressive identities; on the other hand, we find narrative signals that suggest an affinity with more conservative views of U.S. national borders and frontiers, exemplified in the nineteenth-century historian Frederick Jackson Turner's so-called frontier thesis. Turner argued that the frontier of the United States was a space where differences and conflicts would be absorbed, or assimilated—as in a crucible—to generate the new nation.[24] *Almanac* represents the "frontier" in Tucson as an outlaw region where U.S. and transamerican history come together at the "edge" of the nation, generating a "new" transnationally hybrid site.

This border region is an exaggeration of necropolitics—resonating with the reign of violence at the actual U.S.-Mexico border—and yet also a space "at the edges" in which the social formations of the United States crack open, where both illegality and indigeneity can do their work under the radar of state and capital power. This double meaning of the allegorical chronotope of marginality figures the border as both an apocalyptic dead or death zone which promises no forms of safety or security for its inhabitants, but also as the incubator of revolution—a place where Indians and other subversives can more easily operate outside the "law" of a corrupt and dead-end social order. This double signification reiterates the problem of allegory (and the stereotype) in that the narrative ultimately is constrained to tell a story that we know already, at least at some level. In her discussion of Ciudad Juárez and the ongoing epidemic of murders of young women in the maquiladoras (factories) at the real-life border, Zebadúa-Yañez notes that the murders illustrate how a "global unequal distribution of vulnerability is replicated within the community" so that particular spaces in the city come to "represent the very border between inside and outside, between relative security and probable death" (14). *Almanac* likewise posits Tucson and El Paso and the environs around Mexico City and the outlying areas of Chiapas as national spaces that demarcate the "inside and outside" of the civil order and manifest such a "global unequal distribution of vulnerability." As Lecha notes, "Life has always been cheap in Tucson" (165). Therefore, too, we see how these chronotopes and the plots and images they convey operate at this other level as an allegory of necropolitical capitalism. But the shadow of that allegory is precisely its familiarity and real-life resonance with, and performative repetition of, "what we know" about the U.S.-Mexico border.

This revised frontier operates as both a space and an edge and is figured primarily in relation to "MEXICO" (note that the United States is not named on the map). In this map and in the text as a whole, the U.S.-Mexico border is thus a trope of transamerican historical and cultural syncretism—where white, Indian, and Mexican all come together—but is also a point of transition and exchange at this edge, a point or zone characterized by anarchy, violence, and dissolution of the nation-state and other forms of security and civil life. For example, the arrows that point "South to Cartagena and Buenos Aires" come with captions such as "torture video tapes" and "military arms, aircraft to private army," and those that point north come with captions such as "cocaine to finance arms." These images of "the other side" of the border resonate in particular with the long history of Anglo national fantasies of Mexico, and Central and South America, as the origin points of a contagion of brutality and disorder that could easily sweep northward into the United States.[25] In deploying images that coincide with such dominant white nationalist discourses of "tropicalization" together with a critical destabilizing of the very notion of a United States and of the nation-state itself, we see how *Almanac's* representation of "MEXICO" and the "SOUTH" can figure both the revolution that is coming as well as the origin point of reactionary violence and chaos.

IV. Revolutionary Time

In addition to its interrogation of spatial imaginaries and the ontologies attached to them, *Almanac* also addresses the temporal aspect of history—particularly how Euro-American modernity presumes specific temporalities and relations, including terms such as "progress" or "premodern." A number of critics have noticed the various representations and narrative restructuring of time in the novel, generating what critics such as Caren Irr have called its oppositional and alternative, or "indigenous," narrative temporality. Irr notes that "against [a] decomposing Eurocentric subject," Silko's text elaborates indigenous perspectives on time and history and produces a revolutionary temporality (233): "Silko narrates into being a 'tidal wave of history' . . . [in which] parallels and simultaneities make it possible to imagine a hybrid temporality composed of an inevitable history leading up to a transformative, mythic, and widely extensive 'now'" (236). This wide and inevitable "rush" of time to a teleological endpoint set by prophecy and myth further indicates the ways that the "apocalypse" in Silko's novel is quintessential of the prophetic genre.[26]

However, the "mythic and widely extensive now" of *Almanac of the Dead* is in fact decidedly apocalyptic, portraying the decadence and brutality of the "end times" of the epoch of the Death-Eye Dog in ways that further reflect its preoccupations with questions of collectivity and the ontologies of identity, particularly in these juxtapositions of the "decomposing Eurocentric subject" with the temporality of revolution. Revolutionary time, in fact, has been the constant "now" for indigenous persons in the Americas since the Conquest, according to the novel—a revolution figured by "the great war to take back the land," also known as the "war against the United States . . . the same war it had always been; the people were still fighting for their land"(631). The character Calabazas, a Yaqui Indian smuggler living in the desert around the Arizona-Mexico border, is often credited as one of the text's key voices of indigenous tactics of opposition and alterity— both as a storyteller and as a smuggler. Acting as the main spokesperson for the "war against the United States," Calabazas describes the philosophy of time, and of history, that the revolutionary temporality in *Almanac* inscribes: "He did not think time was absolute or universal; rather each location, each place, was a living organism with time running inside it like blood, time that was unique to that place alone" (629). By yoking temporality to "each location, each place," Silko emphasizes the transamerican context of her apocalypse and its insistence on a prophetic "great now" in the Americas. This revolutionary temporality is narrativized through various scenes that highlight the confluence—unplanned and primarily mystical or spiritual—of a wide array of indigenous collectivities from Mexico, up and down the Americas, Alaska, and beyond; all of which share the sense that the moment for a total revolutionary uprising has arrived.

The Anglo-European decadence against which this revolutionary time is represented occupies the other chapters, which also emphasize an equally extensive "now" that is structured through the interplay of various plots of local criminality in Tucson, Las Vegas, Los Angeles, and Mexico City. These plots are populated almost exclusively by characters whose relationships are mute, violent, and brutally instrumental, in both familial and romantic contexts. As noted, these relationships and characters are also marked by extreme sexual deviancy and violence, particularly the vividly repugnant and bloody fetishistic practices of various white male characters—especially but not exclusively homosexual ones.[27] I have suggested that the novel figures these affective disorders through their constitutional ties to global capitalist social formations as manifested in the murderous conspiracies of nation-states, criminal gangs, the police, the military, and multinational business interests. One of *Almanac*'s especially prescient forecasts, for example, is of the growing reliance, in the United States and elsewhere, on independent contractors who provide private armies of mercenary soldiers, torturers, and weapons to ensure "security" for rich persons, corporations, and countries.[28]

This generative relation between global capitalism, the state, and necropolitical death-worlds is developed predominantly in the deployment of virulent discourses of race and sex in the novel. For example, when one of the main bad guys in Tucson, Judge Arne, reflects on his sexual use of "brown boys" (in the context of a similar use of his "beloved" basset hounds), he also articulates these connections between ontologies of race and large-scale political economies:

> The brown ones knew their place, the white ones didn't. But wasn't that what increased police spending was for? Alleys and vacant lots across Florida and the Southwest were littered with human refuse from the Midwest and Northeast—cast-off white men, former wage earners from mills and factories . . . Now there was the chaos spreading across Mexico. The refugees were thick as flies in barbed-wire camps all along the U.S. border. (461)

This brutal but grotesquely plausible sociopolitical analysis by Judge Arne, coupled with his character filter, highlights the interaction of a language of instrumentality in politics with an instrumentalized "use" of sex and other intimacies for a depersonalized bodily satisfaction, a satisfaction that is twisted by sadistic and bloody desires and orientations. This example reiterates how the language of specific narrative filters throughout *Almanac* conveys the extent of necropower's operations in the interior lives of human individuals as well as in public spheres of politics and population shifts, again underlining the corruption and horror of contemporary Euro-American sociality.

In the chapters that feature the revolutionary momentum against this sociality, the critique of nation-state borders takes on a foundational cast through its articulation of a scathingly ironic dismissal of the territorial claims and philosophical concepts of sovereignty and juridical legality that underwrite Euro-American modernity. Reflecting on what notions of "law" and sovereignty have meant for Native Americans, she notes that "there was not, and there never had been, a legal government by Europeans anywhere in the Americas. Not by any definition, not even by the Europeans' own definitions and laws . . . Because stolen land never had clear title . . . Every waking hour Zeta spent scheming and planning to break as many of their laws as she could" (133). Using the empirical logic of Western thought itself, Silko exposes the ruses of discourses of Euro-American modernity that rely on notions of property rights and the sacred sovereignty of the individual.

The apocalyptic scenario narrativized in the plot of *Almanac* involves the hemispheric "great war" to take back the land, which comprised a number of distinct armies, or battalions: indigenous tribes scattered from Chiapas to Alaska; the homeless in Tucson, Los Angeles, and New York; and the slum dwellers of Mexico City. This alliance across ontologies of race and geography between indigenous collectivities and the poor and homeless of the Americas indicates one of the novel's early and explicit deviations from its implied racial Manicheanism, though the binary division of good against evil is maintained. The fact of cross-identity alliances is clearly articulated by Clinton, an African American Vietnam vet and organizer of the "Army of the Homeless," who notes, "After the riots and Vietnam War, there had been no more university funding for black studies classes. That was no accident. The powers who controlled the United States didn't want people to know their history. If the people knew their history, they would realize they must rise up" (401, 431). Clinton and the Mayan revolutionary leader Angelita La Escapía (the Meat Hook) thus share the ethical-political imperative to "know their history" across the distinct contexts of African American and Native American revolutionary social movements. Such alliances have been read as Silko's advocacy of an antiessentialist concept of oppositional social movements, though the apocalyptic narrative push seems to fold even these crossings of identity and history into the Manichean race war. As the revolutionary narrative of "the war to take back the land" nears a climatic endpoint late in the novel, it promises to end in vast bloodshed and a rather large die-off of European Americans on the two continents of the Americas. Calabazas describes the plot handed down by the old-time people: "The prophecies said gradually all traces of Europeans in America would disappear and, at last, the people would retake the land" (632).

These examples highlight how throughout *Almanac* the specter of an apocalyptic war organized through relations to race and property awakens the officially repressed history and memory of racial violence in the Americas. Silko confrontationally stages the dominant deployments of racial conflict and violence in official national history by reversing and inverting precisely the terms of that Manichean "ideological narrative."[29] Through this inversion, *Almanac* resurrects the specter of indigenous uprising: a haunting of the U.S. national imaginary that has served historically to mobilize white anxiety about "social order" and legitimize the various defensive mechanisms that protect white Euro-Americans' social dominance in discursive, juridical, and bodily spheres of public life. Such national narratives of social order are deployed in the United States and in Latin America as bulwarks protecting the dominant social formations and their privileges. They are also the foundation of a collective national imaginary of racializations (and rationalizations) built on disavowed histories of violent conquest and theft. *Almanac of the Dead* pushes against these national imaginaries (shared by the United States, Mexico, and much of Latin America) with a liberatory allegorical narrative of "race war" in the

Americas, a narrative that participates in the tradition of anticolonial revolutionary violence. Inverting the colonialist binary logic of the "Manichean allegory" that opposes European civilization to the savagery and backwardness of conquered peoples, *Almanac* rewrites the hemisphere's colonial script in terms of Silko's revised, transamerican conceptualization of the Americas.

V. Allegory as Technology of Selfhood: Multiplying Allegorical Effects

Exposing the inadequacy of rational logocentrism and Euro-American neoliberal individualism in both politics and personal relationships across the Americas, *Almanac of the Dead* opens conceptual room for a revised understanding of allegory, one that operates via an alternative logics and works through prophecy and montage.[30] *Almanac* consistently advocates for storytelling as a means of revolution, an investment in narrative that Silko uses to highlight the links between her *Almanac* and Marx's *Communist Manifesto*. Like the "stories of depravity and cruelty" that Marx related to factory workers to animate the class struggle in nineteenth-century Europe, *Almanac* offers the hope of a worldwide uprising that takes light because of the revolutionary fervor, the affect, generated by stories and by writing. As La Escapía explains,

> Marx had understood stories are alive with the energy words generate. Word by word, the stories of suffering, injury, and death had transformed the present moment, seizing listeners' or readers' imaginations so that for an instant, they were present and felt the suffering of sisters and brothers long past. The words of the stories filled rooms with an immense energy that aroused the living with a fierce passion and determination for justice. (520)

In claiming that such stories are the very key to revolutionary historical transformation, *Almanac* raises the expectation that the novel itself will provide its readers with this transformative affective connection to the suffering of others and a "determination for justice."

As I've suggested, however, this connection to the suffering of others does not occur through the customary realist narrative technologies of identification and conventional narrativity (Brooks; de Lauretis). *Almanac's* experimental narrativity is established precisely through its excessive use of free indirect discourse and a dizzying juxtaposition of narrative filters—filters characterized by an equally striking absence of "feeling" and identificatory options for the reader. The text's passionate advocacy for justice rubs against this performative narrativity and its production of the affect of *affectlessness* as figured in the "dead" and flattened voices of its characters and the narrative focalization through them. This flattening of the human individual into a "type" or plot function is a key tactic, and effect, of the allegorical mode. Even the apparent protagonists of *Almanac* are represented through narrative focalizations that convey a violence and disgust that permeates the character filters, including those characters who might be expected to be privileged in the binary ideologies indicated in the text's ontological racial "schema." The Yaqui protagonist Lecha, for example, often seems most characterized by her drug use, which is described in the novel through the eyes of her son: "Ferro says the needle slips in like a lover's prick and shoots the dope in white and hot. That's why Lecha wants them all to watch her get off, Ferro says, but *he* doesn't watch junky orgasms not even for his *own* mother" (20). Ferro's hateful but astute observations show again how language itself symptomatically reflects a sociality that promotes the violent instrumentalization of human beings and relations in the service of greed and sensation.

Because the focalization through Ferro includes his reported speech, addressed to no one in particular in the kitchen, it holds to James Phelan's emphasis on the multiple tracks of such "character narration." In the gap between what Phelan calls the "disclosure functions" and "telling functions" of narration, an array of complex vectors can arise, particularly in this situation in which the information disclosed by Ferro is further doubled: we learn both that Lecha likes to shoot up in front of her family and that Ferro harbors a deep, dense hatred of her that is sexualized as well as brutal in its language. The reader thus learns to "read" Ferro's emotional landscape as likewise brutal, deadened, and unfamiliar in its darkness. *Almanac* thwarts the novel's generic leanings toward a psychological seduction of the reader, a seduction that normally occurs in a readerly identification with a character that is enabled by that character's psychological mimesis, or reality effect.[31] In that Ferro's interior life is represented as bleak and bereft of "normal" feeling and relations, it fails to be mimetic. But in staging his character narration within the text, Silko suggests that the affective norms of psychological realism are being transformed under the conditions of necropower.

Almanac's refusal of psychological and mimetic depth further signals its allegorical status. Benjamin emphasizes that allegory pushes against the bourgeois individual subject and his [*sic*] "beautiful soul." In his argument against Romanticism's privileging of the symbol over the Baroque emphasis on allegory, Benjamin notes a dynamic that articulates some generic-historical reasons for Silko's resistance to character narration:

> What is typically romantic is the placing of this perfect individual within a progression of events which is, it is true, infinite but is nevertheless

redemptive, even sacred. But once the ethical subject has become absorbed in the individual, then no rigourism—not even Kantian rigourism—can save it and preserve its masculine profile. Its heart is lost in the beautiful soul. And the radius of action—not only the radius of culture—for the thus perfected individual is what describes the circle of the "symbolic". In contrast, . . . the immediate problems of the baroque, being politico-religious problems, did not so much affect the individual and his ethics as his religious community. (160–61)

Silko's shift away from the generic conventions of the novel—particularly the modern realist novel with its consuming interest in the development of the individual—reflects the primary concern of *Almanac* with collectivities and populations, rather than with the individual subjects of bourgeois capitalism. Throughout the majority of its 763 pages, *Almanac* traces various incarnations of a "politico-religious" community that overshadow any particular narrative of individual growth or transformation. In place of such transformations, *Almanac* confronts the reader with the very images of apocalyptic violence and disorder that haunt Euro-American modernity's dream of democracy and progress and insists throughout most of the novel that what we are reading is a reflection of the Europeans' own apocalyptic modernity: one that reflects a love of death, of dismemberment, and is on a road to total self-annihilation; this apocalyptic scenario seems to move inexorably toward an endpoint that will signify justice, return of the land, and redemption for "the dead" and the oppressed.

Another key function of allegory emerges in *Almanac* proliferation of allegories embedded within allegories. That is, some stories told by or to Lecha and Zeta include narratives that involve and incorporate specific diegetic elements from the novel's story-world into other allegories that operate simultaneously as stories told to or by characters and as allegories of Native American history. These overlapping circles of narrative interconnection participate in a baroque aesthetics of narrative recycling and also suggest the complexity of *Almanac*'s references to a real world culturalism and the logic of national, racial, or ethnic differences.[32] For example, the first allegorical story told by the old grandmother character Yoeme (long dead but recalled here by Lecha) addresses key questions about the cultural work of the "old notebooks". Though fictionally represented in the text, *Almanac* features these other "Almanacs" to raise questions about books, what they can do, and how do they operate in the long history of indigenous collectivities. This intradiegetic scene of storytelling highlights the links between these Almanacs and what Benjamin explains as a Baroque aesthetics of "ruins" and "encrypted" mythography that manifests history itself.[33] The various complexities of this embedded tale also recalls

Murrin's prophetic dilemma: the diligent reader puzzles and rereads the allegorical tale, quite separating it from the plot threads of Lecha and Zeta and the ranch. But Silko recycles for the reader a particularly tricky parable of collective history, its cycles of loss and preservations, and the function of non-culturalist differences in that history.

This story "The Journey of the Ancient Almanac" appears fairly early in the text—at the end of Part One—and is framed as a story told by "old Yoeme," Zeta and Lecha's grandmother; the twins "had never been able to get old Yoeme to say much about the old notebooks" (246), but she finally tells ("intone[s]") this tale about "the long journey from the South" back when the last survivors of "the Butcher" debate whether to die together or send a small band of "the strongest" away with the almanac: "Because they were the very last of the tribe, strong cases were made for their dying together and allowing the almanac to die with them . . . Finally, the stubborn voices prevailed and three young girls and a small boy were chosen to carry the almanac North" (246). The elders warn the children that their journey will be difficult and treacherous but that "the 'book' they carried was the 'book' of all the days of their people. These days and years were all alive, and all these days would return again. The 'book' had to be preserved at all costs" (247). Yoeme then says that the story of the journey itself is "somehow" included in the notebooks, so that she can be telling the story to Lecha who will also be able to read it. Here the multiple tracks of narrator/narratee, implied author/authorial audience, and authorial audience/allegorical signification illustrate their complex intertwining. Yoeme's story suggests another example of "redundant telling," in which certain plot elements are reiterated by a character for the benefit of the authorial audience, even when the narratee might already know the story (Phelan). In this instance, recalled many years later by Lecha, both the reader and the narratee are hearing the allegorical tale for the first time. The redundancy is perhaps in the act of recollection, through which the reader/authorial audience witnesses and absorbs the story as important both to Lecha and to the argument that Silko is making about the Americas as well as about human existence.

The apocalyptic landscape of this narrated "journey" is emphasized in the devastation and hunger the children encounter as they walk north. On the few occasions they meet other people, they "saw there was little food to be had. They were told the aliens had stolen their modest harvests year after year until the people could hardly keep enough to seed the gardens the following season" (247). So the apocalypse that is recorded in the notebooks is thinly veiled to suggest a period after the colonial conquest of the Americas, after "the Butcher" and "the aliens" have exploited and devastated the land and the people. Both in the almanac and in *Almanac,* then, the destructive power of colonialism occurs simultaneously on a geologic scale and in the human communities that are brutally killed, tortured, or left to starve after all their food and resources have been stolen. But the simple binary in Yoeme's parable of a Euro-American "Butcher" and its victims is further complicated by the tale's focus on the band of children and their actions and choices. A particular character, identified only as "one of the younger girls," emerges as a foil for the leader, "the eldest girl," who becomes suspicious of tears shed by the younger girl, claiming extreme hunger. In a story that emphasizes the anonymity of "the people" in order to depict the desolation as collective and historic, and perhaps even hemispheric, the main character conflict and plot line nevertheless focuses on two specific girls: one stoic and rather bossy and the other plaintive and weak. The third character who takes on a key role in this story of the old notebooks is an old woman they find "singing" in an abandoned village along a river: "She was a hunchbacked woman left behind by the others when they fled the invaders and their soldiers" (248). This old woman who moves "along the ground like a spider" and the younger girl are surprisingly linked in the story as distinct but related portrayals of the darkest aspects of human selves, as presented through allegory's particular ability to historicize and universalize simultaneously.

The old woman appears to be "crippled" and cruelly "left for dead" by her own people, but she proves to be a horrific figure; she is only singing happily because the arrival of the children promises her both food and entertainment for her unspeakable cannibalistic pastimes. But the reader and the children learn the old woman's secret only after they've all eaten from a big pot of stew. The eldest girl had secretly slipped a page of the almanacs into the stew because, being written on "membrane," the almanac turns out also to be a source of nutrition and flavor. The other children have an anguished debate after eating the stew because they come to understand that the reason the stew tastes so good and makes them feel so much stronger is that it contains this page of the old notebooks. We likewise come to understand the extent to which the children have internalized the relationship between the notebooks and their tribe's history when the sole little boy worries that "he might be eating the passage of the story that describes the return of the spirits of the days who love the people" (250). The eldest girl, however, announces, "'I remember what was on the page we ate. I know that part of the almanac—I have heard the stories of those days told many times. Now I'm going to tell you three. So if something happens to me, the three of you will know how that part of the story goes'" (250). Here, the "Journey of the Ancient Almanac" seems to have fulfilled its deepest purpose: to convey the strange and crucial power of stories to keep both the past and the future alive, as well as to be a source of strength and survival in extreme times. However, the story does not end with the children eating, remembering, and retelling the stories of the almanac.

This tale also highlights a gender division that often emerges in the stories: women in *Almanac* are often tougher, more ruthless than men—or apparently, boys. However, that sly mocking of male weakness and sentimentality—as opposed to discipline and self-control—can be undone by other forms of weakness and arrogance. This parable's surreptitiously gendered allegory also highlights aspects of an otherwise occluded gender discourse that runs within *Almanac*, which at times figures the female body, and sexuality more generally, to express the paradoxical pull of evil, greed, and other weaknesses of the flesh. The old woman and the tale itself reiterate the centrality of women in the events of the novel—suggesting perhaps that women are both more sensitive to the impending transition, but also perhaps more vulnerable to the effects of the epoch of Death-Eye Dog (as Lecha/Yoeme will insist, "She did not start out that way" (273)).

We see the allegorical embodiment of specific "revolutionary" virtues when the eldest girl begins to worry that "she must not have her willpower fade at the thought of leaving the comfort of the shady cottonwood trees and the water at the little house of river reeds" (250). The question of will and strength in the face of the seductions of material comfort runs throughout *Almanac of the Dead* and links it to anticolonial literature and thought around the world.[34] As the eldest girl decides that they must not eat any more of the almanac, the reader learns that the children had been warned about the epoch that was dawning: "Death-Eye Dog" in which "human beings . . . would become obsessed with hungers and impulses commonly seen in wild dogs" (251). The culturalist logic of the tale's opening thus gives way to another kind of historicism that might be called epochal, or even spiritual. While the "Epoch of the Death-Eye Dog" ostensibly refers primarily to colonialism, this allegorical story—told in the first part of *Almanac*—signals that the concerns of the text are likely to swerve away from conventional history and into other registers and logics.

When the eldest girl decides it is time to travel on, she makes a plan so that the old woman cannot try to stop them. However, the younger girl who had secretly "chewed the edges of the pages she carried hesitated. She had also had her first menstruation because of the food and the rest, and she wanted to show the others, especially the eldest, she was not a child" (251). Even when the eldest tries to warn her and asks her to at least take off the dress to protect the almanac, "the girl refused that too because she was confident of herself" (251). This disastrous break in the group's collective discipline leads to the younger girl's horrific death, which the eldest discovers on sneaking back to retrieve the pages. But the eldest girl has been schooled by the epoch of Death-Eye Dog and so "did not hesitate at what she saw hanging from the crossbeams of the roof" (252). Instead, she slips on the other girl's dress, still with the pages sown into its seams, and walks back to rejoin the others.

In the space of these few paragraphs, Silko maneuvers through several allegorical/encrypted messages. The younger girl's arrogance and stupidity lead to a brutal and literally unspeakable death. Further, Yoeme explains to her granddaughters another key lesson from the story:

> You see, it had been the almanac that had saved them. The first night, if the eldest had not sacrificed a page from the book, that crippled woman would have murdered them all right then, while the children were weak from hunger and the longer journey. As long as all our days belong to Death-Eye Dog, we will continue to see such things. That woman had been left behind by the others. The reign of Death-Eye Dog is marked by people like her. She did not start out that way. In the days that belong to Death-Eye Dog, the possibility of becoming like her trails each one of us. (253)

As in the totality of *Almanac of the Dead,* the diegetic allegory of "The Journey of the Ancient Almanac" communicates multiple narrative lessons and messages simultaneously, so the reader must puzzle through the paradox of an epoch in which chance and brutality are the causal elements that tether individuals to historical forces that they can only hope to learn to navigate: "A human being was born into the days she or he must live with until eventually the days themselves would travel on" (251). But it is also a story in which the younger girl makes fatal mistakes based on a combination of the moral weakness of pride and the less easily categorized mistake of youthful heedlessness. And the final paradox: that in such "times," individuals must be vigilant because the possibility of becoming like the cannibal cripple hag "trails each one of us."

The layers of framing narratives—the novel's and Yoeme's—emphasize the allegorical nature of the story, which encapsulates the paradoxes of individual and collective, and of logical causality and historical contingency, that structure the text as a whole and guide its narrative pedagogy. The receding horizon of that narrative logic and pedagogy also conveys the layers that are operating within the seemingly explicit allegories and binaries of *Almanac of the Dead.* But the most explicit statement of the book as a whole—the horrific "possibility of becoming like her"—emerges in the context of indigenous characters engaged in sacred and seemingly benign, even sanctified, activities (making food for starving children, comforting an abandoned old woman). Here, the function of allegory moves concretely away from the logic of cultural differences and identity swerves into another logic and scale. As in later allegorical fragments about "the Gunadeeyahs" that preoccupy the final sections of *Almanac,* this allegory leaps above the fray of identities and histories to posit other differences of evil and nonevil that are even more profoundly ontological but that do not easily conflate into the explicit culturalizing logic of national allegories.

This other, perhaps more Benjaminian type of allegory works both within and against such cultural versions of difference through the various embedded allegories of the almanacs themselves and signals the equally Benjaminian move to redemption that will end *Almanac of the Dead.* That is, if a discourse of necropolitics in *Almanac of the Dead* intensifies the reader's sense of the "rush of time toward its end," it may also generate the hesitancy and stalling that derails the apocalyptic narrative trajectory toward the novel's end. As in all apocalyptic narratives, according to Lois Zamora, the text itself regards the final sweeping apocalyptic event with ambivalence. And as is also characteristic of the genre, this ambivalence produces a narrative that "both describes and forestalls" the apocalyptic moment (Zamora 14). Here, the foundational relations between *ends* and *endings*—between the narrative's structure and its apparent development toward key goals or ideas and the final events and enunciations of the text—come to the fore in allegory and especially in *Almanac.* Both in structure and theme, the suspicion arises that a Manichean race war is not in fact to be the end, that is, the purpose or goal, sought by Silko's narrative pedagogy. The embedded allegorical enunciations in *Almanac* ultimately indicate that there are other lessons to be learned from its apocalyptic narrativizations of a transamerican past, present, and future and that the significance of the allegories' encoded understanding is in what lies beyond, or perhaps within, the story of impending apocalypse and the sins of necropolitical selves and collectives.

Zamora suggests that like Murrin's prophecy, apocalyptic narrative relies on a division between elect readers and those who are not able to decipher the "truth" conveyed, which is finally a question of language and of reading. "The apocalyptist consoles his readers by letting them see, beyond the landscape of catastrophe, the small elect community of those who write and those who read. Again, the power of language is at issue: The shared secrets of the apocalyptic text itself, perhaps as much as what it explicitly describes, afford the means to rise above the banality of evil" (Zamora 15). So it happens that the righteousness of its battle, or war, is perhaps ultimately thrown into question in *Almanac* precisely at the moment of its impending fulfillment. It almost seems as if Silko abandons the apocalyptic allegory in order to illustrate the likewise exhausted logics of its defiant inversion of the Manichean allegory into a narrative of violent revolution. And so Zeta agonizes,

> She and Calabazas had been fools. Their lives were nearly over and what had they done? What good had all their talk of war against the United States government done? What good had all their lawbreaking done? The United States government intended to keep all the stolen land. What had happened to the earth? The Destroyers were killing the earth. What had happened to their sons? She loved Ferro; she didn't want him to die. (702)

In Zeta's unexpected and uncharacteristic doubts and expressions of "love" for the bizarre and stunted nephew she has raised, the narrative preparation for a cleansing, if violent, inauguration of a new epoch begins to waver from its teleological course. This sudden wavering and derailment is actually one of the first signs that Silko is adhering even more rigorously than one would expect to the fundamentally theological character of allegory, particularly the generic requirement that within its representations of "evil," "allegory goes away empty-handed" (Benjamin 233).

A forceful interrogation of the teleology of allegory in fact preoccupies the final sections of *Almanac*, so that the question of *ends* and *endings* emerges as central to the very mechanisms that have propelled the narrative toward the coming apocalypse.[35] The text begins to include threads and voices that articulate the reader's growing question: What exactly is being narrated—an apocalypse or its deferral? Interestingly, Silko begins to veer her "prophecy" away from the destruction of a hemispheric apocalypse through the voice of Calabazas, who is one of the book's main proponents of "great war" (631). But toward the text's end, Calabazas is having second thoughts, in part because "he couldn't stop thinking about Mexico."

> Rumors and conflicting reports came from village couriers, and from Salvadorian and Guatemalan refugees. Mexico was chaos. The Mexican economy had collapsed, and fleeing government officials had stripped the National Treasury for their getaway. The army and police had not been paid for weeks. Battles had broken out between the Federal police and the local police. The citizens were fighting both the army and the federal police. Fighting between the Citizens' army and the Mexican army had cut off the Federal District from deliveries and food supplies. Electrical power lines and water-main lines to the center of the city had been dynamited. Thousands in Mexico City were starving each day, but Mexico's president had refused the people emergency food. The Mexican air force had opened fire on thousands of squatters rioting for food at the entrance to the city's main dump. Hundreds of squatters, women and children, had died as army bulldozers had leveled miles and miles of shanties and burned lean-tos.

> Within hours of the big fire at the city dump, hundreds of thousands of rats had swarmed through Mexico City, where starving people in the streets had caught the rats and roasted them. There were rumors of bubonic plague and of cholera. (631)

Such images of chaos and plague are tied to an image repertoire of "the South" in the U.S. national imaginary as a place filled with Mbembe's "living dead."[36] But in these double-voiced articulations of "the South" as an origin point of chaos and contagion, the reader notes that a distinct logic of salvation and redemption begins to emerge within the allegory of historical failure and loss. This unexpected turn back onto itself within Silko's narrative actually reflects the ways in which the logic of allegory, according to Benjamin, must necessarily enact this reversal of direction: "on the second part of its wide arc it returns, to redeem" (232).

> Allegory, of course, thereby loses everything that was most particular to it: the secret, privileged knowledge, the arbitrary rule in the realm of dead objects, the supposed infinity of a world without hope. All this vanishes with this *one* about-turn, in which the immersion of allegory has to clear away the final phantasmagoria of the objective and, left entirely to its own devices, re-discovers itself, not playfully in the earthly world of things, but seriously under the eyes of heaven. (232)

Now it seems that Silko's wry admonition, "Everything in *Almanac* is not quite realism" (Arnold 10), accrues an explicitly and profoundly spiritual significance when placed in the context of Benjamin's scenario of what allegories, like almanacs, are really made for—the exposure and redemption of evil here on earth.

VI. Conclusion: Sterling's Redemption

Although in its first 620 pages or so, the text seems to build a carefully and intricately structured panorama of the Americas and an impending apocalypse instigated by the "Armies of Justice," the last 100 pages, especially "Part Five: One World, Many Tribes," tend to derail the apocalyptic rush of time to its end. One result is that many of the narrative's main characters are dumped into renewed states of suspension and waiting, and the narrative enthusiasm for "war" seems to evaporate. *Almanac of the Dead*'s oscillation between the logic of racial ontologies and the allegorical logic of divine apocalypse and redemption converge toward the novel's end, though without a total collapsing of these narrative poles. That is, concerns with time and certain ontologies of spirituality reemerge out of a muck of death and endings, but that seems to be because the logic of allegory has been stretched to its own ending point, as the final and resounding allegory of the Gunadeeyah seems to attest.

Coming at the very end of *Almanac,* Silko uses this parable to signal a new direction and idea behind the novel's movement, one that denies the logic of a Manichean conflict and its binaries to underline the fundamental use of allegory. According to Benjamin, this foundational purpose is to stage evil and death in order to show them as overcome, and as fundamentally "profane" and therefore illusory: "Evil as such, which it [allegory] cherished as enduring profundity, exists only in allegory, is nothing other than allegory, and means something different from what it is. It means precisely the non-existence of what it presents. The absolute vices, as exemplified by tyrants and intriguers, are allegories" (233). In the last pages of the text, Sterling recalls a story told by his Aunt Marie and the old people about when "sorcerers called Gunadeeyahs or Destroyers had taken over the South" (759). This "story," also learned at the knees of older members of his tribe, is being remembered after a long dormant period. By staging its retelling at the end of *Almanac,* Silko places heavy weight on the tale of the Gunadeeyahs, who predate the colonial conquest of the Americas and thus are part of another genealogy, and allegory, of evil: "Long time ago, long before the Europeans, the ancestors had lived far to the south in a land of more rain, where crops grew easily. But then something terrible had happened, and the people had to leave the abundance and flee far to the north, to harsh desert land" (759). The people are deeply scarred by this encounter with the blood-lusting Gunadeeyah. Their alarm resonates with Yoeme's warning about the old cannibal woman: that in these times, this epoch known as modernity, "the possibility of becoming like her trails each one of us" (253).

Silko thus turns away from the novel's dominant-seeming Manichean culturalist logic to explore an entirely different register: "The people were cautioned about disturbing the bodies of the dead. Those who touched the dead were easily seduced by the Gunadeeyahs, who craved more death and more dead bodies to open and consume" (760). The technologies of touch and craving now take the place of the specularizing instrumental logics of industrial technologies and capital. This turn also bespeaks the profound religiosity with which *Almanac* stages its final focus on Sterling and his quiet, melancholy style of redemption—one that posits and underlines the unknowable nature of evil.

> Now the old story came back to Sterling as he walked along. The appearance of Europeans had been no accident; the Gunadeeyahs had called for their white brethren to join them. Sure enough the Spaniards had arrived in Mexico

> fresh from the Church Inquisition with appetites whetted for disembowel-
> ment and blood. No wonder Cortés and Montezuma had hit it off together
> when they met; both had been members of the same secret clan. (760)

With this tale, *Almanac* replaces the allegory of race war; that is, a war that
operates through revolutionary prophecy and a historicist counternarra-
tive of cultural temporalities and geographies in the Americas. Rather, the
allegory of a lust for blood and its contagious danger to "the people"
bespeaks a profound transformation in the character Sterling, one that
the novel does not trace or seek to "prove": it bursts onto the final pages
as a new given of what the reader, like Sterling, has absorbed in the process
of the text's unraveling. As Sterling returns to his Laguna reservation in
New Mexico and walks to the uranium mine site where the stone snakes
emerged many years ago, he expresses and acknowledges what Benjamin
calls "knowledge of evil" (233).

Sterling's narrative trajectory thus holds more significance than its banal
tone and lack of incident would suggest. This final scene encompasses nothing more startling than his being dropped off near his Laguna town by
Lecha, so that he must walk to his aunt's old house and put together a quiet,
reclusive life for himself. After the novel's primary actors and horrific set
pieces have swirled around him, Sterling emerges in this ending as *Almanac*'s
witness and as a quintessential Benjaminian allegorist: "Knowledge of
good and evil is, then, the opposite of all factual knowledge. Related as it is
to the depths of the subjective, it is basically only knowledge of evil. It is
'nonsense' . . . in the profound sense in which Kierkegaard conceived the
word. This knowledge, the triumph of subjectivity and the onset of an arbitrary rule over things, is the origin of all allegorical contemplation" (233).

Sterling's experiences as witness to evil, to the "nonsense" of contemporary sociality, have cut him loose from his old habits. He is no longer waiting to be told what to do, or consulting his *Reader's Digest*: "The magazines
referred to a world Sterling had left forever, a world that was gone, that safe
old world that had never really existed except on the pages of *Reader's Digest*
in articles on reducing blood cholesterol, corny jokes, and patriotic anec-
dotes" (757). *Reader's Digest* is also the oracle that had kept Sterling from
thinking or feeling anything in the beginning of the story when "so often
his brain had gone numb and lost track" (31). In particular, Sterling had
used the crutch of the magazines to avoid considering his own collectivity,
indigenous people, and their long history of loss and defeat:

> He needed to get his mind off such thoughts—Indians flung across the
> world forever separated from their tribes and from their ancestral lands—
> that kind of thing had been happening to human beings since the beginning

of time . . . He needed to get his mind off this subject. All the magazine articles he had ever read on the subject of depression had urged this. (88)

In following the transformation in Sterling—who goes from avoiding such
dark thoughts and the depression they bring to taking a long meditative
walk back to the scene of his own humiliation and expulsion from the tribe
at the uranium mine where the stone snake appeared decades before—the
reader experiences a transformation, albeit not at the "scale" anticipated.
This return to a human scale, as embodied in an individual character, seems
to suggest an evasion of politics as well as a redemption of humanity.
However, if Sterling becomes the figure of the reader, as well as the allegorist, then it is also possible to understand that narration itself is the performative, revolutionary act in *Almanac of the Dead* and its main point.
Sterling then becomes a figure for the reader—a witness to the apocalyptic
allegory of transamerican history and futurity that the text has staged for
his/our benefit. In that witnessing, Sterling—like the reader—understands
that we must veer away from, and out of, the logics of that contemporary
sociality of necropolitics. Literally and figuratively, Silko makes allegory
the ending and the endpoint of the novel, thus encoding her narrative
pedagogy one final time.

4

Allegory and Transcultural Ethics: Narrating Difference in Rosario Castellanos's *Oficio de tinieblas*

Modern totalitarianism can be defined as the establishment, by means of the state of exception, of a legal civil war that allows for the physical elimination not only of political adversaries but of entire categories of citizens who for some reason cannot be integrated into the political system. Since then, the voluntary creation of a permanent state of emergency . . . has become one of the essential practices of contemporary states, including so-called democratic ones.

(*Giorgio Agamben*)

Faltaba mucho tiempo para que amaneciera.
[It would be a long time before dawn.]

(*Oficio de tinieblas*)

I. Transcultural Aesthetics and *Indigenismo*: Raising Questions of Difference

The apocalyptic significance of indigenous uprising takes another cast in the work of writer Rosario Castellanos, renowned Mexican poet, journalist, novelist, and diplomat. In this chapter, I continue to analyze the narrative strategies that offer these counterstories and counterhistories of the Americas and to underline their challenge to Euro-American discourses of the liberal individual subject. As in Chapter 3, I am again considering a text that highlights how this liberal subject emerges under specific and delimited geohistorical locations and generates its own particular modes of subjectivity and selfhood. In her influential "Chiapas novels" *Balún Canán* (1957) and *Oficio de tinieblas* (1962),[1] Castellanos explores the multiplicity of modes of subjectivity available in the Americas by staging a narrativization of cross-cultural ambivalence in the contact zones between indigenous collectivities and the Euro-American modernity of Mexican whites, or *Ladinos*.

While *Almanac of the Dead* often posits a transamerican indigeneity that is directly oppositional to Euro-American modernity, Castellanos's *Oficio de tinieblas* highlights the ambiguity of these contacts and attends to the paradoxes of intimate knowledge and violent othering that mark this quintessential "contact zone" of transamerica. In staging such contacts in the anachronistically feudal colonialism of early twentieth-century Mexico, *Oficio* emphasizes contingencies of history and geography that echo the focus on populations and large-scale social turmoil in *Almanac*. However, the complexity of the cross-cultural and transcultural dynamics depicted in *Oficio* shifts the focus away from revolutionary possibilities and toward concerns about the relations between narrative form and the ethics, as well as the politics, of literary representation.

In spite of *Oficio's* explicit and clearly well-intentioned depiction of an indigenous uprising, a series of questions about these ethics continues to divide Castellanos's readers. This ongoing interrogation of her tactics of translation and her politics of location underline the complexity of the novel's attempt to narrativize the links between modes of communal and individual consciousness. As the discussion of *indigenismo* below illustrates, the ventriloquism performed by Castellanos in her representation of Mayan "speech genres" participates in a tradition of efforts to capture and represent cultural difference in literary language.[2] However, that literary language inevitably uses the dominant, colonizing "national" language (in this case, Spanish) that has played a significant role in the subjugation and violence perpetuated against these very collectivities. Therefore, the well-intentioned writer faces the linguistic conundrum of cross-cultural representation as appropriative violence. Castellanos's ventriloquism of the Chamula "voice" in a lyrical and ritualistic syntax offers a recognizable citation of various stereotypes of indigenous others as established in part by a long tradition of such representations. But this language use also adheres to an ethics of representation that acknowledges and works to account for the profound implications of ontological differences between collectivities. Like Mikhail Bakhtin, Castellanos holds that the form of expression reflects the fundamental constitution of the speaking subject, who emerges out of a specific world and totality of available languages or speech genres.

The poetic and political risks that Castellanos takes by knowingly "citing" these discursive traditions also mark the text's ironic aesthetics,

which signal to the cosmopolitan liberal reader a surreptitious acknowledgment of its complicity in this tradition. The novel stages as well competing notions of history and political agency. Exploring in detail
antagonistic collectivities bound within one nation—in this case, Mexico—
Oficio encapsulates the dialectics of narrative representation and political
discourse as they occur in the novel form. For example, in its critique of
particular forms of political agency and conceptions of justice and the rule
of law associated with Euro-American modernity, *Oficio* underlines the
role of specific discourses and speech genres as themselves technologies of
the self. These discursive technologies promise liberation and above all
"justice" to indigenous subjects previously abjected by the social inequal-
ities of colonial Mexico but now newly interpellated into self-possessive
liberal citizenship. However, the novel maintains a rigorous skepticism
in its narration of these "benign" impositions of languages and forms of
selfhood—narrations that convey the many possible varieties of bad faith
embedded in these efforts. Thus, its narrative performance of key questions of translation, representation, and cross-cultural ethics explains why
Oficio has generated controversy over how it should be read and about
whether its ultimate effects can be characterized as good for progressive
politics.

Although speaking from and to a very different time and place,
Castellanos's and Leslie Marmon Silko's novels share a surprising number of narrative tactics and political discourses in their representations of
indigenous and Euro-American collectivities. Most crucially, in both
works the social, geographical, and racial genealogies of indigeneity—as
liminal to the nation and its social imaginary—occupy a central function
in the text's contestatory narrativizations of discourses of political history and juridical legitimation. Both authors are concerned with the histories that structure their narrative confrontations between "the Indian"
as the impossible, excluded citizen-subject, and the modern nation.[3] For
Castellanos, this exclusion from representation, as well as enfranchise-
ment, generates a profound grappling with the narrative and linguistic
dimensions of writing the excluded other into the narrative of the
nation. Moreover, I argue that *Oficio de tinieblas* textually performs the
impossibilities of translation that generate an impasse in cross-cultural
representation and communication—an impasse for which her novel
proposes gender and allegory as a potential avenue to an otherwise
impossible futurity.

I've suggested that Silko's allegory makes a quintessentially Benjaminian
shift to a scenario of redemption and in the process shows how the text's
baroque and allegorical sensibility is a carefully calibrated response to the
times in which we live. Castellanos, on the other hand, puts allegory in a

more Bakhtinian conversation, or dialogue, one that underlines the competing demands of specific "speech genres" as they are deployed within the totality of the novel. In his later work, Bakhtin developed the concept of speech genres to trace how "language enters life" through concrete utterances, that is, his insistence on a dialectic of language, style, and history: "Historical changes in language styles are inseparably linked to changes in speech genres. Literary language is a complex, dynamic system of linguistic styles. The proportions and interrelations of these styles in the system of literary language are constantly changing" (*Speech Genres* 65). Thus, Castellanos's precise efforts to render the languages of the Chamula, the Ladino, and other distinct collectives that coexist in the world of Chiapas reflect the novel's cultural work as an index of these communities and their worldviews, their languages. Furthermore, by staging ironic scenarios of reading and writing, *Oficio* ultimately displays and enacts the limits of the novel form and its narrative ethics. And finally, Castellanos holds out an allegorical option that might lead to an opening or a redemption of the apocalypse the novel narrates.

The linked plotlines of the novel follow an array of characters—some from the Chamula indigenous community, some in the Ladino ruling classes of Ciudad Real, and a few outcast and marginal characters who move between these two communities. In particular, the novel stages a series of events through which the repressed and exploited Chamula are motivated to resist and strike back against the Ladinos, an uprising that Castellanos bases on historical events. However, the title *"Oficio de tinieblas"* suggests that these events will be rendered as complex and ambiguous. The word *"oficio,"* found both in official juridical language and in religious ceremony, suggests an "official report" or proceedings, as well as a ritual. *"Tinieblas"* can mean dark places or the shadows, but the word can also mean "confusion." So although the narrative moves toward a scene of apocalyptic violence, and its ecumenical promise of redemption, Castellanos defers that alternative future to an even more distant horizon, a far-off "dawn" of the new day. However, this possible future is firmly, if painfully, in the hands and under the watch of the most subaltern and excluded character-agents in the entire narrative: two women—one Ladina and one Chamula—who are bound together by disastrous circumstances and who find that their only access to social power has been in writing or telling tales. Thus, Castellanos stages a less transformative narrative of apocalyptic indigenous uprising, but then uses various forms of storytelling to highlight the crucial function of gender and particularly the work of opening (of scripts, of borders between collectivities, and of possible meanings) done by the woman who betrays.

II. *Indigenismo* and Transamerican Fiction

The sympathetic preoccupation with indigenous conditions and realities has often garnered Castellanos's Chiapas novels the categorical designation of *indigenista* narrative, which inscribes these novels, and her, into a long Latin American literary and cultural history of the representation and appropriation of the indigenous collective as "Other" to Euro-American modern society and subjectivity. But this designation has presumed that Castellanos and her narrative writing remain bound by her biographical location in and social affiliation with the elite European-identified sectors of Mexican society that she came from. The combined explanatory power of Castellanos's personal social position and the generic overdeterminations of the novel in Latin American literary history have worked to render her early prose works profoundly "under-read," as Debra Castillo memorably puts it.[4] I argue that these narratives index a complex matrix of literary and cultural-political dynamics, even to the extent of offering an understanding of the role of narrativizations that resonates with, perhaps prefigures, the radical antihumanist poetics of *Almanac of the Dead.*

Latin American *indigenismo* first emerges in high colonial ideologies of indigeneity, such as Rousseau's "noble savage": a romantic, largely fictional portrait of human origins and innocence as manifested in the "premodern" figure of "the Indian." These fictions are often characterized by their *criollo* (of "pure" Spanish blood) nationalist intentions and their fleeting grasp of cultural differences and ethnographic content—as being only superficially concerned with the Indians, without penetrating their problems, culture and psychology, or languages. These self-aggrandizing and romantically colonialist idealizations are reappropriated by the Latin American Independence movements of the nineteenth century as part of their attempts to resolve the identity crises that plagued the foundation of Latin American nationalisms and independence from Spain. These crises and their supposed reconciliations often centered on the concept of *mestizaje* as a category of identity that sought to acknowledge the cultural and racial heterogeneity of the "New World." Yet this acknowledgment was not without its own vexing problems. The question raised by *mestizaje* (was and still is): How does the nation account for an American "difference" vis-à-vis Europe when the mutually exclusive poles of European/civilized versus Indian/barbaric are so fully established through colonial discourse and history?[5] The polarization of these culturalist definitions of collectivities becomes its own allegory of colonial temporal logics (premodern, civilization, etc.) and reveals the ideological underpinnings of deeply held chronologies of modernization in the Americas.

Oficio de tinieblas is a text that has been accused of reproducing the hierarchies that generate these culturalist definitions, particularly the relations of orality to literacy and of the oral, indigenous languages to the European colonizers' languages—in Castellanos's and Mexico's case, Spanish. North American critics such as Linda Burdell suggest that *Oficio* upholds an understanding of identity that "depends on the contrast between an oral culture and a writing culture" and that tacitly supports "the authority and power associated with writing" (32, 33). These accusations echo an important structural as well as political concern that *Oficio* illustrates and that is a defining feature of cross-cultural aesthetics, especially in Latin American cultural production and even more pointedly in literatures considered *indigenista*. Burdell focuses on the problem of writing and representation, which she concludes invalidates Castellanos's narrative project: "Approaching marginated or nonliterate communities through the medium of the text creates an inherent authority imbalance between the characters and the reader, who engages in obvious literary complicity with the author" (37). Like Burdell, I am interested in how literature produces "social positions for the reader within the arena of cultural identity and difference" (31). However, in *Oficio,* I see Castellanos reworking the given generic structures of the novel in ways that force the reader to acknowledge, and remain ironically aware of, the complicities of the novel's representations of both Ladino and Chamula "others." This narrative pedagogy of ironic, and generic, self-reflection makes *Oficio de tinieblas* a key text for my theorization of narrative tactics that generate specifically literary responses to the challenges and goals of transamerican minority cultural politics.[6]

Coinciding with the Mexican Revolution (1910–17) and its disruption of a *criollo* hegemony in thought and politics in Mexico, early- to mid-twentieth-century *indigenismo* becomes an avenue for the expression of desires for social transformation, or at least socialist reform, particularly in Mexico and in the heavily indigenous nations of the Andes such as Peru, Ecuador, and Bolivia. Yet despite this work toward goals of social reform and justice, *indigenista* writers sometimes repeat the nineteenth-century *indianista* (Indianist) discourses that represented an indigenous past as a crucial and idealized national heritage, but one that has been tragically lost.[7] This nostalgia and its tragic narrative arc thus figure indigeneity as a foundational but excluded "Other" to a national imaginary that centers on a Euro-American modernity and notions of national unity and progress, notions that disavow any agency or social function to indigenous social organizations, persons, or cultures. That this Latin American national ideology of modernity becomes known as *mestizaje* in the twentieth century, particularly in Mexico, illustrates the complicity, and complexity, of narrativizations of cross-cultural relations in the Americas.

Interestingly, it is precisely the *indigenista* writers of the mid-twentieth century who connect their interest in endangered cultures to the discipline of anthropology, and some of them, such as the Peruvian José Marie Arguedas, become influenced by Cuban anthropologist Fernando Ortiz's theory of transculturation. The "problem" of a national cultural heterogeneity and the promise of a more harmonious synthesis of differences find an apparent resolution in Ortiz's specifically Latin American reformulation of the processes of cultural contact and reciprocal influence that mark the post-Conquest Americas. Rather than presenting a disparaging or superficially romantic view of indigenous culture and the potential "humanity" of indigenous persons, texts from this mid-period in literary *indigenismo* focus on a thick description of indigenous culture, usually portrayed sympathetically, in which the goal is to illuminate the characteristics and conditions of a downtrodden people and to document their ways of living. Social theory, political reform efforts, and anthropology often share a presumption of stable ontological cultural differences, and the ways in which *indigenismo* becomes an official government project in Mexico and elsewhere often reinforce these discourses of rigid, eternal cultural differences. In literature, the period from 1900 to 1950 has been sometimes named "social realist *indigenismo*" for its affirmation and participation in national efforts to incorporate indigenous cultures into the modern nation and to improve the living conditions of these collectivities at the margins of that nation.[8] It is also not accidental that Castellanos herself participated in these government initiatives when she returned to Chiapas in the 1950s and worked for the Mexican government organization aimed at the improvement and development of the Maya and their living conditions, the National Indigenist Institute, or INI.[9] These experiences clearly inform Castellanos's Chiapas novels, though there is some debate over the extent to which she emerged from them disillusioned by the progressive ideals and missionary projects of the INI and exactly how she understood the patent failure of the INI's mission to assimilate the Indians.[10]

The last stage of *indigenismo*, the "new *indigenismo*," has been credited with an attempt to both acknowledge and represent aesthetically the distance between the *indigenista* writer and an actual indigenous consciousness or individual character. This textual interplay of cultural heterogeneities led critics such as Angel Rama to evaluate these "new" *indigenista* narratives both for their accuracy and sensitivity and for their ability to use literary techniques to convey processes of transculturation. Understanding transculturation as a process of cross-cultural synthesis, or fusion, Rama celebrates the works of Arguedas and Castellanos as exemplary of the new *indigenismo*. Arguedas's and Castellanos's novels reflect their authors' more accurate and intimate understanding of indigenous culture and often incorporate elements of indigenous myth, as well as work to approximate a Spanish-language version of indigenous language style and syntax. Critics who take this positive view of *indigenismo* in literature often have a much more sophisticated understanding of both transculturation and *indigenista* writing than is ascribed to them. In fact, many advocates of the more aesthetically and politically progressive versions of *indigenismo* articulate and confirm the depth and distance of the divides between the cosmopolitan mestizo writer and the indigenous object of representation. This acknowledged difference and segregation means that writers and critics alike accept that the closest their literary representation can come to capturing indigenous reality will occur through a kind of poetics of approximation. As defended by Jose Carlos Mariátegui, a Peruvian writer and critic involved in the debates around *indigenismo* and socialism in the 1920s, the best *indigenista* writing manifests a central contradiction in Latin American societies and in literature itself:

> The greatest injustice a critic could commit would be to condemn *indigenista* literature for its lack of integral autocthonism, or for the presence of elements of artifice in interpretation and expression . . . The writer must idealize and stylize the Indian. Neither can the writer offer us his/her own soul. It is still a literature of Mestizos. That is why we call it indigenist and not indigenous.

What Mariátegui allows for, and what critics like Burdell do not, is the inherently fictional status of novelistic representation; though to give Burdell credit, she does focus on the extent to which such fictionality—and thus its status as ideologically produced and inflected—is acknowledged or not. And yet, as Mariátegui suggests, and Antonio Cornejo-Polar reiterates, indigenismo remains an inescapably "Westernized" and colonial discourse and optic: "Indigenista works assume, even in their formal structure, the Westernized sign that dominates its productive process; in effect all the genres employed by indigenismo correspond to Western literature and mark, with the gaps that characterize Latin American literature in its totality, the same historical rhythm" (Cornejo-Polar 1989, 23). By asserting that the very "formal structure" of the works manifests the "Westernized sign" that is itself the mark of "the gaps that characterize Latin American literature," Cornejo-Polar articulates an important formulation of the role of genre, and of language, as an index of the contradictions and impasses of crosscultural knowledge that structure the very fabric of Latin American society, as well as its literature.

Genres, then, will reiterate/reproduce the social, economic, and political inequities of social spheres, especially to the extent that they rely on the same cultural and racial ontologies of identity, such as "indigenous" and "mestizo."[11] And as Burdell indicates, the literary text inevitably reproduces some of the hierarchies of representation (oral/written, knower/known) that it ostensibly works to transcend. Both Mariátegui and Cornejo-Polar suggest that this literary reproduction signifies the real content and value of "the best" indigenista literature: it "not only adopts— modestly or audaciously—the interests of the indigenous peasantry in varying degrees, it also assimilates certain literary forms that organically correspond to the referent. This double assimilation of aesthetic forms and social interests correlates dialectically to the imposition of indigenism's productive system on the indigenous universe" (Cornejo-Polar 25). By acknowledging the primarily rhetorical purposes of the aesthetics of indigenista fictions—especially when they work to convey the interiority of an indigenous consciousness—these critics illustrate that the questions raised by indigenista literature are not actually about that interiority, nor about "culture" or "knowledge," but rather about the ethics of representation enacted in and by the text.

The representation of *mestizaje* in literature has been foundational to the concept's public life, as exemplified in the literary criticism of Rama and Cornejo-Polar.[12] Cornejo-Polar in particular traces a conflictive and irreconcilable heterogeneity in Latin American societies—particularly as it impacts the production of Latin American literature—that is exemplified in the difficult nuances of concepts such as *mestizaje* and transculturation. Ultimately, Cornejo-Polar argues that both *mestizaje* and transculturation are inevitably folded into the dominant, or "hegemonic," and therefore "Westernized" signifying system that necessarily overwhelms and erases what is not within that system:

> *Transculturation* would imply, in the long run, the construction of a syncretic plane that finally incorporates a more or less unproblematic totality (in spite of the conflictive character of the process) of two or more languages, two or more ethnic identities, two or more aesthetic codes, and historical experiences. I add that this synthesis would be configured in the space of the hegemonic culture and literature. (Cornejo-Polar 2004, 117)

While not wanting to dismiss transculturation, or even *mestizaje,* from all discussions of Latin American literature and society, Cornejo-Polar holds out for "another theoretical device . . . in which the dynamics of the multiple intercrossings *do not* operate in a syncretic way, but instead emphasize conflicts and alterities" (117, his italics).

Like *mestizaje,* the concept of transculturation remains central to contemporary discussions of both Latin American and more general transamerican dynamics of cultural contact, and as such it plays a key role in both the ethics and aesthetics of narrative cross-cultural representation.[13] However, the negativity and violence that mark Ortiz's portrayal of the cultural contact and impact between European and indigenous collectivities have at times been overlooked: "They were two worlds that discovered each other and collided head-on. The impact of the two on each other was terrible" (100). Although Ortiz coined the term "transculturation" to convey processes of cultural transmission without the imposed unidirectionality of "assimilation," the term does not posit the idealized reciprocity that is often attributed to it. Ortiz and writers such as Arguedas and Castellanos seldom underestimate the violence and extreme power inequities that persist within these transformations of indigenous, Euro-American, and mestizo societies and culture; nor do they mistake their own position at the privileged end of those racialized cultural inequities. The narrative tactics of Arguedas's *Los ríos profundos* (*Deep Rivers*), for example, figure the near impossibility of translation and dialogue, even as the novel deploys an aesthetic transculturation that emerges in narrative structures, poetic syntax, and linguistic innovations that are the result of what Rama called Arguedas's personal and cultural "pelea infernal con el idioma" ("infernal struggle with language"), which results in an *español quechizado* (Quechua-fied Spanish).[14] It is precisely such literary innovations that complicate easy dismissals of Euro-American fatalism or nostalgic pessimism.[15]

The oscillations and ambivalences that crosscut such theorizations of an aesthetics of transculturation highlight the central function of indigeneity as both interior and Other to the nation and its languages. And from their shared roots in nation-making projects and the discourses of early ethnography, *indigenismo* and transculturation, like *mestizaje,* become foundational tropes in the modern Latin American nation. Castellanos's particular formation as the daughter of an elite landowning family in Chiapas, a functionary in the *indigenista* reform efforts of Mexico's socialist governments, and an intellectual and creative writer obsessed with both the stark ethnic divisions of her natal region and their implications for the nation as a whole coincided to give her a deeply informed and yet implicated perspective on these key debates in Mexican social and political discourse. Following the publication of the more directly autobiographical novel *Balún Canán, Oficio de tinieblas* figures another return to her place of origin, which Castellanos represents from a much more wide-scale narrative vantage point in the second novel.

The narrative style of *Oficio* was in fact deemed anachronistic by some because of its apparent revival of social-historical realism and its perceived links to *indigenismo,* both of which marked the novel as regressive and uninteresting, particularly in the context of the New Narrative innovations

of the Latin American "boom" writers.[16] Interestingly, the narrative innovations that Castellanos does deploy continue to be interpreted in diamet-
rically opposing readings of the novel: (1) as an "interesting failure"
(Sommers 1978) that illustrates the limits of Castellanos's ability to transcend the ideologies of her own social location or (2) as narrative disruptions of the discourses of that social hegemony and the conventions of
indigenismo itself. Other less polarized assertions have also emerged, particularly those that underscore the novel's focus on gender difference,
which recent critics have argued offers an alternative optics for its interpretation.[17] But in contrast with the notion of gender as a distinct and separate discursive code through which we should read *Oficio*'s narrative of
cultural conflict, I argue that Castellanos's narrative tactics consistently
highlight a complex and dialectical imbrication that binds ethnicity, gender, and a variety of other social coordinates within the novel's narration
of the interdependent (but possibly still tragic) social totality that is
Ciudad Real and its environs—and Mexico itself.

Oficio insists on a heteroglossic narrative representation of relations
among identities and discourses. This heteroglossia offers an allegory of
gender, and a gendered allegory, as the novel's final response to the problems of cultural translation and mistranslation. Castellanos thus posits
gender as a figure operating at the center of any mediation, complicit or
otherwise, among the collectivities and modes of communication that
constitute the national totality.

III. Dialogic Narrations and Narrative
Authority/Authoritative Narrative

The plot of *Oficio de tinieblas* recounts the story of a Tzotzil uprising in the
southern state of Chiapas, which Castellanos models on a historical event
in the same region of Mexico, during what is known as the Caste Wars of
1867–70. Though now considered to be a fictional justification for Ladino
brutality, the key event in this nineteenth-century uprising was long considered to be the apparent crucifixion of a young boy by his own Tzotzil
tribe, which supposedly believed that ritualistically creating their own
"Christ" would lead them to achieving the power of the Ladino ruling
classes. The novel displaces this event to the 1930s, when the newly formed
Cárdenas government was sending officials to Chiapas, and all over
Mexico, to implement state-run initiatives and reforms, including the
redistribution of the land held by the big *haciendas* (large land holdings).

The novel juxtaposes a large array of characters from three distinct
groups and chronotopes. This juxtaposition emphasizes the dialogic

structure of the novel as a reflection of the dialogic interactions and differences that shape these collectivities and signal their imbrication in a single social totality, which Castellanos portrays as fractured by these
differences but bound by their mutual constitution. The three collectivities
portrayed include (1) the Ladino world of Ciudad Real, which includes
landowning elites and poor struggling peddlers of goods and people (all
Ladinos in this part of Chiapas are known as "Caxlans" to the Tzotzil
Indians and as "Coletos" among themselves); (2) the valley of "Chamula"
outside Ciudad Real and its main village, San Juan Chamula, where the
Tzotzil tribe mostly lives (in the novel, they call themselves "Chamula"; the
Ladinos just call them *"indio"* and *"india"* [Indian]); and (3) an array of
mestizo-identified Ladinos who come from outside the region, primarily
the nation's capital, the *Distrito Federal* (DF). Some of these national outsiders represent the interests of the newly formed government of
Cardenas, and the Mexican state more generally. The character who instigates the novel's plot is one of these outside mestizo figures: the educated
and liberal engineer, Fernando Ulloa, who has arrived in Ciudad Real to
implement Cardenas's land reform and, at least in his mind, to promote
social justice and the rule of law.

The omniscient third-person narration that begins the novel is an
incantatory voice invoking the name of an unfamiliar god: "San Juan, el
Fiador, el que estuvo presente cuando aparecieron por primera vez los
mundos" (9). ("San Juan, the Guarantor, he who was there when the
worlds first appeared" [1].) The opening passage thus deploys an omniscient epic tone and style to communicate the collective voice of the
Chamula and their legend of how they come to be under the rule of
the Europeans. The legend explains that San Juan loves the Chamula
valley and wishes to be worshipped there in a white church, no less,
which the god signals by transforming all the white sheep of the valley
into white rocks. But the "poor tribes" of the valley do not understand
this "seña de una voluntad" ("sign of divine desire") and can only produce "balbuceo confuso" ("confused stammerings"), which is why "fue
necessario que más tarde vinieron otros hombres" ("the other men had
to come, later"):

> Y estos hombres vinieron como de otro mundo. Llevaban el sol en la cara y
> hablaban lengua altiva, lengua que sobrecoge el corazón de quien escucha.
> Idioma, no como el tzotzil que se dice también en sueños, sino férreo instru-
> mento de señorío, arma de conquista, punta del látigo de la ley. (9)

> [And it was as if they came from another world. They carried the sun
> in their faces and spoke an arrogant language, a language that wrenches
> the hearts of those who hear it. A language not like Tzotzil (which is also

spoken in dreams), but like an iron instrument of mastery, a weapon of conquest, the striking lash of the law's whip. (1)]

This explanation highlights the deep penetration of processes of transculturation as cultural domination into the bedrock of Chamula legend
and myth. In working to explain their total and seemingly fateful oppression, this
myth also reveals how the Chamula's absorption of colonial discourses and
Euro-Christian cosmologies dialectically upholds and legitimates that
oppression. Castellanos deploys this collective Chamula filter to articulate
two key questions that drive the novel forward: How is power taken and
wielded? And how is extreme domination understood by the dominated?
By beginning with these questions and linking the Chamula perception of
the Spanish language as central to their oppression—as the bearer and the
whip of the "law" the rulers invoke—Castellanos implies that an analytical
understanding of power, especially of its ability to enchant and mystify, is
necessary to overcoming an oppression that is shown here as lodged deep
in a collective psyche.[18]

But this omniscient and collective narrative filter exists alongside other
voices and more specifically individual character filters. The juxtapositions and contradictions that these multiple voices generate throw in
doubt the reader's impression of a dominant narratorial authority, particularly because no specific character or narrative filter proves to "know" or
to understand the totality depicted by the novel itself. Castellanos thus
stages the confrontation between antagonistic collectivities in a narrative
that mixes modes and perspectives and refuses the authoritative judgment
of a monological narrator. Recalling *Almanac*'s narrative tactics of dialogic
excess combined with a seemingly realist third-person narrator, the slant
of the omniscient narrator of *Oficio* seems to maintain a strong purchase
on the totality of the narration. However, that narratorial authority is
repeatedly disrupted and derailed by a cacophony of voices and character
filters located across disparate social locations. This intensely dialogic narrative structure in *Oficio* undermines—even exposes—the omniscient
narrator's presumed function of translation and mediation between
indigenous and Ladino characters and worlds, and between the story-
world and the reader. Read closely, Castellanos's text narratively performs
the violence of transculturation by both conscripting this fractured social
landscape into a novelistic whole and exposing the seams—sociolinguistic
and narratological—that imperfectly suture its representation of totality.

The distinct ritualistic language and syntax of the voice of the Chamula
echoes the tactics of other mid-twentieth-century *indigenista* narrative
projects, such as Arguedas's efforts to refigure the Spanish language in

order to access alternative cosmologies. The novel's numerous character filters include a variety of personages from each community, and in the case of the Chamula, the disembodied voice of the collective itself. In both *Balún Canán* and *Oficio de tinieblas*, Castellanos continues these efforts to harness the power of literary representation to both depict and affect the Mexican social imaginary and particularly the function of indigeneity within that imaginary, as well as in material social conditions. Burdell emphasizes the appropriation, treachery even, embedded in the narrative structuring of cultural difference implicit in Castellanos's use of voice and speech genres. This appropriation is particularly notable in the novel's "transformation of oral discourse into written narrative," which "is a (mis)representation that conceals, to a greater or lesser degree, the impact of the writing authority on the text" (36). Similar efforts—as in Mario Vargas Llosa's 1989 novel *El hablador* (*The Storyteller*)—have been characterized as "postmodern indigenism" (Castillo) and criticized for using this narrative experimentation as a "cover" for a narrative and cultural politics that still encodes and perpetuates Eurocentric and colonial discourses, even—or especially—within the guise of cultural ventriloquism. So just the fact of its heteroglossic narration does not necessarily absolve *Oficio* of the accusation of relying on (neo)colonial representational politics.

However, Castellanos deploys these character filters and narrative chronotopes to generate a particularly complex play among voices and perspectives in *Oficio de tinieblas*. I argue that Castellanos actually performs and acknowledges—structurally—a delegitimation of her own (authorial and mestizo) authority in the process of using the genre of the novel to ironically expose its architecture of speech genres in competition. She does so in a way that renders impossible an ultimate, authoritative judgment, or even understanding, of what the novel itself portrays.[19] Rather than limiting the narration to a single transculturated individual, as in Arguedas's *Los rios profundos*, or between two clearly defined and delineated narrators who "take turns" controlling chapters (as in *El hablador*), *Oficio* shifts among character filters in seemingly haphazard and often unmarked transitions from one perspective to another. These shifts are most likely to occur within scenes of dialogue or via the free indirect and direct discourse of a particular character; so the transfers among distinct character filters and voices tend to rely on a narrative joining figure who binds the characters in question. This diachronic narrative tactic produces a flow among character filters that is often confined to either the Chamula or Ladino chronotope dominating a particular chapter. However, when Chamula and Ladino characters are conversing or interacting in other ways—some diegetic and some generated through the omniscient narrator's agenda and focus— these shifts move just as freely between Ladino and Chamula characters, undercutting the claim that the narrative structures a racialized cultural difference that is never bridged.

Still, because the narration so often oscillates at chapter breaks between the two communities and chronotopes, a symmetry emerges in this narrative excess, in that it establishes a kind of narrative parity between Ladino and Chamula. As Doris Sommer suggests in her discussion of *El hablador,* this narrative attentiveness and attention to the indigenous characters and perspectives enacts a kind of "stalling" that forces the reader to pause and "detains the rush" toward Euro-American modernity "for as long as we read" (242). We have seen how the claims for this "minor" narrative pedagogy can be overstated, recalling Cornejo-Polar's caution that the form of the "Western sign," including and especially the novel, necessarily precludes any actual encounter with indigenous otherness within the text. However, Sommer does remind us that literary representation retains a unique performative agency by staging multiple narrative genres and styles in order to both approximate and perhaps appropriate distinct and different speech genres within the totality of the novel.[20] Thus, the novel literally reinscribes the heterogeneity of the social and historical moment out of which it emerges, which in *Oficio* involves the clashes and transculturations of Chamula and Ladino speech genres, albeit deeply mediated by the novel form and its author. It is also clear that Castellanos deploys the power of narration to underline the importance, even centrality, of a Chamula cosmology and voice in the novel's totality.

So although she claimed to eschew what she called "stylistic architectonics," Castellanos narrates the weeks and days leading up to the crucifixion and indigenous uprising from the perspectives of a great many characters, offering a dizzying and multifaceted dialogic representation of the distinct communities and individuals involved. The opening sequence moves from the epic and mythic register of the origin legend to focalize on and through specific Chamula characters, particularly Catalina Díaz Puiljá, a Chamula *ilol* (priestess), and her husband, Pedro González Winiktón, a young judge for whom the abuses of the Ladinos have generated an insatiable hunger for "justice"—a rage and an overwhelming desire that make him a leader in his community: "La palabra justicia resonaban en su interior, como el cencerro de la oveja madrina. Y él iba detrás, a ciegas, por veedas abruptas y riesgosas, sin alcanzar nunca" (30). ("The word justice resounded inside him like the bell around the eldest ewe's neck. And he walked blindly behind it, along steep and perilous trails, without ever catching up to it" [21].) While this quest for "justice" propels Pedro through the novel, a mix of hungers shapes Catalina—most particularly her frustrated desire to have a child, which leads her to apprentice herself as an *ilol,* "cuyo regazo es arcón de los conjuros" ("a seer, whose lap is a nest of spells"). The knowledge she acquires in her own obsessive quest makes Catalina a different kind of leader in the community: one who works from the other side of rationality, from "un mundo sombrío, regido por voluntades arbitraries" (13) ("a dark world ruled by arbitrary wills" [5]).

Both Catalina and Pedro are portrayed as powerful individuals thwarted in their deepest desires, and each of these characters is traced through a narrative focalization that takes on specific tones, rhythms, and vocabularies to express their ways of thinking and their respective states of mind— states of mind and personal desires that are always strongly differentiated.[21] Brian Richardson's work on experimental narrative suggests the term "subjectivized third-person narration" (from Gordon Collier) to describe the ways "the discourse of the narrator is infiltrated by language typical of the character being described" (9). While this description of internal focalization encompasses both Silko's and Castellanos's narrators, in Castellanos the interiority of each main character is explored in an exhaustive detail that not only "infiltrates" the narrator's discourse, but often takes it over. And unlike the relentless parade of flat and opaque character filters in *Almanac,* the many voices in *Oficio* are particularly startling in their variety as well as in their detailed emotional and psychological verisimilitude.

Catalina, especially, emerges early as a strongly individualized character. Her mode of understanding and thinking about her life is distinguished in language and logics from that of the Ladina female characters such as Isabel Cifuentes and Julia Acevedo, despite the three female characters' shared preoccupation with questions of power and influence throughout the novel. In narrating how Catalina uses her power as *ilol* to manipulate less intelligent, or more submissive, members of her tribe, the novel represents her interior complexity without reductively evaluating her actions. Among the threads that weave in and out of her consciousness are her intertwined desires for more attention and intimacy from Pedro and her overwhelming sense of failure and doom as a childless woman. Catalina manages to "adopt" the child of Marcela, who is raped by the Ladino character Leonardo Cifuentes early in the novel and then forced to marry Catalina's mute and impotent brother, Lorenzo. But after a number of years of extraordinary attention to the adopted boy, Domingo, Catalina eventually realizes, in the kind of temporal compression characteristic of the novel, that the boy is really the property of her husband, who has become a partner in the efforts of Fernando to enact the government's land reforms. She laments this loss in a somewhat unusual instance of direct discourse: "'Lo arrancaron de mi regazo como si ya hubiera crecido y madurado. Me dejaron sola otra vez. Bruja, mala, ilol. Castigan el daño que hice, el que quiero hacer. ¡San Juan fiador, ten compasión de mí!'" (191) ["'They snatched him from my lap as if he were already grown up

and ripened. They left me alone again. Bruja, evil woman, ilol! They pun-
ish the harm I did, the harm I want to do. San Juan Guarantor, have pity
on me!'" (185).][22] This monologue highlights the complex flows of consciousness and association that mark Catalina's character. She often moves
between anger and anguish as she tries to parse out her relationship to
Pedro and to the community as a whole. Also, in seeing/naming herself
"Bruja, mala, ilol" ("Bruja, evil woman, ilol"), Catalina expresses the fundamental ambivalence of her subjectivity, which is shown here to be permeated by guilt, anger, and patriarchal ideologies of gender and
reproduction: ideologies represented as central to female characters' lives
in both Chamula and Ladino contexts. Catalina also further exemplifies
the novel's link between gender and nonnormative or resistant ways of
thinking, feeling, and acting in relation to the collective. Catalina's central
function in the Chamula community as the *ilol* generates a complex
matrix of ambition and political awakening that makes her a powerful collective agent, but also a catalyst for the violent, and failed, confrontation
between the Chamula and Ladino communities toward the novel's end. So
the large sections of narrative devoted to creating a window into her mind
would seem to work toward a kind of narrative "explanation" of Catalina's
role as political and narrative agent. And yet these long sections often serve
more to complicate and obfuscate the source and the direction of her
agency, even with the foreshadowing of "the harm I want to do."

In such scenes of self-reflection, *Oficio* highlights the distinct modes of
perception and theatres of action of its many characters, Ladino as well as
Chamula. More than most characters in the novel, Catalina often talks to
herself in what is presented as her own voice: a voice that is not mediated
by the third-person, narratorial perspective and that can communicate
specific information about her history and emotional distress. The third-
person narration in *Oficio* thus foregrounds exactly what *Almanac* does
not: the rich and elusive inner worlds of particular characters, whose internal experience and personal histories are conveyed through detailed expla-
nations. Such realist representations of human individuals suggest a
particularly conventional mode of novelistic discourse. The constant invi-
tations to enter the interior worlds of specific characters—especially
Fernando, Pedro, Julia (Fernando's Ladina companion), and Catalina—
suture the reader to these characters in a way that is specific to the novel.
But here too the omniscient narrator's authority over the narrative totality
remains questionable due to the conflicting chronotopes inscribed in each
character's voice and filter. And the novelistic immediacy and individuation
of characters and their histories destabilize the imposition of allegorical or
characterological typologies, what Homi Bhabha calls the "fixing" function
of the stereotype.

However, various critics have asserted that *Oficio* does exactly this, fix the Chamula in a narrative of *indigenismo* that ossifies the border between Euro-American modernity and the "premodern" indigenous "other" in a tragedy of inevitable and total miscommunication. Burdell emphasizes the divide between oral and written cultures in the novel and further claims that the text's "portrayal of marginated individuals, a representation of orality, which is often equivalent to illiteracy, provides readers with a comfortable position from which to view the differences narrated" (37). And several of Joseph Sommers's essays condemn what he calls Castellanos's "cultural pessimism" about the Maya people, which she expresses in the novel through the representation of a resolutely "mythical" indigenous consciousness. Joanna O'Connell poses the persistent critical dilemma generated by *Oficio*: "How then to talk about the real differences between the cultural modes of experiencing and knowing history that Castellanos represents in her novel? And how to account for the novel's failure to imagine a revolutionary consciousness?" (140) However, rather than considering the novel's relation to history, and its failures, I suggest that it is precisely in its status as fiction and especially in its triangulation to the position of the reader that Castellanos makes her most subtle revision of dominant narrativities (those of literate, Euro-American, modern, cosmopolitan readers) and the discourses that uphold them. Because the momentum toward an apocalyptic finale in *Oficio* relies on a series of scenes of miscommunication and mistranslation, and as well as writing, a close attention to such scenarios of translation reveals the play between the predictable and the unanticipated in how Castellanos structures these paradigmatic, perhaps allegorical, interactions between Ladino and Chamula. In such details of narrative inflection, I suggest the novel offers more options, both political and literary, than are sometimes ascribed to it.

IV. Allegories of Translation: Narrating the Cross-Cultural Impasse

One scene that encapsulates *Oficio*'s treatment of the question of translation between the Chamula and the Ladino collectivities occurs about halfway through the novel. The arrival of the government engineer and reformer, Fernando, is presented as the catalyst for the apocalyptic violence of the Chamula uprising and its repression toward the novel's end. The seeds of this plot of tragic defeat and disaster are sown long before the actual uprising, when Fernando is explaining to a village gathering of the Chamula why he has come to Chiapas. This scene begins with the omniscient narrator assuming control of the event, however, a juxtaposition of the distinct filters (the narrator's and Fernando's) and narrative levels begins to disrupt the authority of both the narrator and the character filter:

> Fernando habló con lentitud, como si se dirigiera a un niño, escogiendo las palabras más fáciles, repitiéndolas como si la repetición las tornara comprensibles. Dijó que él era un amigo de los indios y que había venido desde muy lejos con un a recomdación del Presidente de la Republica para que les devolvieran la propiedad de sus tiernas; cuando cada uno sea dueño de su parcela es necesario que todo trabajen, que levanten buenas cosechas, que las llevan a vender a los mercados. Con el dinero que consigan, dijo, pueden vestirse major, pueden comprar medicinas, pueden mandara sus hijos a la escuela. (182–83)

> [Fernando spoke slowly, as if he were addressing a child, choosing the easiest words and repeating them as if repetition would make them comprehensible. He said that he was a friend to the Indians and that he had come very far with a request from the president of the Republic that they be given back the ownership of their lands. When each man is the owner of his own plot of land it will be necessary for all men to work, to bring in the good harvests, and to take them to sell in the markets. With the money they receive, he said, they can clothe themselves better, they can buy medicine, they can send their children to school. (176)]

The narration begins as an objective description of the interactions at the meeting focalized through Fernando, but a vaguely unsettling narratorial perspective emerges in the use of tense. The subjunctive clause "como si se dirigiera a un niño ... como si la repetición las tornara comprensibles" interprets Fernando and his official announcement against the grain of his own understanding of his efforts, which we know from other narrative moments that he sees as laudatory and transparent and not futile or naïve as the comment "as if repetition would render them understandable" suggests. Here, the narrator acts more like a classic realist narrator who possesses a reliable authority over the textual world of the novel, because she can describe characters' actions in ways they would not recognize or claim.[23]

The shift to Fernando's direct discourse after this commentary, however, also sheds significant light on the function of the narrator's realist voice of authority. In reporting his actual words, the text shows Fernando unselfconsciously enunciating the presumptive fallacies of Euro-American modernity and its discursive and social violence. He directs the Chamula to assume the subjectivity and desire of "citizens" of the modern Mexican state; in exchange for this generous offer of inclusion, they must become orderly and productive capitalist workers: "Que levanten buenas cosechas, que las llevan a vender a los mercados" (183). As such, their desires are accounted for in advance: "Pueden vestirse mejor" ("They can clothe themselves better"). The implied author/narrator does not endorse Fernando's blindness to the realities of the Chamulas' lives or desires. In fact, Fernando's announcement "I am a friend of the Indians," with which he introduces himself, sets the stage for showcasing his well-meaning but arrogant ignorance. The narrator thus uses her generic authority to ironize Fernando's belief in the benevolent liberal nation and the reliability of the law that he represents, as well as to expose his faulty knowledge of his audience.

Later in this chapter, the status of the law that Fernando brings to the Chamula becomes a real object of diegetic investigation, largely because its self-evident status and nature are so profoundly bound/attenuated by mestizo modernity and privilege. In an important moment Pedro, the young Chamula judge, community leader, and translator for Fernando asks him, "¿Fernando Ulloa ha visto la ley? ¿Dónde está?" (185) ("Has Fernando Ulloa seen the law? Where is it?" [179]) Castellanos uses shifts in chronotope and collective, as well as individual, narrative filters to mark a deep chasm that is emerging and widening between these two men, their communities, and their respective visions of justice. For his part, Fernando sees himself answering "truthfully" all the Chamulas' questions because "sabe que no admitirán evasivas. Y promete. Él, hombre de razón, hablará con las autoridades ladinas. No, no hay que precipitarse, no hay que obrar fuera de la ley porque la ley lo previene todo, lo ampara todo" (186). ("he knows they will not accept any evasions. And he promises. He, a man of reason, will speak with the Ladino authorities. No, they must not rush into anything or go beyond the law, because the law foresees everything, protects against everything" [180].) But this direct discourse gives its own lie because of Castellanos's nuanced portrayal of the totality of competing discourses and modes of understanding at work in the room where this meeting is taking place. Put into this competition and conversation with other myopic versions of the event unfolding, Fernando's direct speech is double voiced. It both articulates his precise understanding of the proceedings and illustrates the blindness inherent in his position within the extended dialogue between himself and Pedro, and between the discourse communities they represent: the new socialist state and the Chamula tribe. By casting Fernando's speech in an unheard and unspoken dialogue of desires and discourses, Castellanos deploys his utterances ironically to reflect critically on the whole speech genre of Western law, justice, and sovereignty.

By the time Fernando is extolling the virtues and status of "the law," the reader has already glimpsed the dynamics of translation that will lead inexorably to the apocalyptic bloodshed. For example, once Fernando introduces himself as a "friend of the Indians," the narratorial perspective

shifts suddenly and without a tag of any sort to the collective perspective
of the Chamula. Again, the narrator's presence is subtly discernable in the
ironic distance between understanding and signification that Castellanos
emphasizes throughout the novel: "Los ancianos escuchaban y de toda la
peroración no sacaron en limpio más que les estaba exigiendo que
pusieron en manos de un extraño los papeles que, de generación en generación, habían atesorado y tranmitido y que para ellos representaban lo
más precioso" (183). ("The old men listened and out of the whole speech
they gathered only that they were being directed to place in the hands of a
stranger the papers that they had treasured up and handed down from
generation to generation, which represented all that was most precious in
their eyes" [177].) Noting both the resistance and incomprehension of "the
old ones," Pedro jumps in to fill his role as an "embodied translator"
between the Chamula worldview and the Ladino nation, and in the process
his own words become an ironic performance of an apparently inevitable
mistranslation.[24]

Pedro has learned Spanish while working on a plantation in the low-
lands, and he has met the new president and shaken his hand. And while
this education and political "enlightenment" are a central narrative element, Castellanos ensures that the dangers of translation and mistranslation are made palpable to the reader:

> Winiktón hablaba convirtiendo las palabras del ingeniero en la expression
> de su proprio sueño. Decía que había llegado la hora de la justicia y que el
> Presidente de la República había prometido venir a arrebatar a los patrones
> sus privilegios y a dar a los indios satisfacción por todas las ofensas, por
> todas las humilliaciones, por todas las infamias. (183)

> [Winiktón had transformed the engineer's words into the expression of his
> own dream. He said that the hour of justice had arrived; that the president
> of the Republic had promised to come, strip the patrons of their privileges
> and give the Indians satisfaction for all the offenses they had endured, all the
> humiliations, all the outrages. (177)]

By this point in the scene of miscommunication and mistranslation, the
word "justice" has accrued fantastic proportions for both men, Fernando
and Pedro. Both the liberal conception of "the law" and the Chamula
expectation of "satisfaction for all the offenses . . . all the humiliations, all
the outrages" are exposed as equally impossible and naïve. Thus the dialogic
narration enables a reciprocal dialectic of ironic narrativity in which both
sides of the cultural equation are shown as "blind," particularly when it
comes to *la palabra justicia* ("the word justice"). In staging this unspoken
dialogue between the two men and the two collectivities, Castellanos

pushes the reader to a critical awareness of the ruses of liberal discourses of law, inclusion, and representativity—a critique and an awareness that the novel as a whole harnesses in order to launch a devastating rethinking of cross-cultural contact and dialogue.

Here, we also see how the omniscient narrator's voice and authority interact with, rather than control, the voice and filter of other characters. This authorial narrator removes herself at the key moment of Pedro's translation, which makes it the reader's job to interpret the characters and the flow of discourse and action among them. Also, the communal plural and its call to violent action and rebellion enunciate a plan whose origin and perspective remain unclear. (Is it Fernando's assistant César Santiago, the Chamula pueblo, or a critical narratorial aside?) This slippage in who makes judgments, particularly in scenes of translation and writing, indicates Castellanos's refusal of the generic authority of narration by revising the genre of historical realism. Such tactics foreground the undecidable nature of events, both textual and historical, suggesting another kind of textual pedagogy at work in *Oficio*. The novel forces its readers to question and to make meaning in the absence of the dependable omniscient narrator characteristic of realism. Missing as well is a dependable or clear understanding of the novel's own version of the truth of narrative events. The reader is thus put into a position that performatively reflects the position of Fernando himself as he struggles to grasp and understand the events unfolding before his eyes.

We see Fernando's struggle to impose narrative sense on unfolding events after Pedro promises his people this emancipatory and complete "satisfaction" for "all the outrages" they have suffered. Although Pedro signs on as interpreter and guide for Fernando and his cynical assistant, César, the scenes that trace the emergence of "una corriente de simpatía y de amistad" (183) ("a current of fellow feeling and friendship" [179]) between Fernando and the Chamula only emphasize the impossibility of the promised moment of cleansing justice. And ultimately it becomes clear that this impossibility will be the seed of the plot's tragic and violent trajectory. For example, once the conversion of the Ladino engineer's "law" into the Chamula judge's "dream" has been accomplished, the new alliance travels around the countryside to expain to teach and reassure the Chamula that the Ladino government official is working in their interests. And as trust is established through contact and ritual and with the guarantee of Pedro's presence, the Chamula men begin to speak:

> Y así, hoy aquí y mañana en otro lugar, cada uno dice lo que ha guardado durante años. Vienen con sus quejas como van al altar de los santos. Y es la

misma salmodia, la misma letanía de abusos padecidos,de pobreza, de enfermedad, de ignorancia. La desgracia de estos hombres tiene algo de impersonal, de inhumano; tan uniformemente se repite una vez y otra y otra. (185–86)

[And in that way, today here and tomorrow somewhere else, each man finally says what he has kept inside himself for years. They come with their complaints as they would go to the altar of a saint. And it is the same monotonous chant, the same litany of abuses endured, poverty, sickness, ignorance. These men's misfortunes had something impersonal and inhuman about it, so uniformly is it repeated again and again. (180)]

These interminable scenarios of a "litany" of misery are communicated through an undecidable filter that slowly fixes itself as the paragraph progresses to its impatient conclusion: "Se repite una vez y otra y otra" ("Repeated again and again"). Such slippages of narratorial filter and voice point to the ambiguity and ambivalence that lodge in the heart of the novel.

In being both "impersonal" and "inhuman," the violations and living conditions of the Chamula are experienced through the thick veil of cosmopolitan repulsion and scripting. In a sense, Castellanos articulates a view of the other that is precisely what Achille Mbembe and Silko critique in the relation between advanced capitalism and the "living dead" it produces. This enunciation of the discourse of the modern, liberal selfhood that Fernando celebrates as "la máquina de la justicia" (the machine of justice) is momentarily unveiled as being embedded in the biopolitics of modernity and modernization, and not a particularly idealized version of these processes either. As the cynical César will say to himself in the same chapter, "¿Cuál ley? . . . no hay más ley que la fuerza" (187). ("What law? . . . there is no law but force" [181].) Beginning in the narratorial third person, the external observation of the "corriente de simpatía y amistad" emerging between men takes on a more specific personal tone, becoming a voice that articulates a viewpoint rather than remaining an impassive omniscient "eye" for the reader: "Que se quejen algunos, bueno; es la costumbre de una raza vencida, de una generación abyecta" (186) ("Yes, some of them complain and that is fine; complaining is the custom of a vanquished race, an abject generation" [180]). Here, the impatient tone of the allowance, "yes . . . that is fine," suggests a growing awareness of the uncanny line that separates "these men's misfortune" from the worldview of this increasingly embodied narrator, who tries to tolerate her (or his?) disdain for the Maya's uniform and interminable litany of "inhuman" suffering. Here, the risks of "fellow feeling" and true dialogue (and perhaps intersubjectivity) are revealed to include such uncomfortable scenes of confrontation between the "I/eye" of a cosmopolitan narrator-observer and the subjectivity and actual voice of the "bare life" of these nameless, indistinguishable— "abject"—others.

All narration in this novel, including that of the narrator, encompasses only a partial view and comprehension of the totality of what is being portrayed. Neither the omniscient narrator nor the characters whose voices are captured here seem able to stay put, in their place, as text shifts and doubles back over the narrative levels and filters that constitute its cacophonic totality. For example, the narrator's condescending repulsion is then interrogated in its turn by yet another inappropriate detail within the same paragraph: "Pero no todos tiene el mismo temple. Los hay que alzan la voz para protestar, para exigir. Y los que proponen medidas para remediar" (186). ("But not all of them are in the same mood. There are those who raise their voices in protest, who make demands. And there are those who propose ways of remedying the situation" [180].) This shift from the scripted understanding of "una raza vencida" to an articulation of protest and action illustrates how Castellanos's narration refuses its own authority in a way that might be called ironically *indigenista*.

Multiplying the ironic effects of the narrator's slippery authority, Pedro suggests in this scene that some of the magic or "aura" of writing has converted him to a Ladino understanding of justice. When he says, "Fernando, saca el papel que habla; apunta lo que oyes para que todo lo tengas presente" (186) ("Fernando, take out that paper that talks; note down what you hear so you can keep all of this in your mind" [180]), he implicitly asserts the extremely circumscribed capacities of Fernando, and by extension the nation-state, to fully comprehend the Chamula reality. But in demanding that Fernando write it down, Pedro seems to hold out hope for some kind of witness or redress for the litany of injustices. This hopeful imperative also directly counters the judgment of the narrator, who dismisses the Chamulas' complaints as inhuman and impersonal— boring and repetitive and relentless.[25] Pedro thus articulates a relation to writing, to Fernando, and to the Mexican state that is not anticipated by the narrator's dismissal. The imperative to "write down" the details of the Chamula's stories of suffering, in spite of their banal uniformity and inhumanity, emerges from Pedro's particularly powerful enunciation and acknowledgment of the very impossibility of both justice and translation:

> Pero ahora, ¿quién devuelve las gallinas robadas, el telar deshecho, la vida de los niños despanzurrados a bayonetazos? Nadie va a devolver a las mujeres aquella mirada sin espanto ni a los varones un ánimo sin rancor. Pero hay que decirlo; apúntalo, Fernando; escríbelo, caxlán. (186)

[But now, who will give back the stolen chickens, the wrecked loom, the life of the children whose bellies were ripped open by bayonets? No one will give an unfrightened gaze back to the woman or a soul without bitterness to the men. [But] It must be told. Note it down, Fernando; write it, Caxlán. (180–81)]

What begins as a request to write and witness the names and the dates of particular incidents becomes a lament at the impossibility of this project—an impossibility that both Pedro and Fernando will at most other times be unable to acknowledge.

The imperative command to "write it, Caxlán" is voiced from the "below" of a subaltern, illiterate speaker and thus reverberates throughout *Oficio* on at least two levels. Pedro accepts the utility of the modern technology of writing as he and his people struggle to assume the status of human beings in the novel, but he also acknowledges the impossibility of his earlier promise of "satisfaction . . . for all the outrages": "No one will give an unfrightened gaze back to the woman or a soul without bitterness to the men." But even though full restitution of soul and life and gaze are impossible, Pedro suggests that what might move them all closer to "justice" is a combined embodied and linguistic act of witnessing that both records and hears the specificities of the community's history of brutal suffering at the hands of the "Caxlán." This command to write it down also draws a line between the two men, forcing a mutual self-recognition of their respective collective identities and historical differences, no matter how much "fellow feeling" they manage to generate personally. Castellanos thus shares with Silko a critique the presumptive fallacies of invoking liberalism, dialogue, or border crossing as necessarily ethical positives. Interestingly, both narratives tether their critique of metropolitan benevolence to the possibility that the related activities of telling stories and writing them—and that *oficios,* books, and almanacs—can be effective where both "fellow feeling" and "the law" have failed.

V. Gender and Allegory: Writing Avenues to Futurity

If there are alternatives to the law, they emerge in the other "cross-cultural" preoccupation in *Oficio de tinieblas:* the staging of the exclusionary chronotopes of the novel's gendered worlds. As the example of Catalina suggests, *Oficio* implicates gendered collectivities within the Chamula-Ladino dualism, highlighting the exclusion of women and their ways of thinking from both Ladino and Chamula public spheres. This exclusion resonates with, but is not equal to or commensurate with, the violent exclusion of indigenous collectivities from the chronotope of the nation. Ultimately in fact, the female chronotope proves to harbor forms of narrative and of subjectivity that may, possibly, survive the apocalyptic failure of all other communicative efforts in the novel.[26] The character of Catalina, among others, also suggests that alternative gendered ways of thinking are to be linked simultaneously to women and to their nonnormative (i.e., subversive) performances of agency within both Ladino and Chamula worlds. This implied logical chain between gender and modes of knowledge that are distinct from Euro-American patriarchal society again involves the technologies of oral storytelling and writing, particularly toward the end of the novel.

The key figure of female writing that emerges in the text is, surprisingly, Idolina Cifuentes, the spoiled and sickly stepdaughter of the (literally and figuratively) rapacious Leonardo, who as the treacherous brother of her dead father is also her uncle.[27] Though she is a teenager and a female, confined by ill-health and habit to her bedroom, Idolina wields a peculiar power throughout the novel, particularly as she directs the household through her whims and ill-health and in her disturbing relationship to her mother, Isabel. Idolina's power comes particularly from her position as the keeper of the household's guilty secret—that Leonardo killed her father and that her mother implicitly, through desire, encouraged and supported this turn of events. Idolina's position in the family articulates the hierarchies of gender and visibility that structure the entire social fabric of the Ladino world, thus indicating how she herself functions as a condensed allegorical figure for the position and isolation of women in the Mexican society. Idolina is hidden away and both figuratively and literally crippled by her experiences of the violence of family, heterosexuality, and power. Her body manifests the suffering, and perhaps also the guilty desires, of her mother as the wife who must tolerate the contempt, the infidelities, and the isolation that come from her marriage to Leonardo.

And to cement this figurative status in relation to Ladino femininity, we learn the story of Idolina's Chamula caretaker and nurse, Teresa. Isabel tells a visitor that years ago, as a new mother, she realized that she did not have enough milk for her baby. She "learns" that a Chamula woman at the ranch has also just had a child, so she forces this new mother, Teresa, to nurse Idolina. Because Teresa fears that she will not be able to provide sufficient milk to her own daughter, she tries to run away. Isabel orders that she be brought back and put in stocks; Teresa agrees to nurse Idolina, but secretly continues to try to save her milk for her own daughter. So, as Isabel puts it, "Tuve que separarlas" (140) ("I had to separate them" [132]), which meant that the other infant girl dies: "¿Y por qué no iba a morir? . . . Teresa no es más que un india. Su hija era india también" (140). ("And why wouldn't she die? . . . Teresa's no more than an Indian. Her daughter was an Indian, too" [133].) The adolescent Idolina's guilty dependence on Teresa, whose daughter was killed so that she should live, and Teresa's dedicated care of Idolina after being expelled from her own home and community, figure the corrupt intimacy of Ladino interactions with the Chamula.

It is not surprising, then, that Idolina's sense of absolute exclusion from the world of her Ladino community and her desire to both hide from and find a place in that society generate a knot of ambivalence about both her mother and questions of power. After her mother relates this story to Julia, a new arrival to Ciudad Real, Idolina switches her primary attachment from Teresa to Julia. Julia is both the companion, thought to be wife, of Fernando and the newest mistress of Leonardo. The narrative never clarifies or explains Julia's motivations for her studious courtship of Leonardo's invalid stepdaughter, but their alliance provides Idolina with a window on society and a sense of participation she had not had through her mother. However, Idolina's mother is jealous of this new attachment and joins forces with the disapproving priest, Don Alfonso, to persuade Idolina that Julia is her traitor. Once Idolina understands the truth of Julia and Leonardo's relationship, she is thrown back onto her isolation and powerlessness—an isolation that subsequently propels her to writing.

In the scene of writing, Idolina overcomes and transcends her abject circumstances, though this crossing into yet another foreign and forbidden world is narrated as primarily an act of supreme and wounded narcissism—to push herself into that world and through the glass that separates her.

> Ansiosamente busca un papel y un lapis. Ella, que apenas sabe escribir, está llenando ahora página y otra con esa letra greande, des gobernando, de quienes están acostumbrados a emlear la mano otros menesteres. Es un relato tumultuoso, una confesión infantil, el último grito del que se ahoga. Cuando termina está jadeante como si hubiera hecho un gran esfuerzo físico. (202)

> [She searches anxiously for paper and a pencil. Then she, Idolina, who can barely write, is filling one page after another with the large shaky letters of someone unaccustomed to doing things with her hands. It is a tumultuous narrative, an infantile confession, a last cry before drowning. When she finishes, she is shaking as if after a great physical exertion. (195–96)]

To grasp the pen and the power that it will ultimately give her, Idolina stages a scenario of being overcome, of not being in control of her actions. And it's true that the impact of those actions, the status of the letter she writes, remains veiled from the reader until the final pages of the novel.

Catalina is similarly possessed, not by writing but by the revelation of truth behind an oral myth, when she finally achieves her goal of rediscovering the stone gods that she believes the community must worship and that she and her brother had discovered as children. Catalina's initial concern is primarily her exclusion from the collective, the loss of both Domingo and Pedro: "Voy a desatar el nudo de mi amor que no gardó más que el aire. Estoy sola. Es preciso entenderlo bien. Sola" (192). ["I am going to untie the knot of my love that held nothing more than air. I am alone. This must be understood completely. Alone" (186).] Her growing sense of cataclysmic failure is rendered as well: "¡Mentira! ¿No ves que te has mentido, durante años y años, Catalina?" (193) ["Lies! Do you not see that you have lied, Catalina?" (188)] This insistent second-person narration voices accusations that are coming from her own head and underlines the agony of self and collective that Catalina is always experiencing. She's being watched and found wanting and then urged on by this same wounded voice of paranoia to find compensation for her failure. In the end, this is her new avenue into the collective, which will be her rediscovery of the stones in the cave and her call to the Chamula community to return to their old ways of worshipping their gods.

Both Idolina and Catalina figure female agency in all its complexity and complicity, figuring the roots of that agency in a dialectic of psychic interiority with social discourses that emerge as a very ambivalent source of political desire and agency. In addition, these scenes of female creativity emphasize the enormous obstacles that each woman faces, in particular the social isolation that comes with being female. As O'Connell argues, Catalina's "function as organic intellectual arises from her attempts to rewrite the trope of female identity from one of reproduction to one of creation" (160). As extended metaphors of creativity, Idolina's writing and Catalina's ritual religious practices encapsulate both the extreme energy necessary to overcome their respective societies' systemic repression and containment of female energy as well as that creativity's murky and somewhat suspect origins in wounded narcissism. Thus *Oficio de tinieblas* is not only a revisionist *indigenista* narrative of misfired cross-cultural translations and a failed Maya uprising; within those concerns emerges a perhaps even more profound preoccupation with the question of an equally excluded and impossible female agency in relation to the social.

Conclusion

The challenge posed by female agency is most clearly manifested in Catalina's ambiguity as a character and agent of change in the narrative. On the one hand, her mode of participating in the Chamula collectivity clearly has catastrophic effects, especially once she translates her obsession with the old ways into story form and links it to her desire to be remembered, to be a leader in the community. Catalina comes to the point where she announces that the only way the Chamula can free themselves from the oppressive dominance of the Ladinos is to hold their own crucifixion ceremony. She indicates that Domingo was born to serve the collective as their sacrifice to the gods. The narratorial commentary indicates a deep authorial condemnation of the way the killing of Domingo instigates a horrific communal killing spree in which "la tribu se movía como un gran animal torpe, desarticulado y acéfalo" (327) ("the tribe moves like a great, clumsy animal, disjointed and headless" [324]). Focalized through the irrational and leaderless collective as it engages in a series of scenes of massacre, rape, and cannibalism, the representation of apocalyptic violence that seems to be the culmination of *Oficio de tinieblas* is unflinching and detailed. And in portraying the aftermath of the "uprising," as one of complete defeat and disaster for the Chamula, the novel emphasizes the uprising's futility.

But after the uprising has been narrated, though not the brutal retaliation of the Ladino who decimate and scatter the Chamula, the novel focuses again on interior spaces and domestic scenes in the Ladino community. First, there is a detailed narration of the meeting between the morally and emotionally destroyed Bishop Don Alfonso and the governor of the state of Chiapas who has come to Ciudad Real in the wake of the Ladinos' ruthless and systematic genocide of all Indians in the region. The governor is concerned about some letters he continues to receive from the city that have denounced its leaders and even led to a delay of federal support for the Ladino during the uprising. On being questioned about these letters, the bishop exclaims enigmatically, "Writing! The mania of lonely women" (358). His opaque "explanation" of the letters articulates a surprising theory of agency and affect, one grounded in the example of Idolina and her letters: "Cuando alguno está solo, solo de raíz y durante mucho tiempo, adivina las intenciones de los demás antes de que cuagen en actos y palpa los delirios ajenos y da nombre y substancia a las criaturas que los otros sueñan din saberlo" (361). ["When someone is alone, fundamentally alone, and for a very long time, they can guess other people's intentions even before those intentions have taken shape in actions; they can feel other people's deliria and give a name and a form to the creatures others dream of unknowingly" (359).] By ascribing a prophetic power to "that girl" and her frantic, late-night letters, the bishop conveys to the reader that Idolina's manic writing has had a reverberating impact on politics and policies at a state, if not national, level.

The bishop also suggests an alternative theory of agency grounded in the marginality of gender—and perhaps implicating the power of other forms of marginality as well, including Catalina's. He proposes that such liminal participation in the collective leads to an intuitive knowledge derived from ephemeral but astute perceptions of other people's hidden motivations and actions—and of the social order itself—which those lodged comfortably within that social order cannot "see." By linking this special perceptivity to both social isolation and a scene of writing, and storytelling, he prepares the narrative ground for the novel's final scene.

The prophetic power ascribed to those outside the circle of community in *Oficio* differs substantially from the way the "almanac" in *Almanac of the Dead* operates. But both novels end with a scattering of the people—a return to "the shadows," or margins, of a society not yet transformed. The Chamula have abandoned their villages and markets in order to seek the safety of the caves: "La busqueada de la tinieblas los conduce a las cuevas" (364). ["The search for darkness leads them to the caves" (361).] In this retreat to the shadows, though, the scattered collectivity finds its own talisman, which again forces the reader to consider the technology of the book, and thus of the law, and the role of both in the brutal decimation that has occurred. The Chamula men huddled in their caves, living the life of animals, engaged in a ritual that centers on a found object—a few pages of "the book" that they pass around, examine, and worship (but can't read). The narrator then reveals the title of this "book," *Ordenanzas militares* (364) (*Military Directives*), which exposes a layer of irony that haunts the final pages of the novel. Leonardo authored *Military Directives,* which provided the ammunition and motivation for the Ladino "victory", particularly through the detailed and brutal elimination of each and every Chamula found in the state of Chiapas provided in the text of Cifuentes's manual of military, and state, power. Thus the very scene of the Chamula in the cave, worshipping the instrument of their destruction, offers another allegorical emblem of the catastrophic vagaries of cross-cultural relations and translations.

How to read this scene has been a controversial point in the characterization of Castellanos's narrative practices. Some critics have suggested that the fact that *Military Directives* is now in Chamula hands means they have access to the same guidelines to armed resistance as the Ladinos, access to the organization and goals that enabled the triumph of Euro-American modernity, once they learn to read the book in their hands. Following that interpretation, Burdell understands this moment as the culmination of Castellanos's bias in favor of writing and, thus, of Euro-American modernity, as well as the culmination of her pessimistic view of the capacity of the indigenous communities and cultures to survive this Euro-American colonial modernity. Castellanos's authorial perspective and narrative focalization in this scene indicate both a searing irony and a crucial ambiguity that manage to support both of these opposing readings. In some readings, Castellanos's irony implies a bitterness as the Chamula once again misrecognize Western modernity and what it can offer them. However, the ruse of modernity may in fact be directed at the reader—who like Fernando is likely to believe in the law and the state. But the scenario of *Military Directives* being displayed around a campfire is not the final emblem of the novel, which gets another coda to the apocalypse—holding forth other possibilities for futurity, as well as translation. The final scene of the novel returns to Ciudad Real, where Idolina is being cared for once again by Teresa. The nurse has returned to the Cifuentes household, again "betraying" her people out of a need to survive the constraints of violence perpetuated in the name of social norms and forces she has no control over. Isabel is busy participating in her corrupt husband's political success and power while Idolina listens for her mother's distant voice as she lies in her darkened room. Teresa has returned to caring for and "serving" Idolina, who is now tormented by visions of brutal violence in fragmented yet accurate flashbacks to scenes from the uprising and its repression. To comfort Idolina and block out these horrific visions, Teresa "le cuenta un cuento para calmarla, para dormirla" (366) ("tells her a story to soothe her and put her to sleep" [364]). The story begins, "En otro tiempo . . . hubó en mi pueblo, según cuentan los ancianos, una ilol de gran virtud" (366). ["In other times—you weren't born yet, child . . . there was in my village, the old people say, an *ilol* of great power" (364).] In this retelling, Teresa displaces the story that the reader has just read to "another time" and so both reclaims and reshapes a memory that has been announced as "lost," producing a narrative form that can be tolerated, and circulated, in place of the impossible events that the two communities, and women, have just lived through.

In Teresa's tale of a powerful *ilol* and her son made of stone, the pair become too powerful and begin to demand human sacrifices. The elders then complain to the "lords of Ciudad Real," asking "'¿Qué hacemos con estos devoradores de gente?'" (367) ("'What are we to do with these devourers of human flesh?'" [366]) The lords and the elders join forces but can only defeat the *ilol* and her son with a trick that murders the son and thereby incites the mother to destroy herself in despair, after which "los cadavers propagaron, a todos los vientos, pestilencia y daño" (368) ("their corpses strewed pestilence and harm to all the winds" [366]). This allegory of a past and inexplicable apocalypse has the following final message: "El nombre de esa ilol, que todos pronunciaron alguna vez con reverencia y con esperanza, ha sido proscrito. Y el que se siente punzado por la tentación de pronunciarlo escupe y las saliva ayuda a borrar su imagen, a borrar su memoria" (368). ["The name of that ilol, which was once spoken by all with hope and reverence, has been outlawed. The man who feels himself stung by the temptation to speak it spits and the saliva helps to erase her image, to erase her memory" (367).]

Here, Teresa goes silent and "goes back to her place. Because it will be a long time before dawn." This image of Teresa and Idolina—enclosed again in their dark complicity and intimacy born of a mutual necessity, in which neither is completely innocent—would seem to signal a shutting down of possibilities, and of futurity for either woman locked in this social and emotional isolation that has been established as near total. If a window is made available out of this enclosed space of the Cifuentes household, it would be in the possibility that one day Idolina will be able to listen to and *hear* Teresa's story and the Chamula will learn to *read* the *Directives*. In each case, narrative itself has proven to hold the capacity to affect, to *move*, the collective: Catalina's vision of a revolutionary new ritual act and Idolina's surprisingly effective letters to the official body of the state are both performative statements that shape the story that remains here— though arguably each had disastrous consequences. And the final two chapters of *Oficio de tinieblas* illustrate the devastating effects of the violent social order that the Chamula, and women, inhabit. Both the ironic pathos of the Maya huddled around the *Military Directives* and the enclosed world of Teresa and Idolina are customarily read as dead-ends— narrations of cultural pessimism or hopelessness. However, each of these scenarios also depends fundamentally on the technology of the story and the relation between storytelling and the potentiality of a new community. In looking again at the narrative performance staged by an apocalyptic allegory, I wonder to what extent Castellanos concurs with Silko that another future is possible, one redeemed from the apocalyptic race war that the text itself depicts?

Unlike Silko, Castellanos assiduously avoids a culturalist ontology of virtue: the many characters in both novels are equally shaped by the sociality of Euro-American modernity's "death worlds," but in *Oficio,* they are also equally duped by that modernity. This difference reflects a profound divergence in the two texts' performative narrativity and pedagogy. One of Silko's goals is to fortify the forces of revolution and rebellion— particularly among the "abjected" populations of the Americas—even as the other goal is to create an "ogre Kachina" of a book that will scare the complacency out of readers soaked in the blood of a contemporary necropolitics that they refuse to see or acknowledge. Castellanos's mid-century novel does not presume this double audience or pedagogy, so her ideal reader is precisely the Ladino "citizen" who unselfconsciously occupies the seat of humanity—energetically drawing lines around "the good life" and the "bare life" of the Mexican nation. Although I have focused on the profoundly dialogical ethics of Castellanos's narrative practice, this pedagogical difference raises interesting questions regarding the performative impact of identity discourses and the extent to which Castellanos's refusal of an ontology of subalternity as perception and/or ethics can be read as a particularly far-sighted indictment of liberalism's easy platitudes, or an inadvertent concession to the logic of "the same" that most fundamentally rules modern sociality?

In each book, however, there is a witness, interior to the text, who mirrors the reader's experience of watching in horror as the apocalyptic plot takes shape. And like Teresa and Idolina (and Sterling), the reader remains somewhat uncomprehending—stunned by the violence and tragic futility of the uprising and its suppression. Here the questions of storytelling and pedagogy do seem to converge, particularly given the uncanny resemblances shared by these final scenes of allegorical narration. Both depict collectives faced with the dilemma, "What are we to do with these devourers of human flesh?" (Castellanos 366). Sterling's response to this revelation of evil in the world, like Teresa's, is to both tell the allegorical story and then to wait. Teresa however, notes the injunction on witnesses of these slices of history and their horrors: "Y el que se siente punzado por la tentación de pronunciarlo escupe y la saliva ayuda a borrar su imagen, a borrar su memoria" (368). ["The man who feels himself stung by the temptation to speak it spits and the saliva helps to erase her image, to erase her memory" (367).] The insistently gendered pronoun in English illuminates the gendered nature of this need to "erase" both the image and the memory of the lost history. Ultimately, Castellanos allegorically encodes her own rebellion against the collective will to forget: against the injunction not to speak the name of the transgressing woman, Castellanos barrages her readers with a tapestry of stories about her, and them.

5

Encrypted Diasporas: Writing, Affect, and the Nation in Zoé Valdés's *Café Nostalgia*

It is easy enough to see that this apparent glorification of the critic-philosopher in the name of truth is in fact a glorification of the poet as the primary source of this truth.

(Paul de Man)

Secular epiphanies reveal the past, but one's personal history is an elusive god.

(Adam Phillips)

I. "Mi cicatriz de nacimiento" (My Birth Mark): Affect and Nation

The ethics of representation and questions of identity and nation formation take a distinct turn in the experimental popular fiction of contemporary Cuban writer Zoé Valdés. Renowned for precisely the stylistic pyrotechnics that Rosario Castellanos claimed to eschew, Valdés has produced a series of novels that highlight a globalized postmodern sensibility. Her stories focus on female protagonists—often implicitly autobiographical—and their various struggles with Cuban history, both on and off the island. Valdés's early novel, *La nada cotidiana* (1995) (*Yocandra in the Paradise of Nada* [1997]), was hailed as the emergence of a new voice in Cuban literature. *La nada cotidiana* follows the thoughts and experiences of Yocandra (née Patria) and provides a stringent, if often hilarious, critique of life in Havana under Castro and especially during the "periodo especial" (special period) that followed the withdrawal of Soviet financial support from Cuba in 1989. Valdés penned most of her subsequent novels, stories, essays, and poems after she left Cuba in the mid-1990s, and these works often depict the condition of exile shared by so many Cubans of that era's "diaspora generation," with a special focus on writers and artists.[1] The cultural work of literature and the condition of Cuba and its generation of contemporary transnational migrants are the explicit and intertwined concerns of Valdés's work, and especially of her 1997 novel *Café Nostalgia*.[2]

Although eminent Cuban American admirers such as Oscar Hijuelos insist that "there is no pro-Castro or anti-Castro agenda here, only the agenda of the self" (back cover of *Yocandra*), Valdés's baroque first-person monologues underline how deeply "the agenda of the self" is compelled to respond to, and be shaped by, political conditions and goals. In fact, how—and to what effect—the traces of history emerge through the narrations of Valdés's politically irreverent and sexually transgressive protagonists is a primary question raised by her work and its reception. Many of these novels also provide an interesting foil for the popular fiction of U.S.-based Latina writers, in that Valdés does not place her migrant narrator-protagonists within a specifically intergenerational familial chain. This U.S.-Latina emphasis on generational and genealogical links to the homeland tends to generate a model of diaspora that focuses on reproductive lineages, underscoring—sometimes intentionally and critically—their imbrication in heteronormative models of migration and exile. Understanding diaspora through the excavations of family histories, many of the most popular fictions, such as those by Julia Alvarez, Cristina Garcia, and Achy Obejas, emphasize the links of blood and history that bind their female protagonists simultaneously across time and space to the island homeland and the "now" of family and community in the United States. One result of this difference is that Valdés's hyperindividualist register appears less explicitly tied to notions of politicized identities or concerns with collectivity. In fact, preemptively foreclosing any discussion of Cuban politics, Marcela, the narrator-protagonist in *Café Nostalgia*, proclaims early on in the novel that she is like Lord Byron in that "ignoraba a todos los políticos" (28) (I know nothing about politicians).[3]

However, Marcela's emphatic assertions that neither her life nor her extended first-person monologue is controlled or determined by "politics" do not necessarily indicate that the narrative itself is apolitical. It's true that Marcela's account of her specifically personal experiences and her insistence on the primacy of individual ethics and the affective registers of her experience take up nearly all of *Café Nostalgia*'s narration: "A mí lo que me interesa es demostrar mis capacidades como ser humano, mi honestidad, ejercer el derecho a mi libertad individual" (28). (What interests me is to demonstrate my capacities as a human being, my honesty, to exercise my right to individual freedom.) But it also becomes clear that *Café Nostalgia* is a text that invites, even insists upon, a figurative understanding of Marcela's emotional states and her pursuit of freedom and "human capacities" as elements that operate in relation to the *logics*, or metaphor, of Cuban exile, as well as the experience of it. The textual *accounting*—a tally as well as a story—that takes place in *Café Nostalgia* raises a number of key questions about the work of writing and reading a "self," particularly the relation of individual "feelings" to collective, or national, affect as they intersect on the pages of the text. Valdés's novel stages these interactions between narrative writing, the personal intensities and upheavals of the text's narrator-observer-agent, and the figuring of history and nation as producing certain conditions for selfhood and thus certain affects or affective tendencies, particularly the nostalgia of the title. In exploring exile as the constitutive contingency of Marcela's personal life experience, Valdés narrativizes the mechanisms of exile as a technology of nostalgic selves and posits the Cuban diaspora as a nation or collectivity of such selves.

That is to say, in *Café Nostalgia* the text's narratorial subjectivity figures the individual and psychic remains of traumatic histories while the discourse of that narrating "self" indexes the geohistorical contexts of those subjective effects.[4] Such coded literary representations of historical conditions and political ideologies indicate the novel's allegorical elements, even as they also bespeak a particular incarnation of the relations between writing, politics, and history that compares suggestively with the mode of allegorical generational memoir in works by U.S.-based Latina writers. Despite their disparate geocultural locations, though, the novels written by these women share many thematic elements, especially a preoccupation with time and memory—both personal and collective—and a recurrent desire to explore the costs and contours of Latina/o diasporas.[5] However, the particularities of such texts' narrative remembering of Cuba, for example, suggest important differences between writers; these differences sometimes reflect their respective locations across the Cuban diaspora—whether that be in the United States, in other Caribbean islands, in Latin America, or in Europe. Valdés currently resides in Paris after temporary stays in New York and her formative years of childhood through early adulthood in Havana—a trajectory that *Café Nostalgia* closely follows in Marcela's narration. This autobiographical element further underlines the narrative's focus on an individual and subjective relation to the hauntings of Cuban national histories and displacements.[6]

Marcela articulates an obsessive attention to both herself—the vicissitudes and experiences of her emotions and her body—and her tight-knit circle of friends, most of whom are the product of intense friendships forged during her adolescence in Havana and who are now "desperdigados por el mundo" [scattered around the world]. In these extended narrations of subjective states, life events, love affairs, and career incidents, *Café Nostalgia* presents to the late modern (and modernist-trained) reader a familiar dilemma: Are we to "read" the text as a narrative of a particular obsession with Cuba that traces the effects of exile on the protagonist's self, effects that the narrator-agent marks through her extended interrogations of her own memory, her reading practices, and her sexuality? Or are we to follow the conventions of poststructuralist reading practices that demand we read "against the grain" of representations and focus on how the novel also works as a startlingly narcissistic document—a testimony to Cuban collective nostalgia as a structure of feeling that produces a particularly "wounded" self? This "Cuban" selfhood emerges not only in the content of what Marcela says and describes, but also in the very structure and grammar of how she says it. What Shoshana Felman calls the "unwritten testimony" thereby emerges in the text's inscription of the traumas of Cuban exile, and this testimony can be interpreted in at least two ways: as a valuable index to those national traumas or as a metaliterary, or allegorical, interrogation of the melancholic selfhood generated by the technologies of Cuban diaspora and exile. This exile selfhood embraces both its traumatized state and the narratives that support it, which suggests that Valdés has encoded within her novel a critique of nostalgia and its role in the collective imaginary of Cuban exiles and their often-provisional communities. However, this "figurative reading" (to use de Man's term) seems to ignore the constative significance of the text's expression of Marcela's own melancholic, traumatized selfhood produced by her distinct personal diaspora— one that demands to be attended to on its own terms. This chapter explores what is at stake in the choice between the former, ironic and post-structurally sophisticated, reading hermeneutic and attending directly to Marcela's articulations as the transparent narratorial voice of the novel.

The space that marks the tension between these reading alternatives— which de Man terms the "figurative" and the "literal"—becomes the space in which to measure the role of irony in *Café Nostalgia*.[7] Although irony is a mode that Valdés clearly embraces, as an author, its relation to Marcela's enunciations is less clear. In novels such as *Te di la vida entera* (1996) *(I Gave You All I Had* [1999]*)*, Valdés mockingly deploys melodramatic genre elements from *telenovela* television serials and sentimental 1950s cinema and raunchily and exuberantly milks their figurative potential while deciphering the farces of sexuality, sentiment, and Cuba's decrepit material conditions.[8] Likewise, *Café Nostalgia* is a novel that marks itself as highly metaliterary, and thus metafigurative, from the very first lines, as when the narrator announces, "Ayer. ¿Cuándo fue ayer? Ayer se me olvidó mi nombre" (9). [Yesterday. When was yesterday? Yesterday I forgot my name.] This abrupt introduction to the character of Marcela and the scene of narration begins the book by disorienting the reader, who is required to participate in Marcela's experience of forgetting her name and then working to recall it. Marcela's claimed amnesia thus provides a narratorial occasion to report her name to the reader and also to signal the multiple meanings of this momentary memory loss. At the gallery reception in which this opening scene unfolds, Marcela is responding to the greetings of a person she does not know, or recognize, but whose questions (never conveyed to the reader) provoke a cascade of sensory impressions and recollections. Among the images and experiences that Marcela narrates in this moment of being a self stripped of memory and name is her perception of a sculpture that stands before her in this gallery, and "en la cual predominaba como sugestión el tema marino me ayudó a que recuperara mi cicatriz de nacimiento, la identidad" (9). [in which a marine theme predominated as a suggestion, it helped me to recover the scar of my birth, my identity.] The "marine theme" leads to further recounting of olfactory and sensory experiences as a series of food and market recall until Marcela is able to recollect her name: "¡Ay, ya recuerdo! Exclamé retando a las neuronas; las tres letras de esta palabra son las mismas que las tres primeras de mi nombre. Mar . . . Me llamo Marcela, respondí titubeando" (10). [Oh, I remember now! I exclaimed challenging my neurons; the three letters of this word are the same as the first three of my name. Mar . . . My name is Marcela, I replied hesitating.]

This opening scene exemplifies Marcela's endless circling through memory and consciousness as she narrates the story—a *bojeo* (circling path) that, as Isabel Alvarez-Borland notes, becomes the guiding metaphor or figure for the novel as a whole. Because Valdés will also make this link between the archaic Spanish verb *bojar* or *bojear* and the plight of Cubans who feel forced to leave their island (as well as the island itself, also floating somewhat aimlessly in the ocean), the metaphor of *bojeo* exemplifies the novel's preoccupation with "return," as well as with "circling." In recounting how both *el mar* (the sea) and "mi cicatriz de nacimiento, la identidad" are connected in a semantic chain, the novel demands to be read figuratively, beyond its literal context of a gallery opening and a chance encounter with a stranger. The very structure of Marcela's consciousness is revealed in the associative wordplay that brings Marcela "back" to herself through a kind of linguistic echolalia that suggests presymbolic subjectivity—or, rather, a breakdown in ordered subjectivity that the novel indicates is characteristic of "exile subjectivity." The predilection for narrative games within the text and with the reader, who like the stranger at the reception remains unclear as to just how sincere this attack of amnesia ever was, also conveys how Marcela operates as a narrator: acutely sensitive but possibly unreliable, as well as deranged or damaged.[9] In representing her sense of self as so tenuous and unstable as to be momentarily misplaced, Marcela communicates and emphasizes her experiences of herself as a misplaced person.

In this discourse of loss and memory, Marcela returns again and again to close descriptions of emotional states and responses, especially her understanding of herself as a "mujer melancólica" (melancholic woman) (69). These detailed and extended portraits of her emotionally wrenching experiences of friendship, love, and family, as well as music, film, art, and literature (particularly Proust) serve as a "close reading" of her subjective states; these states are offered as potentially emblematic of contemporary diasporic Cuban selfhood, of the self produced by "aquella isla" (that island), as Marcela is always calling Cuba, and by the necessity of leaving it. The novel's thick description of this distinct Cuban technology of self-hood entails a particular attention to embodied experiences and the five senses of physical perception. All the details of this consciousness, and of this body, are to be minutely recorded and communicated, and in fact, the classic list of the five senses reappears in the structure of the novel itself as chapter headings that further underline the novel's constitutional fusing of affect and the body: "Capítulo primero: El Olfato, Desasosiego" ("First Chapter: Smell, Restlessness") is followed by Chapters 2 through 5 marked as "El Gusto, Peligro"; "El Oído, Olvido"; "El Tacto, Duda"; and "La Vista, Armonía" ("Pleasure, Danger"; "Sound, Forgetting"; "Touch, Doubt"; and "Sight, Harmony"). In the sixth and final chapter, "A Mi Único Deseo" ("To My Sole Desire"), the various threads of the previous chapters are brought together for the novel's resolution and finale. The first two chapters are structured through a running metacommentary on three topics in particular: (1) the nature of memory, (2) memory in relation to the senses, and (3) the meaning and practice of reading. Marcela represents both her past in Havana and her current life in Paris through the lens of these three thematic foci, with the narrative frequently shifting back and forth in time and across oceans to explore in exhaustive detail her jarring memories of events, often dramatically traumatic, from her formative years in Havana. Thus the novel highlights the structural and everpresent intertwining of a self within multiple locations and temporalities—a diasporic self and chronotope—and suggests that the narrative form of the novel and its representation of scenes of remembering operate as a precise reflection of that multiply constituted self.[10] Interestingly, this chronotope of diaspora and the community that inhabits its "floating" location bespeaks a narrative scene that always comes back to a traumatic origin and event—which suggests that Valdés narrates diasporic selfhood as haunted by, and always inhabiting, a chronotope of trauma.[11]

Marcela explicates her world of emotional intensity, one that "nearly destroys" her, through a minute—though fragmented—reconstruction of the collective history of herself and her friends. Marcela admits, "Yo dependo de la amistad como la araña de su hilo" (19) (I depend on friendship like a spider on its web), which signals the constitutive function of this collectivity forged through intense adolescent friendships in Havana. These experiences of passionate community generate a nostalgic longing for Cuba or "aquella isla"—in time as well as in space—that coheres Marcela's friends as a community whose loss, or breaking apart, is experienced as a foundational trauma that occupies the main narrative thread of the novel. The group itself thus emerges as a metonym for the nation and for the diaspora generation. Hilly Nelly Zamora explains this community formation as follows: "El exilio como condición definitoria de los personajes, los marca de tal forma que constantemente reviven y recapturan cada uno de los rasgos de su patria, para así fortalecer los lazos de unión, creando un nuevo sentido de nación" (125).[12] [Exile as a defining condition of the characters, marks them in such a way that they constantly relive and recapture each one of the characteristics of their *patria* (fatherland), and so strengthen the binding of the union, creating a new sense of nation.] Marcela's monologue thus narrates into existence this particular exilic collectivity, which emerges as a collectivity precisely through a process of loss, the wound of their group's separation. In recalling the details of their *amistad* (friendship) and the specific characteristics of each person in this "web" (name, token smell, and romantic or career history), Marcela sits in her room in Paris, writing and remembering Havana in a narrative project that appears to be a recuperative attempt to forestall forgetting.

That threat of time, of her sense of herself as no longer 20 years old, thus becomes part of a double struggle to "capture" and maintain the lost past and to fight the attrition of memory, a noted element of diasporic memory that also signals its unstable foundation.[13] The cathexis that the novel simultaneously reflects and represents through Marcela's circular autobiographical narrations denotes a suspension of the historical shifts of time and space in order to maintain the desired object—this personal and collective past—and to preserve the libidinal investments that it holds for her. But to what extent does the narrative totality actually fulfill this project of recovery? Alvarez-Borland emphasizes the countermovement within Marcela's monologue and Valdés's narrativizations of the diasporic consciousness: "As tropes of memory, Valdés's islands/tapestries do not perform their expected function of recovery. Instead, like vagrant vessels, they evoke dispersion and loss" (359). Following this eloquent formulation, I suggest that this failure is in fact the content or "proper" meaning of the novel's allegorical figuring—a possibility that most informs and preoccupies my own particular counterreading of Valdés's narrative project in *Café Nostalgia*.

II. Allegories of Reading Nostalgia

Marcela's minutely observed discourse of its life as both a body and a consciousness is elaborated in an extended metonymic chain that juxtaposes both mundane daily experiences and geographical and historical facts with sensory experiences of thinking/feeling, of "living so physically"; this chain often leads Marcela back to literature: "Y claro, vivir de esa manera tan física, tan transcendental, me aniquila; entonces me refugio en los libros" (12). [And clearly, living in such markedly physical way, so transcendentally, destroys me; so I hide myself in books.] In such self-dramatizations, Marcela embraces a narcissistic mode that suggests the clichés of Western adolescence—but also quite possibly a specifically Latina and *"trágica"* register of a self-dramatizing, feminine *latinidad,* which is deployed to characterize a subjectivity that is both suffering and yet ironically self-aware, what Alexandra Vasquez has called "making epic of the everyday."[14] Marcela herself acknowledges and interrogates the notion that her affective life is notably adolescent: "Amar es lo que me impide vivir con rutina. Porque cuando amo me doy demasiado cuenta de lo que estoy sintiendo. Ya que siempre vuelvo a enamorarme con aquella intensidad profética de la adolescencia" (12). [Loving is what keeps me from living routinely. Because when I love I am exceedingly aware of what I am feeling. Because I am always falling in love with the same prophetic intensity of adolescence.] This claim preserves both a past moment and a way of experiencing, of living, in the present that maintains that past self, thus upholding an emotional intensity threatened by the losses induced by isolation, time, and forgetting. But in highlighting the youthfulness, even immaturity, of her deepest feelings—particularly melancholy—Marcela allows for less enchanted interpretations of what these intense feelings signify for this diasporic, and yet adolescent, selfhood.

Marcela's self-dramatizations convey a wealth of information about the relation of aesthetic and sensory experiences, the circulation of affect across time and space, and other preoccupations of Cuban "exilic memory," to use José Muñoz's term. Situating Marcela's supremely individualist consciousness and voice within a specifically "Cuban" context and causal chain transforms her personal experience of exile and diaspora into one that is *exemplary.* In particular, Marcela's sense of an inescapable and ongoing situadedness in both a city and a body emerges as part of her Cuban diasporic experience, but it is a situadedness that is largely imagined, "fantastic" even, in the psychoanalytic sense. Marcela insists that especially while "leyendo y soñando" (reading and dreaming), she experiences herself as always and forever located in her apartment in Havana, with her friends and family: "Es entonces que me despabilo y emerjo de las páginas donde sueño con el océano, con mi madre, con mi cuarto" (14). [At that moment, I wake up and emerge from the pages of the book where I am dreaming with the ocean, with my mother, with my room.] At these moments, Marcela luxuriates in her remembered past, "arrellanaba en él como sobre un tibio sofá, dejando caer mi cuerpo delgado con toda la ligereza de mis viente años" (14). [lounging in it as in a warm sofá, letting my slender body fall with all the lightness of my 20 years.] Reading induces this affective experience of displacement and return—a return that Marcela recognizes as fantasmic and idealized, but also finds profoundly pleasurable.

The suspended dream state that reading produces here stalls, for just a moment, Marcela's abrupt return to her embodied present (and that of Havana), in which both have aged and deteriorated.

> Claro, ya no tengo veinte años y en el presente, este de hoy, he perdido agilidad. Mis padres tampoco viven más en La Habana. Me abandonaron en el año ochenta para irse a Miami. No aceptaron la peligrosa alternativa de esperar a que yo saliera de la beca ni tuvieron tiempo de avisarme. (14)

> [Of course, I am no longer 20 years old and in the present, that of today, I've lost agility. My parents don't live in Havana anymore either. They abandoned me in 1980 to leave for Miami. They didn't take the risky alternative of waiting until I finished my scholarship nor had time to alert me.]

This admission that the whole scene is a fantasy betrayed by her exile, her parents, and the very passing of time highlights Marcela's, and Valdés's, use of memory and nostalgia as keys to a subjectivity that emerges as wounded, and fragmented by that wounding. But this scenario also illustrates the function of reading as a technology of both selfhood and, in a sense, national affection. In linking scenes of reading to Marcela's personal but emblematic nostalgia, Valdés gestures toward the text's collective function as an "affective machine" (Bianco), even when the reading event in question is emphatically private.

Throughout the novel, Marcela oscillates between expressions of an insistent longing and *nostalgia* for Cuba and the life she lost there and lucid and cutting articulations of ironic and pained awareness of the impossibility of going back, of reversing or undoing time itself and the changes and losses it entails. Often these articulations, as in the aforementioned example, suggest that the memories and losses are themselves profoundly distorted by idealizations of a wholeness that never quite existed, such as that with her mother.[15] In this way, the narrative continually presents the reader with an astute commentary on the very structure of nostalgia and melancholy, even as it claims as "real" the profound experiences of insight and suffering that such melancholy has generated. Into Marcela's narrative perambulations and detailed asides, Valdés inscribes a narrative model for the kind of sustained patience and respectful attention that "teaches" the reader how to read *Café Nostalgia,* that is, very much as Marcela "reads" her own life. What, borrowing from J. Hillis Miller, Nattie Golubov has called, "slow reading," can be understood as Marcela's own narrative pedagogy: "Slow reading implies a particular form of respectful attention to the text in which nothing is lost: what matters is how and why the narrative voice or poetic persona articulates every detail and how the textual horizon of meaning allows such an arrangement" (Golubov). The sustained attentiveness that slows the reader's rush to judgment ironically mirrors the psychoanalyst's attentiveness to the discourse of the analysand, as discussed later, but here Valdés and Marcela figure this "slow" reading practice as a way to thwart predetermined "answers" such as those offered in psychologizing (or colonializing) scripts.

Reading itself, then, becomes Valdés's supplement that disrupts the logics of Freudian melancholy with her own, or rather Marcela's, distinct economy of sensation—of touch, sound, and taste—that pushes some of these expressions into unfamiliar territory: an exilic landscape of affect and interpersonal relations that Marcela, and possibly Valdés, distinguishes from the established paradigms of both subjectivity and exile. Marcela's repeated insistence on loving and living "con un exceso de sensaciones" (with an excess of sensation) signals a rebellion against the codes of recovery and "proper" affective relations that are common to discussions of exile as collective melancholy and trauma. Therefore, in a novel that traces a series of personal, largely sexual and intimate, traumatic experiences, the notions of narcissistic wounding are inflected into a particular direction that claims for itself its own specific mode. In so far as Marcela's "exceso de sensaciones" privileges the epistemologies of touch, smell, and taste, rather than vision, for example, these sensorial excursions further suggest that Valdés is working through the familiar materials of exile and subject formation to express a subjectivity that demands to be considered on its own terms.

Marcela's resistant and particularist narration of her experience questions presumptions about the narcissistic economy of her "yo" and suggests narration itself as an alternative to the pathologizing of melancholia as traumatic repetition. In this sense, *Café Nostalgia* can be understood through the kind of reformulation of melancholia advocated by David Eng and David Kazanjian in their influential collection *Loss.* In their introduction, Eng and Kazanjian suggest that "melancholia's continued and open relation to the past finally allows us to gain new perspectives and new understandings of lost objects" (4). In proposing a methodology of "reliving" as a way to "bring the past to memory," they cite a Benjaminian historiography that Marcela, and probably Valdés, would likely embrace for its claim that melancholia operates critically as both a creation and an intensification of meaning and a more profound understanding of the lost object, such as Cuba. But in at least two ways, Marcela's monologue traces a rather classically Freudian path. One, her affective experiences are marked ("scarred") primarily by pain—even melancholy finally becomes more of a burden than a secret pleasure. And two, in its narrative *bojeo* (circling) around this wounded core of selfhood and suffering, the narrative of *Café Nostalgia* structurally encodes the pathological symptoms of melancholia as a stalled, stagnant state of being; one that, Freud cautions, can ultimately lead to suicide.[16]

While this core would seem to be generated by her exile, for Marcela it is also "abandonment" that emerges as her near-unspeakable primary loss and thus melancholic attachment. She expresses this centrality on only a handful of occasions, such as when noting that, she and a friend, "compartíamos de toda la vida un intenso enigma: el del abandono" (35) (we shared all our lives an intense enigma: that of abandonment). Although Marcela admits here that this ongoing experience of abandonment began with her parents' emigration to Miami, she tends to skirt around this originary trauma, so that her story more often slides into a narrative focus, the diaspora itself—the dispersion of a "family" of friends forced to leave "aquella isla" by the nation's figurative abandonment of the hopes and aspirations of an entire generation, particularly its artists. Here, the paradoxes of celebratory rereadings of melancholic attachment also emerge: on the one hand, Marcela encapsulates precisely "that ongoing and open engagement with the past" advocated by Eng and Kazanjian (4) and on the other hand proves to be profoundly incapable of "reimagining the future," an impossibility that haunts the novel right to its very end.

The specific terms of Marcela's embrace of nostalgic selfhood are established early in the long monologue of the novel, particularly in the opening reflections about reading and Proust that return at the beginning of Chapter 2. The meditative tone of these opening chapters turns increasingly toward narrations of events—of key experiences from Marcela's years in Havana and from her ongoing struggle for survival and connection in her current exilic existence in Paris. These distinct but constantly interwoven chronotopes of a past in Havana and recent and current experiences in Paris are ultimately reconciled in a series of "coincidences" that brings Marcela's past into her present in the last two chapters of *Café Nostalgia*.

The multiplying coincidences of the novel's various plotlines layer Marcela's experiences of memory and remembering onto experiences of reading and language, thus indicating the centrality of both writing and memory to the novel's main project of remembering and maintaining emotional connections to her past self and the collectivity of friends that defines and supports her identity as a *Cubana*. Even as the past is increasingly threatened by time, exile, and the political and economic conditions of both, the *bojeo* of Marcela's memory testifies to a "necessity to review, recover, and recount, a need born by the displacement that is at the heart of *Café Nostalgia*" (Alvarez-Borland 350). But as a literary text *Café Nostalgia* also necessarily embodies its own undoing, which means that the possibility of another understanding entirely of this *need* to return to and recover the past always exists. In the first chapter, Marcela articulates a theory of reading that indicates her particular and very paradoxical understanding of the uses of memory and desire for diasporic subjects, particularly *Cubanos*. This link between the self and the nation is one that both Valdés and Marcela return to often; in earlier works, Valdés represents, sometimes ironically, the very characteristics of wounded Cuban selfhood that Marcela plays out in her monologues. And like *La nada cotidiana*, *Café Nostalgia* emphasizes, even exaggerates, autobiographical elements so that the echoes and repetitions appear to weave a complex palimpsest of the subjectivities of the narrator and Valdés herself.

This palimpsestic character of the narrating voice generates a specific reading hermeneutics that is established in part by the novel's ongoing metacommentary on reading and knowledge. Marcela first brings up reading in the context of her name, thus linking it to the question of her identity—as the way that "la etimología de mi nombre me lastima" (the etymology of my name hurts me)—and to the intensity of her suffering. This suffering is manifested as a longing for *el mar*, a specifically Caribbean-Cuban sea: "Y no puedo abrir la ventana y husmear su proximidad . . . pero estoy soñando y leyendo, y más tarde, despierto en el interior de la lectura, o sea en el libro, y me veo en mi cuarto de La Habana" (13). [And I can't open the window and breathe in its proximity . . . but I am dreaming and reading, and later, I wake up inside the reading, or in the book, and I see myself in my room in Havana.] But this deep logic of reading as a kind of dreaming that returns Marcela to her past self is twisted back onto itself in other descriptions of reading as simultaneously return and escape, forgetting and remembering. Again, reading shows itself to be, fundamentally, a machine producing affects. Marcela's remembers these experiences of physical and emotional intensity and connectivity through acts of reading—acts that she suggests can operate as a virtual production of the potentiality of diasporic selves and communities.

In her opening discussions, Marcela initially describes her love of reading as a kind of addiction, a refuge from the sensory and emotional overload in which she exists most of the time:

Entonces me refugio en los libros. Leer me impulsa a leer. La lectura es la señal de que aún poseo inocencia, de que todavía puedo preguntar. Preguntar, ¿à quién? Cuando voy por la mitad de un libro por fin dejo de ser yo. Porque leyendo sueño. Pero leer, soñar y besar en los labios es vivir con mi yo, dentro de mi yo. Aprecio la melancholia del yo. (127)

[So I hide myself in books. Reading pushes me to read. Reading is the sign that I still possess innocence, that I can still question. Question whom? When I am in the middle of a book, I finally stop being me. Because in reading, I dream. But to read, to dream and to kiss on the lips is to live with my "I", inside of my "I". I appreciate the melancholy of my "I".]

Reading functions both to return her to the desired past and place and to allow her to forget herself. Marcela explains that the intensity of her reading experiences can be traced to her need to "burlar dos sentimientos tan opuestos como son el recuerdo y el olvido" (19) (thwart the opposition of two affects as opposed as those of memory and forgetting). This need to "burlar dos sentimientos" reiterates the paradoxes of ambivalence as an oscillation between remembering the self and forgetting the personal past that tyrannizes that selfhood. As theorist and psychoanalyst Adam Phillips notes, "Freud sometimes calls what happens in the gap we call forgetting, 'dream-work'; and at other times, though he does not use this phrase, 'art-work'" (31). So while reading and dreaming appear to return Marcela to an imagined Havana, they are also the subjective states that most allow her a creative forgetting that is, in psychoanalytic versions of melancholia at least, the only avenue to futurity—to something other than an interminable experience of the remembered, and the repressed, past.

As the narrative remembrance of her past and her selfhood, both distant in Havana and immanent in Paris, the trope of reading joins sensory impressions and data as primary transfer points, or scene shifters, between the distinct time periods, friendships, lovers, and cities that constitute the narrative content of the novel. From describing reading as a preferred mode of "dreaming" that returns her to her former apartment in Havana, Marcela switches midparagraph to a conception of reading as the privileged mode of interpersonal, and intersubjective, connection and communication.

Existe una extraña seducción entre tu yo y el mío, entre el yo de aquel que por convencionalismos morales o traumas sociales restará importancia al yo íntimo del otro. Leer es lo único que puede hacer coincidir las soledades sin que nuestro ego predomine por encima de las épocas, los sitios, las costumbres del otro. Aceptar al prójimo no es lo mismo que tolerarlo, es una verdad de Perogrullo que hemos desdeñado demasiado aprisa. En el verbo tolerar está implícita la censura. Todavía el hecho de leer permite, aunque a duras penas, a causa de constituir una vivencia cultural, la aceptación de los casos admitimos mezclarlo con el nuestro.

[There exists a strange seduction between your "I" and mine, between that "I" of her who for reasons of moral conventionalism or social trauma substracts importance from the intimate "I" of the other. Reading is the only thing that can bring together solitudes without letting our own ego predominate over the epoch, the places, the customs of the other. To accept this proximity is not the same as to tolerate it, this is a truism of Perogrullo that we have abandoned too quickly. Censorship is implied in the verb to tolerate. Still the fact of reading permits, even with some difficulty, because of building a cultural life, the acceptance of the other in those cases where we allow it to mix without own. (13–14)]

In this long quotation, Marcela makes a claim for the radical power of reading to enable an acceptance, a kind of embrace and incorporation of the other that is not possible in other mediums. Reading alone overcomes the ego's control of these interactions, perhaps precisely through the dreamlike state of openness that it generates. Marcela's descriptions coincide strongly with influential theories of reading as a radical subjective engagement with the other. In addition to such theories by Mikhail Bakhtin and Emmanuel Levinas, we also note the resonance with Golubov's conception of "slow reading" as a cross-cultural pedagogy that also can help "the narcissistic self . . . to break free of the restriction which is itself" (Golubov). Doris Sommer has likewise argued for "respect" as a requirement for reading practices that can suspend monolingual and monocultural judgment (1999). As an allegory of her selfhood, Marcela's narration of reading suggests that intersubjective connection, an ecstatic intertwining of selves and subjectivities, is her primary goal.

And yet reading, like writing, is a solitary activity, one that maintains and enforces the isolation and lack of connection that plague Marcela throughout the novel. This problem of both imagined and embodied connections preoccupies her discourse and structures the monologue as she weaves between various scenes and characters to recreate, and often to relive, the "web" of *amistades* that supports her even as she struggles with the isolation and anonymity of life a Cuban exile in Paris. But here and elsewhere Marcela will also clearly assert reading as the privileged mode of communication that underlines the inadequacy of technologies such as the telephone, answering machine, and fax. In her comparing technologies of connection and communication, reading maintains its primacy perhaps precisely because of its silence and isolation, invoking a state similar to the "listening" of psychoanalysis, which Phillips describes as a "free-floating or evenly suspended attention" (31). Furthermore, Phillips suggests, "It is only when two people forget themselves in each other's presence that they can recognize each other. Because we can only communicate underground—only recognize each other in spite of ourselves" (31). In understanding reading as a kind of "dreaming" that releases the ego from its predominance, and thus a practice of forgetting that momentarily releases her from a life of compulsive remembering, Marcela emphasizes that it is only within this gap in the ego's self-domination that connection and recognition with the other can occur.

But *Café Nostalgia* maintains and repeats the compulsion to overcome separations of time and space through memory and other forms of compulsory communication that are embedded throughout the novel. So Marcela's interior monologue can move from a seemingly meditative consideration of how "we" exiled Cubanos are "ilusoriamente libres" (illusorily free) to a free, direct address to her friend Ana: "Ana, te amo, airado jazmín . . . Quiero conocer a tu hija, Ana, pero ahora sería imposible, no tendría fuerzas para viajar en avión hasta Buenos Aires" (20–21). [Ana, I love you, angry jasmine . . . I want to meet your daughter, Ana, but right now that would be impossible, I don't have the strength to travel by plane to Buenos Aires.] This desperate call to the absent friend is followed by a litany of similar remembrances of her friends Enma and Andro, whom she describes as "Andro es mi alma gemela. Mi parte masculina. Estamos conectados por telepatía, por magia, por el no se qué de san Juan de la Cruz" (21). [Andro is my twin soul. My masculine part. We're connected by telepathy, by magic, by the I-don't-know-what of San Juan de la Cruz.] These monologues both express and testify to the emotional intensity of her lived relations with the collectivity of friends "scattered around the world" and her desire to saturate the field between her and this network of friends with words and communications. Such direct addresses that foreclose the possibility of response (because they are written in her room or take place within the pages of a book) recall Marcela's store of unsent letters and her intense preoccupation with one-sided communications sent out into the ether, where this web must be constantly spun and maintained.

III. Ambiguous Narrativities of Individual Desire and Collective Affect

The paradox generated by Marcela's theory of reading as a "dream" of the exilic self and as a means of "accepting" the "other" ultimately shapes the reader's experience of both Marcela's monologues as well as the various "interior texts" that punctuate the novel and supplement Marcela's dominant voice. Including the utterances of others would seem to build a dialogic whole out of the novel. But whether these intertexts ultimately contest or affirm Marcela's point of view and the validity of her claims is another key question raised by her self-representations and their problematics of narrative levels and the role of irony. For example, Marcela admits that she is a voracious letter-writer, and the novel is full of plotlines that involve letters (and other missives) that are not sent, or that get read by the "wrong" person. But, the status of those unsent letters remains undecidable and for the most part unknowable. Are such communiqués the material evidence that manifests the connections upholding this collectivity, a group of friends whose "scattered" status indicates its allegorical function for the kind of collectivity the nation of "Cuba" has become? Or rather do such dialogic intertexts illustrate the phantasmatic nature of those connections and of Marcela's efforts to maintain this collectivity in the face of its "real" destruction by time and migration? In many ways, the novel holds in suspension the status of Marcela's entire worldview; both her "ignorance" and ours sustain the possibility of recuperation but also signal the reality of loss. Into this textual miasma of desire and communications not completed, the function of "interior texts"—both Marcela's and those of other characters—takes on special weight in *Café Nostalgia*.

The "interior texts" of others are often incorporated into the novel; these other texts include various letters, faxes, and telephone messages from "mi grupo de amigos" (my group of friends) that often confirm and supplement Marcela's (and Valdés's) portrait of Cuba as crumbling and of the diaspora generation as a fragmented community struggling to keep its links alive. Alvarez-Borland sees these diverse confirmations as further illustration of the hardships of life in Cuba, especially during the "período especial" (special period);[17] however, she also notes that the epistemological value of their inclusion is that "the novel's modernistic narrative strategies question the readers' own models of judgment" (352). Some of these dialogic commentaries occur in the direct dialogue that Marcela reports, as in a debate about emigration between herself and one of her best friends when they were in the eighth grade: "Enma, a pesar de todo yo creo que es aquí donde hay que estar. Es mejor tratar de cambiar esto que cambiar algo que no nos pertenece. Yo creo en esto, éste es mi sol, mi cielo, mi mar. Mis padres están aquí. Mis amigos también. Yo creo en todo eso" (104). [Enma, in spite of everything I believe that I must stay here. It is better to try to change things here than to change something that isn't ours. I believe in this, this is my sun, my sky, my sea. My parents are here. My friends too. I believe in all of this.] Enma, interestingly, responds with a precocious cosmopolitanism that is equally emphatic: "¿Y qué es lo que es tuyo? ¿Qué es lo que debe pertenecerte? Pero qué manía de propietario de esta isla tiene todo el mundo aquí. Yo no quiero que ningún país sea mío. Yo solo quiero que sea mío lo que me gane con el sudor de mi frente" (105). [And what is this that is yours? What is the thing that must belong to you? But, why does everyone here have a fixation on owning this island. I do not want for any nation to be mine, I only want to own what I earn with the sweat of my brow.] In this dialogue, Marcela stages two principal illusions of the Cuban diaspora: first, that one can choose to stay, believing in "todo esto" (all this) when the conditions and contingencies of life on the island force so many to leave; and second, that one can refuse to claim a country or anything else that "pertains to you" by maintaining the fictions of a self-possessive, liberal individual untouched by the webs of history and material contingency.

Some of these intradiegetic intertexts are written by Marcela herself, who avows her penchant for writing unsent letters (the negative consequences of which she slyly foreshadows in Chapter 1). One of her earliest, and ultimately most persistent, traumas is set in motion by such floating communiqués that are misplaced or misread, in this case tragically so. This tale takes up a central portion of Chapter 2 (titled "El Gusto, Peligro") and instigates one of several narrative threads that are ultimately incorporated into the novel's ending. As a teenager, Marcela develops a crush on an older man whom she knows only from watching him pass by her friend Mina's apartment on the way to the park with his young son. She writes this unknown man a string of love letters as a way of distracting herself from her infatuation with a close friend who sees her only as a buddy. The unlikely tragedy occurs when it seems that her letters are read by the man's wife, who sets fire to her husband in their bed for his supposed adultery. A stricken, adolescent Marcela watches the man being taken to the hospital and is then viciously attacked by Mina who accuses her of destroying this family by using her sexuality in a vindictive and amoral bid for attention. Because Mina's accusations echo Marcela's own anguished thoughts, they underline both the brutality of this supposed friend and the deeper significance of the event, which links sexuality and desire with violence and guilt as an inexorable and interminable "mark" on Marcela—who not coincidentally has announced in Chapter 1 that "Soy frigida" (38) (I'm frigid).

The horror of the immolated husband stays with Marcela, who admits, "No niego que asumí la historia como una marca del destino que debía aprovechar para alimentar mis estados melancólicos" (112). [I don't deny that I took on this history as a mark of destiny that I had to take advantage of as food for my melancholic states.] However, she also understands that the hauntings of personal trauma have wounded her in ways that cannot be "appreciated" or taken advantage of and that still thwart her experiential horizons and especially her experiences of sexual desire and romantic satisfaction: "Pero el malestar no siempre fue favorable y caía en profundas depresiones. Lo peor es cuando aún vivo aquel suceso como si hubiera ocurrido en una pesadilla diabólica que me alienó las futuras relaciones amorosas" (112–13). [But unhappiness is not always favorable and I fell into profound depressions. The worst is when I still experience that event as if it had occurred in a diabolic nightmare that alienated me from all future love relations.] This specter of endless romantic failure and isolation haunts the novel and is especially notable in the repeated cryptic references to her longing for her "amor platónico" (platonic love), Samuel, whose importance she continues to underline, though without offering much information until much later in the novel.

Samuel is also the author of the most extensive and climactic interior text that Valdés includes in Marcela's story of remembering and reading. Finally, in Chapter 4 (titled "El Tacto, Duda") the reader is presented with a coherent description of the neighbor and romantic interest, Samuel, whose arrival Marcela anticipated with intense desire and anxiety. In this instance, Marcela doesn't just read the other; here, she actually steals the writing of the other. As she waits and watches his apartment during move-in day, Marcela sees that a large manuscript has fallen from Samuel's things onto the shared hallway. So before she has even met her new neighbor, Marcela peers uninvited into this textual window on his soul. What she finds signals a shift in the narrative totality of all of Marcela's little stories as well as the multiple narrative threads woven by the collective of friends "scattered around the world." This manuscript turns out to be a long film script whose main characters are a group of friends in Havana, including Samuel, Monguy (Gago), and Andro. As Marcela reads the script in her own closed apartment, Valdés intersperses the italicized story of the three friends and their raft "adventure" with Marcela's astonished realization that Gago and Andro are the same persons that she knows and loves (and left behind) in Cuba.

This script, whose reading is itself a key transitional event in Marcela's experience and in the narrative, reflects the circular narrative structure of *Café Nostalgia,* underlining the novel's thematic and structural articulation of the Cuban diaspora as a *bojeo.* In fact, the three men announce that they are planning a literal "bojeo," a journey around the island of Cuba that they claim is just for fun and "adventure," but which transforms into a miniature epic portrait of contemporary Cuba. Among other events included as the friends attempt to set off in their small raft are various meetings with an array of characters and intimate conversations that reveal previously hidden personal stories and information. And in tandem with these intradiegetic revelations, a strangely enormous chunk of information directly relevant to Marcela is also communicated in the various dialogues and false starts that mark the men's symbolic, and ultimately aborted, trip. For example, Nieves, the African Cuban lover of Monguy, is an old friend whom Marcela has already discussed, and it turns out that Samuel is seeing a "Mina"—the name of the girlfriend who blamed Marcela for the violent death of her neighbor. Then, even more uncannily, Samuel makes a few comments that suggest that he has his own tragic past that has estranged him from his mother—a foreshadowing of more coincidences and connections to come. Ultimately, the adventure, and its filming by Andro on Super Eight, is likewise revealed as a deeply serious and perhaps tragic enterprise, especially once Monguy admits at the last moment that he is planning to use the raft to leave Cuba for good. After a series of revelatory proclamations the script ends with the terrible failure of the whole adventure. Ansiedad, one of the key figures of their daylong odyssey and a kind of outcast urban prophetess, has died and Gago is in custody. Andro and Samuel are pictured as two distraught figures beyond whom the entire panorama of Havana, of the Malecón, opens before the camera. The script ends with the enigmatic words "Pantalla a blanco. Fin. O tal vez no" (244). [Fade to white. End. Or maybe not.] This ending on whiteness and silence echoes the ending of several key chapters in *Café Nostalgia* in which silence and the blankness signified by whiteness overtake the relentless commentary of Marcela's voice. In this ending scene, Marcela, exhausted and overcome by the reading of the script, returns slowly to her present in her apartment in Paris, where she notes, "La flecha es la profecía, el arquero es el destino. El blanco: yo" (245). [The arrow is the prophecy, the archer is destiny. The target (white): me.] Underlining the shared "prophetic" and thus allegorical nature of her reading of both the script and her own life, Marcela sets up the final two chapters as figurative responses to the texts' unspoken questions about destiny and the future, as well as the past.

Among its other functions, Samuel's film script also encapsulates several aspects of the novel's slippery relation to Cuba. Throughout *Café Nostalgia,* Valdés expresses a distanced relation to patriotic feeling as well as nostalgic longing in ironic critiques of nationalist platitudes, whether they be of the Castro government's revolutionary rhetoric or the exilic communities' own nationalist fantasies. The meticulous descriptions that dominate *Café Nostalgia* do not convey or uphold that discourse of a "lost paradise" that has marked other well-known examples of Caribbean exile literature in English and French, as well as in Spanish. Evading announcements of national feeling that are more obviously scripted, Marcela nevertheless persistently indicates that the fundamental affect of her self and her collectivity is a longing and a traumatic experience of loss that are constitutional to this shared exile subjectivity: "Cada vez somos más numerosos los desperdigados por el mundo. Estamos invadiendo los continientes; nosotros, típicos isleños que, una vez fuera, a lo único que podemos esperar es al recuerdo" (126). [Each time we the scattered around the world are more numerous. We are invading continents; once outside, the only thing that we, typical islanders, can expect or hope for is memory.] But memory is something that Marcela has expressed a significant amount of ambivalence about, which again poses the problem of irony and raises the question of how transparent these pronouncements of collective and individual desire actually are.

The question of exilic, or diasporic, affect and its relation to reading hermeneutics thus also operates as a commentary on Cuba that the novel likewise does not seem inclined to resolve. The rhetorical question bitterly asked early in the novel by an unidentified interlocutor indicates the black humor and despair that characterize Cuban affect both on an off the island: "No hay de nada, Marcela, pero la gente se diverte. Coño, ¿y qué quieren, que se suiciden en conglomerado? ¿O no les bastan nuestros océanicos desaparecidos?" (36) [There isn't anything, Marcela, but people entertain themselves. Hell, what do they want, that they all commit collective suicide? Or is it not enough our oceans of disappeared people?] This angry rebuke to a "they" includes not just dispirited exiles or eager capitalists but the entire international community's refusal to attend to and act upon Cuba's plight. The Cuban collective, or nation, becomes in this formulation another dead zone, a territory of the "living dead" in a global imaginary. Such scenes indicate that the betrayal of Cuba extends beyond the Castro regime and the nation's borders. Likewise, in the film script, Samuel and the others who have stayed in Cuba echo this address to a "deaf" world that is beyond the reach of those floating in the hyperisolation of the small island nation; as the aptly named Ansiedad demands, "Por qué carajo nadie en el mundo nos oye? ¡Esta isla es una mierda, nadie nos oye!" (235) [Why the hell doesn't anyone in the world hear us? This island is shit and no one hears us!] Considering Ansiedad's death at the end of the script and the context of the Cuban raft crisis of 1994, her invocations of death and disappearance and a crisis of international proportions are not necessarily overly dramatic characterizations of the Cuban condition. And yet she too will turn back on her own protests ironically, saying in effect, it's not all bad, "Me encanta estar traumatizada" (235) (I adore being traumatized). These ironic commentaries on the national affects generated by Cuban poverty, isolation, and loss consistently block the appropriative reading that would allow readers to dismiss Marcela and her friends, or Valdés for that matter, as just more duped victims of the crises of late global modernity.

IV. Writing the Unwritten Testimony and Allegorical Encryption

The "fade to white" that ends Chapter 4 signals a repeating motif of whiteness and silence as emblems of blankness and absence in *Café Nostalgia*, further suggesting the unarticulated significance of Marcela's monologue and its explicit struggle with memory and connection. In ending Chapter 1 and describing herself as "una neurótica leyendo" (a neurotic woman reading), Marcela emphasizes the intensity as well as the suspect nature of her desires—for memory, for reading, and for the past and Havana: "Con los ojos aguados de lágrimas por la nostalgia de aquellas citas adolescentes con la literatura, lo menos que podía hacer era un homenaje silencioso a mi Habana" (65). [With eyes swimming in tears from the nostalgia for those adolescent encounters with literature, the least I could do was to pay a silent homage to my Havana.] The silence, like the whiteness, figures reading as an invitation to the future, to the unexpected, though it is a future that mostly terrifies Marcela. However, these moments of silent reading can also intimate to her "futura madurez sin temor" (future maturity without fear). But the last commentary on this silence and this reading underscores the counterimpulses at work within Marcela's monologue and the haunting of her desires: "De contra, mi problema consiste en que me regodeo en la tristeza, disfruto con el tremendismo de los estados melancólicos" (65). [In contrast, my problem consists in how I take pleasure in sadness, I tremendously enjoy my melancholic states.] And as she describes her experiences of frustrated desire and loss in such delicious and vibrant detail, questions begin to arise regarding the relation between the explicit and the implicit in Marcela's amazing personal history of near-unrelenting trauma and difficulty.

When Marcela begins reading Samuel's script, she questions herself—rather disingenuously—"¿Por qué me gustó Samuel y no otro?" (20) (Why did I like Samuel and not another?) In this way, Marcela acknowledges that before she has even met her new neighbor and fellow Cuban exile, he has become the obsessive and sole object of her desire, and that before this sudden and unprecedented cathexis, she has gone "months and years" without significant sexual or romantic involvements. This estranged relationship to her own desire returns both the narrator and the reader to the gaps that pocket Marcela's access to her own life and also indicate her narrative strategies' combination of a disarmingly frank acknowledgment of difficult feelings and experiences with a cagey withholding of the kind of information that is readily available in more conventional narratives. Throughout the novel, Samuel's name constitutes a mystery to be revealed and hopefully solved—the narrative promise of information to come. So when it becomes clear through the script that Samuel is a figure who encompasses several of the key traumatic events of Marcela's past as well as an unsuspected link to her entire web of *amistades*, the snowballing cascade of revelations and resolutions itself becomes a kind of mystery or problem to be solved.

In her work on trauma and narrative, Felman cautions against a literal or transparent understanding of the text as testimony. She reminds readers that in psychoanalysis, "the *testimony* differentiates itself from the content of the *manifest confession* which it uses as its vehicle, the confession is *displaced*, precisely, at the very moment we think we grasp it, and it is in this surprise, in this displacement, that our sense of testimony will be shifted once again" (23). Freud's implicit theory of an unconscious of the testimony indicates to Felman the analogous functions of literary representation and the discourse of the analysand, even to the extent that she asserts that the literary act can be said to participate in the psychoanalytic testimonial process. This possibility of an "unconscious testimony" haunts Valdés's novel: a testimony that the reader traces by "reading" the effects and apparent process of production of the written testimony and that produces an "unconscious, unintended, unintentional testimony [that] has, as such, an incomparable heuristic and investigative value" (24). Hence, Felman asserts,

> Psychoanalysis, in this way, profoundly rethinks and radically renews the very concept of testimony, by submitting, and by recognizing for the first time in the history of culture that one does not have to *possess*, or *own* the truth, in order to effectively *bear witness* to it; that speech as such is unwittingly testimonial, and that the speaking subject constantly bears witness to a truth that nonetheless continues to escape him, a truth that is, essentially, *not available* to its own speaker. (24)

Reading *Café Nostalgia* for the truth that is "not available to its own speaker" offers us access to a world of possible meanings and ironies embedded in Valdés's narrative practice as a reflection *of*, as well as on, the Cuban diaspora and its reverberations at psychic and historical levels.

In the gaps between memory and forgetting, then, Freudian psychoanalysis has located the operations of an always already guilty, or at least unconscious, desire as the tyrant of the individual subject's life. By suggesting, as Felman does, that important, if unwanted, information is often encoded in contingencies, in the events that subjects allow/invite into their life in the form of "accidents," psychoanalysis, like most good readers, holds that there are no real "accidents." *Café Nostalgia* both invites and thwarts this reading habit, especially when it comes to Marcela's narration of her sexual history as a palimpsestic allegory of her exile history. Because so much of the narrative focuses on Marcela's experiences as a sexual subject and their particularly unfortunate character and outcomes, sexuality emerges in the novel as a primary scene of her life's "accidents." As a kind of foreshadowing of the traumatic experiences to come, Marcela notes in Chapter 1, "Yo gozo dilatando el tiempo de la entrega.

Tal vez por eso nunca ha tenido un orgasmo, soy frígida" (38). [I enjoy stretching out time of surrender and union. Maybe that's why I have never had an orgasm, I'm frigid.] In this announcement, Marcela indicates that her desires are perhaps aimed at something other than satisfaction. She also claims that that this ongoing "dilation" of her desire—like the suspension and expansion of particular moments of her personal history—is a pleasure to her. As discussed above, a similar, though contradictory, announcement will claim that she embraces the tragic implications of the immolated husband as "una marca del destino" (a mark of destiny)—a destiny that is seemingly romantic but can also expand, vertiginously, to include all her possible "fates."

That is, Marcela and Valdés deploy sexuality allegorically to figure Marcela's thwarted relationship to desire, and thus to futurity, but this allegory does not necessarily imply a condemnation of her desire. In fact, the call "Á mi único deseo" (To my only desire) in the title of the last chapter signals that this coincidence of sexuality and exile experiences is deeply intentional, which suggests that the novel's uncanny denouement is an explicitly strategic response to the scripts of desire—as well as to those of the nation. For example, the burning of her supposed boyfriend in Chapter 2 is followed by a harrowing scene of first intercourse in Chapter 3. This tale recalls how Marcela's encounter with "Cheny" on a rooftop leads to a game of real-life Russian roulette and then back to more rough sex that includes the ex-friend Mina and a shadowy observer standing by the fire escape. This intensely erotic but tormented narration is followed by the teenage Marcela walking home alone and being beaten by another group of youth: "El goce se castiga, pensé resignada" (153) (Pleasure calls for punishment, I thought resignedly). And the chapter continues to relate the rather awful story of her visit to an abortion clinic with her friend Ana, so that there is no doubt concerning the myriad ways in which "pleasure punishes."

Furthermore, the melodrama around Marcela's "love" for Samuel seems to follow this pattern of frustrated and hopeless love, which Marcela connects to her history of abandonment (parental and national) and to the way in which the injuries of exile leave their marks, particularly on sexuality and desire. Thus, desire is acceptable only as nostalgia, as desire for "aquella isla"—an impossible situation for Marcela that she resolves by latching onto Samuel. He quite literally and consciously "stands in" for Cuba and for all it signifies to Marcela. However, the narrative also begins to raise the question of which version of success Marcela will most cling to: the romance narrative that would reunite her with Samuel or the more persistent narrative of *nostalgia* as a suspension and dilation of her thwarted relationship to desire (the metonymic displacement and unwritten testimony to her parents' abandonment and failure, as much as the nation's failure). This narrative and affective structure constitutes the engine of her pleasure in seeing herself as a "mujer melancólica" and illuminates how the accidents of her life have become conscripted into the imperative to nostalgia. Whether that imperative version of Cuban exile success—forever ensnared in a past that is absent—is imposed by a personal or national agenda is not clear.

In Chapters 5 and 6 of *Café Nostalgia,* a series of revelations brings the past into the present via Samuel. It turns out that a slightly younger adolescent, Samuel himself, was the fifth person watching on that rooftop when she lost her virginity—a shadowy figure and witness who has haunted Marcela like so much else in her experience. But even more shockingly, Samuel is revealed to be the unnamed son of the man who was burned to death by his jealous wife on account of a supposed affair with a teenaged Marcela. Once they both realize who the other is, and just when Samuel had about convinced Marcela that the intensity of his love could overcome her apparent frigidity, Samuel leaves for New York. This gap between a now in Paris and the return of Samuel is where the narration and the narrative converge in Chapter 6, and the reader waits with Marcela to learn what is to become of her true love for the compatriot exile, Samuel.

One important revelation occurs in this process of waiting and unveiling: Marcela discovers that one of her most formative and painful "traumas" is based on a lie. The immolated husband is both the avowed source of her reluctance to experience sexual satisfaction and her claimed reason for never sending all those copious and carefully written letters. Her guilt over this event is particularly keen when she considers his son, the boy she used to watch walk to the park with his father. And now that son turns out to be Samuel, the "amor platónico" (platonic love) who haunts the temporal perambulations of Marcela's entire narrative. Samuel now figures Cuba as well as a miraculously recovered link to her lost group of friends. Once he has left Paris and reached New York, Samuel learns and then reports to Marcela the "true story" of his father's death. In another unlikely coincidence linking the two thwarted lovers, the bitter and vengeful "friend" Mina turns out to be Samuel's ex—who in New York admits to him that she herself was the unnamed lover of his father. While Marcela and Samuel understand this secret to release them from the guilty association, it's interesting that those misread letters she had sent his father are never discussed. The knot of guilt and causality is narrated as an unraveled mystery even as the "truth" of those letters (they mistakenly led Samuel's mother to "know" her husband was having an affair) remains disavowed by both even as it remains an unspoken current in the novel's resolutions of Marcela's traumatic relation to the past. In this final chapter and its various "resolutions," Samuel now proves to have a cauterizing effect on Marcela and her "open" melancholic relationship to her history of loss and abandonment. In displacing her cathexis from that melancholia onto Samuel, Marcela seemingly finds her pathological relationship to happiness, desire, and satisfaction healed in a final scene of sexual union and ecstasy.

What to make of this astonishing resolution of the narrative's myriad details and far-fetched coincidences? The melodramatically farcical aspects of Valdés's narrative structure are not commented upon in the narratorial discourse or filter, but only emerge through the extreme repetition of so many exile clichés. Meanwhile, the tone and content of Marcela's narration remain deadly earnest, particularly as the dispersed threads of the novel come together in the final two chapters. That earnestness is exactly what hooks the reader and raises my questions about the role of irony in Valdés's narrative practice and its effects. At stake in this question is a fuller understanding of the "cultural politics of affect," as Sara Ahmed puts it. Valdés's work as a whole is often read as a kind of "mapa textual de la experiencia cubana" (González-Abellás) (textual map of the Cuban experience), so the questions of exilic subjectivity raised in *Café Nostalgia* involve a pointed understanding of what that *cicatríz* (mark) of Cuban identity actually signifies: the "Cuban experience" as a national trauma that requires global attention combats with the novel's rather critical and ironically distanced relationship to the nostalgia generated by that traumatic technology of selfhood.

The relationship to the past that Marcela articulates is both uniquely individual and grandly, collectively, shared—so that the narrative itself operates as an interrogation of the term "nostalgia" and its status as both national affect and personal haunting. In generating a series of paradoxes about self, collectivity, and the questionable, ironic status of her—or any character's—knowledge, Marcela's monologue positions her as an allegorical figure for this national trauma and simultaneously questions that national affect of nostalgia. The collective character of memory and its ruses emerge surreptitiously in this narrative, behind or through the veil of Marcela's own carefully arranged words and recollections. *Café Nostalgia* thus offers a narrative that manages to both attend to the specific, local knowledge embedded in her individual nuances and logics but also signals how Marcela remains a stranger to herself.[18]

This problem of authorship and authority over one's self echoes also a suggestive reading of another famous novel of Cuban exile written in Paris, Severo Sarduy's *Cobra* (1972). Vilashini Coopan argues that while *Cobra* is clearly a "work of mourning" as well as a classic of Cuban literature, its experimental form employs the "metalanguage of kitsch" and ultimately refuses the "mimetic compact between the nation and novel form" in favor of an aesthetic "emblematization of national loss" (253, 255). Embracing the baroque aesthetic of emblems and kitsch and metonymic displacements, Sarduy's novel manifests a revised understanding of Cuban exile by transforming "exile's ontology (being away)" into "exile's epistemology (seeing and knowing an object from a distance)" (256). Using Coopan's reading of Sarduy as a kind of template, it becomes easier to recognize the baroque and "emblematic" aesthetic that Valdés deploys in *Café Nostalgia* and to understand the novel's performative "rereading" of nostalgia as an interrogation of the affective script of Cuban identity—one that refigures the operations of national affect and thus individual and collective relations to *cubanidad* (Cuban identity) as well as to the past.

To claim a kind of analogy between the kitsch of postmodern writings of mass culture and Valdés's melodramatic narrative elements as borrowed from pop genres of cinema and television (and eighteenth-century picaresque novels) perhaps points to the false choice in my opening questions about literal and figurative interpretations of *Café Nostalgia*. I have tended to argue that the novel enacts a critique of the nostalgic structure of Marcela's selfhood, one which implicates the nation itself—as a concept, a specific and failed regime, and a lost "home"—in her affective structure of pleasure and pain and stasis. However, the suggestion that Marcela's nostalgia is in and of itself the object of interrogation—rather than "Cuba" or *cubanidad*—enables a more nuanced reading of the novel's content as well as its ironic allegorical aesthetics. The final scene further indicates the novel's primary investment in these allegorical modes that challenge both identity logics ad their prescriptive coding of experience. This scene features Marcela and Samuel engaged in an extended lovemaking that Valdés narrates as a mutual consuming of each body by the other, but then they are interrupted by the telephone. Even as Marcela participates in the most direct union or "entrega" (surrender) possible, she finds that her desire's satisfaction is stretched out and delayed—showing how her "único deseo" (only desire) is perhaps to be interrupted to defer satisfaction indefinitely.

In response to this phone call, the couple rushes to "resinsertarnos los órganos, cada cual toma lo que puede, sin prestar atención, en medio del sangriento desorden. Ya no distinguimos más si él soy yo, si yo soy él" (359). [reinsert our organs, each one taking what they can, without paying much attention, in the midst of that bloody disorder. Still not distinguishing if he is me or if I am him.] What follows and ends the novel is the interior text of Andro's voice on the answering machine—a technological interruption and connection that ironically comments on Marcela's many despairing expressions of the disconnection and mediation generated by the technologies of communication that are poor substitutes for physical presence and contact. To further underline this final ambiguous commentary on the novel's staging of a nostalgic logics of loss and longing, Andro wants now to talk about the future, though one that involves a drawing together of the whole diasporic collective in his gossipy chatter. His newfound optimism and excitement focus on notions of "love" and on all the friends he has seen recently, generating a sense of new possibilities for their dispersed group. Translating Rainer Maria Rilke, rather loosely, Andro exclaims, "¡La juventud fue un sueño cabrón!" (Youth was a dream, asshole!) Also, in the midst of this performative monologue on the answering machine—one that invokes Cuban pop music traditions and asks Marcela to "sing along with me"—Andro announces a plan to close his popular bookstore in Miami in order to "fundar una especie de salon para apacuguar la agonía de la espera, y mientras tanto se baile, se canta, se goze, se quiere. Le pondré *Café Nostalgia*" (361). (establish a kind of salon to relieve the agony of hope [also "waiting"], meanwhile many will dance, sing, enjoy, and love. I'll call it *Café Nostalgia*.)

The dialogic structure of *Café Nostalgia* only puts further into question the status of exilic desires for a place of belonging and return, as well as the now compensatory vision of a refuge from the agony of waiting/hoping for that impossible return. As interrogated through the novel's ironic scenarios, the discourses of exile and the novel's textual performance of a diasporic *bojeo* figure the diaspora itself as a perpetually receding horizon marking the phantasmic return that constitutes desire, that is, nostalgia. If its status as a *desire* can be taken seriously, then the shared nostalgia that defines and constitutes this collectivity is exactly what Valdés offers as the allegorical truth hidden from its protagonists and encrypted within the testimony of its many speakers. But the narrative spirals that have been so crucial to this structuring of exilic desire seem to become increasingly "straightened out" in the second half of *Café Nostalgia* and ultimately appear to be resolved into a neat and complete narrative "circle" that draws all the missing pieces back together. However, both the cannibalistic love scene and Andro's romantic call to "live and dance" refuse to announce a full release from the suffering that marks a specifically and foundationally Cuban "agony of hope," which defines the novel's understanding of the Cuban condition and its dominant affect. In fact, Valdés seems to imply that Marcela's "único deseo" may in the end be embedded in these two juxtaposed scenarios: one of yet another delayed satisfaction and the other, an exuberant celebration of tenuous connections and unstable collectivities. Ultimately, neither scenario of union and connection claims to fully heal the psychic and material suffering produced by that Cuban condition, but both offer a metaphoric map for survival and life amid the ruins of longing.

6

Performing Suspended Migrations: Novels and Solo Performance Art by U.S. Latinas

There was always this place, this Emerald city where I believed I would finally belong. I was fascinated by this ultimate place, the Havana of my dreams.

(*Achy Obejas*)

Many of the Dominican passengers of American Airlines Flight 587 were headed home for the holidays when it crashed in Queens on November 12, 2001. As the trauma of that crash reverberated both in New York and in Santo Domingo, newspaper accounts illustrated the long-standing links between the Upper Manhattan neighborhood of Washington Heights and the Dominican Republic from where a large portion of its residents hailed. These interconnections were further highlighted when New York politicians, including Mayor elect Michael Bloomberg, Governor George Pataki, and Governor-candidate Andrew Cuomo, made official visits to Santa Domingo in the following months. This dramatic illustration of the diasporic web of relations of family, national and local politics, and both micro- and macroeconomics underscored the connections between New York and Santa Domingo, ties that bind U.S. cities to Havana and San Juan as well.

These binding emotional and economic ties are complicated by various histories of imperialist incursions and local despotisms, migration and return, and exile and economic opportunity. Such histories have produced an emerging generation of artists and writers preoccupied by questions of place and history, memory and return, and home and belonging. As I discussed in Chapter 2, contemporary Latina artists and writers, including

Cherríe Moraga and Gloria Anzaldúa, focus simultaneously on the operations of cultural memory and identity as they relate to sexuality and gender. These writers highlight how sexual practices and deviations from heteronormative paradigms constitute a central concern for U.S. Latina subjects. This chapter engages these questions through a comparison of the genres of fiction and solo performance and considers artists' respective generic strategies for raising and exploring Caribbean Latina diasporic experiences as articulated in stories of belonging that are crosscut by gender and sexuality.

Again, the allegorical figuring of individual experience as a template for the history of the collective proves to have a profound connection to discourses of gender and sexuality. So following both the artists and influential critics, I return to the persistently central position of gendered sexualities within discussions of cultural politics, and particularly in the figuring of collective memory and the reverberations of history. Recalling the allegorical cultural work of female sexuality in Chicana/o public spheres, the narrative texts and performance of Achy Obejas, Julia Alvarez, and Carmelita Tropicana illustrate how generational and collective memory becomes allegorically condensed in the figure of the "daughter" in narrativizations of intergenerational projects of nation-formation and identity preservation. But this array of Latina cultural production also signals the contested and paradoxical operations of such allegories within these female artists' representation of their protagonists' negotiations of the demands for memory and "witnessing."

In the epigraph, from an interview following the release of her successful 1996 novel *Memory Mambo,* the Cuban American and lesbian writer Obejas explained the role of memory in the exile mythography of her family (Harper 1996). Obejas's invocation of "the Havana of my dreams" suggests how the continued struggles over national and cultural belonging in the Hispanic Caribbean diaspora take on particular resonance in the work of lesbian writers and artists residing in the United States, particularly through the imbrication of sexual identities and intergenerational dynamics of memory and collective cohesion. Obejas's apparent enchantment by nationalist memorial projections of the homeland might seem ironic, especially since so-called sexual deviants are exactly the people who would ostensibly have the least investment in this nostalgia, termed "exilic memory" by José Muñoz. By virtue of their sexual identities and marked bodies, these people are the not-quite-citizens who should find a return to the "homeland" especially difficult and undesirable.[1] And it is true that such "outsider sexualities" (to borrow a phrase from Moraga) have often acted as the ground for resistant or disidentificatory relations to home and homeland communities, particularly those communities that advertise their territorialized ideologies of race, ethnicity, nationalism, and heterosexism.

However, recent theorizations of "queer diasporas" have contested these seemingly exclusive identity constructs by highlighting the variety of links possible between those who claim the insurgency both of their sexual identities and practices and of their hybrid national and cultural allegiances as diasporic subjects. This chapter examines this disruptive yoking of sexual and national identities in the work of Cuban Americans Tropicana and Obejas and Dominican American Alvarez. These artists create work—performance pieces and novels—that is increasingly recognized for its challenge to conventional understandings of both Hispanic Caribbean and U.S. national belonging. And by emphasizing the cultural baggage of particular, often racialized, sexual identities, such artists open discussions of belonging, citizenship, and nationality to include sexuality and gender in emerging diasporic or transnational configurations of identity and community. The point of such discussions is not to embrace an endlessly fluid or dehistoricized understanding of transnational identities and migrations between specific national spaces. As Lisa Lowe puts it, "Hybridity in this sense does not suggest assimilation . . . of immigrant practices to dominant forms but instead marks the history of survival within relationships of unequal power and domination" (67). In these works, constructs of identity, selfhood, and community can be understood as commentaries on the ways that sexuality and national and familial histories become inextricably imbricated in Caribbean Latina imaginaries of home and belonging.

For example, the "queering" of Cuban diasporic consciousness in Obejas's fiction (*We Came All the Way from Cuba So You Could Dress Like This?* [1994], *Memory Mambo* [1996], *and Days of Awe* [2001]) and in the film and performance pieces of Tropicana/Alina Troyano (*Carmelita Tropicana: Your Kunst Is Your Waffen* [1992] and *Milk of Amnesia/Leche de Amnesia* [1994]) suggests the central roles that can be played by alternative gender and sexual identities in constructions of "the nation," as well as of class and ethnic identifications. In theorizations of queer diasporas, the term "queer" is used to highlight a function specific to sexuality in the dynamics of diasporic migrations, often with the double purpose of exposing and interrogating the heteropatriarchal underpinnings of more dominant models of diaspora, as well as sexual identity.[2] As Cindy Patton and Benigno Sánchez-Eppler note, "Against current poles of discussion about sexuality . . . examination of specific modes and effects of incremental displacement—bodily, discursive, and/or territorial—*on* or *as* sexuality, reveals an extraordinarily complex picture of the frictional relation between geopolitics and embodied desires" (3). Considering how the figuring of female sexualities might be understood through its intersection with projects of cultural memory and questions of geocultural belonging in the Americas, this chapter asks how we might describe the dynamic relations between diasporic and sexual histories.

That question proves to be a slippery one, at best. Feminist anthropologist Louisa Schein has called for attention to the materiality of "the homeland" and suggests that "thinking diasporic sex" illuminates the dynamic intersection of geographical, economic, and historical opportunities with sexuality and gender, understood as desires that shape the movements of both migrants and transnational capital (723). However, in the work of the three artists discussed in this chapter, the desire or the act of going "back" to the Caribbean, be it Cuba or the Dominican Republic, is primarily about familial pasts and cultural memory and not about erotic (or economic) futures. So even though these artists implicate their protagonists' sexual personas and histories in their imagined return trips to the supposed homeland, desire diverges from a specifically sexual history and recedes into the familial and communal fold. These works thus seem to participate in a conventional plot of immigrant narrative in that the discourses of family, exile, and cultural identity overtake concerns with sexual identities, histories, or romances. Such narratives can operate, and be read, as allegories of Caribbean Latina belonging, but they are allegories in which the narrative pedagogy works through conflicting vectors.

These works illustrate how in both writing and performance the uses of sexual and romantic themes and subplots serve an overarching paradigm of migrant belonging and memory in which the protagonists' experiences of sex and gender are secondary effects of a national and cultural trauma of displacement that is the narrative's main concern. As in Chapter 2, an analogy between sexual rebellion and resistance to collective norms determines the apparent parameters of the narrative template for the terms of female belonging. And the question of sexuality does insistently mark these female protagonists' relations and struggles with intergenerational and nationalist demands for allegiance and compliance. However, each of these texts takes the "predetermined signified" of sexual transgression as a figure for marginalization and betrayal of the collective and scrambles the narrative development of that plot. In Alvarez's autobiographical novels, female sexual liberation sometimes manages to uphold the hybrid standards of specifically diasporic Latina/o codes of behavior and allegiance—signaling a new diasporic collective that maintains unique sexual as well as cultural codes. Likewise, the sexual "transgression" of lesbianism does not in and of itself translate into betrayal and expulsion in the work of Obejas and Tropicana (not to mention Moraga, Anzaldúa, and Terry de la Peña). These texts illustrate that the primary preoccupation and focus of sexual narratives often returns to the fold of the family, and the nation. In revising the presumed allegories of belonging of Latinas, these are texts that both mark newly solidified sites of the recuperation and preservation of the collective as well as gesture toward emerging spaces and modes of freedom within reconfigured contexts of collective belonging and preservation/memory.

I. *Memory Mambo*: Nostalgia, Collectivity, and Bad Witnessing

Each of these Latina artists underlines that collective memories are both necessary and imaginary and illustrates how they operate in the simultaneous construction of personal and national histories. Obejas, however, almost immediately challenges conventional understandings of what, exactly, it means to be connected through memory and history. This trope of connection—especially as structured in a generational narrative—is also embedded in Alvarez's narratives of cultural memory and its transmission and becomes an even more pointed figure for political and personal work in Tropicana's *Milk of Amnesia*. However, the lesbian protagonists in Obejas's work suggest a particularly ambiguous function for both sexual and cultural histories and identities. In *Memory Mambo,* the relation between Juani de las Casas's sexuality and her cultural memory is complicated by its embeddedness in the patriarchal family and its legacies, further underlining the deceptive nature of memory as a primary means of understanding experience and raising some serious questions as to what that cultural memory does to and for Obejas's conflicted protagonist. The novel chronicles, in fact, a collision of the domains of sexual and "exile" communities and spaces, emphasizing Juani's inability or refusal to, in effect, re-member—to put those domains together. Or as Juani puts it, "I often wonder just how distinct my memories are . . . sometimes other lives lived right alongside mine interrupt, barge in on my senses, and I no longer know if I really lived through an experience or . . . became the lens through which it was captured, retold, and shaped" (9). In portraying herself as permeated by the memories of others—their instrument, in fact—Juani gestures toward the underside of diasporic remembering.

In *Memory Mambo,* the various communal and personal acts of memory that maintain this Cuban exile community in Chicago rely on a dynamic of familial and communal witnessing in which Juani is required to validate and perform repetitively specific memorializations of their shared trauma of exile. However, as she becomes skeptical about whose memories are whose, Juani starts to wonder: What kind of memory project, exactly, has she been conscripted into? Such questions illustrate the critical thrust of Obejas's narrative of the collective and personal meaning of being connected through memory and community. In a sense, Juani finds that she has become a mouthpiece, or reservoir, for the desires and memories of others, and the inherent duplicity of these desires undermines the more positive cast to her role. Juani thus struggles with the meanings of her function as a "witness" for her family, and especially for her father, in the ongoing project of remembering their past, figured essentially as their traumatic exile from Cuba. Theorizations of collective trauma, such as those by Mieke Bal, Ann Kaplan, and Marianne Hirsch, have emphasized the interlinked need to both integrate traumatic events into narrative and have a "witness" confirm this "painfully elusive past" (Bal 1999, x). I argue that *Memory Mambo* extends this discussion of the uses of memory and narrative in negotiating traumatic histories in ways that illustrate a constitutional ambivalence that can undercut the "integrative" function of cultural memory.[3]

Like Carmelita in *Milk of Amnesia*, Juani is desperate enough to appropriate the memories of others in this quest to "know what *really* happened." For Juani, however, these appropriations are often involuntary; they emanate from an uncertainty about origins, identities, and boundaries that spreads from within and touches on all aspects of her individual memory and her obsessive efforts of reconstruction. Juani's ambivalent relation to her Cuban exile community, and especially to her own family, and its store of collective memories finds its roots in the combined function of both memory and the mourning processes that accompany the trauma of exile. If mourning is something that claims you, seizes you, and indicates that you are not in control of your affective relationship to loss, experiences of exile produce a generational cascade of such seizures, what Hirsch has called "postmemory."[4] Juani is frustrated by the ambiguities between whose memories are "real" and whose memories are merely in the service of personal and national fantasies. But as *Memory Mambo* demonstrates, she is already too implicated in those fantasies and has already gone too far down the path of making her own fantasy memories to be able to find a reliable answer to her persistent question: "What *really* happened?"

Memory Mambo thematizes the distance that separates Juani's two worlds—a Latina lesbian community and her familial Cuban exile community, both in Chicago—and their ensuing dangerous collision via a plot that centers not only on memory but also on violence. On one track is the story of how her relationship with her Puerto Rican activist girlfriend, Gina, ended in a nasty fight that put them both in the hospital. On the other is her skeptical and troubled quest to unearth the truth about her family's past—especially about her father's claim that he invented duct tape and that the Central Intelligence Agency (CIA) stole the formula from him when he fled Cuba along with his family. The father's nostalgic and clearly exaggerated laments form a sardonic backdrop for Juani's quest to "find out what really happened," as well as an ironic commentary on the politics of nostalgia in Cuban exile communities. This quest for knowledge and a suturing of the gaps created by diasporic wanderings is one that each text mirrors in particular ways. For Obejas and Alvarez, in particular, the desire to know and remember the past emerge within a familial and inter-generational dynamic that shapes the narrative structure of their allegories of belonging.

Juani's family offers a textbook demonstration of how the inaccessibility of the past is further distorted by the idiosyncratic ways each person's recollections reflect personally and ideologically overdetermined fantasies of what was lost. As a result, Juani complains, she has memories of their life in Cuba and of planning their family's escape by boat that can't possibly be hers, and asks, "If these aren't my memories, then whose are they? Certainly not my father's . . . If these were my father's stories, they would be wholly congratulatory and totally void of meaningful detail. My cousin Patricia says this is because his tales are almost always lies" (11).

Often understood as tied to nostalgia, collective remembering attempts to fix "the ultimate uncertainty of the past" through acts of "saturation" of the present with the remembered past (Bal 1999, xii). Obejas explores both the productive and the incapacitating aspects of these nostalgic projects and their effects on subsequent generations. Although Juani's quest for knowledge seems all-too-familiar, Obejas highlights its multivalent negotiations and implications with narrative tactics that derail the possibility of a linear narrative of self-discovery through historical reconstruction and return. Instead, she weaves a story that unravels on multiple tracks, in a "mambo," as it were. The main storyline ultimately seems to posit the aftermath of Juani's traumatic fight with Gina as the beginning of her desire to know the real story of her family's exile from Cuba. Here, Juani's questioning of "true" histories emerges in the hinge between her sexual and familial ties and the role of politics in both. Although Juani insists on a clear demarcation and separation between these two spheres of romance and lesbian sexuality and family and community belonging, the narrative brings them together through two scenes of rather shocking violence. This violence announces a contagion that threatens to explode Juani's careful maintenance of the two distinct problems with memory, exposing them as one.

The narrative figure who acts as the fuse to the explosive collision of Juani's two worlds is "Jimmy," the abusive husband of her cousin, Caridad. In tracing the emergence of the paradoxically sexualized identification that Juani and Jimmy share, *Memory Mambo* also highlights the ambiguities of

Juani's various identities, the way her sexual and diasporic histories have led her to an impasse of seemingly conflicted allegiances and affiliations. This identification with Jimmy, who is described as "disgustingly Cuban," contributes to, and perhaps constitutes, the climax of the novel's narrative of memory and violence and sexual and cultural identities.

Memory Mambo underlines these conflicts not only through portrayals of her family's somewhat dubious acceptance of her as a lesbian, but also through the way Juani's Cubanness is read in Gina's crowd of activist Latinas.[5] Hence, though Juani denies any interest in "politics," the novel emphasizes how her personal dilemmas have their source in the intersections of politics, history, and sexuality. For example, Gina, who is explicitly "political" in the Chicago Puerto Rican community, prefers to remain ambiguous, even closeted, about her sexual identity:

> "Look, I'm not interested in being a *lesbian*, in separating politically from my people," she'd say to me, her face hard and dark. "What are we talking about? Issues of *sexual identity*? While Puerto Rico is a colony? . . . You think I'm going to sit around and discuss *sexual identity*? Nah, Juani, you can do that—you can have that navel-gazing discussion." (77)

Juani notes that because she is Cuban she is "pinned with this topic" since she is seen as "automatically more privileged," or as Gina says, "'That's so white, this whole business of *sexual identity*,' . . . 'But you Cubans, you think you're white'" (78). Gina's comment exposes the various differences that mark intra-Caribbean politics in the Caribbean Latina/o diaspora, particularly the general understanding of the politically conservative, and upwardly mobile, nature of Cubans who left after the socialist revolution. This belief—that Cuban Americans are "in collusion, not collision" with dominant U.S. culture (Perez-Firmat, 6)—has specific intradiasporic repercussions in Juani's attempts to negotiate her ethnonationalist and sexual affiliations.

The novel shows what Juani does not narrate explicitly: the many ways that her political affiliations and allegiances are in fact complex and contradictory. Juani insists that she is apolitical: "I know all too well how the world of politics with its promises and deceptions, its absolute values and impersonal manifestos, can cut through the deepest love and leave lovers stranded" (87). *Memory Mambo* chronicles, however, a collision between the world of politics and the world of love, and this violent collision reflects the results of Juani's inability or refusal to, in effect, re-member—to put them together. As Kate McCullough observes, "Obejas's text demonstrates that even the formulation of sexual orientation as a subject position—whether dominant or deviant—is interwoven with and produced out of colonial matrices" (579) or, in other words, that claims to sexual identities emerge out of histories that involve national as well as personal events and fantasies. And as McCullough points out, the novel "precludes any reconciliation of political trauma by means of personal romantic narrative" (594). Obejas seems intent on exposing the deceptive nature of romances of the self, whether they be familial and oedipal or sexual, and thus supposedly independent of history.

In the end, Juani's collusions with familial exilic delusions and the political repercussions of upholding nationalist nostalgia and familial, and especially patriarchal, pride—albeit very ambivalently—lead her into an impossible, and intolerable, place. The macho Cuban American Jimmy becomes the figure for this intolerable conflict, and interestingly, his character and Juani's lesbianism are introduced on the same page of the novel. Jimmy sees Juani as masculine competition and is repeatedly shown confronting her in a way that is both sexualized and masculine posturing (with him often "rubbing his dick"). Juani's response is likewise ambiguous: on one hand she sees such encounters as a "stand off" and on the other, "I went home that night and got off a dozen or so times just playing that scene over and over in my head" (20).

The way that Juani misrecognizes herself in Jimmy has much to do with her father, exile, and the impasse that her "mambo" with memory has led her to.[6] In trying to explain Jimmy's hold over his wife, Caridad, one of her sisters calls him "Jimmy Frankenstein" and another notes that "there is something disgustingly Cuban about him, and I think that appeals to her, like a primordial memory" (60). This lurking image of a hidden memory of Cuba and of a masculine, and fatherly, figure apparently bewitches Juani as well. In particular, Jimmy shares with her father an ability to incapacitate Juani by demanding what I call "bad witnessing," the saturation of her present with stories of the family's past. We see this call to bad witnessing too in her family members' demand for the repetition of particular stories and specific fantasies. Her father especially remains obsessed with his imagined loss and demands sympathy and support from everyone who enters his home. And it seems that the responsibility for upholding this wounded patriarchy often falls on Juani ("I was still comforting Papi about the duct tape" [71]). For his part, Jimmy uses Juani's propensity for such misremembering to demand her silence and her complicity in a steeply escalating war of distorted histories.

Jimmy's claim that "'Juani's just like me, we're two of a kind . . . She'd do *anything*'" (20) haunts the novel and becomes the vehicle for a series of crises that calls into question Juani's agency and complicity in painful confrontations with both familial and sexual communities and the memories that have shaped her relationships to those communities. Jimmy provokes

Juani, but with the result that she is too often, in her words, "hypnotized" and "mesmerized." Throughout *Memory Mambo* being "hypnotized" denotes Juani's tendency to disconnect from events as they are happening to her. The novel suggests that this catatonic disassociation is the result of Juani's years of trying to acquiesce in the official versions of her family's exilic history. Although at many points in the novel she is called upon to witness, to account for herself and *tell* what really happened, it is at exactly these moments that Juani is, in her words, "paralyzed," "mesmerized," or "unable to speak." Hence, Juani oscillates between a deep interest in "what really happened" in the interpersonal and collective realm of cultural memory and an apparent inability to remember key events in her own life, as well as an inability to act—to be either her own or others' "witness." In a sense, Jimmy's assumption that she won't tell on him—neither about their sexualized encounters nor about his wife-beating—is a perverted reflection of what her family has asked of her.

If the traumatic history of her family's exile, and of Cuba's colonial history more generally, has damaged Juani's relationship to memory, her relationship to Jimmy suggests a dissociative splitting that enacts her wounded relationship to speaking memory (and to sexuality). As in Zoé Valdés's work, the allegorical figuring of a Cuban diasporic selfhood indicates the traumatic foundation of that self and the community; though in Obejas, the generational and pathological aspects of her relation to memory and history are underlined in a tone that is ultimately anti-ironic. Jimmy's expanding importance in the novel reflects the increasing tension in Juani's conflicted psyche, where the collision between spheres of memory and social connection seems to barrel down on her. That is, as *Café Nostalgia* develops toward a phantasmic moment of reconciliation and reparation, *Memory Mambo* is toward a nightmare of dissolution and violent fragmentation.

Memory Mambo takes on added momentum when it turns out that Jimmy is the only witness to what Juani did to her girlfriend. At the end of the novel, Juani confronts Gina with her perennial demand, "I want to know what happened" (229), but neither she nor Gina has a satisfying explanation for the explosion of violence that overtook their relationship. The narration of this fight occurs in the middle of the novel, and it provides at least one central piece of Juani's puzzled dance with memory. In particular, it shows again how the realms of memory, politics, and sexuality are overly intertwined for Juani, even though she denies these overlaps, and how deeply traumatic this material actually is. The episode occurs after Juani again encounters the open contempt of Gina and her friends, who mock Juani as a "baaaaad Cuban." When Juani tries after the dinner party to get an explanation from Gina, Gina first responds sympathetically and then more antagonistically, giving Juani "just a little push" (134). Juani describes how in response, she rolled up her fist "into a wrecking ball" and "I don't know why or how but I smashed it into her . . . and I felt the bones of her face collapse under my hand" (134). After a shocked pause, the two begin to fight on the floor of Gina's apartment. At one point, Juani notes, Gina is "like a rabid dog on my breast, even as blood came gushing though my shirt" (135). At the hospital, Juani wakes up to find "Jimmy, gloating over me" (137). In addition to coming up with the lie that will presumably "save" Juani further humiliation, Jimmy has bribed the cops to not pursue the incident ("just a little domestic violence"). This way, Jimmy says he is assured that now Juani understands that she is deeply in his debt.

This language of debt and payoff becomes central to their relationship. Here again, the demand for complicity and bad witnessing with which Juani has struggled begins to reach fantastic proportions, literally and figuratively. Jimmy is now also a bad witness, lying in order to protect someone else to whom he is bound, but in this case the binds are explicitly grounded in an economy of blackmail and coercion. The complicity this information uncovers between Juani and Jimmy illuminates the exponential nature of this economy: each exchange both covers and generates more lies and more violence until Juani cannot tolerate the bargain she has made. It is also important that though this event is remembered halfway through the novel, it precedes Juani's narrative and to an extent instigates it. The fight with her lover combines with her devil's bargain with Jimmy to act as a "multiplier" of Juani's crisis of memory and agency. For example, Juani marvels—in a deeply alarmed way—that her descriptions of her fight with Gina in her own journal reflect Jimmy's false story, not her complicated memory of the event. These narrative moments suggest both the importance and the failure of memory and productive witnessing for Juani, who does not experience collective remembering as an affirmation or catharsis that might ratify her traumatic experiences. Rather the fantastic dimensions of memory expand exponentially to force her entire, previously carefully compartmentalized, existence into a totality of lies.

The sort of "traumatic (non) memory" that collective trauma, such as exile, can theoretically produce has been described as that which resists integration and is doomed to cycles of traumatic repetition; that is, in Freud's work, trauma actually blocks memory—the conscious mind has no access to the traumatic event. In the context of Cuban exile and its generational legacy of "postmemories," the wounds of exile are shared collectively by subsequent generations, whose identification with these wounds can be seen as "based on overidentification and repetition . . . [on] the constitution of one's self as a surrogate victim" (Hirsch 16). Hence, whereas in *Milk of Amnesia* Carmelita needs to recover her memory of

Cuba—as well as the memories of others of Cuba—Juani is unable to move around the behemoth weight of such memories. She seems driven by a dynamic that Ricardo Ortiz describes as endemic to exilic nostalgia: "The larger guilt built into the structure of exile, the guilt of abandoning the motherland . . . the guilt one bears for that loss, the sneaking suspicion of complicity and culpability that weighs the mourner down" (64).

More than anything, Juani fears losing her connections to others—to Gina and to her family. Not only is much of her wandering and paralysis caused by the terror she has of ending up alone, but she admits to resorting to trickery because otherwise "that lock will remain shut, and I'll be left out here in the cold" (228). The imagery of cold, with its emotional and geographical connotations, plays a large role in Obejas's representation of Juani's fears of isolation. Comparing herself to an admired cousin, called "the Fortress of Solitude" because "our parents often found her so distant and cold," Juani says, "I didn't have an escape and I didn't want to be rejected" (124). Thus, Juani's life is stalled, suspended between an obscure past and a future she shuns, between the family's dramas and her own. The climax of the novel occurs just as Juani has allowed herself to be comfortable in this stasis, even to the extent of relying on Jimmy to lend her his car. Obejas shows how Juani's complicity with Jimmy is normalized, though as one cousin says dryly, "Yeah, . . . and what do you have to do for it?" (214). The cousin's question takes on special weight as it immediately precedes the last and most horrific of Juani's traumatic calls to bad witnessing.

Left with Jimmy and her baby niece Rosa, Juani falls asleep on the couch, where she has a dream about not being able to save the baby. When Juani does manage to wake up, "I open my eyes and the scene is clear, as clear as anything I've ever witnessed in my life . . . His head is back, ecstatic, lips red and shiny. One hand is on the back of Rosa's puny head, pushing her down; the other is on his cock, inflamed and purplish, its glossy tip disappearing into her tiny, tiny mouth" (221). Though Juani acts decisively and quickly to separate Jimmy from the child, she is almost immediately "caught" by her own imaginative collusions when Jimmy asks her to defend him against Rosa's enraged parents: "'Juani . . .' Jimmy says. 'Tell them . . . tell them what really happened . . . Juani, please . . .' he pleads" (224). Although the scene had been "as clear as anything I'd witnessed in my life," Juani cannot speak in response to the combination of Jimmy's pleas and her sister's questioning. As Jimmy begins to taunt her, and then attack her, Juani runs away from all of these demands: "I'm faster than him, faster than all of them . . . and I'm out of there, out of that furnace of all their passions and tempers, out of that sucking spiral to hell, out of their circle of darkness and fire" (226).

Although Juani runs into the night away from this scene to find Gina and come to a provisional truce with at least *that* past, the novel does not end with any resolutions of "what really happened" or even what these traumatic reenactments have meant for her. She never discovers the "truth"—or a story that makes sense to her—or her father's relationship to duct tape nor the end of her relationship with Gina, and she rails against the option that she could "accept it" because "to accept it, I think, is to lose hope. I don't mean hope about us, but about *me*" (233). As Juani contemplates herself numbly, she notes, "I'm stuck here"; she finally admits, "It is possible—it is entirely possible—that I need to see it this way and that need dictates what I remember" (234). This acknowledgment of memory's instrumentality speaks to the intervention made in Obejas's novel—one related but distinct from the work of Tropicana's more positive invocation of cultural memory. Obejas critiques the presumptive coherence of memory and community, of the "imagined community" of Cuban exiles in the novel, but she also shows and, in a sense, celebrates aspects of Juani's cultural, and exilic, memory that produce community and family for her. Nonetheless, the image of Juani, "stuck" and confused, persists.

For Obejas, the terms of collective and personal memory share a similar unspoken ethos with other reconstructive projects around familial, national, and exilic memory: "That need dictates what I remember" (234). *Memory Mambo* ends with a consideration of the impossibility of exilic memory, of its impartial and complicit dimensions. The narrative seems at first to judge Juani harshly for her inability to act independently and speak against the call for traumatic repetition, but it also shows the power of the familial scenario. Within the last few pages, it is clear that the extended family and community quickly normalizes the sexual abuse of the baby Rosa and plans to go on, more or less, as before: Jimmy's wife defends him, and Rosa is "fine, actually" (235). Juani is left with some vague sense of an impasse and a plan to visit Cuba. When asked why, she answers in riddles: "'For belonging,' I say. 'To get away,' I admit" (235).

If the "not-knowing" that de Man describes as the "driving allegory of reading" can be transposed to *Memory Mambo*, we see the significance of Juani's continued ignorance and confusion. She embraces the anxiety of ignorance, in spite of her protestations, and never learns (or asks for that matter) what "really happened" either with her father or with her girlfriend. In fact, Juani occupies a kind of oscillation between trajectories of going back and moving forward. The emblematic scene of sexual violence that rips her out of her mesmerized identification with Jimmy suggests that Juani may be mobile, but the muted and irresolute ending indicates that she remains deeply embedded in certain familiar scenarios of family and community. Sexuality subsides as an issue—suspended, if not cut short entirely, though the ghost of her lesbianism is faintly decipherable in her conversations with Patricia, one of her cousins. What resolution the novel does offer lies in its cautionary tale about the effects of suspended migrations—hanging hopefully between homelands and identities—and the uses of memory.

II. Alvarez and Narrative Fantasies of Return

The protagonists in Alvarez's popular novels *How the García Girls Lost Their Accents* (1991) and *¡Yo!* (1997) remember and return to "the island" in order to preserve a past that they often did not have. In these apparently autobiographical fictions, Alvarez emphasizes the fantastic nature of memory, especially as it is inscribed in narrative, in ways that underline the intersections of its productive, or integrative, function with the necessarily imaginative nature of both remembering and telling stories. By showing how such stories fulfill the need to make the past available to succeeding generations and against the imperatives of immigrant forgetting, Alvarez's perspective on cultural memory recalls Chicana narratives of community and cultural identity as resistance. Both tend to rely on a positive, productive dynamic between community, culture, and self—offering a memory "product" at key moments. This need for memory is a direct result of histories of migration, including colonialism and exile, which create linguistic, cultural, geographical, and sexual confusions and paradoxes for the many protagonists and narrators of both novels. For example, in *How the García Girls Lost Their Accents* and on the occasion of her first return to "the island" in five years, the novel's first and primary narrator, Yolanda García, announces her desire, "Let this turn out to be my home" (11). That wish is soon thrown into question, however, when a flirtatious poet asks her the key "mother tongue" question: "What language, he asked, looking pointedly into her eyes, did she love in?" (13) Yolanda does not answer him. As in this example, Alvarez punctuates her first novel with provisional or unsuccessful returns, particularly to "the island," and it seems that their failures might have something to do with the other deeply felt wish of at least two other García women, who both say, "I want to forget the past" (50, 60).

In these novels, as in those by Obejas, an interrogation and rewriting of the patriarchal family becomes a meditation on the allegorical function of daughters in narratives of exile. And in that meditation, the tropes of memory and return emerge as powerful agents in ambivalent inscriptions of gender and sexuality as imbricated in family and nation. Interestingly, a comparison between the heterosexual paradigm that dominates Alvarez's work and the "queer" rewriting of ethnicity and exile in Obejas's work suggests that the conventions of allegorical narratives of return (e.g., nostalgic national mythologies and family romance) are deployed in similar ways. However, the distinct relations to sexuality, and perhaps to patriarchal or paternal authority, that emerge in these writers' respective bodies of work indicate a possible reading of the differences between what we might call a "queer" attitude toward memory and a "feminist" one.

Inscriptions of return in *García Girls* occur narratively to the past and geographically to the island. These stagings are used to represent how the various "girls" grapple with the familial nostalgia for the lost privileges of wealth, a paternal legacy of revolutionary activism, and a patriarchal tradition of control over female sexuality. Much of the novel chronicles the four daughters' struggles with their parents on this last score, especially with their father whose attitudes toward their sexual behavior as teenagers and adults in the United States are encapsulated by his fury at one adult daughter: "Has he deflowered you? . . . Have you gone behind the palm trees? Are you dragging my good name in the dirt, that is what I would like to know!" (30) The father's spatial and temporal, as well as cultural, displacement is exposed in how his attitudes toward his daughters' sexuality are grounded in a past time and lost place: they joke that they are more likely to become virgins again than find palm trees where they live in the United States. Return to the island in this context becomes a parental and national threat, one their parents make when the girls are behaving in ways that are too "American."

However, when one sister, Fifi, is actually sent back to the island for a year (after being caught with marijuana), she falls victim to an unforeseen danger: she falls in love with an illegitimate cousin, Manuel, who "looks like a handsome young double for Papi and a lot like us" (119). The cultural and filial promise of this return through heterosexual coupling and blood reunion turns sour when the other sisters decide that "Manuel is quite the tyrant, a mini Papi and Mami rolled into one" (120). In this section, the first-person plural narrator of "we" contrasts the girls' acquired American politics of "women's liberation" with Fifi's deluded acquiescence to cultural standards of gender and sexuality that are "foreign" to her. The rest of the sisters had already viewed Fifi's new romance as "dangerous to the rest of us. With one successfully repatriated daughter, Papi might yank us all out of college and send us back. Not to mention that it's out and out creepy that Fifi, the maverick, is *so* changed. Carla, in fact, says it's a borderline schizoid response to traumatic cultural displacement" (117).

This chapter, "A Regular Revolution: Carla, Sandi, Yoyo, Fifi," is narrated in a first-person plural that refers to each sister by name when she speaks, leaving no indication of a singular narrator apart from the group. Each chapter of *García Girls* has a title and a subheading that indicates which sister or sisters will be the protagonist and viewpoint of its subplot.

The novel as a whole is organized in a backward chronology from most recent to most distant past, which formally reiterates the thematic emphasis on cultural and familial memory and the integrative effect of narrating that familial past. This structure carries the reader and the "girls" back to a kind of origin point in their early childhoods in the Dominican Republic, becoming a counterpoint to the novel's initial themes of sexual and romantic behavior and cultural and generational conflict with their parents. The three sections of the novel would seem to further inscribe this trajectory from fragmentation and division within the family to a kind of cultural harmony between the girls and their parents that could be possible when they were all still Dominican. However, in the last vignettes, as in the novel as a whole, Alvarez shows how such suppositions of harmony are illusory. These final stories of childhood desires gone awry within a household riven by differences of class, race, and generation demonstrate that fragmentation was a constitutional fact of her narrators' early lives on "the island," as well as an effect of cultural and geographical displacement.

The collective "we" used in "A Regular Revolution" resonates with the theme of revolution, which plays out on several different levels and is part of this middle section's emphasis on the conflicts brought on by adolescence and the move to the United States. These various revolutions include a "small" but real revolution on the island that persuades their parents to stay in New York, the girls' revolution against parental control and traditional behavior for "girls," their mother's "own little revolution" (which consists of attending real estate and business classes), and finally, the women's revolution in whose name the sisters act together to "save" one of their own. Alvarez emphasizes irony in this chapter, particularly in that "the revolution" in question retains a sly ambiguity that reminds the reader that this narratorial "we" remains a highly constricted point of view and that what "the girls" *say* happened to Fifi reflects only what they experienced and saw—or even only what they will claim to have seen. The possibility of selective narration lurks behind all the disclosures in the novel, generating interesting layers of narrative meaning.

Although their concerns that Fifi has changed are momentarily relieved when they learn that her new boyfriend, Manuel, is an illegitimate son of one of their uncles. "We sisters give each other the V for victory sign. It's still a guerrilla revolution after all. We were afraid that Fifi was caving into family pressure and regressing into some nice third-world girl. But no way. She's still Ye Olde Fifi" (118). But it turns out that Fifi is in fact much changed, and most disturbingly, she "is letting this man tell her what she can and cannot do" (121). When the sisters confront Manuel, insisting that "even Dominican law grants" women rights, his dismissive response instigates an open battle "for our Fifi's heart and mind" (122). The following paragraphs then paint a picture of Fifi as seriously deluded against her own best self-interest, slipping further and further from the ironic tone of the chapter's early pages. This shift in strategy reflects a hierarchy of values in Alvarez's descriptions that assumes the benefits of American-style feminism and the rightness of a cause that involves getting their sister, who's been "brainwashed," to leave the island (126). The offensive behavior of a favorite male cousin who "turns macho" on the island further underlines the importance of geography in this scenario of return as a regression into "nice third-world" womanhood.

Ultimately, the narratorial "we" suggests that this was a real and necessary "revolution" after all. To prevent Fifi from having more unprotected sex with Manuel and perhaps staying on the island forever, the sisters betray her to their parents, albeit surreptitiously. This betrayal, even when acknowledged, becomes further evidence justifying the sisters' cause: an effort to win the personal freedom that necessarily can only happen in America. Confronted with her accusation of being "traitors," the narratorial "we" explains Fifi's romance with Manuel as a symptom of "her fear of her own life. Like ours, it lies ahead of her like a wilderness just before the first explorer sets foot on the virgin sand" (132). In this tale, the intersection between patriarchal authority, diasporic identity, and the policing of female sexuality converges on Fifi's complicitous desires for return. This final narratorial pronouncement clearly characterizes those desires as regressive and motivated by fear, not the courageous and adventurous spirit needed by an "explorer" in her own life. In this way, Alvarez subtly upholds certain hierarchies of modernity: the individualist character traits that bode success in the New World and the ways that gender liberation and personal freedom conflate to denote a metropolitan modernity and not the traditional values and gender options of "the island."

That is not to say that Alvarez is blasé about the psychic and sexual costs of this cultural and geographical displacement, however "liberating" it might be. The first section of the novel relates the various breakdowns, the cultural and emotional unmooring, and the romantic failures that plague the four sisters. As the opening section of the novel comes to a close, moving backward in time from adulthood to adolescence, the last two chapters recount Yolanda's sexual coming-of-age. In reflecting on her early attempts at both sex and love—one in high school and the other in college—Yolanda sadly realizes "I saw what a cold, lonely life awaited me in this country. I would never find someone who would understand my peculiar mix of Catholicism and agnosticism, Hispanic and American styles" (99). Alvarez insistently links linguistic, cultural, and sexual facility, and so it is particularly interesting how two of the sisters experience almost total linguistic breakdowns. These near-psychotic episodes illustrate the tenuousness of the García girls' grip on their place in the world, specifically as women. Thus the novel oscillates between modernity's conventional Euro-American presumption of the sexual and personal liberation that accrues to a cosmopolitan belonging in the United States and a more nuanced accounting of the losses and gaps left behind by such a personal history of displacement and language shifting.

Thus, sexual styles and their relations to various diasporic and patriarchal histories of loss, violence, and repression are a major theme in *How the García Girls Lost Their Accents*—a theme that the novel presents to the reader allegorically via a series of scenarios that narrativize the same elements in different order. The elaboration of this allegory of confused or difficult experiences of sexuality as the sign of diasporic suspension results in a text in which every impulse toward an integrative or harmonious model of diasporic subjectivity is undermined by a narrative fragmentation that occurs both thematically and formally. For example, in the central (literally and figuratively) chapter of *Garcia Girls*, Yo experiences a linguistic meltdown that mirrors and allegorizes her experience of monolingual and monocultural sex and love with her first husband, John. But the relationship itself can also be said to stand in for her impossible location between nations, identities, languages, and "sexual styles," which clearly precipitates Yo's crisis of language. By "regressing" back to an origin state of reestablishing the relations between words and things, Yo also figures the epistemological privilege of her diasporic self—of the technologies of selfhood that have produced her.

In *¡Yo!* however, the focus shifts more overtly to questions about the uses of memory, and although this novel is formally just as fragmented as Alvarez's first, a more recuperative impulse reveals itself in relation to the demands of memory and cultural histories. The final section of *¡Yo!* returns to the figure of Yolanda's father, who narrates a dream he has for his daughter, which constitutes the novel's last word on the links between cultural memory and the losses of migration. Because this section is told in the father's voice, various ambiguities remain as to what extent Alvarez is articulating a theory of memory and of writing. However, the father establishes both an identification and a continuity between himself and his daughter, the writer and authorial alter ego, Yo: "I am blessed—and sometimes cursed—with a child who understands my secret heart" (292). Yo has become worried that she will never have children, a "decision" that seems linked to her vocation as a writer. In the father's reverie, he wants to reaffirm Yo as a writer by telling her a secret story about her childhood when they were living in fear of the dictatorship: "It is a story I have kept secret because it is also a story of my shame which I cannot disentangle from it. We were living in terror and I reacted with terror. I beat her. I told her that she must never ever tell stories again . . . I have to tell her I was wrong. I have to lift the old injunction" (296). In a novel that is structured around Yo but never features her voice, the father's final section is in dialogue with all the other sections, many of which reflect her family's resentment of how she has exposed them in her successful novels and stories.

The father, too, is sophisticated about the relation between narrative and memory, saying, "It's also because I have read the story of those years over and over as Yo has written it, and I know I've substituted her fiction for my facts here and there" (299). But although the father knows that the new fictions replace the old memories, he insists that Yo is fulfilling a crucial function—one that will link the generations across time and space and that will allow them all to survive.

> We left everything behind and forgot so much. Ours is now an orphan family. My grandchildren and great grandchildren will not know the way back unless they have a story. Tell them of our journey. Tell them the secret heart of your father and undo the old wrong. My Yo, embrace your destino. You have my blessing, pass it on. (309)

In these final words, Alvarez expresses a positive understanding of stories about memory, of writing memory even with the distortions of desire and transcription. Interestingly, this utopian vision of healing "the old wrong" through renarrativizations of the past positions Yo firmly in a reproductive function, vis-à-vis her father and the family. The heterosexual paradigm that dominates Alvarez's representations of the García girls' sexualities emerges again (returns) in a new form: the terms under which Yo will be the chronicler of herself and the extended history that constitutes her.

Alvarez generates an allegory of writing and remembering through the father's closing tale about Yo, and such allegories reveal much about the desires embedded in narratives of diaspora and return. Here, the past that will bind and ground the family, and the paternal legacy, must be renarrated and re-membered by the writing daughter. As such, the desire for memory recalls other reconstructive national and cultural projects that enlist memory in necessarily fantastic versions of history and identity. The issue of collective memory's therapeutic and historical functions is a central topic of investigation for all three artists: Alvarez, Obejas, and Tropicana. This attention manifests itself, for example, in the way *García Girls* reads chronologically in reverse, toward the past of Yolanda's earliest childhood memories of the island. Both thematically and structurally, then, Alvarez foregrounds a dialectic relation between the lived past and the invented past that is crucial to how her novels conceive of diasporic Latina subjectivity. An acknowledgment of the role of fantasy is further confirmed when their Haitian maid prophesies toward the end of the novel that the García girls "will be haunted by what they do and don't remember. But they have spirit in them. They will invent what they need to survive" (*García Girls* 223).

Discussions of cultural memory have often turned on understanding's Freud's theory of mourning and the possibilities of working through traumatic material. Such therapeutic notions of "working through" confront, however, the oft-noted dangers of memory's nostalgic reconstructions. Mieke Bal, for instance, discusses the fine line between memories that remain fixed, unavailable to narration, and therefore condemned to a non-therapeutic and neurotic cycle of repetition and those that effect psychic healing. In contrast to the therapeutic model of memory as mourning, psychoanalyst Adam Phillips points out how concepts of "working through" traumatic memory actually require a special kind of forgetting. What preoccupies Phillips is a crucial ambivalence both in Freud's theory of mourning and of psychoanalytic practice in which memories are necessarily "screen memories": they express the subject's desires but not her "real" past. This fantastic structure of memory suggests that working through memories is about the desires that are left behind as the residue of the past; desires for memory are about memory, but not memories themselves.

Thus, the past generates desires—sexual desires as well as desires for origin, return, and history—but in a displaced fashion that camouflages and conflates the facts of history and their effects. In *Memory Mambo*, a related understanding of memory and history occasions a narrative acknowledgment that sexual and familial relations and identities are generated by all our histories—histories that are distant and political, as well familial and intimate. Such acknowledgment involves a skepticism toward both memory and love, one that is less evident in Alvarez's work. However, the final moment of ¡*Yo!* can be understood as a more subtle critique of the father's appropriation of the daughter's energies than the one in *Memory Mambo*. Like Juani's, Yo's father also conscripts her into his own project of cultural memory, albeit in a way that camouflages the possible violence of his appropriation. Therefore, the narrative loop around the tropes of writing and memory in Alvarez's novel ultimately throws into question the novel's discourse of reconciliation and working through. Although ¡*Yo!* stages a series of such reconciliations, particularly at Yo's late-in-life multicultural wedding, Alvarez leaves open the possibility of reading against the father's desires for reproduction through his daughter's cultural work of storytelling. Alvarez highlights this possibility by structuring the novel so that Yo's desires—cultural and oedipal, as well as sexual and intellectual— remain inferred; the voice of "Yo" (the novel's "I" or central self) is never heard directly. Yo, as the novel's protagonist, emerges only through the voices of others, playing on the reader's impulses toward coherence and conventional narrative trajectories. That is, Alvarez stages a recuperative model of memory and narration but in way that opens both to various readings, countering the text's apparent affirmation of a transparent understanding of the uses of familial and cultural memory.

III. Performative Poetics and the Collective Unconscious Memory Appropriation Attack (CUMAA)

One thing that emerges in these allegorical narrativizations by Obejas and Alvarez of intergenerational collective memory and its coercions is how the questions of memory and nation emerge via a palimpsestic layering with another story about fathers and fatherlands. That is, in these texts, the possibilities and fantasies generated by the dreamed-of return to the *patria* (fatherland/country) are surreptitiously figured through the father himself. In *Milk of Amnesia,* a parody of this diasporic and patriarchal "not-knowing" also sets off Tropicana's quest. The amnesia that instigates this performance piece likewise involves a father figure, but "Pingalito" (little dick) as a paternal/patriarchal authority and the protagonist's anguished negotiations with that authority are both performed as warm-hearted parody, using the alternative logics of embodied queer performance and the registers of farce and kitsch enabled by the stage. *Milk of Amnesia* thus remixes the familiar allegory of female sexuality and belonging to figure a rather different story about memory, trauma, and migration in the Americas.

While the novels by Obejas and Alvarez focus on the personal functions of memory for the protagonist—its ideological function for herself and her family—Tropicana's performance piece *Milk of Amnesia* reflects critically and politically on the loss of memory generated through diasporic and immigrant experiences. That is, where the protagonists in *Memory Mambo* and *How the García Girls Lost Their Accents* might question memory and exilic fantasies of the lost homeland in order to analyze its role in intergenerational histories and issues of posttrauma (Hirsch), Tropicana "recovers" personal and collective memory in order to wield them in a liberatory struggle against the coerced forgetfulness of immigrant assimilation. Hence, in *Milk of Amnesia* the privileged exilic allegory of return as recovery and reparation is deployed in a double articulation that allows for the lived power of that return even as it is ironically mocked and undercut within the performance. I suggest that this twist on allegories of belonging and their cultural work reflects a generic difference between performance and the novel. The novels by Obejas and Alvarez may question the exilic fantasy of return but the mode of novelistic discourse does not allow for the explicit uses of parody and stereotypes that Carmelita conscripts into her appropriation of return as a scenario that enables new political formations rather than a generational family plot.

Carmelita's "queerness" is especially underlined in the performance of *Milk of Amnesia*, which features several queer, cross-dressing, and parodic characterizations that accumulate in a composite tableau of the nation's expelled bodies, memories, and sexualities. Tropicana uses what Muñoz describes as "*Cubana* dyke camp" to assert class, sexual, and national bodies that have been "forgotten" and that undermine simultaneously Cuban, Cuban American, and American models of identity and belonging.

Milk of Amnesia is a one-woman show with three main characters: the writer (Troyano), Pingalito Betancourt, and Tropicana. It weaves among these three personas and between New York, Miami, and Havana to tell the story of how Carmelita (and, in a different sense, Troyano) was struck with amnesia and how both Carmelita and Troyano regained their memory—specifically through a trip "back to Cuba," "the place I was born in" (Troyano 2000). As this summary indicates, memory is seen to have a deep relationship to space, as well as identity, in this plot. The therapeutic nature of Carmelita's trip to Cuba, participating in "the diaspora that's going back" underlines the hybrid spatial imaginary of the performance—one embedded in the ambiguities of Cuban diaspora politics and its sense of geographical home. Tropicana suggests her movement through this space by describing the ingenuity of diasporic Cubans in the Miami airport, "holding onto plastic bags with medicines and the most magnificent hats" as part of their strategy to avoid airline weight limits on baggage (59). Carmelita then models her own magnificent hat, claiming "Soy una tienda ambulante . . . I'm a walking Cuban department store. Tampons and pearls, toilet paper, stationary supplies. What a delight" (60). Tropicana uses the performance medium and plays with audience expectations by adopting and dropping the thick "Cuban" accent of Carmelita to address them in more Americanized tones, which are presumably more "realistic" and hence believable. She assures the audience that the story of the hats is true, referencing *New York Times,* and concludes, "Next to me was a woman with a pressure cooker on her head. A pressure cooker. These people are going to survive" (60). These interplays of accent, language, dress, and imagined location generate a specifically performative hybridity that both references political and economic realities and parodies audience assumptions about national identities and embodied behaviors.

The stage of Carmelita's "performance art" enables Tropicana to convey simultaneously the material conditions of exile, diasporic travel, and

Cubans living through the "special period." Obejas too relies on an assumed relation between self, memory, and the geographical and national place of "Cuba" in her own political and communal imaginary: this "place . . . where I would finally belong" as she puts it, somewhat ironically. For Troyano/Tropicana, however, the return is not about belonging but about forgetting, specifically the immigrant forgetting demanded by U.S. discourses of assimilation. Muñoz argues that such forgetting is resisted in the specific identity and hybridized spatial imaginary of the "exile." The distinct tactics that each of these artists adopts in her exploration of diaspora, exile, and the geographies and sexualities of memory differ in important ways. I argue that although both Tropicana and Obejas confirm Muñoz's characterization of a Cuban exilic imaginary, they also contest the cultural and geographical meanings of "exile" and the role of memory in constructions of national identities and histories; as does Alvarez in her narratives of exile and return, if somewhat more ambivalently. In Obejas and Tropicana, and even in Alvarez, functioning collectivities and selves actually emerge in spite of the logics of exilic nostalgia. As in Valdés, nostalgia's cohering force across time and space shows itself to be profoundly destructive of individuals and even the diasporic collectivities that are the "real" against which the nationalist fantasies of return and recuperation are staged.

Milk of Amnesia portrays personal and collective re-membering through its participation in the performative genre of "camp," a mode related to irony and parody in its political resonance—resonances that the generic conventions of narrative fiction find much harder to generate.[7] For example, the performance triangulates the three characters of Carmelita (signaled by her thick accent and the occasional outrageous costume), the writer (never seen but heard as a voice broadcast during costume changes), and Pingalito (who is seen, effectively, as Carmelita in male drag). In this way, Tropicana also circumvents some of the dramatic plot conventions of autobiographical fiction. Such games of appearance and authorship (Whose voice is most "truly" the artist's? Which story most evocatively hers?) blur other kinds of categories and boundaries and their presumed "scripts," including the nation-states of the Americas and their respective histories and cultural memories. That is to say, Carmelita's message is ultimately aimed at a multiple audience that extends far beyond the Cuban exile community into publics that encompass notions of a transnational and transethnic *latinidad* (Latin-ness), and perhaps even the Americas as an emerging public in and of itself.[8]

As a way of introducing her theme of personal memory and the collective meaning of its loss, Troyano begins *Milk of Amnesia* by relating a scene of her early years in school in the United States, where, she tells us, she was having some difficulties fitting in because she didn't like peanut butter and jelly (preferring peanut butter and tuna) and because she never drank her milk. One day she spills this milk in the cafeteria, which leads to a confrontation:

> The nun came over. Looked at me and my milk. Her beady eyes screamed: You didn't drink your milk, Grade A pasteurized, homogenized, you Cuban refugee.
> After that day I changed . . . If I closed my eyes and held my breath I could suppress a lot of the flavor I didn't like. This is how I learned to drink milk. It was my resolve to embrace America as I chewed on my peanut butter and jelly sandwich and gulped down my milk. This new milk that had replaced the sweet condensed milk of Cuba. My amnesia had begun. (53)

We see here how Tropicana/Troyano highlights the suppression of self, of bodily senses and desires, as well as memory, which is necessary for her to "embrace America," and the demands for "pasteurization" that she must negotiate. As Muñoz points out, "Dominant culture is suspicious of the exile's double residency both inside and outside the nation . . . Nations, especially the U.S., . . . understand the ambivalence, indeterminacy of exile and hybridity as a threat to the fiction of national unity and cohesion" ("No es fácil" 77).

This rooting of the subject in a conception of exile that rejects the claims of a monological U.S. identity underlines the importance of the hybridity of Cuban American experiences. However, in insisting that it is the U.S./Cuba dyad that organizes the state of "exile," Muñoz pushes Tropicana toward a more contained political vision than her work actually performs. Rather than understanding the trip "back to Cuba" as itself the catalyst for Carmelita's political agency, I see *Milk of Amnesia* as a performative unveiling of the complex mechanisms that work on and through Carmelita as simultaneously American, Cuban, Latina, and queer. And yet the journey itself does seem to be necessary to this process of working through her multiple (as opposed to dual) sense of belonging. Muñoz describes "exilic memory" as that which binds the imaginary and material domains of a fraught identity: "The ephemera and personal narratives that signify 'Cuba' for me [and] resonate not only as possessing a certain materiality, but also providing a sense of 'place'" (76). This "sense of place" is distinctly different, however, from the ways that Carmelita describes her loss of memory and identity, though it is only through an experience of "place" that she is able to repair the damage done by her personal and cultural amnesia. Carmelita's loss of a simultaneously lived and imaginary connection to "Cuba" lands her in the hospital, suffering from a total loss of self-recognition. From her hospital bed Carmelita announces that since Pingalito tells her she is from

Cuba, "maybe there is only one way to find out. To go back to the place I was born in. My homeland" (59). So, Carmelita uses this trip to Cuba—in which she "will cross an ocean of years"—to tell two stories: one about how she is cured of her amnesia and another about contemporary transnational migrations and diasporic histories in the Americas.

Muñoz has suggested that the act of going back to Cuba and regaining her memory is precisely what allows Troyano/Tropicana to articulate a politics, which she does by calling for an end to the embargo against the Castro regime, and thus the people of Cuba, in the final monologue of *Milk of Amnesia*. But though Tropicana relies on the materiality of her specific diasporic experience of travel and return to Cuba, she also communicates beyond an exclusively Cuban diasporic public: "We are all connected," she insists in her final monologue (69). Michael Keith and Steve Pile suggest that the circulation of diasporic cultural productions, such as music (and, I would argue, including exilic memory and Tropicana's performance art), link both within the diaspora and outside it, underlining the epistemological questions raised by the cultural politics of diaspora (19). Thus Tropicana legitimizes the importance of "local knowledges" but then ultimately gestures outside notions of "Cuban exilic memory" to less nationalized, and static, diasporic constructions of the Americas (e.g., linking a pig in Castro's Havana to Cortez's horse at the time of the Conquest to Carmelita's up-to-the-minute New York Latina kitsch). The relation between space and memory is reiterated throughout *Milk of Amnesia* in a way that confirms Muñoz's most important point: Carmelita's performance is aimed against a "corrosive forgetting, codified as 'assimilation'" ("No es fácil" 69). However, Muñoz's emphasis on the category of "exile" seems to lock Carmelita and Troyano into a nationalist politics of memory and space that *Milk of Amnesia* ultimately undoes.

While Tropicana and Obejas underline the idea of memory in these works—as is apparent from their respective titles—they also demonstrate how memory is a treacherous, if necessary, domain for the foundation of national and/or personal identities. Although, as *Milk of Amnesia* demonstrates, the presumed alternative of immigrant assimilation signifies self-erasure and a devastating forgetting that ultimately places one in an intolerable isolation. Such questions of memory and nostalgia and the links they foster within communities have dominated discussions of diasporic and nationalist imaginaries, where as Keya Ganguly says, "Recollections of the past serve as the active ideological terrain on which people represent themselves to themselves. The past acquires a more marked salience with subjects for whom categories of the present have been made unusually unstable or unpredictable, as a consequence of the displacement enforced by postcolonial and migrant circumstances"

(Ganguly 1992, 29). Similarly, Schein has explored the dynamic that produces nostalgia as a by-product of the "discursive construction of homeland," which becomes the obsessive interest of diasporic subjects for whom that past and that place of "the homeland" has become inaccessible (Schein 1999, 703). For both Ganguly and Schein, the categories "past" and "present" are deeply spatialized for diasporic and migrant subjects. That is, the inaccessibility of a grounding experience of the place of the past—in this case Cuba—becomes the catalyst for imagined reconstructions of that lost home, "the Havana of my dreams," as Obejas confesses. The role of fantasy, of dream and desire, in these efforts to remember and put back together both past and present and here and there is highlighted in *Milk of Amnesia*, in which the inaccessibility of the past becomes a symbolically saturated amnesia that erases all of Carmelita's "identity." Carmelita complains that as a result of this amnesia, "I want to remember so much I get these false attacks. In desperation, I appropriate others' memories" (58).

Thus the communal nature of memory, its fantastic impulse to create something for the self to claim, becomes for Carmelita both tool and trickery. Carmelita's quest to regain her memories is itself an allegorical narrativization with both personal and political significance. The narrative force of a "return to the homeland" underlines the authenticating function of a firsthand experience of Cuba, one that will imprint and connect her to lost memories of Cuba, "the place I was born in." On the other hand, Carmelita confesses to a tendency toward appropriating others' memories—a habit that will persist when she arrives in Havana and makes a humorous and revealing ironic commentary on both memory and the politics of exile and return. *Milk of Amnesia* is thus simultaneously a trenchant critique of the politics of nostalgic reconstruction and a performative negotiation that refuses the dominant models offered, which the piece approaches from multiple vantage points.[9] In particular, both Tropicana and Obejas show how a particularly nationalist Cuban diasporic politics of nostalgia carries the double burden of maintaining the "homeland" through the collective memory of Cuban exiles in the United States and of asserting that this homeland was effectively "lost" with the advent of socialism.

Thus, there is a double attack in *Milk of Amnesia* that operates through a simultaneous parody of Cuban bourgeois nostalgia and an intervention in the likewise exclusionary nationalist discourses of U.S. citizenship and belonging. Tropicana deploys performative incarnations of irony and comedy to portray Cuban life on the island in a different register from what is normally found in the United States, subversively confirming what Gayatri Gopinath has called the need to understand "not only that diaspora be seen as part of the nation but that the nation be rethought as part of the diaspora as well" (1995, 304). That is, the way Carmelita returns to

Cuba—with the guidance of a parodic and queer version of a national father-figure, Pingalito, and the heard-but-not-seen commentary of the cosmopolitan voice of a U.S.-Cuban "writer" (herself)—demonstrates how Cuba can be reframed and reconceptualized outside of nationalist rhetoric and via a queer diasporic rhetorics of sexual and cultural hybridity. Tropicana consciously intends this double address to Cuban and U.S. audiences and its ironic invocation of an array of allegories of belonging. All of Tropicana's audiences are challenged by what she calls elsewhere her *"chusmería"* ("shameless, loud, gross, tacky behavior, in short tasteless with attitude" 77). In her introduction, Troyano tells the story of the Cuban couple who gave her a ride in their limousine: "Even though I said I was Cuban in my routine, the Cuban couple still could not believe it and asked, 'You are Puerto Rican, aren't you?' They did not see the fruits, the accent, the loud behavior reflected in their own Cuban mirror" (2000, xxv).

While it offers audiences an alternative picture of Cuba, as well as of migrant belonging in the United States, *Milk of Amnesia* also parodies various sexual and ethnic identity categories. For example, the first persona to appear on stage is Carmelita's spoof of Cuban masculinity, Pingalito (who in spite of the moniker "Pingalito," or "little dick," calls himself "the Cuban Antonio Banderas"). Chomping on his cigar and wearing a *guayabera* (a white shirt typically worn by Cuban men), Pingalito introduces himself as a former bus driver from Havana who adores Carmelita. He is the one to visit her in the hospital after the accident that caused her to lose her memory (which we find out happened while she was "chocolate-pudding wrestling," 58). As a man, Pingalito embodies the Cuban national subject while undermining the racial and national purity of that subject through the performance mediums of accent, dress, and music (as Pingalito enters the stage, a mambo tune that was actually most popular in the United States is played) (Yarbro-Bejarano 205). So, although Pingalito attempts to cure Carmelita's amnesia and begins as a kind of commentator and "Cuban" guide for the audience, as well as for Carmelita, the performance undermines in various ways his claims to representing Cuba and his paternal ability to "help" Carmelita. The irony explicit in Tropicana's drag king performance of Pingalito further undercuts the way he occupies the role of the "real" Cuban, making the performance simultaneously a national parody and a loving invocation of Cuba.[10]

Because figures of stereotypical "island" Latino masculinity also play an important role in the novels by Obejas and Alvarez, these three writers and their works raise questions about the intersections of gender and sexual politics in diasporic imaginaries. Interestingly, in both *Milk of Amnesia* and the 1992 film *Your Kunst is Your Waffen* (directed by Ela Troyano, Tropicana's sister), Carmelita's cross-dressing performance of "the Cuban man" signals an imagined return to the past and the geographical space of Cuba, as well as a critique of Cuban masculinity. As Yvonne Yarbro-Bejarano notes, Tropicana actually embodies "the symbolic fathers of Cuban identity on stage" (2000, 200). In both Tropicana and Obejas, the culturally hybrid lesbian protagonist turns to masculine stereotypes in ways that suggest an appeal to a legitimating national discourse of *cubanidad* that is at least partly ironic and critical. On one hand, such masculinity articulates and guarantees a claim to "Cuba" that operates without the ambivalence of the female and queer Cuban American artists, for as Gopinath notes, there is a "difficulty in thinking diaspora outside of a patri-lineal genealogical economy" (306).[11] On the other hand, although the fatherly concern and attention that Pingalito offers Carmelita plays a key role in her imaginative reconstruction and recovery of the homeland, the parodic register of Tropicana's performance works on the heteropatriarchal underpinnings of the national subject—making even this good-natured, if buffoonish, icon a queer on the stage.

The ways that gender play and infusions of sexual feeling lead to such ambiguities of both sexual and cultural personas have been central to the development of Tropicana's performance art, and of the Carmelita Tropicana persona in particular. In an interview with David Roman, Troyano emphasizes how a queer context of sexual and gender differences informed her performance work from the start:

> In 1983 Holly [Hughes] put me in her show The Well of Horniness. She had me doing things that were so heavy for me! I had to play a man and a butch girl. That was hard. I can't be butch! I had to shut up all these voices in my head that said I couldn't be loud, that I had to be a nice girl. But the voices in my head were silenced as soon as I stepped onstage wearing this tiny T-shirt . . . flexing my muscles. All the girls went nuts and I thought, "It's not so bad to be butch!" That's how my career began. (Roman 1995, 86)

The "voices in [her] head" that Troyano silences through performance—what she calls "putting the mask on"—are implicitly tied to family and community. Against the admonition to behave herself (as a "girl" and as a Cuban American), the hyperbolic and performative *cubanidad* that per-meates both Carmelita and Pingalito's personas enables Tropicana's "return" to Cuba in *Milk of Amnesia*.

Early in the performance of *Milk of Amnesia*, Troyano/Tropicana uses "the writer's voice" to explain again how she came to be a performance artist, and specifically how she came to be Carmelita Tropicana:[12]

> But it wasn't me. I couldn't stand in front of an audience, wear sequined gowns, tell jokes. But she could. She who penciled in her beauty marks, she

who was baptized in the fountain of America's most popular orange juice, in the name of Havana's legendary nightclub, the Tropicana, She was a fruit and wasn't afraid to admit it. She was the past I'd left behind. She was Cuba. Mi Cuba querida, el son montuno . . ." (Troyano 2000, 57–58).

Carmelita is "the fruit" who goes against "the voices in my head" that insist she must be a nice girl, as well as the assimilating rhetoric of the United States. The "fruit" thus becomes a place, "the past," that had been left behind, or rather that had been disciplined out of Troyano in the United States. This emphasis on the ways that performing Carmelita has always been an act of recovery for Troyano—a recovery of simultaneously queer and Cuban selves, as well as repressed memories—shows the intricate relations between sexual and cultural identities and memory that *Milk of Amnesia* traces. And yet by splitting her performative persona, Carmelita Tropicana, from Alina Troyano, the writer, and in emphasizing that performer's sexual and ethnic markers, Troyano/Tropicana also articulates an ambivalence that links sexual and diasporic histories.

In yet another ironic twist, Tropicana uses Carmelita's journey "back to Cuba"—a place she cannot remember—to mock the right-wing nationalist Cuban American political myths of return. When she does visit the house she was born in, for example, it's a construction company and the secretary follows her suspiciously through its rooms, asking "'Hey, you're not one of those Cubans who plans to come back and take over their house.' I say, 'Oh no, we only rented.' The moment I say this I feel like I'm not like one of those Cuban who left—who never would have said they rented . . . Are you kidding me, we owned the whole block" (65). In this instance, Tropicana acknowledges the deceptive role of memory in consolidating national and communal mythologies (such as repatriation)—her difference from "those Cubans" who would never remember that sticky detail of renting. In acknowledging the material tenuousness (renting, not owning) of her ties to Cuba, Tropicana must acknowledge that her sense of belonging, of being "one of those Cubans," is likewise tenuous.

In diasporic and postcolonial contexts where memory is threatened and distorted by the double work of the politics of nostalgia at one end and a politics of assimilation at the other, cultural memory offers the promise of epistemological grounding. So Carmelita appears "cured" of her amnesia by the "healing" power of memory in a way that affirms the collective and political nature of both history and memory. However, this final therapeutic episode is also rendered in the register of parody, and with a thick layer of irony that distances Tropicana from the scene she recounts. Her big breakthrough occurs when she undergoes another CUMAA in which two events and subjectivities converge: that of a pig being raised for food in a Havana apartment in the 1980s and of Carmelita having her tonsils out as a child in Havana. After her CUMAA brings back her memories of Cuba and the United States (as well as of the Conquest and Mexico), Carmelita emerges onstage in her full regalia and admonishes her audience, "We are all connected, not through AT&T, e-mail, Internet, but through memory, history, herstory, horsetory. I remember" (69). In explicitly articulating the webs of connection that cohere a "we all" of the Americas, Troyano articulates an allegory of belonging that expands beyond the nation-state discourse of even diaspora. Offering the picture of Carmelita in a hospital gown and her department store hat (one that Troyano emphasizes in performance and describes in detail in the script), *Milk of Amnesia* works against the logic of the bildungsroman and the romance of the individual in ways that the first-person narration of novels cannot.

The ironic mocking of developmental narratives of nostalgia and its healing in Tropicana's performance art shakes up the exilic story and presents it on a stage as the emblem or image of Tropicana in various forms of drag. This register of "*Cubana* dyke kitsch" (Muñoz) also highlights her generic departure from the narrative figuring of diasporic selfhood as tragically, and irremediably traumatized that we see in Valdés and in the generational narratives of U.S. Latina writers such as Obejas and Alvarez. So although each of the protagonists of these narrativizations of Latina selfhood finds herself suspended between places, sexual histories, and nation-states in ways that reflect their specific experiences of displacement, distinct lessons are learned and particular pedagogies are enabled by differences between the popular novel and iconic performance art.

Hence, though Juani, Yolanda, and Carmelita all find themselves suspended between places, sexual histories, and nation-states in ways that reflect their experiences of displacement, Tropicana queers—and diasporizes—Cuban exile, allowing for a generic tone beyond the traumatic and tragic. This new kind of diasporic cultural production speaks beyond even the categories of diaspora and to the need for alternative configurations of selfhood, space, and sexuality in relation to cultural and ethnic histories. Tropicana illustrates how performance operates as an allegorical mode that can activate other kinds of thinking/feeling about identity and experience. The visual composition of elements complements the juxtapositions of narrative scenarios that don't quite fit together. Both combine, as Robert Hariman might put it, into a "paradoxical whole" that does not work through the conventions of narrative development, even as it invokes the stereotypes, emblems, and scripts of both *cubanidad* and assimilationist United States. Like Obejas, Tropicana works to expose the coercive operations of cultural memory even as she also acknowledges and deploys collective memory and its inscriptions of trauma in order to work pedagogically on audiences.

As I have argued throughout this book, such performative pedagogies generate a narrativity—or relation and affect among performer, audience, and discourses—that is distinct from the identitarian, and somehow melodramatic, vectors of narrative fiction. The genre of the minority memoir/ novel has perhaps become overly conscripted and saturated with the logics of traumatic feelings and events, as well as of the progressive individual personality development that are the currency of mimesis in realist novels. Tropicana is able to leap out of that logic and use the media of performance art to push her aesthetic encapsulation and representation into another direction—one that the tools of kitsch and the absurd make possible. Tropicana pushes that parodic suspension of identity to the limit in performances that queer—and diasporize—Cuban exile and transamerican communities, allowing for a generic tone beyond the traumatic and tragic. And this new kind of cultural production blurs even the categories of diaspora, speaking to the need for alternative configurations of, and connections between, selfhood, space, and sexuality in relation to the cultural and national histories of the Americas.

Notes

Preface

1. Writing in the January 2005 North American Congress on Latin America (NACLA) Report, anthropologist Shane Greene makes this argument in some detail, noting that indigenous groups in Latin American countries such as Bolivia and Peru "are careful to define collective rights in concert with the West's historically dominant notions of human and individual rights" (Green 38). So the "circuit" here is one that includes indigenous collectivities who are now strategically negotiating with both the legal and political structures of what Negri and Hardt would call "Empire." Green goes on to emphasize the role played by environmentalist discourses and issues in gaining Latin American indigenous activist groups further UN support and visibility.
2. See Norma Alarcón's seminar essay, "*Traditora/Traiditora*: A Paradigmatic Figure of Chicana Feminism."
3. Discussed especially in Chapter 3, "necropolitics" extends the Foucauldian term, biopower, to theorize its relation to contemporary conditions of "terror" and global "necropolitics," Mbembe defines necropolitics as "contemporary forms of subjugation of life to the power of death" (39) and argues that the Enlightenment subject of contemporary philosophy and political theory is actually a "fantasy" of reason and truth, whose purpose is to cover and camouflage the real mechanisms and interests of biopower, or further, of *necropower*.

Chapter 1

1. *New York Times* film critic A. O. Scott has been analyzing the rise of allegory in popular, often Hollywood-produced films for several years. See his review of *28 Days Later* for a useful example (June 2007).
2. See "Ethnographic Allegories" by James Clifford and *Foundational Fictions* by Sommer.
3. Williams emphasizes that "this is a way of defining forms and conventions in art and literature as inalienable elements of social material process; not by derivation from other social forms and pre-forms, but as social formations of a specific kind which may in turn be seen as the articulation (often the only fully available articulation) of structures of feeling which as living processes are much more widely experienced" (*Marxism and Literature* 133).

4. José Muñoz has discussed the stereotype of "Latino as excess" as one that U.S. Latina/o artists work through "rather than trying to run away from" in order to negotiate an official "national affect" of whiteness. Muñoz argues that "Latina/o citizen-subjects find their way through subgroups that perform the self in affectively extravagant fashions" that should be understood as "an important mapping of the social" ("Feeling Brown" 70). Agreeing heartily with this diagnosis, I suggest that in addition to a distinct mapping or negotiation, these performances of minoritarian affect also point to the ways that such affects impact and circulate beyond a specifically "ethnic" sphere, even as they may remain implicated, and not simply oppositional to, dominant affective structures.

5. See Ian Watt's influential arguments in *The Rise of the Novel*. Ann Laura Stoler's seminal explication of the late writings of Foucault on race and biopower in *Race and the Education of Desire* are key to current discussions of technologies of selfhood. Stoler parses through Foucault's final lectures to illuminate the role of racism in his understanding of the "technologies of selfhood" of modernity and the state's concern with "the management of life" or biopower (81).

6. As Ana del Sarto explains, "Cultural Critique construes its locus from aesthetic materiality, in order to 'critically transform the real' . . . while Cultural Studies construes it from social materiality, in order to produce social reality" (quoted in Nelson and Tandeciarz, xv). This emphasis on reading and textual exegesis relies on Latin American theories of "cultural critique" as opposed to the more dominant Anglo paradigm of cultural studies.

7. Regarding these local contexts and the languages of the Americas, this book focuses primarily on U.S., Latin American, and Latino connections, so the main languages at issue are English and Spanish. If a source is available in translation, I use the published translation. And if a secondary source is available in translation, I use only the translated text—unless the original version conveys key information not available otherwise. Primary sources are quoted first in the original language and followed by the translation in paranthesis.

8. An important theory of this cultural work has been José Muñoz's work on "disidentification" and performance, which clearly informs aspects of the arguments here. Notions of the performative are key to Muñoz's and other influential efforts to dislodge identity and identify politics from its position as the centerpiece of a dominant political repertoire of social transformation, and particularly though its links to narrative and film theory's emphasis on the identificatory processes that bind the self in aesthetic spectatorship.

9. Taylor's invocation of a concept of "scenarios" as a central trope for performance art and performance studies is aimed precisely at dislodging the hegemony of text-based "close reading" methodologies that reiterate the primacy of writing and reading over embodiment and transmission. While such theoretical paradigms specific to performance studies promise to be very productive, the comparative nature of this study has generated a vocabulary that probably remains bound within the metaphors and logics of writing, though I try to break away from that epistemological habit. See Taylor, *The Archive and the Repertoire: Performing Cultural Memory in the Americas*.

10. In fact, Hansen claims a radical opportunity is opened by the "emptying out" of the raced image produced both by its "interpellative failure" and the extent to which "images of the ethnic Other can be nothing but fantasy projections of the same" (109). For Hansen, the possibilities opened by the suspension and even total evacuation of identity takes on a redemptive potential through the workings of "affectivity." One question raised by *Def Poetry Jam* is whether its project of audience participation and community building is fully co-opted into the failure of "the raced image" or if it produces something else, an excess and potentiality embedded in both the images and the contagions circulated through the show, the audience, and the television.

11. The notion of the "assemblage" in recent cultural theory suggests a shift to the logic of "affect" away from what cultural theorist Jasbir Puar calls "an intersectional model of identity, which presumes components—race, class, gender, sexuality, nation, age, religion—are separable analytics and can be thus disassembled" (127). Puar specifically refigures queerness away from the logic of identity, explaining "Queerness as an assemblage moves away from excavation work, deprivileges a binary opposition between queer and non-queer subjects, and instead of retaining queerness exclusively as dissenting, resistant and alternative (all of which queerness importantly is and does), it underscores contingency and complicity with dominant formations" (*Social Text* 121).

12. In addition to its publications in Nelly Richard's journal *Cultural Critique,* the CADA has received sustained critical attention in the United States by scholars such as Alice Nelson and Silvia Tandieciearz.

13. Villarejo explains further: "The collective faces a society in which the functional mode of interpellation—through ideological apparatuses, through the institutions of civil society (including family and kinship)—has changed, insofar as capital has been invested at an affective level . . . The labor of the production, circulation, and manipulation of affects, with its emphasis on the corporeal (not simply 'the body' but subindividual bodily capacities and also machinic assemblages of bodies), becomes crucial in understanding contemporary networks of biopower; it compels a shift in thinking from the bounded, identitarian body to an intensification of the perception of the body, its capacities and assemblages" (136).

14. The notion of the "assemblage" in recent cultural theory suggests a shift to the logic of "affect" away from what cultural theorist Jasbir Puar calls "an intersectional model of identity, which presumes components—race, class, gender, sexuality, nation, age, religion—are separable analytics and can be thus disassembled" (127). Puar specifically refigures queerness away from the logic of identity, explaining "Queerness as an assemblage moves away from excavation work, deprivileges a binary opposition between queer and non-queer subjects, and instead of retaining queerness exclusively as dissenting, resistant and alternative (all of which queerness importantly is and does), it underscores contingency and complicity with dominant formations" (*Social Text* 121).

15. In her introduction to *The Affective Turn,* Clough explains the shift in late modernity from discipline societies to control societies and why it's important: "Disciplining engages a politics of representation; it forms part of a cinematic

regime of representation" that operates through the ideological apparatuses of family, nation, etc, in a subject formation grounded in identities (19). In contrast, Clough continues, control "aims at a never-ending modulation of moods, capacities, affects, and potentialities . . . in bodies of data and information (including the human body as information and data" (19).

16. Miranda Joseph critiques the concept of "community" in ways that resonate with my sense of a mixed productivity in these emergent political art projects: producing both well-worn and reductive "identities" and "communities" but in tandem with a supplement of affect and a shift in public feeling that also carries the traces of the ironies and disclaimers of the Def Poets' negotiation with ethnic identity scripts. See Joseph, *Against the Romance of Community*.

17. See also Mireille Rosello, *Declining the Stereotype: Ethnicity and Representation in French Cultures*.

18. Jameson in fact argues that "all such group or 'cultural' relations" cannot operate without the stereotypical because "relations between groups . . . must always involve collective abstractions of the other group, no matter how sanitized, no matter how censored and imbued with respect" ("On Cultural Studies," 274). Chow emphasizes how Jameson's bracing contrarian statements force us to understand that stereotyping is "an encounter between surfaces rather than interiors" in both linguistic and political terms (57). Jameson notes that "what it is politically correct to do under such circumstances is to allow the other group to elaborate its own preferential image and then to work with that henceforth 'official' stereotype" ("On 'Cultural Studies'" 274).

19. Irony is thus a performative act in the sense that "it is what speech-act theory would call a 'perlocutionary' act as well, for it produces 'certain consequential effects upon the feeling, thoughts, or actions of the audience, or of the speaker, or of other persons' (Austin 1975: 101)" (Hutcheon 39).

20. As Kierkegaard also says, ironic communication *requires* distinctions and even hierarchies between groups and their knowledge of one another in that irony "travels in an exclusive incognito, as it were, and looks down from its exalted station with compassion on ordinary pedestrian speech" (Kierkegaard 1971, 261, quoted in Hutcheon).

21. Notes taken during an April 2003 performance of Def Poetry Jam on Broadway in New York City.

22. Teresa de Lauretis further reminds readers of Vladimir Propp's structuralist poetics of the folktale, in which he cautioned, as she puts it, that "plots do not directly 'reflect' a given social order, but rather emerge out of the conflict, the contradictions, of different social orders as they succeed or replace one another; the difficult coexistence of different orders of historical reality in the long period of transition from one to the other is precisely what is manifested in the tension of plots and in the transformations or dispersion of motifs and plot types" (113).

23. Trinh T. Minh-ha adapted the term "image repertoire" to describe the discursive operations of colonial thought, which are deeply tied to Rey Chow's discussion of the stereotype; both interestingly work through what Eva Cherniavsky calls "specular epistemology" (for more on the links between narrative style and

questions of epistemology, see Chapter 3). In pinpointing the gendering, racializing, and hierarchizing functions of anthropological discourse, Minh-ha analyzed key cultural work done by the stereotype in a global division of discourse, labor, and the power to name. Thus del Valle talks back to that discursive history, even as she threatens to slip into its parameters.

24. See again José Muñoz, "Feeling Brown," for a related reading of Latina/o performance.

25. See, too, Susan Sulieman, Judith Roof, and Homi Bhabha.

26. Chow also recently furthered this argument: "The more resistive (that is, on the outside) X is imagined to be, the more unavoidably it is to lose its specificity (that is, become appropriated) in the larger framework of the systemic production of differences, while the circumstances that make this framework possible (that is, enable it to unfold and progress as a permanently self-regulating interiority) remain unchallenged" (*The Age of the World Target* 68).

27. "Biopower" is a term from the later work of Michel Foucault that Stoler links to technologies of the self and the role of the state in managing populations, particularly through discourses of race and sexuality. Also a key concept in Chow and Puar, biopower is the undercurrent that generates the sovereign right of the state "to kill and let live," which becomes in modernity "the right to make live and let die" (TM: 38, qtd. in Stoler 81). For Foucault and Stoler, the central paradox of this inquiry is how does the biopower of the state, "a power invested in augmenting life and the quality of life," become "the means of introducing . . . a fundamental division between those who must live and those who must die" (TM: 52–53, qtd. on 84). In addition to its analysis of the function of racism in the modern political imaginary and the "permanency of war-like relations inside the social body" (84), this question highlights the processes of expulsion and boundary-making that characterize modern community formation and identity discourses (see Brown, Butler, Chow, Puar, and Riley).

28. "Moreover, in the process of literary creation, languages interanimate each other and objectify precisely that side of one's own (and of the other's) language *that pertains to its world view*, its inner form, the axiologically accentuated system inherent in it . . . what stands out is precisely that which makes language concrete and which makes its world view ultimately untranslatable, that is precisely the *style of the language as a totality*" (Bakhtin, *The Dialogic Imagination* 62).

29. See in particular, Mikhail Bakhtin's discussions of "speech genres" in *Speech Genres and Other Late Essays*.

30. See Judith Butler's description of subjectification in Althusser in *The Psychic Life of Power*.

31. Like Chow's, my understanding of the linguistic and sociopolitical processes of identity formation remains fundamentally "poststructuralist" and therefore often challenges the liberalist tradition in its understanding of social action and political agency. For counterarguments to these positions, see work on "realist identities," particularly by Paula Moya and Satya Mohanty.

32. Raymond Williams uses "structure of feeling" to interrogate the psychic effects of social formations at both individual and collective levels, to account for the

ways that "all that is present and moving, all that escapes or seems to escape from the fixed and the explicit and the known, is grasped and defined as the personal: this, here, now, alive, active, 'subjective'" (*Marxism and Literature* 128).

33. My understanding of "assemblage" is derived from Puar's recent work on queer politics in her essays in *Social Text* and book, *Terrorist Assemblages: Homonationalism in Queer Times*. Puar emphasizes that processes of assemblage "underscore contingency and complicity with dominant formations" even as they articulate new political formations (xx). I posit that a similar dynamic is at work in the "identity phenomena" that are put into motion by *Def Poetry Jam* and other performative narrative texts. However, because Puar is explicitly arguing through a Deleuzian theory of "assemblages" as effects within biopolitics, it is important to emphasize that "identity phenomena," as I use the term, is not to be confused with identities or even identitarian collectivities, but rather implies the effects or mirages of such coherent and stable collectivities.

34. "An intellectual history of loss must apprehend itself as an act of provisional writing against the conformism of unwavering historical truths that claim to blot out the present" (Eng and Kazanjian, "Introduction: Mourning Remains" 6).

35. See Gregory Forter for his astute critique of the discourses of racial melancholy. "Against Melancholia:Contemporary Mourning Theory, Fitzgerald's *The Great Gatsby,* and the Politics of Unfinished Grief" in *differences: A Journal of Feminist Cultural Studies* 14.2 (2003): 134–70.

36. In his description of particular writers, such as the Argentine Tununa Mercado and Chilean writer and artist-activist Diamela Eltit, Idelbar Avelar links the decline of "storytelling" (more specifically, of the "auratic" era of literature in Latin American society most familiar as "the boom") to a denial of this erosion of the role of narrative literature: "Only by ignoring the imperative to mourn, only by repressing it into neurotic oblivion, can one proceed to narrate today without confronting the epochal crisis of storytelling and the decline in the transmissibility of experience. This has been, of course, the hegemonic strategy, the victorious version" (20).

37. This explanation strikes me as a reductive rendering of the relation between "story" and the past—not to mention the future. In place of the therapeutic language of accomplishing mourning, other critics such as Richard, and Avelar himself, have contrasted the aesthetics of melancholic allegory with the transparent collective function attributed to *testimonio* (testimonial nonfiction writing). In such cases, literature and especially allegory, prove capable of manifesting the most convoluted—baroque, even—matrices of social, personal, and ideological experience, without necessarily being conscripted into notions of sociological or transparent "truth."

38. Subjectivation as constituting both the surface of the ethnic stereotype in cross-cultural representation and the interiority of a categorically "ethnic" experience of selfhood.

39. See Rafael Pérez-Torres on the generative ambivalence, and the poetics, of mestizaje in Chicano literature.

40. Gloria Anzaldúa makes this point in *Borderlands/La Frontera* when she admonishes, "Admit that Mexico is your double . . . Gringo, accept the doppelganger in your psyche" (86), in a passage that explicates dominant processes of scapegoating, or what Cheng calls the melancholic operation of dominant white identity in America: "An elaborate identificatory system based on psychical and social consumption-and-denial" (11).

41. Chapter 2 addresses this question in relation to Cherríe Moraga and a larger body of Chicana lesbian feminist theoretical and fictional texts from the 1990s.

42. For further analysis of this confluence, see Román de la Campa's "Comparative Latin American Studies: Literary and Cultural Theory," in *Comparative Cultural Studies and Latin America,* ed. Sophia A. McClennen and Earl E. Fitz, 56–67.

43. See in particular, Deborah Madsen, *Rereading Allegory: A Narrative Approach to Genre,* where she discusses the history of allegory criticism that goes between reading allegory as working through the substitutive logic of metaphor or through the diachronic, that is, *historical,* logic of metonymy.

44. The metacritical work of Clifford, Minh-ha, and Mary Louise Pratt helped establish the genre of ethnography as an exemplary model in cultural and literary studies for how certain plots, or repeatable narratives, operate through unconscious ideological investments to shape and contain the lessons of particular narratives for both the consumers and producers of "knowledge."

45. See Chow, Shu-Mei Shih, and Gayatri Spivak and also Lori Ween's "This is Your Book" in the Publications of the Modern Language Association of America (*PMLA*) issue on "America: The Idea, the Literature." Ween persuasively links the demands of publishing markets to the emergence of special imprints for "ethnic literature" that ultimately serves to reify and compartmentalize racialized discourses of difference and belonging.

46. See, in particular, recent essays by Haun Saussy, Bill Brown, and Julie McGougal.

47. This presumption draws on a long history of dismissing allegory as mechanical and reductive, inferior aesthetically and philosophically to the symbol. Walter Benjamin explains that this verdict on allegory originated with the Romantics and persisted unchallenged into the twentieth (and now twenty-first) century, establishing an aesthetic bias and hierarchy that he links to questions of linguistic temporality and duration, as well as the history of criticism.

48. See the work of Richard, whose promotion of "cultural critique" is discussed in the Preface.

49. Laura García-Moreno notes that Avelar's study "foregrounds the need to situate itself in relation to a neoliberal present, the double imperative to mourn a recent catastrophic past and at the same time resist passive forgetting or accepted modes of memory, and the critique of modern narrative modes and literary legacies such as magical realism and testimonial narratives that ultimately assume a compensatory or reconciliatory role in relation to the contradictory experiences of modernity in Latin American countries" (2). Similarly, the testimonial function could be said to participate in, even invite, the Western appetite for traumatic memoirs, such as those of the Japanese occupation of China that are criticized by Shih.

50. In *The Cultural Politics of Emotion,* Sara Ahmed articulates a theory of affect that focuses on the naming of emotions at the contact between the individual and the social: "Even though I am challenging the idea that there simply 'are' different emotions, 'in here', or 'out there', I also want to explore how naming emotions involves different orientations towards the objects they construct. In this sense, emotions may not have a referent, but naming an emotion has effects that we can describe as referential" (14).

51. See Jamie Skye Bianco's "Zones of Morbidity and Necropolitics" in *Rhizomes* 8 (Spring 2004).

52. I would like to thank Jane Elliott for calling my attention to Brown's essay and his important contribution to rethinking allegory and its related questions. See also her book *Popular Feminist Fiction as American Allegory.*

53. Brown characterizes Jameson's critical work through its ongoing effort "to convey cultural phenomena in all their concrete immediacy while at the same time fixing them squarely within the cultural logic of late capitalism" (738). In his reading, Brown describes capitalism as "the econo-cultural system here taking the place of a divine system in which paradise is unrepresented and perhaps unrepresentable but known (axiomatically and unequivocally) as the collectively effaced socialization of the means of production" (738).

54. For further examples of the controversies over what is involved when activist political theories are debunked, particularly by poststructuralist destabilizations of any possibility of totality, see Carine Mardorossian on Wendy Brown and Paula Moya on Norma Alarcón.

55. Benjamin also writes, "The measure of time of the experience of the symbol is the mystical instant in which the symbol assumes the meaning into its hidden and, if one might say so, wooded interior. On the other hand, allegory is not free from a corresponding dialectic, and the contemplative calm with which it immerses itself into the depths which separate visual being from meaning, has none of the disinterested self-sufficiency which is present in the apparently related intention of the sign. The violence of the dialectic movement within these allegorical depths becomes clearer in the study of the form of the *Trauerspiel* than anywhere else" (165).

56. Peter Hallward is especially scathing about theorizations of politics as a component of aesthetics. He argues for the clear demarcation of a universal-rights-based sphere of political discourse that is delineated from the critiquing function of aesthetic work, particularly literature. Likewise, Frederick Luis Aldama critiques the "ontology" of contemporary ethnic criticism and its conflation of ethnicity and writing.

Chapter 2

1. See Marta Sanchez (1998), as well as Norma Alarcón (1989), for discussions of the prominence of *Malinche* in the imaginations of Chicana feminists and their differing interpretations of various Chicana rewritings of the *Malinche* allegory as emancipatory and regressive.

2. See Daniel Cooper Alarcón's discussions of Mexico as a palimpsest for concepts and representations of Chicano identities, particularly during the Chicano *movimiento* of the late 1960s and early 1970s in *The Aztec Palimpsest.*
3. For example, in their seminal 1986 essay "Feminist Politics: What's Home Got to Do with It?" Biddy Martin and Chandra Mohanty interrogate the political and discursive creation and maintenance of "home" as necessarily one of masculinist and often racist exclusions that ultimately turn back on antiracists, feminists, and queers.
4. Lora Romero's analysis in "When Something Goes Queer" (1993) focuses on the unintended consequences of this rhetoric of *familia,* especially in the work of Cherríe Moraga. See also Norma Alarcón (1990) on the need for an alternative figure for Chicano community.
5. These salient economic characteristics of Chicana/o communities and political identities have motivated a powerful Chicana/o critique of dominant white culture and its political economy. Rosa Fregoso and Angie Chabram (1990), for example, emphasize that oppositional relation to dominant Anglo culture remains crucial to the politics of Chicana/o writers and activists—without it, the term "Chicano" loses both its historical basis and its radical political significance and agency.
6. *Mestizaje*—the cultural and racial mixing or hybridity of individuals and the collective identified as "Latinas/os"—is often theorized as a fundamental and specific problem in Chicano theory and identity. See Rafael Pérez-Torres's recent book, *Mestizaje: Critical Uses of Race in Chicano Culture* (2006).
7. Avery Gordon's work on haunting is particularly useful in elucidating these dynamics as well. See *Ghostly Matters: Haunting and the Sociological Imagination* (1997).
8. Ironically, it is Frantz Fanon himself who has most influentially articulated these traps of postcolonial communal and political life in "On National Culture" (Fanon 1963). See also Pérez-Torres's discussion of "On National Culture" in the context of Chicano and Latino aesthetics where he emphasizes the need to articulate Chicana/o subjectivity, and understand the Chicana/o novel, in "a postcolonial register" (Pérez-Torres 2000, 545).
9. That is, as Caren Kaplan, Norma Alarcón, and Minoo Moallem have stated, "Women are both of and not of the nation" (Kaplan, Alarcón, and Moallem 1999, 12), and this inside and outside location creates several tensions and discontinuities between women and the consolidating force of nationalist narratives.
10. For further theorizations and discussions of shame, see Sara Ahmed, Ann Cvetkovich, and Eve Sedgwick.
11. Dionne Espinoza and Paula Moya touch on the long-standing discussions of white feminist appropriations of the texts of women of color in order to "lend materialist credibility to their arguments" (Espinoza 1998, 47). For example, Moya, like Lora Romero and Espinoza, critiques Donna Haraway's deployment of Moraga and Chicana feminism in her "manifesto" of a feminist utopia, claiming that it erases or ignores the specific histories and subject positions that inform Chicana feminism (Moya 1996).

12. In this vein, Rosaura Sánchez makes a materialist argument against ahistorical discourses of *indigenismo,* especially in its more spiritually focused inscription in Ana Castillo's *Massacre of the Dreamers: Essays on Xicanisma* (Albuquerque: University of New Mexico Press, 1994) (Sánchez 1997).

13. As discussed in detail in Chapter 3, *indigenismo* denotes the popular aesthetic and cultural revaloration of indigenous culture in Latin American societies, beginning in the colonial era. Roughly translated as "indigenism," this often condescending celebration of Native American culture has been criticized for its appropriation of the image or idea of Indians in order to bolster other, liberal or colonial, agendas.

14. Rita Felski (1995) suggests that a mainstream Anglo-European tradition of modernity and modernism exists in an obscured tension with contemporary oppositional or "subversive" discourses of gender and ethnicity. Tracing the impact of literary modernism and the representations of female sexuality in fin-de-siècle avant-garde literature, Felski highlights fundamental links between political discourses of modernity and the textual politics of modernism and cautions against "generalized claims for the subversive nature of experimental forms" (Felski 1995, 27).

15. I emphasize this realist element in Chicana writing generally and Pérez in particular in order to undercut a prevailing opposition between realist (and therefore more "ideological") novels and experimental, or postmodern, fictions that are necessarily disruptive of preconceived identity categories. In Chicana writing, such identity categories can emerge in the midst of experimental narrative (as in *Borderlands,* at least according to some readers), and some realist fictions produce deeply subversive and noncommodifiable characters, for example, in the short stories of Sandra Cisneros's *Woman Hollering Creek* (1991).

Chapter 3

1. The term *"estadounidense"* is the Spanish word preferred in Latin America to designate the adjectival form of the United States—thereby avoiding *"americano,"* which only reiterates this arrogance linguistically.

2. Echoing the influential cultural critiques of Walter Mignolo and José Rabasa regarding the "invention of America," such narratives prefigure the originary relation between Western nation-state modernity and the conquest and occupation of the Americas, and particularly the crucial role of contact with—and exploitation of—the iconic "Other" of this modernity: the original, indigenous inhabitants of the Americas.

3. For further discussion of prophecy as a political and aesthetic mode, see Kirsten Silva Gruesz's essay "Utopía Latina: *The Ordinary Seaman* in Extraordinary Times" and Hazel Carby's essay "Figuring the Future in Los(t) Angeles."

4. Thus enacting a literary negotiation with "the disappearance of the question of the future" in late modernity (Morris 31).

5. *Almanac's* refiguring of the realist novel genre also coincides with Deleuze and Guattari's definitions of "minor literature," particularly in the move away from

designation and metaphor ("Kafka deliberately kills all metaphor, all symbolism, all signification" (22)) to work toward language's "extremities or its limits" (23). Their emphasis on a literature that resists mimetic representation brings Deleuze and Guattari's "minor literature" into the realm of allegory as discussed here and in Benjamin, Avelar, and Richard: both deploy abstract or disruptive aesthetics to resist figuration and co-optation into the "same." Deleuze and Guattari, "What Is a Minor Literature" from *Kafka: Towards a Minor Literature.*

6. The opening scene also illustrates the text's multiple disruptions of "scale" to indicate the shifts and recombinations of the language and image repertoire of geographies, identities, and economics that *Almanac* deploy. See Ann Bingham's "Productions of Geographic Scale and Capitalist-Colonialist Enterprise in Leslie Marmon Silko's *Almanac of the Dead.*"

7. In explaining this delineation of political belonging, Agamben draws from Arendt in *The Origins of Totalitarianism,* noting "the fiction implicit here is that birth immediately becomes nation, such that there can be no distinction between the two moments. Rights, that is, are attributed to man only in the degree to which he is the immediately vanishing presupposition (indeed, he must never appear simply as man) of the citizen" (Agamben, "We Refugees." *Symposium* 49.2 (1995): 114–19; 118).

8. The note has not been provided yet.

9. Cherniavsky asserts that these identity markers operate within the novel as "exploitable simulacrum produced by a system of abstract equivalence," which the tribal protagonists, at least, simply appropriate and manipulate to work within the commodifying logic of capitalism in order to move toward other kinds of sociality and relation (113). "The simulated regime of European identity overwrites the material world, imposing its discipline on living persons it so stunningly fails to represent. Identity in *Almanac* thus functions on the order of Baudrillard's 'object-sign' as that which supports a thoroughly dehumanized version of social relations. . . . From the tribal vantage point, the commodification of historical identity associated with late capitalism is simply redundant, since identity itself mediates and substitutes for the irreducible heterogeneity of historical existence" (Cherniavsky 113).

10. See Rey Chow's "Where Have All the Natives Gone?", David Johnson and Scott Michaelson's "Border Secrets: An Introduction" in *Border Theory: The Limits of Cultural Politics* (1997), and Elizabeth Povinelli's "Settler Modernity and the Quest for an Indigenous Tradition."

11. "In contrast to ethnonationalisms, and their sustaining rhetoric of cultural purity, tribal knowledges in *Almanac of the Dead* are avowedly impure, non-organic, and non-innocent, and their subjects are media-savvy talk-show queens, computer hackers, high-tech smugglers, and smart shoppers. This positioning of the novel's tribal protagonists, immersed in the circuits of information and commodity exchange, supplants the primitivist imaginary and its association of the tribal with peripheral space and anterior time" (Cherniavsky 111).

12. The notion of a colonial Manichean conflict between races is grounded in Hegel's master/slave paradigm and is first introduced in the colonialist

analysis of A. O. Mannoni and then more famously critiqued in Abdul JanMohammed's *Manichean Aesthetics: The Politics of Literature in Colonial Africa.*

13. Michael Murrin discusses the roots of allegorical pedagogies in Renaissance allegory in *The Veil of Allegory* (1962), beginning with an explanation of Spenser: "The reality of the Queen, like the sun, blinds—so he enfolds her light in a veil 'That feeble eyes your glory may behold' (Pro. 5, Spenser). He substitutes for the veil in the minds of his audience his own veil, through which the sun may at least shine, though faintly . . . The few, however, can with difficulty pierce the cloud bank and see the truth, and this is the most important function of the veil. It makes truth valuable for a few people in the poet's audience. In oral communication truth has no power; the speaker must make it valuable for his auditors. The veil of allegory creates the value truth needs by setting up difficulties for the understanding" (11).

14. As will be discussed later, the dilemma produces a variety of divisions and conundrums, particularly in terms of audience and narrative strategy: "The prophet in his failure . . . wavered between dismay at the impossible revelations which he received from Yahweh and rage at the blindness of his audience" (Murrin 34).

15. See Jane Elliott's *Popular Feminist Fiction as American Allegory* and her discussions of allegory as narrativization of cultural imaginaries of temporality and history, particularly the function of feminism and women's novels in the 1970s and 1980s. As discussed in Chapter 1, Benjamin's famous "death's head" of history and the link between allegory and narratives of historical failure are particularly apt for allegory as the genre of mourning and of prophecy. The special link between allegory and historical failure and loss is one that Benjamin returns to again and again.

16. Furthermore, by bringing the status of "stories" and of writing itself to bear on the emergence of this necropolitics, Silko resituates literary expression in the center of these contemporary historical processes at the precise moment when the social relevance of fiction is increasingly under fire. That is, if the question of contemporary criticism is, as Bill Brown suggests, "How to articulate our cultural predicament" (737), then the increased questioning of the status of literature, and of aesthetics more generally, illustrates a contemporary crisis of faith, of influence, in both the enterprises of literature and academia.

17. I would like to thank Elizabeth Freeman for her astute comments as a respondent to our 2003 American Studies Association panel on "Race War in the Americas" and for underlining the cathartic and containing function of narrative, of telling stories, in my reading of *Almanac.*

18. Idelber Avelar has likewise asserted that as the genre that "voices mourning," allegorical narrative in Latin American postdictatorships has become a means to "reactivate . . . the hope of providing an entrance into a traumatic experience that has seemingly been condemned to silence and oblivion" (4, 10).

19. See the discussion in Chapter 1 and further explication of the link between these normative modes of signification and the neocolonial-biopolitical logics of culturalism in Chow, *The Protestant Ethnic.*

20. See Brian Richardson's *Unnatural Voices* for a full overview of the modernist and postmodernist array of antihumanist narrative techniques. However, the majority of Richardson's examples are texts that take the avant-garde, and elite cosmopolitan, path in that their narrative experimentation works as a rebuke to, and refusal of, more popular modes of signification. Silko on the other hand exploits those modes and then shifts their terms—*Almanac* is not aimed above the popular modes, but right at the center of it, even as it appropriates aspects of experimental highbrow fiction. It is no accident that originally *Almanac* was contracted and planned as a "genre style" detective fiction, explicitly popular, and as a respite from her more literary works, such as *Storyteller* (see German interview).

21. In occasionally offering the adjectives "baroque" and "neobaroque," I am describing Silko's aesthetic strategies as nonlinear and anticlassical (against Aristotelean poetics), which positions *Almanac* within the emerging field of a "New World Baroque" aesthetics as described in the work of Monika Kaup and Lois Parkinson Zamora, and also signals the archaic nature of the narrative of *Almanac*. Its literally "baroque" elements echo Benjamin's treatise on allegory as a specifically and historically (seventeenth-century) "baroque" art form relying on the alternative, and medieval, aesthetics of the emblem and the ruin.

22. This example also indicates the complexity of the narrating functions in *Almanac*. Here, we see an instance of what James Phelan describes as when "the implied author's indirect address to the authorial audience can interfere with the narrator's address to the narratee" (*Living to Tell about It: A Rhetoric and Ethics of Character Narration*, 12).

23. See also Henry James on the novel form, especially his classic polemic on realism versus more popular novels in "The Art of Fiction," in which he deplores the high sentimental mode of fiction with its dominance of melodrama and event over the realist (more scientific and objectively true to human psychology and event, and less popular) emphasis on character.

24. See Amritjit Singh and Peter Schmidt's Introduction, "On the Borders between U.S. Studies and Postcolonial Theory" in *Postcolonial Theory and the United States: Race, Ethnicity, and Literature.*

25. On "tropicalization," see Stephen Benz's "Through the Tropical Looking Glass: The Motif of Resistance in U.S. Literature on Central America" in *Tropicalizations: Transcultural Representations of Latinidad*, ed. Frances R. Aparicio and Susana Chávez-Silverman. Also see Daniel Cooper Alarcón's extensive analysis of the invention of "Mexico" in *The Aztec Palimpsest.*

26. As discussed in the Preface, the notion that Baroque aesthetics operate as a particularly "American" mode of artistic expression has been deeply discussed in Latin American literature and philosophy. Recent critics to take up this genealogy include Monika Kaup and Lois Parkinson Zamora in her book *The Inordinate Eye: New World Baroque and Latin American Fiction.*

27. The identitarian implications of the novel's suggested ontology of sexual practices—queerness as corrupt, unnatural, and grotesquely sadistic behavior—continue to be a problem for many of Silko's readers, myself included.

28. See Bianco's essay for a thorough and suggestive explication of the discourses of "security" in both necropolitics and *Almanac*.

29. Ideological narratives, as defined by Wahneema Lubiano, rely on "cover stories" that mask and deflect our attention away from a hidden ideological purpose. Lubiano explains, "Cover stories are faces of other texts, different texts. They are pretexts that . . . protect the texts of the powerful" (Lubiano 324).

30. Benjamin writes, "The desire to guarantee the sacred character of any script . . . leads to complexes, to hieroglyphics. This is what happens in the baroque. Both externally and stylistically—in the extreme character of the typographical arrangement and in the use of highly charged metaphors—the written word tends towards the visual. It is not possible to conceive of a starker totality, than this amorphous fragment which is seen in the form of allegorical script" (175–76).

31. Phelan defines mimetic as "that component of character directed to its imitation of a possible person. It refers, second, to that component of fictional narrative concerned with imitating the world beyond the fiction" (216).

32. For further explanation of the connection between the baroque and "trash," see recent and forthcoming work by Patricia Yaegar. Also, various Chicano critics such as Laura Pérez have written of the *rasquache* aesthetics of taking what is found, figuratively or literally, to re-make the world in ways that would contest hegemonic representations (of a U.S. national imaginary of whiteness, etc); such aesthetics have likewise been related to Baroque or "Neobaroque" tactics in visual and other arts.

33. Benjamin famously theorizes allegory as an aesthetic mode that materially manifests a specific slice of history: "When, as is the case in the *Trauerspiel,* history becomes part of the setting, it does so as script. The word 'history' stands written on the countenance of nature in the characters of transience. The allegory physiognomy of the nature-history . . . is present in reality in the form of the ruin . . . Allegory thereby declares itself to be beyond beauty. Allegories are, in the realm of thoughts, what ruins are in the realm of things" (177–78).

34. Both in the anticolonial writing on "national culture" by Frantz Fanon and in the postcolonial literature by writers such as Ama Ata Aidoo and Ngugi Wa Thiong'o (and perhaps more recently Tsitsi Dangarembga) the theme of being seduced and corrupted by the luxuries of Euro-American modernity and cosmopolitanism resurfaces as a cautionary tale for those working toward large-scale social change and to preserve the traditions and cultures of colonized societies. It's also interesting that the little boy is portrayed as emotional and panicky and the girls as "brutal."

35. In her classic work on apocalyptic narrative *Writing the Apocalypse,* Zamora notes that "while any narrative text may be said to disclose its full meaning only at its point of closure, apocalyptic narrative makes the conjunction of meaning and ending its theme, both in its expressed understanding of history and in its own narrative procedures . . . Apocalyptic narrative moves toward an *ending* that contains a particular attitude toward the goals of the narration, and toward the *end* that implies an ideology" (14).

36. This is a discourse that *Almanac* deploys allegorically but also counters dialogically with the "alternative" allegorical plot of the revolutionary "Great March Northward" of indigenous peoples and their armies.

Chapter 4

1. *Balún Canán* was translated as *The Nine Guardians* in 1963 and *Oficio de tinieblas* as *The Book of Lamentations* in 1964.
2. I use the term "speech genres" following Bakhtin's later work in *Speech Genres and Other Late Essays* and its emphasis on the heterogeneity of speech forms available to any speaker at any specific point in time. Bakhtin explains that "Language is realized in the form of individual concrete utterances (oral and written) by participants in the various areas of human activity . . . All three of these aspects—thematic content, style, and compositional structure—are inseparably linked to the *whole* of the utterance and are equally determined by the specific nature of the particular sphere of communication" (*Speech Genres* 60).
3. See Mexican feminist theorist Marisa Belausteguigoitia's "Zapatista Women: Place-based Struggles and the Search for Autonomy" on the relations between the discursive and juridical exclusion of both indigenous collectivities and women and questions of nation and subject formation in Mexico. Her work on subaltern subjects, narrative and images, and "the law" articulates some of these key dynamics in the context of contemporary indigenous women artists and activists in Chiapas, as well as Chicana writers.
4. See Castillo's essay, "Rosario Castellanos: 'Ashes without a Face,'" which focuses primarily on the first novel, *Balún-Canán*, in *De/Colonizing the Subject: The Politics of Gender in Women's Autobiography,* ed. Sidonie Smith and Julia Watson.
5. These questions of national identity and foundations involved a wide array of political as well as cultural projects. The key role of "creoles" who identified against both European colonial centers and the indigenous majority they lived with played a key if ambivalent role in the development of a distinctly "American" collective identity in Latin America. See also Doris Sommer, *Foundational Fictions.*
6. Much of my sense of this narrative pedagogy is indebted to the work of Doris Sommer, particularly her own related argument in *Proceed with Caution, When Engaged by Minority Writing in the Americas* (Harvard University Press, 1999).
7. Such is a central complaint about Mario Vargas Llosa's *El hablador* and an implicit critique of the cultural "fatalism" of both Vargas Llosa and Castellanos; particularly in *El hablador,* the reader is presented with a scenario that understands Euro-American modernity as an inevitable, if probably tragic, ongoing process of obliteration. For a useful comparison of readings of *El hablador,* see Castillo and Sommer (1999). The rhetoric of the tragically "dead Indian" is a familiar conceit in the United States and has been thoroughly analyzed in works such as *Border Matters* by José David Saldívar and *The Insistence of the Indian* by Susan Scheckel.

8. Jean Franco outlines the three main categories, loosely chronologically organized, that I am signaling in this discussion: the exoticizing *indianista* period in the late nineteenth century; social realist *indigenismo* up to 1950; and *nuevo* (new) *indigenismo* after 1950. (*The Modern Culture of Latin America* 162–67). O'Connell also cites this periodization in her discussion of "Castellanos and Indigenismo in Mexico" in *Prospero's Daughter: The Prose of Rosario Castellanos.*

9. O'Connell describes in some detail Castellanos's biographical experience with the INI in *Prospero's Daughter: The Prose of Rosario Castellanos,* 54–57.

10. Questions of modernization and cultural survival thus have a deep history in Mexican society and government, and as O'Connell notes, "The INI program fits in with a long history of efforts to domesticate this indigenous labor force from colonial times" in which "policies are formulated in the language of solving the 'Indian problem'" (57).

11. For an overview of these debates and their chronology, see Cornejo-Polar, "Indigenist and Heterogeneous Literatures: Their Dual Sociocultural Status," *Latin American Perspectives.*

12. The discourse of *mestizaje* is likewise central to discussions of Latino/a identities in the United States, particularly in Chicano literary and cultural theory. See especially Rafael Pérez-Torres, "Ethnicity, Ethics, and Latino Aesthetics" in *American Literary History.* And his more recent book *Mestizaje: Critical Uses of Race in Chicano Culture*

13. Many English language readers were first introduced to Ortiz and the theory of transculturation through the work of Mary Louise Pratt, particularly her essay, "Arts of the Contact Zone," and her seminal work, *Imperial Eyes.* In addition to the large body of critical work by Antonio Cornejo-Polar, Silvia Spitta and among others, Pratt has have written important essays tracing the processes of transculturation in various transamerican contexts.

14. In underlining the linguistic innovation and transculturation of Arguedas's work, Rama—and Arguedas himself—argued that this "Quechua-fied" Spanish language indexes the processes of transculturation as they emerge in speech genres of the everyday language spoken by Peruvians. This representation of the mutual impact and interdependence of Ladino, mestizo, and Quechua populations in Peru thus relies on both literary and sociological concepts of "representation." See Rama, *Transculturación narrativa en América Latina.*

15. See Sommer's argument in her chapter on Llosa, "About Face: The Talker Turns toward Peru," where she underlines the productive capacities of narrative "stalling" in *El hablador,* so that even while clearly reflecting Llosa's ambivalence about indigenous culture's ability to integrate into 'the nation' of Peru, the text performs a long and ethical attentiveness to indigenous culture and perspective, albeit totally through fiction, appropriation, and ventriloquism. See *Proceed with Caution, When Engaged by Minority Writing in the Americas.*

16. Castillo and Laura García-Moreno have written about the commodification of this Latin American imagery as exotic "other" in the consumerist global marketplace and its constraints on representations and dialogue concerning the social realities of specific Latin American collectivities, as well as on the literatures that

would address them. See Castillo's essay in *De/Colonizing the Subject: The Politics of Gender in Women's Autobiography* and García-Moreno's review of Idelbar Avelar's *The Untimely Present*.

17. In "Sexualidad femenina y patriarcado en *Oficio de tinieblas* de Rosario Castellanos," Consuelo Navarro writes, "La trayectoria literaria en prosa de Rosario Castellanos se inserta en la tradición indigenista estableciendo, sin embargo, una distancia frente a ella. Esta distancia está marcada por su papel de precursora del feminismo en México" (29). [The literary trajectory of Rosario Castellanos's prose participates in the *indigenista* tradition, establishing however a distance from that tradition. This distance is marked by her role as a precursor to feminism in Mexico.]

18. Also, as the medium of communication *and* domination, the imposition of Spanish on the Chamula reflects the hegemony of the logics of "the Western sign" as discussed by Cornejo-Polar in "Indigenist and Heterogeneous Literatures: Their Dual Sociocultural Status."

19. See Bakhtin's theory of dialogism in *The Dialogic Imagination* and his later revision of these theories in his discussions of "speech genres" in *Speech Genres and Other Late Essays*. The later work transcends the context of the genre of the novel to become a theory of language and society.

20. In his theory of "speech genres," Bakhtin suggests that living within a social totality means that *all* subjects are to some extent permeated by *all* the speech genres that constitute that totality; a dynamic in language, sociality, and literature that I suggest can be translated into the concept of transculturation. And yet he also holds that these languages maintain their own integrity when in contact with one another, thereby preserving their specific genealogies and cosmologies. See *Speech Genres and Other Late Essays*.

21. O'Connell notes that this individuation of indigenous characters emerged as a dominant narrative tactic of the more reform-minded *indigenista* writers in the mid-twentieth century, in Mexico as well as across Latin America (61–62).

22. Catalina's thoughts are marked initially by quotation marks in the text that signal, or "tag," her interior first-person monologue as she watches Pedro and the men of the community hatch their plans. But within a few paragraphs, these tags disappear and the narration returns to the free direct discourse that dominates Castellanos's transitions between character filters. As discussed in Seymour Chatman (*Story and Discourse: Narrative Structure in Fiction and Film*) and in Gerard Genette (*Narrative Discourse: An Essay on Method*), the distinction between "free" and "direct" discourse is the presence of these punctuation or phrases (he said, etc.) that play this tagging role. In "free" direct and indirect discourse, the reader must rely on the shifts in syntax and point of view to trace the character subjectivity in question. See Gerald Prince's *Dictionary of Narratology* for succinct discussions of these terms.

23. In this layering of narratorial commentaries and voices, Castellanos's narrative practices involve what Genette means by "narrative levels" in *Narrative Discourse*.

24. See E. Ann Kaplan's work on the mediation of "embodied translators" in contemporary processes of cultural translation and transculturation in *Trauma and Cinema: Cross-Cultural Explorations*.

25. See Jane Elliott's chapter on static time and the stalling of historical transformation in *Popular Feminist Fiction as American Allegory: Representing National Time*.
26. Lois Parkinson Zamora notes that the narrating agency and the reader share both a vision and a message that will survive the apocalypse, in the form of the prophetic narrative itself.
27. O'Connell notes that in much of Castellanos's prose works, "the position of women of the privileged class as female is cast in terms of an incestuous complicity," which here applies directly to Isabel's marrying Leonardo, who likely killed his brother/her husband. O'Connell notes that Idolina's later ambivalent regard for Leonardo takes on a peculiar, sexualized cast (154).

Chapter 5

1. The "raft crisis" of 1994 was one event in the general migration out of Cuba that followed the economic crises of the early 1990s (Martínez-San Miguel 2003). The "impossibility" of living, and staying, in Cuba remains one of Valdés's recurrent lamentations in fiction and in interviews; so it is not surprising that her work generates some controversy, especially among defenders of Castro's postrevolutionary regime.
2. Alvarez-Borland notes that "*Café Nostalgia*, a pivotal work within Zoé Valdés's own literary trajectory, embodies the concerns of the Cuban immigration of the 1990s, also known as the 'diaspora generation.' In her novel, the author poses a central question of diaspora aesthetics and, by extension, of Cuban identity: Is a community still a community when its members are dispersed throughout the world?" (347).
3. All translations of *Café Nostalgia* are my own and are aimed primarily at conveying, without artistic flourish, the precise meaning of Valdés's phrases. As in the rest of the book, when secondary sources are available in translation, I use those published documents. If not available, I quote the original source and follow with my translation in paranthesis.
4. See Idelbar Avelar's *The Untimely Present*, Kazanjian and Eng's edited book *Loss: The Politics of Mourning*, and Sophia McClennen's *The Dialectics of Exile*.
5. This phrase "desperdigados por el mundo" (scattered around the world) appears repeatedly throughout *Café Nostalgia*, most notably in the dedication, and on pages 126 and 345.
6. The relation between collective affect and notions of collective "haunting" is explored in Avery Gordon's book, *Ghostly Matters: Haunting and the Sociological Imagination*. Likewise, this chapter considers how Valdés represents displacement and diaspora as individual experiences that reflect and refract public histories.
7. De Man on the literal and figurative modes that opens *Allegories of Reading*.
8. These conditions vary over time and span Valdés's own lifetime, encompassing the Cuban Revolution, the U.S. embargo, and particularly the "periodo especial" that sets in after the fall of Soviet Russia in the early 1990s.

9. To use Wayne Booth's classic narrative terminology, Marcela is established as a "self-conscious narrator-observer" who may or may not be "unreliable." Booth distinguishes between narrator-observers, who are "aware of themselves as writers," and those, who do not discuss or mark the writing, or literary, nature of the narrative. Booth acknowledges that the question of reliability is particularly complex and a discussion of the "norms of the work (which is to say, the implied author's norms)" in *Café Nostalgia* will be important later in the chapter. See Booth's *The Rhetoric of Fiction,* 153–59.

10. Although Marcela insists on the trope of "exile," her structuring of time and place also suggests what Carine Mardorossian calls the shift from "exile to migrant literature"(115). However, although she reframes contemporary Cuban identity as migratory and in some ways deterritorializes it, Valdés does not show any interest in "a coming together of cultures" and splits Mardorossian's distinction by both "foregrounding what was left behind" (as in exile literature) and emphasizing a migrant sense of "the dynamic relationships between the past and present and the impossibility of return" (*Reclaiming Difference: Caribbean Women Rewrite Postcolonialism,* 117). Sophia McClennen's *The Dialectics of Exile: Nation, Time, Language, and Space in Hispanic Literature* suggests that tropes of multiplicity and fragmentation have long been part of the repertoire of characteristics associated with "exile" and exile literatures, which places Valdés's aesthetics of exilic subjectivity in a tradition of Hispanic exile literature.

11. Special thanks to Adrián Pérez-Melgosa for underlining the link between my reading of Valdés's narrativizing of exile as a technology of traumatized selfhoods and the significance of the diasporic chronotope as itself characterized by, and generated through, trauma.

12. Zamora links this "new sense of the nation" to Homi Bhabha's theorization of "nation and narration."

13. See my essay, "Migratory Sexualities, Diasporic Histories, and Memory in Queer Cuban-American Cultural Production," *Environment and Planning-D: Society and Space;* special topic issue on "Sexuality and Space," ed. Jasbir Puar, Dereka Rushbook, and Louisa Schein, vol. 21 (2003): 461–77; see as well the discussions on this topic in Chapter 6. Also see Ricardo Ortiz, "*Café, Culpa* and *Capital:* Nostalgic Addictions of Cuban Exile," *The Yale Journal of Criticism* 10.1 (1997): 63–84; and also *Cultural Erotics in Cuban America, 2007.*

14. I would like to thank Vasquez for her "polemic" at the 2007 New York Metro American Studies Association meeting at Columbia University, in which she called for a closer attention to the genesis of this "epic everyday" that generates a seemingly farcical "way of being so *trágica*" that marks Latina femininity in both racist stereotypes and the lived incarnations of embattled negotiations with white-identified and "proper" dominant society. See also Muñoz on notions of Latina/o affect and racist social formations ("Feeling Brown: Ethnicity and Affect in Ricardo Bracho's *The Sweetest Hangover (and other STDs)*" in *Theatre Journal* 52.1 (2000): 67–79). Chapter 6 discusses the work of Carmelita Tropicana, who also uses parody and exaggeration to underline the productive and astute critiques of dominant culture enabled by such performances of ethnic affect.

15. For an illuminating discussion of Latina writing and the role of such melancholic negotiations with an introjected but "lost" relation to the mother, see Benigno Trigo, *Remembering Maternal Bodies*.

16. See Greg Forter's "Against Melancholia" for his detailed analysis of the ways that recent efforts to "rehabilitate" the political valence of melancholy tend to be "strangely out of touch with the *affect* of melancholia," which Forter comments, "*feels* . . . about as far from freedom as it is possible to be" (139).

17. The "special period" is what Cubans call the years immediately following the fall of the Soviet Union—and the loss of Soviet economic support for Cuba. For most of the 1990s, Cuba experienced severe national privation that included widespread shortages of food and medicine. The U.S. trade embargo is understood to have played a central role in this economic crisis."

18. In *On Flirtation*, Adam Phillips's meditation on memory, forgetting, repeating, and contingency, he suggests that notions of "success"—such as valuing the "working through" of grief over the suspended state of melancholia—manifest individual relations to the past and to collective ways of seeing that past that define the individual relation to collective imperatives. Phillips suggests that one of the problems of "success" for individuals is how to revise the story/memory of their own past so that it can be made to coincide with "the ideals of our culture. Fantasies of success are given to us—our inheritance but not our invention—and, much like our gender identities, from which they are inextricable, constructed" (51).

Chapter 6

1. See M. Jacqui Alexander, "Not Just Any *Body* Can Be a Citizen: The Politics of Law, Sexuality and Postcoloniality in Trinidad and Tobago, and the Bahamas," *Feminist Review* 48 (Autumn 1994): 5–23.

2. See Gopinath's discussion of these heteropatriarchal underpinnings, especially in relation to the theories of Paul Gilroy in "'Bombay, U.K., Yuba City': Bhangra Music and the Engendering of Diaspora," *Diaspora: A Journal of Transnational Studies* 4.3 (1995): 303–22. Jasbir Puar has incisively critiqued the imbrication of "queer" diasporic cultural politics with nationalist projects and the Anglo-American hegemony of "rights" discussions and the uses of sexual identity in international politics. Jasbir Puar, "Global Circuits: Transnational Sexualities and Trinidad," *Signs* 26.4: 1039–66.

3. Bal further asserts that the edited volume, *Acts of Memory: Cultural Recall in the Present*, "is predicated" on this understanding of memory as productive integration of traumatic material. As in Chapter 5, these works all engage with other psychoanalytic understandings of the fantastic aspects of memory, individual or collective, and therefore of narrative and history. Fantasy in this sense is understood as "all those representations, beliefs, or bodily states that gravitate toward . . . the preservation of the status quo" (Abraham and Torok 1972, 125). See also Cathy Caruth, ed., *Trauma: Explorations in Memory*. Baltimore: Johns Hopkins University Press, 1995.

4. Hirsch refers to the context of the Holocaust to explain "the relationship of
    children of survivors of cultural and collective trauma to the experiences of
    their parents, experiences that they 'remember' only as the stories and images
    with which they grew up, but that are so powerful, so monumental, as to con-
    stitute memories in their own right" (1999, 8).

5. Even though Juani casts herself as a political observer—a lover, not a fighter—
    she is the one who ultimately explodes with a rage that is sparked by these polit-
    ical conflicts with Gina's Puerto Rican activist circle, who refer to her as a
    "gusano". "Gusano" literally means "worm" and was a term supposedly coined by
    Castro to refer to Cubans who left after the revolution, thus betraying the nation.

6. In contrast to such misrecognition, or "misidentification," Muñoz explicates a
    concept of "disidentification" as a liberatory strategy for minority subjects who
    "are outside the purview of dominant public spheres" and "encounter obstacles
    in enacting identifications" (8). Hence, "to disidentify is to read oneself and
    one's own life narrative in a moment, object, or subject that is not culturally
    coded to 'connect' with the disidentifying subject . . . it is the reworking of those
    [politically dubious and shameful] energies" (12). Or as Muñoz says later, it is
    to "desire . . . with a difference" (15).

7. In his hybrid critical piece "De un Pájaro las dos Alas: Travel Notes of a Queer
    Puerto Rican in Havana," Lawrence La Fountain-Stokes attests the limits of auto-
    biography through his mix of postmodern narrative pastiche and critical reflection
    in order to convey the emotional, economic, and political complexities of his own
    trip to Cuba and its significance in terms of queer travel, intra-Caribbean relations,
    the U.S. embargo, and other aspects of queer mobility and globalization.

8. Carmelita has discussed the emphasis in her work on a "Latina" perspective
    rather than a "Cuban" one. The inclusiveness of a non-nationally specific
    "latinidad" (Latin-ness) focuses on what is shared: language, media, and other
    commonalities of culture (Performance talk, Yale University, November 1, 2007).

9. María de los Angeles Torres chronicles the paradoxical effects of both govern-
    ments' cold war strategies and state policies, which have been implemented to
    divide Cuban exile communities in ways that refuse their possible claims of cit-
    izenship and belonging in Cuba, as well as in the United States (de los Angeles
    Torres 1999).

10. Yarbro-Bejarano suggests that such male-gendered embodiments by
    Tropicana work as "drag-on-drag metaperformances, in which the male roles
    are actually performed by Carmelita, not the actress playing Carmelita" (203).

11. Not coincidentally, Obejas's second novel Days of Awe (2001) chronicles the
    female protagonist's return to Cuba as a journey made in the shadow of her father,
    whose desires, friends, and links to Cuba preoccupy the narrative throughout.

12. Troyano is the performance artist's given name and the listed author of this
    collection of Tropicana's performance scripts. In her interview with Roman,
    Troyano/Tropicana emphasizes the deep psychic and cultural split between
    Carmelita and Alina, but the fact of the book yet again collapses this supposed
    distinction in Tropicana's work. Given such ambiguities, I have chosen to
    retain the name "Tropicana" to refer to both the main character and the
    "author" of her performance work.

Bibliography

Abraham, Nicolas, and Maria Torok. "Mourning or Melancholia: Introjection versus Incorporation." In *The Shell and the Kernal: Renewals of Psychoanalysis,* translated and edited by Nicolas Rand, 125–38. Chicago: University of Chicago Press, 1994.

Agamben, Griorgio. *The Coming Community.* Trans. Michael Hardt. Minneapolis: University of Minnesota Press, 1993.

Ahmed, Sara. *The Cultural Politics of Emotion.* New York: Routledge, 2004.

Alarcón, Daniel. *The Aztec Palimpsest: Mexico in the Modern Imagination.* Tucson: University of Arizona Press, 1997.

Alarcón, Norma. "Chicana Feminism: In the Tracks of 'the' Native Woman." *Cultural Studies* 4 (1990): 248–55.

———. "Cognitive Desires: An Allegory of/for Chicana Critics." In *Chicana (W)rites: On Word and Film,* edited by María Herrera-Sobek and Helena Viramontes. Berkeley: Third Woman Press, 1995.

———. "*Traddutora, Traditora*: A Paradigmatic Figure of Chicana Feminism." *Cultural Critique* 13 (1989): 57–87. Reprinted *Dangerous Liaisons: Gender, Nation, and Postcolonial Perspectives,* edited by Anne McClintock, Aamir Mufti, and Ella Shohat, 278–97. Minneapolis: University of Minnesota Press, 1997.

Aldama, Frederick. *Postethnic Narrative Criticism: Magicorealism in Oscar "Zeta" Acosta, Ana Castillo, Julie Dash, Hanif Kureishi, and Salman Rushdie.* Austin: University of Texas Press, 2003.

Alexander, M. Jacqui. "Not Just Any Body Can Be a Citizen: The Politics of Law, Sexuality and Postcoloniality in Trinidad, Tobago, and the Bahamas." *Feminist Review* 48 (1994): 5–23.

Alvarez, Julia. *¡Yo!* New York: Plume Books, 1997.

———. *How the García Girls Lost Their Accents.* New York: Plume Books, 1991.

Alvarez-Borland, Isabel. "'A Reminiscent Memory': Lezama, Zoé Valdés, and Rilke's Island." *Modern Language Notes* 119 (2004): 344–62.

Anzaldúa, Gloria. *Borderlands/La Frontera: The New Mestiza.* San Francisco: Spinsters/Aunt Lute Book Company, 1987.

Aparicio, Frances, and Susana Chávez-Silverman, eds. *Tropicalizations: Transcultural Representations of Latinidad.* Hanover: Dartmouth University Press, 1997.

Arguedas, José. *Los ríos profundos.* Translated as *Deep Rivers* by Frances Barraclough. Austin: University of Texas Press, 1978.

Arnold, Ellen. "Listening to the Spirits: An Interview with Leslie Marmon Silko." *Studies in American Indian Literatures* 10.3 (1998): 1–33.

Arrizón, Alicia. *Latina Performance: Traversing the Stage*. Bloomington: Indiana University Press, 1999.

Avelar, Idelbar. *The Untimely Present: Postdictatorial Latin American Fiction and the Task of Mourning*. Durham: Duke University Press, 1999.

Bakhtin, Mikhail. *The Dialogic Imagination: Four Essays*. Translated by Caryl Emerson and Michael Holquist. Austin: University of Texas Press, 1981.

———. *Speech Genres and Other Late Essays*. Translated by Vern McGee. Austin: University of Texas Press, 1986.

Bal, Mieke. "Introduction." In *Acts of Memory: Cultural Recall in the Present,* edited by Mieke Bal, Jonathan Crewe, and Leo Spitzer, ii–xvii. Hanover: University Press of New England, 1999.

Balibar, Etienne. *Masses, Classes, Ideas: Studies on Politics and Philosophy before and after Marx*. New York: Routledge, 1994.

Belausteguigoitia, Marisa. "Rebeliones en la frontera sur: las mujeres y la construcción de la ciudadanía en los limites de la nación." In *Fronteras, violencia, justicia: nuevos discursos,* edited by Marisa Belausteguigoitia y Lucía Melgar, 177–208. Mexico City: Universidad Nacional Autónoma de México, 2007.

Belausteguigoitia, Marisa. "Zapatista Women: Place-Based Struggles and the Search for Autonomy." In *Women and the Politics of Place,* edited by Wendy Harcourt and Arturo Escobar, 190–205. New York: Kumarin Press, 2005.

———, and Araceli Mingo, eds. *Géneros Prófugos: Feminismo y educación*. Mexico City: Editorial Paidós Mexicana, S. A. and Programa Univesitario de Estudios de Género, UNAM, 1999.

Bell, Virginia. "Counter-Chronicling and Alternative Mapping in *Memoria del fuego* and *Almanac of the Dead.*" *Multi-Ethnic Literatures of the United States* 25.3/4 (2000): 5–30.

Beltrán, Rosa. *América sin americanismos: El lugar del estilo en la épica*. Mexico City: Facultad de Filosofía y Letras, Universidad Nacional Autónoma de México, 1996.

Benjamin, Walter. *The Origin of Tragic German Drama*. Translated by John Osborne. London: Verso Press, 1998.

Benz, Stephen. "Through the Tropical Looking Glass: The Motif of Resistance in U.S. Literature on Central America." In *Tropicalizations: Transcultural Representations of Latinidad,* edited by Frances Aparicio and Susana Chávez-Silverman, 51–66. Hanover: Dartmouth University Press, 1997.

Bianco, Jaime. "Zones of Morbidity and Necropolitics." *Rhizomes* (8 spring 2004). http://www.rhizomes.net/issue8/bianco.htm.

Bingham, Ann. "Productions of Geographic Scale and Capitalist-Colonialist Enterprise in Silko's *Almanac of the Dead.*" *Modern Fiction Studies* 50.2 (2004): 304–31.

Booth, Wayne. *The Rhetoric of Fiction*. Chicago: University of Chicago Press, 1961.

Brown, Bill. "The Dark Wood of Postmodernity (Space, Faith, Allegory)." *Publications of the Modern Language Association of America* 120.3 (2005): 734–50.

Brown, Wendy. *States of Injury: Power and Freedom in Late Modernity*. Princeton: Princeton University Press, 1995.

Burdell, Linda. "Writing Cultural Identity: Strategies for Authorizing Difference." *Cincinnati Romance Review* 16 (1997): 31–37.

Butler, Judith. *Bodies That Matter: On the Discursive Limits of "Sex."* New York: Routledge, 1993.

———. *The Psychic Life of Power: Theories in Subjection.* Palo Alto: Stanford University Press, 1997.

Carby, Hazel. "Figuring the Future in Los(t) Angeles" *Comparative American Studies* 1.1 (2003): 19–34.

Caruth, Cathy, ed. *Trauma: Explorations in Memory.* Baltimore: Johns Hopkins University Press, 1995.

Castellanos, Rosario. *Oficio de tinieblas.* Mexico City: Editorial Planeta Mexicana, 1962. Translated as *The Book of Lamentations* by Esther Allen. New York: Penguin Books, 1988.

———. *Balún Canán.* Mexico City: Fonde de Cultura Económica, 1957. Translated as *The Nine Guardians* by Irene Nicholson. Columbia, Louisiana: Readers International, 1992.

Castillo, Debra. "Quez." "The Tropics of the Imagination: Quetzalcoatl and All That." In *Tropicalizations: Transcultural Representations of Latinidad,* edited by Frances Aparicio and Susana Chávez-Silverman, 67–98. Hanover: Dartmouth University Press, 1997.

———. "Rosario Castellanos: 'Ashes without a Face.'" In *De/Colonizing the Subject: The Politics of Gender in Women's Autobiography,* edited by Sidonie Smith and Julia Watson, 242–69. Minneapolis: University of Minnesota Press, 1992.

Chabram-Dernersesian, Angie. "I Throw Punches for My Race, but I Don't Want to Be a Man: Writing Us—Chica-nos (Girls, Us)/Chicanas—into the Movement Script." In *Cultural Studies,* edited and introduced by Lawrence Grossberg, 81–111. Routledge, 1992.

Chatman, Seymour. *Story and Discourse: Narrative Structure in Fiction and Film.* Ithaca: Cornell University Press, 1978.

Cheng, Anne Anlin. *The Melancholy of Race: Psychoanalysis, Assimilation, and Hidden Grief.* London: Oxford University Press, 2000.

Cherniavsky, Eva. "Tribalism, Globalism, and Eskimo Television in Leslie Marmon Silko's *Almanac of the Dead." Angelaki: Journal of the Theoretical Humanities* 6.1 (2001): 111–26.

Chow, Rey. "Where Have All the Natives Gone?" *Writing Diaspora: Tactics of Intervention in Contemporary Cultural Studies.* Bloomington: Indiana University Press, 1993.

———. *Ethics after Idealism: Theory-Culture-Ethnicity-Reading.* Bloomington: Indiana University Press, 1998.

———. *The Protestant Ethnic and the Spirit of Capitalism.* New York: Columbia University Press, 2002.

———. *The Age of the World Target: Self-Referentiality in War, Theory, and Comparative Work.* Durham: Duke University Press, 2006.

Cisneros, Sandra. *Woman Hollering Creek and Other Stories.* New York: Vintage Books, 1991.

Clough, Patricia. *Autoaffection: Unconscious Thought in the Age of Teletechnology.* Minneapolis: University of Minnesota Press, 2000.

———. "Future Matters: Technoscience, Global Politics, and Cultural Criticism" *Social Text* 22.3 (2004): 1–24.

———, edited with Jean Halley. *The Affective Turn: Theorizing the Social.* Durham: Duke University Press, 2007.

Coopan, Vilashini. "Mourning Becomes Kitsch: The Aesthetics of Loss in Severo Sarduy's *Cobra.*" In *Loss: The Politics of Mourning,* edited by David Eng and David Kazanjian, 251–77. Durham: Duke University Press, 2002.

Cornejo-Polar, Antonio. "Indigenist and Heterogeneous Literatures: Their Dual Sociocultural Status." *Latin American Perspectives* 16.2 (1989): 12–28.

———. "Mestizaje, Transculturation, Heterogeneity." *The Latin American Cultural Studies Reader,* edited by Ana del Sarto, Alicia Ríos, and Abril Trigo, 116–19. Durham: Duke University Press, 2004.

Cvetkovich, Ann. *An Archive of Feelings: Trauma, Sexuality, and Lesbian Public Cultures.* Durham: Duke University Press, 2003.

de la Campa, Román. "Comparative Latin American Studies: Literary and Cultural Theory." In *Comparative Cultural Studies and Latin America,* edited by Sophia McClennen and Earl Fitz, 56–67. West Lafayette: Purdue University Press, 2004.

de Lauretis, Teresa. *Alice Doesn't: Feminism, Semiotics, Cinema.* Bloomington: Indiana University Press, 1984.

———. *Technologies of Gender: Essays on Theory, Film, and Fiction.* Bloomington: Indiana University Press, 1987.

de Man, Paul. *Allegories of Reading: Figural Language in Rousseau, Nietzsche, Rilke, and Proust.* New Haven: Yale University Press, 1979.

Derrida, Jacques. "Law of Genre." Translated by Avital Ronell. *Critical Inquiry* 7.1 (1980): 55–81.

Elliott, Jane. *Popular Feminist Fiction as American Allegory: Representing National Time.* New York: Palgrave Macmillan Press, 2008.

Eng, David, and David Kazanjian, eds and intro. *Loss: The Politics of Mourning.* Durham: Duke University Press, 2002.

Espinoza, Dionne. "Women of Color and Identity Politics: Translating Theory, *Haciendo Teoría.*" In *Other Sisterhoods: Literary Theory and U.S. Women of Color,* edited by Sandra Stanley, 44–62. Urbana: University of Illinois Press, 1998.

Fanon, Frantz. "On National Culture." In *The Wretched of the Earth,* translated by Constance Farrington, 206–48. New York: Grove Press, 1963.

———. *Black Skin, White Mask.* New York: Grove Press, 1967.

Felman, Shoshana. "Education and Crisis, or the Vicissitudes of Teaching." In *Trauma: Explorations in Memory,* edited by Cathy Caruth, 13–60. Baltimore: Johns Hopkins University Press, 1995.

Felski, Rita. *The Gender of Modernity.* Cambridge: Harvard University Press, 1995.

Fletcher, Angus. *Allegory: The Theory of a Symbolic Mode.* Ithaca: Cornell University Press, 1964.

Forter, Greg. "Against Melancholia: Contemporary Mourning Theory, Fitzgerald's *The Great Gatsby,* and the Politics of Unfinished Grief." *differences: A Journal of Feminist Cultural Studies* 14.2 (2003): 134–70.

Fox, Claire. "Comparative Literary Studies of the Americas." *American Literature* 76.4 (2004): 871–86.

Franco, Jean. *The Modern Culture of Latin America.* London: Penguin Books, 1967.

———. *The Decline and Fall of the Lettered City: Latin America in the Cold War.* Cambridge: Harvard University Press, 2002.

Freeman, Elizabeth. "Packing History, Count(er)ing Generations" *New Literary History* 31 (2000): 727–44.

Freud, Sigmund. "The Uncanny." In vol. 17 (1919) of *The Standard Edition of the Complete Psychological Works of Sigmund Freud,* edited and translated by James Strachey, 217–56. London: Hogarth Press, 1955.

———. "Mourning and Melancholia." In vol. 14 (1914) of *The Standard Edition of the Complete Psychological Works of Sigmund Freud,* edited and translated by James Strachey, 237–58. London: Hogarth Press, 1957.

Fregoso, Rosa, and Angie Chabram. "Introduction: Chicana/o Cultural Representations: Reframing Alternative Critical Discourses" *Cultural Studies* (2001): 203–12.

Fusco, Coco, and Brian Wallis, eds. *Only Skin Deep: Changing Visions of the American Self.* New York: International Center of Photography/Harry N. Abrams, Inc., Publishers, 2003.

Ganguly, Keya. "Migrant Identities and the Constructions of Selfhood." *Cultural Studies* 6.1 (1992): 27–50.

García-Moreno, Laura. Review of Idelbar Avelar's *The Untimely Present. Bryn Mawr Review of Comparative Literature* 2.2 (2001).

Genette, Gerard. *Narrative Discourse: An Essay on Method.* Translated by Jane Lewin. Ithaca: Cornell University Press, 1980.

Golubov, Nattie. "Feeding on Alterity: Reading in a Knowledge Society." *Trans: Revue de littérature générale et comparée* 4 (2007). http://trans.univ-paris3.fr/.

González-Abellas, Miguel. "'Aquella isla': Introducción al universo narrativo de Zoé Valdés." *Hispania* 83 (2000): 42–50.

Gopinath, Gayatri. "'Bombay, U.K., Yuba City': Bhangra Music and the Engendering of Diaspora." *Diaspora: A Journal of Transnational Studies* 4.3 (1995): 303–22.

Gordon, Avery. *Ghostly Matters: Haunting and the Sociological Imagination.* Minneapolis: University of Minnesota Press, 1997.

Greene, Shane. NACLA Report on the Americas, Jan–Feb, 2005. 34–39.

Hallward, Peter. *Absolutely Postcolonial: Writing between the Singular and the Specific.* Manchester: Manchester University Press, 2001.

Hansen, Mark. "Digitalizing the Racialized Body, or The Politics of Universal Address." *SubStance: A Review of Theory and Literary Criticism* 33.2 (2004): 107–33.

Hariman, Robert. "Allegory and Democratic Public Culture in the Postmodern Era." *Philosophy and Rhetoric* 35.4 (2002): 267–96.

Harper, Jorjet. 1996. "Dancing to a Different Beat: An Interview with Achy Objeas (Lesbian Hispanic Writer)." *Lambda Book Report* 5.2: 1–4.

Hirsch, Marianne. "Projected Memory: Holocaust Photographs in Personal and Public Fantasy." In *Acts of Memory: Cultural Recall in the Present,* edited by

Mieke Bal, Jonathan Crewe, and Leo Spitzer, 3–23. Hanover: University Press of New England, 1999.

Honig, Bonnie. "Difference, Dilemmas, and the Politics of Home." *Social Research* 61.3 (1994): 563–98.

Hutcheon, Linda. *Irony's Edge: The Theory and Politics of Irony.* New York: Routledge, 1994.

Irr, Caren. "The Timeliness of *Almanac of the Dead*, or a Postmodern Rewriting of Radical Fiction." In *Leslie Marmon Silko: A Collection of Critical Essays*, edited by Louise K. Barnett and James L. Thorson, 223–44. Albuquerque: University of New Mexico Press, 1999.

JanMohammed, Abdul. *Manichean Aesthetics: The Politics of Literature in Colonial Africa.* Amherst: University of Massachusetts Press, 1983.

———. "The Economy of Manichean Allegory: The Function of Racial Difference in Colonialist Literature." *Critical Inquiry* 12.1 (1985): 59–87.

Jameson, Fredric. *The Political Unconscious: Narrative as a Socially Symbolic Act.* Ithaca: Cornell University Press, 1981.

———. "Third World Literature in the Era of Multinational Capitalism." *Social Text* 15 (1986): 65–88.

———. "On Cultural Studies." In *The Identity in Question*, edited by John Rajchman, 251–95. New York: Routledge, 1995.

Johnson, David, and Scott Michaelson, eds. "Border Secrets: An Introduction." In *Border Theory: The Limits of Cultural Politics*, 1–39. Minneapolis: Minnesota University Press, 1997.

Joseph, Miranda. *Against the Romance of Community.* Minneapolis: Minnesota University Press, 2002.

Kaplan, Caren. *Questions of Travel: Postmodern Discourses of Displacement.* Durham: Duke University Press, 1996.

———, Norma Alarcón, and Minoo Moallem, eds. and intro. *Between Woman and Nation: Nationalisms, Transnational Feminisms, and the State.* Durham: Duke University Press, 1999.

Kaplan, Ann. "Traumatic Contact Zones and Embodied Translators, with Reference to Australian Texts." In *Trauma and Cinema: Cross-Cultural Explorations*, edited by E. Ann Kaplan and Ban Wang. Hong Kong: Hong Kong University Press, 2004.

Kaup, Monika. "Becoming Baroque: Folding European Forms into the New World Baroque with Alejo Carpentier." *CR: The New Centennial Review* 5.2 (2005): 107–49.

———. "Neobaroque: Latin America's Alternative Modernity." *Comparative Literature* 58.2 (2006): 128–52.

Keith, Michael, and Steve Pile. "Introduction Part 1: The Politics of Place . . ." In *Place and the Politics of Identity*, edited by Michael Keith and Steve Pile, 1–21. New York: Routledge, 1993.

Kutzinski, Vera. "Borders and Bodies: The United States, America, and the Caribbean." *CR: The New Centennial Review* 1.2 (2001): 55–88.

La Fountain-Stokes, Lawrence. "*De un pájaro las dos alas:* Travel Notes of a Queer Puerto Rican in Havana." *GLQ: A Journal of Lesbian and Gay Studies* 8.1–2 (2002): 7–33.

Lowe, Lisa. *Immigrant Acts: On Asian American Cultural Politics*. Durham: Duke University Press, 1996.

Leys, Ruth. *Trauma: A Genealogy*. Chicago: University of Chicago Press, 2000.

Lubiano, Wahmeena. "Black Ladies, Welfare Queens, and State Minstrels: Ideological War by Narrative Means." In *Race-ing Justice, En-gendering Power: Essays on Anita Hill, Clarence Thomas, and the Construction of Social Reality*, edited by Toni Morrison, 323–63. New York: Pantheon Books, 1992.

Madsen, Deborah. *Rereading Allegory: A Narrative Approach to Genre*. Macmillan Press, 1995.

Mardorossian, Carine. *Reclaiming Difference: Caribbean Women Rewrite Postcolonialism*. Charlottesville: University of Virginia Press, 2005.

Mariátegui, José. *Siete ensayos de interpretación de la realidad peruana*. 1928. Lima: Biblioteca Amauta, 1973.

Martin, Biddy. "Lesbian Identity and Autobiographical Difference[s]." In *Life/Lines: Theorizing Women's Autobiography*, edited by Bella Brodzki and Celeste Schenck, 77–103. Ithaca: Cornell University Press, 1988.

———, and Chandra Mohanty. "Feminist Politics: What's Home Got to Do with It?" In *Feminist Studies/Critical Studies*, edited by Teresa de Lauretis, 191–212. Bloomington: Indiana University Press, 1986.

Martínez-San Miguel, Yolanda. "Balun Canan y la pespectiva feminina como traductora/traidora de la historia." *Revista de Estudios Hispánicos* 22 (1995): 165–83.

———. *Caribe Two Ways: Cultura de la migración en el Caribe insular hispánico*. San Juan: Ediciones Callejón, 2003.

Mbembe, Achille. *On the Postcolony*. Translated by A. Berrett, Janet Roitman, Muray Last, and Steven Rendall. Berkeley: University of California Press, 2001.

———. "Necropolitics." Translated by Libby Meintjes. *Public Culture* 15.1 (2003): 11–40.

McClennen, Sophia. *The Dialectics of Exile: Nation, Time, Language, and Space in Hispanic Literatures*. West Lafayette: Purdue University Press, 2004.

McCullough, Kate. "'Marked by Genetics and Exile': Narrativizing Transnational Sexualities in *Memory Mambo*." *GLQ: A Journal of Lesbian and Gay Studies* 6.4 (2000): 577–608.

Mirzoeff, Nicholas. "The Shadow and the Substance: Race, Photography, and the Index." In *Only Skin Deep: Changing Visions of the American Self*, edited by Coco Fusco and Brian Wallis, 111–28. New York: International Center of Photography/Harry N. Abrams, Inc., Publishers, 2003.

Moraga, Cherríe. *Loving in the War Years: Lo que nunca pasó por sus labios*. Boston: South End Press, 1983.

———. *The Last Generation*. Boston: South End Press, 1993.

Moraña, Mabel. "Baroque/Neobaroque/Ultrabaroque: Disruptive Readings of Modernity." *Hispanic Baroques: Reading Cultures in Context*. Edited by Nicholas Spadaccini and Luis Martín-Esudillo, 241–82. Nashville: Vanderbilt University Press, 2005.

Moya, Paula. "Chicana Feminism and Postmodernist Theory." *Signs* 26.2 (2001): 441–83.

———. "Postmodernism, 'Realism,' and the Politics of Identity: Cherrié Moraga and Chicana Feminism." In *Feminist Genealogies, Colonial Legacies, Democratic Futures,* edited by M. Jacqui Alexander and Chandra Mohanty, 125–50. New York: Routledge, 1996.

Muñoz, José. "Feeling Brown: Ethnicity and Affect in Ricardo Bracho's *The Sweetest Hangover (and Other STDs)." Theatre Journal* 52.1 (2000): 67–79.

———. *Disidentifications: Queers of Color and the Performance of Politics.* Minneapolis: University of Minnesota Press, 1999.

———. "*No es fácil:* Notes on the Negotiation of Cubanidad and Exilic Memory in Carmelita Tropicana's 'Milk of Amnesia'" *The Drama Review* 39.3 (1995): 76–83.

Murrin, Michael. *The Veil of Allegory: Some Notes toward a Theory of Allegorical Rhetoric in the English Renaissance.* Chicago: University of Chicago Press, 1969.

Navarro, Consuelo. "Sexualidad femenina y patriarcado en *Oficio de tinieblas* de Rosario Castellanos". *Explicación de textos literarios* 31.1 (2002–03): 29–37.

Niemann, Linda. "Narratives of Survival: Linda Niemann Interviews Leslie Marmon Silko." *Women's Review of Books* 9 (1992).

Norell, Brenda. "Apaches Rise to Defend Homelands from Homeland Security." In *Americas Program, Center for International Policy* (CIP) online newsletter. January 10, 2008. http://www.Américas.irc-online.org.

Noriega, Chon. "Editor's Introduction: Very Good with the Tongue." In *I, Carmelita Tropicana: Performing between Culture* by Alina Troyano, iv–xii. New York: Beacon Press, 2000.

Obejas, Achy. *We Came All the Way from Cuba So You Could Dress Like This?* Pittsburgh: Cleis Press, 1994.

———. *Memory Mambo.* Pittsburgh: Cleis Press, 1996.

———. *Days of Awe.* New York: Ballantine Press, 2001.

O'Connell, Joanna. *Prospero's Daughter: The Prose of Rosario Castellanos.* Austin: University of Texas Press, 1995.

Oliver, Kelly. *Witnessing: Beyond Recognition.* Minneapolis: University of Minnesota Press, 2001.

Ortiz, Ricardo. *Cultural Erotics in Cuban America.* Minneapolis: University of Minnesota Press, 2007.

———. "Café, Culpa and Capital: Nostalgic Addictions of Cuban Exile" *Yale Journal of Criticism* 10.1 (1997): 63–84.

Patton, Cindy, and Benigno Sánchez-Eppler. "Introduction: With a Passport Out of Eden." In *Queer Diasporas,* edited by Cindy Patton and Benigno Sánchez-Eppler. Durham: Duke University Press, 2000.

Pérez Firmat, Gustavo. *Life on the Hyphen: The Cuban-American Way.* Austin: University of Texas Press, 1994.

Perez-Torres, Rafael. "Ethnicity, Ethics, and Latino Aesthetics." *American Literary History* 12.3 (2000): 534–53.

———. *Mestizaje: Critical Uses of Race in Chicano Culture.* St. Paul: University of Minnesota Press, 2006.

Phelan, James. *Living to Tell about It: A Rhetoric and Ethics of Character Narration.* Ithaca: Cornell University Press, 2005.

Phelan, Peggy. *Unmarked: The Politics of Performance*. New York: Routledge, 1993.

Phillips, Adam. *On Flirtation: Psychoanalytic Essays on the Uncommitted Life*. Cambridge: Harvard University Press, 1994.

Povinelli, Elizabeth. "Settler Modernity and the Quest for an Indigenous Tradition." *Public Culture* 11.1 (1999): 19–48.

Pratt, Mary. *Imperial Eyes: Travel Writing and Transculturation*. London: Routledge, 1992.

Prince, Gerald. *Dictionary of Narratology*. Lincoln: University of Nebraska Press, 1987.

Prosser, Jay. *Second Skin: The Body Narratives of Transsexuality*. New York: Columbia University Press, 1998.

Puar, Jasbir. "Global Circuits: Transnational Sexualities and Trinidad." *Signs* 26.4 (2001): 1039–66.

———. "Queer Times, Queer Assemblages." *Social Text* 84–85 (2005): 121–40.

———. *Terrorist Assemblages: Homonationalism in Queer Times*. Durham: Duke University Press, 2007.

Quintana, Alvina. *Home Girls: Chicana Literary Voices*. Philadelphia: Temple University Press, 1996.

Rama, Angel. *Transculturación narrativa en América Latina*. Mexico City: Siglo XXI, 1982.

Ramírez, Liliana. *Entre fronteras latinoamericanos y literaturas: Balún Canán, Dreaming in Cuban, y Chambacú*. Bogotá: Editorial Pontificia Universidad Javeriana, 2006.

Reagon, Bernice. "Coalition Politics: Turning the Century." In *Home Girls: A Black Feminist Anthology*, edited by Barbara Smith, 356–68. New York: Kitchen Table Press, 1983.

Richard, Nelly. *The Insubordination of Signs: Political Change, Cultural Transformation, and Poetics of Crisis*. Translated by Alice Nelson and Silvia Tandeciarz. Durham: Duke University Press, 2004.

Richardson, Brian. *Unnatural Voices: Extreme Narration in Modern and Contemporary Fiction*. Columbus: The Ohio State University Press, 2006.

Riley, Denise. *The Words of Selves: Identification, Solidarity, Irony*. Stanford: Stanford University Press, 2000.

Rios, Katherine. "'And You Know What I Have to Say Isn't Always Pleasant': Translating the Unspoken Word in Cisneros' *Woman Hollering Creek*." In *Chicana (W)rites on Word and Film*, edited by María Herrera-Sobek and Helena Viramontes, 200–23. Berkeley: Third Woman Press, 1995.

Roman, David. "Carmelita Tropicana Unplugged." *The Drama Review* 39.3 (1995): 83–94.

Romero, Lora. 1993. "'When Something Goes Queer': Familiarity, Formalism, and Minority Intellectuals in the 1980s." *The Yale Journal of Criticism* 6.1 (1993): 121–41.

Roof, Judith. *Come as You Are: Sexuality and Narrative*. New York: Columbia University Press, 1996.

Saldaña-Portillo, María. *The Revolutionary Imagination in the Americas and the Age of Development*. Durham: Duke University Press, 2003.

Sanchez, Marta. "La Malinche at the Intersection of Race and Gender in *Down These Mean Streets.*" *Publications of the Modern Language Association of America* 113.1 (1998): 117–28.

Sánchez, Rosaura. "Reconstructing Chicana Gender Identity." *American Literary History* 9.2 (1997): 350–63.

Schein, Louisa. "Diaspora Politics, Homeland Erotics, and the Materializing of Memory." *Positions: East Asia Cultures Critique* 7.3 (1999): 697–730.

Shih, Shu-Mei. "Global Literature and the Technologies of Recognition." *Publications of the Modern Language Association of America* 119.1 (2004): 16–30.

Silko, Leslie Marmon. *Almanac of the Dead.* New York: Penguin Books, 1991.

Simmons, Danny, ed. *Russell Simmons Def Poetry Jam on Broadway . . . and More.* New York: Atria Books, 2003.

Singh, Amritjit, and Peter Schmidt, eds. and intro. "On the Borders between U.S. Studies and Postcolonial Theory." *Postcolonial Theory and the United States: Race, Ethnicity, and Literature.* Jackson: University Press of Mississippi, 2000.

Sommer, Doris. *Foundational Fictions: The National Romances of Latin America.* Berkeley: University of California Press, 1991.

————. *Proceed with Caution, When Engaged by Minority Writing in the Americas.* Cambridge: Harvard University Press, 1999.

Sommers, Joseph. "El ciclo de Chiapas: Nueva corriente literaria." *Cuadernos Americanos* 133 (1964): 246–61.

————. "Rosario Castellanos: Nuevo enfoque del indio mexicano." *La Palabra y el Hombre* 8 (1964): 83–88.

————. "Forma e ideología en *Oficio de tinieblas* de Rosario Castellanos." *Revista de Crítica Literaria Latinoamericana* 7–8 (1978): 73–91.

————. "Literatura e historia: Las contradicciones de la ficción indigenista." *Revista de Crítica Literaria* 10 (1979): 9–39.

Spitta, Silvia. *Between Two Waters: Narratives of Transculturation in Latin America.* Houston: Rice University Press, 1995.

Spivak, Gayatri. *Death of a Discipline.* New York: Columbia University Press, 2003.

Stoler, Ann. *Race and the Education of Desire: Foucault's History of Sexuality and the Colonial Order of Things.* Durham: Duke University Press, 1995.

Sugg, Katherine. "'I Would Rather Be Dead': Nostalgia and Narrative in Jamaica Kincaid's *Lucy.*" *Narrative* 10.2 (2002): 156–73.

————. "Migratory Sexualities, Diasporic Histories, and Memory in Queer Cuban-American Cultural Production," Special topic issue on "Sexuality and Space," edited by Jasbir Puar, Dereka Rushbook, and Louisa Schein. *Environment and Planning-D: Society and Space* 21 (2003): 461–77.

————. "'The Ultimate Rebellion': Chicana Narratives of Sexuality and Community." *Meridians: Feminism, Race, Transnationalism* 3.2 (2003): 139–70.

————. "Literatures of the Americas, *Latinidad,* and the Re-formation of Multi-Ethnic Literatures." *Multi-Ethnic Literatures of the United States* 29.3/4 (2004): 227–42.

Suleiman, Susan. *Authoritarian Fictions: The Ideological Novel as a Literary Genre.* Princeton: Princeton University Press, 1983.

Taylor, Diana. *The Archive and the Repertoire: Performing Cultural Memory in the Americas.* Durham: Duke University Press, 2003.

———. "Remapping Genre through Performance: From 'American' to 'Hemispheric' Studies." *Publications of the Modern Language Association of America* (2007): 1416–30.

———, and Roselyn Constantino, eds. *Holy Terrors: Latin American Women Perform.* Durham: Duke University Press, 2003.

Tierney-Tello, Mary. *Allegories of Transgression and Transformation; Experimental Fiction by Women Writing under Dictatorship.* New York: State University of New York Press, 1996.

Thomas, Brook. "Civic Multiculturalism and the Myth of Liberal Consent: A Comparative Analysis." *CR: The New Centennial Review* 1.3 (2001): 1–35.

Torres, María de los Angeles. *In the Land of Mirrors: Cuban Exile Politics in the United States.* Ann Arbor: University of Michigan Press, 1999.

Trigo, Benigno. *Remembering Maternal Bodies: Melancholy in Latina and Latin American Women's Writing.* New York: Palgrave Macmillan, 2006.

Troyano, Alina. *I, Carmelita Tropicana: Performing between Cultures.* Boston: Beacon Press, 2000.

Trujillo,Carla. "Chicana Lesbians: Fear and Loathing in the Chicano Community." In *Chicana Lesbians: The Girls Our Mothers Warned Us About,* edited by Carla Trujillo, 186–94. Berkeley: Third Woman Press, 1991.

Valdés, Zoé. *Café Nostalgia.* Barcelona: Actes Sud, 1997.

———. *La nada cotidiana.* Barcelona: Actes Sud, 1995. Translated as *Yocandra in the Paradise of Nada* by Sabina Cienfuegos. New York: Arcade Press, 1997.

———. *Te dí la vida entera.* Barcelona: Actes Sud, 1996. Translated as *I Gave You All I Had* by Nadia Benabid. New York: Arcade Press, 1999.

Villarejo, Amy. "Activist Technologies: Think Again!" *Social Text* 22.3 (2004): 133–50.

Williams, Raymond. *Marxism and Literature.* Oxford: Oxford University Press, 1977.

Yarbro-Bejarano, Yvonne. "Gloria Anzaldúa's *Borderlands/La Frontera:* Cultural Studies, 'Difference,' and the Non-Unitary Subject." *Cultural Critique* (1994): 5–28.

———. "Traveling Transgressions: *Cubanidad* in Performances by Carmelita Tropicana and Marga Gómez." *Reading and Writing the Ambiente: Queer Sexualities in Latino, Latin American, and Spanish Culture.* Madison: University of Wisconsin Press, 2000.

Zamora, Hilly. "La memoria del exilio y el abismo de la destruccion en *Café Nostalgia* de Zoé Valdés." *Expicación de Textos Literarios* 28.1–2 (1999–2000): 125–32.

Zamora, Lois. *Writing the Apocalypse: Historical Vision in Contemporary U.S. and Latin American Fiction.* New York: Cambridge University Press, 1989.

———. *The Inordinate Eye: New World Baroque and Latin American Fiction.* Chicago: University of Chicago Press, 2006.

Zebadúa-Yañez, Verónica. "Killing as Performance: Violence and the Shaping of Community." In *E-Mespherica* (2005).

Index

affect: collective affect, 9, 15, 137, 143,
196n4; identity and, 11–2, 197n11;
melancholy and, 24–6; named
emotions and, 202n51; narrative
techniques and, 71, 75; as
political logic, xiv; production of
affectlessness, 88; social control and,
12, 197n14. *See also* structures of
feeling
Agamben, Giorgio, 10–1, 73, 205n7
Ahmad, Aijaz, 31
Ahmed, Sara, viii, 4, 45, 159, 202n51
Aidoo, Ama Ata, 208–9n34
Alarcón, Norma, 35, 40, 65, 203n9
Aldama, Frederick Luis, 36, 202–3n57
allegory: allegorical logic, x, xiii, 4–5, 7,
32, 33–4, 98; allegorical pedagogy,
vii, 77, 93, 206n14; allegorical
representation, 69, 80, 202n56;
allegorical revolution, vii, 76, 79–87,
133; characterization in, 78–9, 88,
175, 183; ethnographic allegory, 31;
gender and, x, 35, 41, 50, 164, 176;
genre theories of, 3, 29, 30, 32–3, 42,
201n48; history and, 30, 31, 32, 78,
90, 206n15, 208n33; identity and,
29–30, 73–4, 75–6, 87–90, 137,
205n9; memory and, 141, 156, 161,
175, 183; "not-knowing" status of
characters, 175, 183; prophecy and,
xiii, 67–9, 71–2, 77, 206n14;
redemption in, 94–7; social
transformation and, x–xii, 69. *See
also* apocalyptic narrative;
Benjamin, Walter; Jameson,

Frederic; *La Malinche*; Manichean
allegory; Third World allegory
Almanac of the Dead (Silko):
allegorical revolution in, vii, 76,
79–87; allegory and, 73–4, 75–6,
87–90, 205n9; apocalypse and, 94–7;
"bare life" in, 73; cultural critique
in, 72–3; feminine characters, 91–3;
indirect discourse in, 87, 90;
intradiegetic "almanac" device in,
75, 80–1, 90, 93; irony/hyperbole in,
4, 32, 71, 77–8, 205n6; narrative
pedagogies of, vii, 6, 68–9, 73, 74–5,
77–9, 81, 91–3, 206n16; overlapping
narratives/genres in, 70, 71–2, 43–94,
207n20; parable of the
Gunadeeyahs, 97; as prophecy, 67–9,
71–2, 77, 80–1, 206n14; racial
ontology in, 76, 79, 103; realism
and, 69–70, 205n5; sexuality in,
208n27; transamerican dead zones
in, 72–5, 96, 123; tribal
epistemology in, 68, 75–6. *See also*
Manichean allegory
Althusser, Louis, 21
Alvarez, Julia, 136, 164, 175–6
Alvarez-Borland, Isabel, 139, 141, 150
Anzaldúa, Gloria: allegorical practices
in, 30, 65; on Chicana lesbian
identity, 39, 41, 164; Chicana
multiplicity/fragmentation in, 61–2;
on Chicana/o racial genealogies, 58;
on Chicana/o stereotype, 27; on the
pocho (cultural traitor), 42; sexual
transgression in, 63, 166–7

apocalyptic narrative: allegory and, 68–9, 76–81; meaning/ending conjunction in, 209n35; reader/ witness role in, 98–9, 133, 212n26; revolutionary time in, 83; teleology and, 94–7
Arendt, Hannah, 73, 205n7
Arguedas, José Marie, 107, 110, 113–4, 210n14
assemblage, 9, 12, 197n12, 197–8n15, 200n34
assimilation: Chicana/o identity and, 52–3, 58, 65; diaspora and, 165, 187; discourse of contamination and, 27–8; *indigenista* literature and, 109; transculturation compared with, 110. *See also* belonging/betrayal; transculturation
authenticity: ethnonationalist cultural purity, 206n11; Euro-American Otherness, 105–6; *indigenismo*, 57–61; indigenous groups as precontact other, 105, 198n19, 204–5n2, 211n17; preassimilationist past, 27–8; revised ethnicity and, 44; ventriloquistic voicing, 102
autobiography, 8–9, 69, 142–5, 215n7
Avelar, Idelbar: on allegory as resistance, 5, 7, 31–4; cultural critique in, 72–3; on ironic narrative, 35; on Latin American literature, 200n37; on literary imagination, 79; on mourning, 26–7, 206n16, 207n18; on narrativity in allegory, xii–xiii; sexual violence/trauma in, 65; on *testimonio*, 200–201n38, 202n50

Bakhtin, Mikhail, 18–20, 26–7, 102–4, 148, 209n2, 211n20. *See also* dialogism
Bal, Mieke, 168, 215n3
Balibar, Etienne, 51–2
baroque, xii, 5, 36, 79, 81, 88–9, 207n21, 208n30, 208n32
Belausteguigoitia, Marisa, xiii, 209n3

belonging/betrayal: Chicana sexuality and, 39, 41, 44, 52, 164; community and, 39, 42, 54, 63, 201n39; *gusano* term and, 215n5; *La Malinche* and, 40, 49–50, 52; sexuality of displacement and, 179–80; sexual transgression and, 166–70, 174–5; shame, 56, 58–9; *vendidas* (sell-outs), 53. *See also* community
Benjamin, Walter: on the aesthetics of ruins, 90, 207n21, 208n33; on allegorical representation, 69, 202n56; on the allegorical subject, 88–9; on allegory as reductive, 201n48; on allegory criticism, 30; on baroque allegory, xiii, 4–5, 80–1, 207n21, 208n30; on epistemological crisis, 33, 35; on history, xii, 31, 90, 206n15; on identity, 18; melancholia and, 144–5; on narrative pedagogy, 77; on redemption in allegory, 94, 96–7
Bhabha, Homi, 117
Bianco, Jamie Skye, 75, 143
bicultural body, 56–7
binary paradigms, 8
biopolitics, 10, 12
biopower, 19, 21, 22, 34, 195n3 (Preface), 196n5, 197n14, 199n28
Blount, Rosie Molano, viii
body: control of affect and, 197n14; feminine body, 91–2; instrumentalization of life, 73; racialized body, 11–2, 27–8, 56–7; visibly marked body, 10–2
Booth, Wayne, 213n9
borders/boundaries: *Almanac* critique of, 81–2; Anzaldüa on, 30; Ciudad Juárez femicides and, 73–4, 82; Mexico-U.S. border, viii, 71, 73, 83; national sovereignty and, 85; racial contact zones in *Oficio*, 102; racialized body as, 28; racial melancholia and, 25; threshold areas, 73, 82
Brown, Bill, x, 33, 206n16

Brown, Wendy, xi, 20–1, 59, 202n54
Burdell, Linda, 106, 108–9, 118, 130

Café Nostalgia (Valdés): depiction of
    reading, 146–8, 154–5; as diaspora
    novel, 136–8, 153–5, 212n2, 213n10;
    exilic romance in, 151–2, 155–6,
    172; exilic subjectivity in, 21, 137,
    139, 160–1; interior texts in,
    149–152, 160–1; nostalgia/memory
    in, 143–7, 157–9, 161; political
    stance of, 136
"camp" performative genre, 185
capitalism: affective control and, 10,
    12, 197n14; commodification of
    culture, 26, 211n16; Jameson on,
    202n54; late-capitalist identity
    formation, 8; late-capitalist state
    violence, 72–4
Castellanos, Rosario, 101–2, 105, 107,
    110, 210n7, 211n17, 212n27. *See also*
    Oficio de tinieblas
Castillo, Ana, 39
Castillo, Debra, 105, 211n16
Castro, Fidel, 135–6, 153–4
Chabram, Angie, 203n5
Chamula, 102, 104, 106, 112–32,
    211n18
Chatman, Seymour, 211–212n22
Cheng, Anne Anlin, 21, 23–4
Cherniavsky, Eva, 68, 75–6, 199n24,
    205n9
Chicana feminism, x, 39, 41, 44–50,
    52–4, 164, 204n11. *See also La
    Malinche*
Chicana lesbian identity, 39, 41, 44–50,
    54, 56–7
Chicana/o movement: Aztlán/México
    as homeland, 57–9; critique of white
    culture, 203n5; cultural nationalism
    in, x, 53, 57–61; patriarchal ideology
    and, 42–3, 48–9, 50–3, 56; racial
    categories and, 54–6; racialized body
    in, 27–8; realism in, 204n15
Chow, Rey: on biopower, 199n28; on
    colonialist residue, 52; critique of

culturalism, 6–7, 18–20; on ethnicity,
    21; on identity, 22, 200n32; on
    liberalist alibi, 19; on narrative
    instrumentality of women, 35; on
    resistance, 21–2; on stereotypes, 14,
    198n19, 199n24, 199n27
chusmería, 188–9
Cisneros, Sandra, 39
Clifford, James, 3, 31, 201n45
Clough, Patricia, 12, 198n16
Colectivo Acciones de Arte (CADA), 10
collective/collectivity. *See* community
colonialism: anthropological discourse
    and, 199n24; appropriation of
    native lands, 85; colonialist history
    in *La Malinche*, 52; creoles and,
    209n5; fatalism and, 210n7;
    indigenous groups as cultural other,
    76, 105, 198n19, 204–5n2, 211n17;
    Manichean binary logic and, 87;
    modernity and, 208–9n34; parable
    of the precolonial Gunadeeyahs in
    Almanac, 97; racial ontology in, 79
community: collective identification,
    20; collective remembering, 169;
    crises of equilibrium in, 51–2; exile
    communities, 59, 141, 148–55,
    168–9, 212n2, 215n9; femininity
    and, 42–3, 48–9, 68, 125–6, 136, 166;
    irony as social differentiation, 14–6;
    masculinist/heterosexist community
    coherence, 41, 44, 50, 60–1;
    oppositional identity and, 44–50, 54,
    59, 61–2; performance and, 11–3;
    productive vs. reductive production
    of, 1–2, 198n17; racial genealogy
    and, 57–60, 136; sent/unsent letters
    and, 149–52; shame and, 56, 58–9;
    tribal community, 60, 67–8, 75–6.
    See also belonging/betrayal
Coopan, Vilashini, xiii, 159–60
Cornejo-Polar, Antonio, 108–9,
    115
Cortéz, Hernán, 98
cover stories, 208n29
criollo (Spanish purity), 105–6

cultural criticism: Chilean *crítica
cultural* movement, 72; critique as
allegory, 33; cultural studies and,
196n6, 197n10; disidentification, 22;
importance of genre in, 29; status of
allegory in, 7
culturalism, 6–7, 18–20, 30, 105, 199n27
cultural studies, 2, 36–7, 196n6, 197n10

Dangarembga, Tsitsi, 208–9n34
Def Poetry Jam: allegorical
irony/hyperbole and, 6; audience
affect shifts and, 9, 15; identity in,
1–2, 35, 69, 198n17, 200n34; ironic
distancing and, 7–8, 10, 13, 15–6;
technologies of selfhood and, 21
de la Peña, Terri, 39, 43–51, 60, 65, 69,
166–7
de Lauretis, Teresa, 17, 198–9n23
Deleuze, Gilles, 12, 205n5
de los Angeles Torres, María, 215n9
del Sarto, Ana, 196n6, 197n10
del Valle, Mayda, 17–8, 35, 199n24
de Man, Paul, 138, 175
Derrida, Jacques, 17
dialogism: dialogic structure in *Café
Nostalgia*, 161; dialogic voicing in
Oficio, 113–7, 121–4, 211–12n22;
letters as dialogic commentaries,
149–52; in novelistic discourse,
19–20. *See also* Bakhtin, Mikhail
diaspora: allegory and, 21, 30, 159–60;
collective trauma and, 173–4; Cuban
diaspora, 136–8, 150–5, 159–60, 164,
166, 168–9, 173–4, 184–7, 191,
212n1–2, 215n5, 216n11; cultural
amnesia, 185–6, 191; diasporic
cultural production, 187; diasporic
sexuality, 151–2, 155–6, 166;
Dominican diaspora, 163, 166,
176–9; exile communities, 59, 141,
148–55, 168–9, 212n2; local vs.
diasporic knowledge, 187; "lost
paradise" discourse, 153;
memory/nostalgia and, 63–4,
139–41, 143, 169, 176, 183–8, 191;

queer diasporas, 165; racialized
body as marker, 59; witness role in,
164, 167–8. *See also* exile
Díaz, Junot, 30
disidentification, 22, 42, 196n8, 215n6

Elliott, Jane, 202n53, 206n15
Eltit, Diamela, xi, 200n37
emblem-books, 5
Eng, David, 24–5, 144–5
epic everyday, 142, 214n14
epistemological crisis, 33–5, 51–2
Espinoza, Dionne, 57, 204n11
ethnicity: aesthetic theories of,
202–3n57; categories of naming
and, 13; diaspora narratives and, 30;
epistemological understanding and,
48; ethnic identity politics, 68;
ethnic literature, 29–30, 201n46,
202–3n57; ethnic masculinity, 8,
171; ethnonationalism, 206n11;
indigenismo, vii, 57–61; oppositional
identity and, 44–50, 54, 59, 61–2;
racialized body in, 6, 27–8, 47;
reproduction by genres, 108–9; self-
representation and, 17;
transnational *latinidad*, 142, 185,
215n8. *See also* racial identity
ethnography, 31, 110, 201n45
exile: exile communities, 59, 141,
148–55, 168–9, 212n1–2, 215n9;
exile wounds, 144, 173; exilic
melancholy, 156–9; exilic memory,
164, 167, 168, 186, 188; exilic
romance in *Café Nostalgia*, 151–2,
155–6, 172; exilic subjectivity, 21,
137, 139–41, 160–1, 175–6;
"migrant" compared with, 213n10.
See also diaspora

familia, 42–3, 50–3, 56, 58, 136–8.
See also home
Fanon, Frantz, 52, 208–9n34
fascism, xii
Felman, Shoshana, 138, 156
Felski, Rita, 204n14

feminine/femininity: body alienation and, 56–7; Chicana sexual identity, 40, 44; community and, 42–3, 48–9, 68, 125–6, 136, 166; female agency in *Oficio*, 128; feminine characters in *Almanac*, 91–3; Latina sexual stereotype, 17–8, 142, 214n14; transgressive female sexuality, 41, 44, 51–2, 61, 166, 212n27. *See also* Chicana lesbian identity; *La Malinche*; lesbian identity; sexual identity
feminism, ix–x, 35–6, 40–4
Fletcher, Angus, 29
Foucault, Michel, viii, xv, 4, 12, 13, 19, 59, 195n3 (Preface), 196n5, 199n28
Fox, Claire, xi
Franco, Jean, 210n8
Fregoso, Rosa, 203n5
Freud, Sigmund, 23–4, 145, 147, 156, 182
frontier thesis, 82
Fusco, Coco, ix–x

Ganguly, Keya, 187
Garcia, Cristina, 136
García-Moreno, Laura, 202n50, 211n16
gavacho cultural type, 53, 54, 58
gender: *Almanac* as gendered allegory, 91–2; Asian American masculinity, 8; exclusion of women in *Oficio*, 125–8, 209n3, 211n15; *La Malinche* as paradigm, viii, 50, 60; Latino masculinity, 189–90; Tropicana drag-on-drag metaperformances, 216n10; woman as betrayer in *Oficio*, 104
Genette, Gerard, 211–212n22
genre, 17, 29–30, 69, 108–9, 207n20. *See also* literature
George, Rosemary, 49
Golubov, Nattie, 144, 148
Gopinath, Gayatri, 188–9
Greene, Shane, 195n1
Grewal, Inderpal, 35

Guattari, Félix, 205n5
güera racial category, 54–5

Hallward, Peter, 36, 202–3n57
Hansen, Mark, 1–2, 10, 11, 197n11
Haraway, Donna, 204n11
Hardt, Michael, 195n1
Hariman, Robert, x, 192
Hegel, Georg Wilhelm Friedrich, 206n12
Hijuelos, Oscar, 136
Hirsch, Marianne, 168, 215n4
history: allegorical appropriation of, 32, 78, 90, 206n15, 208n33; colonialism in *La Malinche*, 52; female identity and, 36; historical crisis, 33–5; historical truth, 31, 200–1n38; historical vs. revolutionary time, 83–5; memory and, 167–8; narrated selfhood and, 137; as unsymbolizable global process, x. *See also* mourning; trauma
home: Chicana/o political discourse of (Aztlán), 57–9, 60–1; Chicanas and, 48–9, 62–6; as masculinist discourse of exclusion, 203n3; narratives of, 42–3, 63–4, 65, 143, 176, 212n1, 213n10, 216n11; as narrative teleology, 49, 70; nostalgia/memory and, 143–4, 160, 164. *See also familia*
homophobia, 63
Honig, Bonnie, 60, 62–3
How the García Girls Lost Their Accents (Alvarez), 176–8, 181–3
Hutcheon, Linda, 14–5
hybridity, 25, 27, 165, 189

identification: assemblage, 9, 12, 197n12, 197–8n15, 200n34; collective identification, 20, 36, 60–1; conflicts in, 42–3, 48, 54; disidentification, 22, 42, 196n8, 215n6; "home" image and, 42; identificatory logic and, 21, 51, 76; melancholy subjectivity and, 25;

identification (*cont.*)
as narrative technology, 87–8; raced image and, 1–2, 11, 197n11; reading and, 27, 88; self-enclosure in, 44–5; self-identification discourses, 17, 22; suspension and, 27, 54–5; wounding and, 173. *See also* identity; stereotype; subjectivity; suspension

identity: aesthetic supplement/excess in, 34–5; allegorical identity/subjectivity, 29, 73–4, 75–6, 87–90, 205n9; binary paradigms of, 8; diasporic selfhood, 21; *familia*/home image and, 62; identity binding, 9; identity politics, 23, 34; images as basis of, 10–1; in indigenous social movements, vii; liberalism and, xiii–xiv, 12, 20; narrative writing/reading and, 137; oscillation and, 21, 30, 186; postidentity, 29; poststructuralist identity, 200n32; self-dramatization, 142–6; self-representation, 8–9, 13–4, 16–17; "simulated regime" of, 75–6; structures of feeling and, 3–4, 20, 22, 195n3 (Chap. 1), 200n32; subjectivation and, 201n39; suppression of exilic self, 186; technologies of the self, xv, 4, 13, 17, 19, 196n5; in transamerican dead zones, 75; wounded attachments and, 20–1, 25, 59. *See also* ethnicity; identification; lesbian identity; racial identity; stereotype; subjectivity; suspension

indigeneity: absorption of colonial discourses, 112–3; in *Almanac*, 69, 76, 85–6; Chamula, 102, 104, 106, 112–32, 211n18; discourses of exclusion and, 103, 209n3, 211n15; human rights paradigm and, vii, 195n1; liberalism and, vii, 118–25; mythical thought and, 79, 83; *Oficio* racial categories and, 103; premodern "Indian" figure of, 105, 204–5n2, 210n10; representational

strategies in, xiii, 106, 108, 118. *See also mestizaje*; racial identity

indigenismo: Chicano/as and, 57–61, 204n13; *indigenista* narrative, 105–7, 211n17; materialist critique of, 204n12; new *indigenismo*, 107–8; as Westernized discourse, 108

intersubjectivity, 147–8

irony: community solidarity and, 14–6; figurative vs. literal reading and, 138–41; ironic distancing, 7–11, 14–5; ironic performative citation, 2, 7, 14–5, 34, 77–8; kitsch, 159–60, 193; media affect and, 12–3; narrative tone in *Café Nostalgia*, 159; omniscient narration and, 119, 124; oscillation and, 2; parodic irony in *Milk of Amnesia*, 188–9, 192; as performative act, 71, 77–8, 198n20, 205n6; prophecy and, 77–8; self-representation and, 13–4, 16–7; social hierarchies and, 198n21; stereotype compared with, 14–5

Irr, Caren, 83

James, Henry, 207n23

Jameson, Frederic: on allegory, 3, 5, 6, 31, 78; capitalism as paradigmatic in, 202n54; on epistemological crisis, 33–4; on identity and language, 18; on stereotypes, 14, 198n19

JanMohammed, Abdul, 76, 206n12

Joseph, Miranda, 198n17

Kaplan, Ann, E., 168

Kaplan, Caren, 203n9

Kaup, Monika, xii, 207n21

Kazanjian, David, 24–5, 144–5

Keith, Michael, 187

Kierkegaard, Søren, 98, 198n21

kitsch, 159–60, 193

Ladinos, 102, 104, 111–30

La Fountain-Stokes, Lawrence, 215n7

La Malinche: Chicana lesbian bicultural body and, 56–7; Chicano cultural nationalism and, x, 60–1; as gender allegory, viii, x, 40–1, 50, 52, 60; *Gulf Dreams* narrator as, 64; narrative reappropriation of, 45; Veronica (*Margins*) as, 49–50. *See also* Chicana feminism

language: allegorical subversion of, 29–30; collective "we" narrator voicing, 177–9; culturalized identity and, 18–19; dialogism and, 19–20; direct discourse in narration, 119, 211–212n22; *español quechizado* (Quechua-fied Spanish), 110, 210n14; in *indigenista* narratives, 113–4; interanimation and, 199n29; language of return in *García Girls*, 176; Mayan speech genres in *Oficio*, 102–4, 114–5, 209n2, 211n20; paternal voicing in *¡Yo!*, 180, 182–3; perlocutionary acts, 198n20; Spanish language, 102, 110, 113, 121, 210n14, 211n18

late modernity, 51–2, 72–5, 78, 81, 154, 207n20. *See also* modernity

Lathan, Stan, 7

Latina/o identity: indigenous social movements and, vii; Latina sexual stereotype, 17–8, 142; "Latino as excess" stereotype, 196n4; racial categories and, 170; trauma/melancholia and, 26

latinidad, 142, 185, 215n8

lesbian identity: masculine competition and, 171; oppositional identity and, 61–2; as outsider sexuality, 54, 164–5; sexual transgression and, 166–70. *See also* Chicana lesbian identity; sexual identity

Levinas, Emmanuel, 148

liberalism: allegory and, 3, 34; "cathartic" literary experience and, 32; Chicana feminism and, 41, 43; culturalism and, 19, 199n27; *Def Poetry Jam* pedagogical intent and, 7–8; ethnographic study of, 201n45;

feminism and, ix; identity and, xiii–xiv, 12, 14, 17, 19–21, 65; indigenous groups and, vii, 118–25; individualism and, 80, 87; Latin American critique of, vii, 72; liberal reading in *Oficio*, 102–3; postsubject technologies and, 13, 19; raced images and, 15, 197n11; War on Terror and, ix–x. *See also* multiculturalism

literature: canonical citation in *Def Poetry Jam*, 15–6; ethics of representation in *Oficio*, 102; ethnic literature, 29–30, 201n46; interanimation of languages in, 199n29; as mirror of reality, 48–9; novelistic discourse, 19–20; as performance, xiv, 99–100; as resistance, 206n16; social realist *indigenismo*, 107; storytelling and, 200n37. *See also* allegory; apocalyptic narrative; genre

Lowe, Lisa, 165

Lubiano, Wahneema, 208n29

Madsen, Deborah, xiii, 30

Manichean allegory: colonialism and, 87; ideological narrative, 86, 208n29; Manichean epistemology in *Almanac*, 68; Manichean race war in *Almanac*, 72, 79, 86–7, 95, 97–8, 206n12; racial ontology and, 76, 79; subversion/reversal strategies for, 6, 80

Mannoni, A. O., 206n12

Mardorossian, Carine, 213n10

Margins (de la Peña), 43–51, 65, 69. *See also* de la Peña, Terri

Mariátegui, José Carlos, 108–9

Martin, Biddy, 49, 62

Marx, Karl, 33, 87

Massumi, Brian, 12

Mbembe, Achille, xi, 70, 72, 74, 96, 123

McCullough, Kate, 170–1

melancholia: cultural trauma and, 21–6; dominant identity and, 201n39;

melancholia (*cont.*)
 exilic sexuality and, 157–9; exilic
  subjectivity and, 140, 144–5, 151;
  melancholic allegory, 200–201n38;
  memory and, 24–5, 144–5, 214n18;
  resistance and, 24–7; structures of
  feeling and, 22
memory: capitalist logic of substitution
  and, 26; collective remembering,
  169; Collective Unconscious
  Memory Appropriation Attack
  (CUMMA), 183–93; cultural
  amnesia, 185–6, 191; as destructive
  to identity, 185, 187, 191; in diaspora
  narrative, 139–40, 143–7; diasporic
  loss and, 168–9, 172, 174–5, 180–3,
  191; diasporic sexuality and, 166;
  exilic memory, 164, 168, 186, 188;
  forgotten (unconscious) desire, 156;
  home/*familia* in diaspora narrative,
  30, 36, 136–8, 143–4, 160, 164;
  melancholia and, 24–5, 144–5,
  214n18; memory/identity "screens,"
  21, 182; postmemory, 168, 173–4;
  "queer" vs. "feminist" approach to,
  176–7; reading as nostalgic practice,
  142–4, 146–7; transmission vs.
  representation of, xiii–xiv. *See
  also* history; mourning; nostalgia;
  trauma
Memory Mambo (Obejas), 21, 166–70,
  172–3, 183
Mercado, Tununa, 200n37
mestizaje: Chicana/o identity and, 27,
  40, 203n6; *criollo* (Spanish purity)
  and, 105–6; cultural authenticity
  and, 47; hegemony of genres and,
  108–9; mixed-race body, 56–7, 59;
  racial/historical burden and, 55–6,
  60–1; racial melancholia and, 25.
  See also indigeneity; racial identity
Milk of Amnesia (Tropicana), 165,
  167–8, 173, 183–93
Miller, Hillis, 144
Minh-ha, Trinh T., 199n24, 201n45
Moallem, Minoo, 203n9

modernity: colonialism and,
  208–9n34; cultural survival and,
  107, 210n10; fatalism and, 210n7;
  historical time and, 83; *mestizaje*
  affiliation with, 106; national
  sovereignty and, 85;
  oppositional/subversive discourses
  and, 204n14. *See also* late modernity
Mohanty, Chandra, 49
Mohanty, Satya, 200n32
Montezuma, 98
Moraga, Cherríe: allegorical practices
  in, 65; on Chicana lesbian identity,
  39, 41, 44, 164; on Chicana/o racial
  categories, 54–6; on Chicano
  cultural nationalism, 53, 57–62;
  critique of hybridity, 27–8; on "la
  Chicanada," 45, 57–8; on materialist
  identity scripts, xv; on outsider
  sexualities, 54, 164–5
Moraña, Mabel, xii
Morris, Rosalind, 69
Morrison, Tony, 28
Mos Def, 10, 15
mourning, 23–6, 27, 182, 200n35,
  206n15, 207n18. *See also*
  melancholia; memory; trauma
Moya, Paula, 200n32, 204n11
multiculturalism, 7–8, 19, 41, 56–7,
  199n27. *See also* liberalism
Muñoz, José, xiii–xiv, 142, 164, 184–7,
  196n4, 196n8, 215n6
Muñoz, Ricardo, 72
Murrin, Michael, 77–8, 90, 94, 206n13
myth, 79, 83, 112–3, 118, 128, 164, 167

naming, 13, 65
narrative: allegory as reductive mode
  of, 3; antihumanist techniques,
  207n20; author vs. narrator voicing,
  207n22; character density, 71;
  character subjectivity, 87–9;
  collective "we" narration, 177–9;
  damaged/unreliable narrators,
  139–41, 213n9; dialogic voicing,
  113–7, 121–4, 211–12n22; diasporic

memory loss and, 180–3; direct
discourse in, 119, 211–212n22;
home image as narrative teleology,
70; ideological narrative, 86, 208n29;
indigenista narrative, 105–7, 211n17;
interior texts, 149–52, 160–1;
narrative authority, 103–4, 114–7,
121–4; narrative recycling, 89,
208n32; narrative tone, 159;
omniscient narration, 112–3, 118–9,
123–4; palimpsestic narration, 146,
183; progress narratives, 45, 50–1,
63–5, 80, 83; self-dramatization as
exemplary experience, 142–5;
sexuality as narrative disruption,
64–5; social transformation and, 41,
64–5, 69, 87, 198–9n23; storytelling,
200n37; suspension and, 26–7; text
as unconscious testimony, 156;
textual accounting, 137;
transnational pathways of, vii–viii
narrativity, xii–xiii, 16–7, 20–1, 34–5
National Indigenist Institute (INI),
107, 210n10
nation/state: allegory and, xii–xiii;
Almanac critique of, 81–2; in
Anzaldúa, 61–2; biopower and,
199n28; birth as enactment of,
205n7; colonialism and, 208–9n34;
creoles and, 209n5; diaspora and,
141, 146, 153–4, 160, 213n10,
213n12; ethnonationalism, 206n11;
identity and, 20–1, 165; laws as
discursive forms, 118–25; literary
novel and, xiii, 159–60; sovereignty
and, 85; threshold areas of, 73, 82;
transculturation and, 110; women in
patriarchal nationalism, 53, 203n9
Native American holocaust, 78–9
necropolitics, 70, 82, 84–5, 195n3
(Preface), 206n16
necropower, xi, 195n3 (Preface)
Negri, Antonio, 195n1
neoliberalism. *See* liberalism
New World Baroque. *See* Baroque
Ngugi Wa Thiong'o, 208–9n34

nostalgia, 139–41, 142–4, 146–7, 169.
See also Café Nostalgia; melancholia;
memory
novels: allegorical appropriation of, 32;
Almanac as realist novel, 205n5;
ideological novels (*romans à thèse*),
51, 204n15; nation and, xiii, 159–60;
novelistic discourse (Bakhtin),
19–20; psychological mimesis in, 88,
208n31; as a "Western sign," 115

Obejas, Achy, 136, 164, 166–7, 216n11.
See also Memory Mambo
O'Connell, Joanna, 118, 128, 210n10,
212n27
Oficio de tinieblas (Castellanos):
alleged culturalism of, 105–6, 132;
apocalyptic conclusion, 128–32;
critical responses to, 110–1, 118,
130–2; dialogic voicing, 113–7,
121–4, 211–12n22; discourses of
exclusion in, 103, 125–8, 209n3,
211n15; hegemonic discourses in,
112–3; plot synopsis, 111–2; racial
categories and, 102–3; significance
of title, 104
oppositional identity, 44–50, 54, 59,
61–3
Ortiz, Fernando, 107, 110
Ortiz, Ricardo, 174, 213n13
oscillation: allegorical logic and, x, 96;
identity oscillation in *Def Poetry
Jam*, 2; narrative oscillation and the
self, xv, 29–30, 147; racial and sexual
identity oscillation, 46, 54;
suspension as, 26–9, 54–5. *See also*
suspension

parody, 183
passing, 27
Patton, Cindy, 165
Paz, Octavio, 40
Perdomo, Willie, 6
Pérez, Emma, 39, 64–5, 204n15
Pérez, Laura, 208n32
Pérez-Torres, Rafael, 44–5, 48

performativity: acts of violence as, 74; anti-positivist approach in, viii; audience affect shifts and, 9, 15, 18–9; "camp" performative genre, 185; ironic performativity, 2, 7, 14–5, 34, 77–8, 198n20; narrative performativity, 115; performative techniques in *Milk of Amnesia*, 186–91; perlocutionary acts, 198n20; scenarios, ix, 9, 196n9; suspension and, 14; Tropicana drag-on-drag metaperformances, 216n10

Phelan, James, 88, 90, 207n22, 208n31
Phillips, Adam, 147–8, 182, 214n18
Pile, Steve, 187
postidentity, 29
postmemory, 168, 173–4, 215n4
postmodernity. *See* late modernity
poststructuralism, 200n32
Pratt, Mary Louise, 35, 201n45
predetermined signified: allegorical representation and, 30–3; identity narratives and, 21; in minority fiction culturalist narrative, 80; narrative suspension of, 4; overlapping narrative in *Almanac* and, 71–2; in progress narratives, 45, 50–2; sexual transgression as, 166
prophecy, 67–9, 71–2, 77–8, 206n14
Propp, Vladimir, 198–9n23
Prosser, Jay, 56–7
Proust, Marcel, 140, 145
psychoanalysis, 20, 156
Puar, Jasbir, 11–2, 65, 197n12, 197–8n15, 199n28, 200n34
public sphere: capitalism and, 19; democratic culture and, xi; exclusion of women in *Oficio*, 125–8, 209n3; privileged discourses in, 4; progressive artist collectives and, 10; transamerican dead zones, 73–4; transgressive sexuality and, 51; trauma/melancholia and, 26, 202n50

queer: anticolonial nationalism and, 55, 58, 60; authenticity and, 43;

chusmería, 188–9; home/*familia* and, 42, 62–3; insider/outsider discourse and, 44–50, 61; *La Malinche* and, 40, 61; in *Milk of Amnesia*, 184, 190; queer autobiography, 39–40, 215n7; queer diasporas, 165; queerness as an assemblage, 197n12, 197–8n15, 200n34; transgressive identity and, 25

racial identity: allegorical performance of, 1–3; categories of naming and, 6, 13; Chicana feminist writing and, 40–1; creoles, 209n5; *criollo* (Spanish purity) and, 105–6; cross-racial desire, 45–7, 49–50; culturalism and, 6–7, 18–9; *indigenismo*, 57–61; Ladinos, 102, 104, 111–30; Latina/o racial categories, 54–6, 170; Mexican racial categories, 102; mixed-race body, 56–7, 59; oppositional identity and, 62; passing, 27; raced images in *Def Poetry Jam*, 15, 197n11; race war in *Almanac*, 72, 79, 86–7, 94–5, 97–8; racial "double bind" in the United States, 42; racial melancholia, 22–5; racial visibility, 11; reproduction by genres, 108–9. *See also* ethnicity; hybridity; *mestizaje*; racialization
racialization: community/collective and, 28, 68, 86; mixed racialization, 55; racialized body, 23, 27–8, 47, 59; racial melancholia, 23–4; sexual desire and, 47, 55–6. *See also* ethnicity; hybridity; *mestizaje*; racial identity
Rama, Angel, 107, 108, 110, 210n14
rasquache aesthetics, 208n32
reading: allegorical irony/hyperbole and, 4, 6; apocalyptic narrative and, 99–100, 133, 212n26; discursive citation and, 102–3; as dreaming, 148–9; intersubjectivity and, 147–8, 152; late modern reading practices, 138; as nostalgic practice, 142–4, 146–7; performance vs., xiv; as

psychoanalysis, 156; reader/character social imbalance, 106, 108, 118; reader/witness role, 99–100, 133; slow reading, 144. *See also* literature; writing

Reagon, Bernice Johnson, 65

realism, 70, 107, 110–1, 200n32, 204n15, 205n5, 207n23

recognition theory, 1–2, 21–2, 125, 149

representation: aesthetic supplement/excess in, 34–5; allegorical representation, 69, 80, 202n56; autobiographical self-representation, 8–9, 69, 142–5, 215n7; diasporic emblematization, 159–60; historical truth, 31, 200–1n38; images as basis for, 10–1; literature as mirror, 48–9; "master code" interpretive approach, 33; narrative transmission compared with, xiv; reader/character social imbalance, 106, 108, 118; suspension as device of irony, 13–4. *See also* predetermined signified; stereotype

resistance: aesthetic production and, 36–7, 202–3n57; allegorical aesthetics and, vii, 5, 7, 34–5, 76, 79–87; identity and, 20–2, 59, 61–2, 164–5; melancholy and, 24–6; modernity and, 204n14; narrative as, 74–5, 78–9, 206n16, 207n18, 208n29; predetermined signifieds and, 31–2; realism and, 204n15; revolutionary consciousness, 118; revolutionary time, 83–5; sexual transgression and, 51–2, 166; suspension and, 26–7; to "terror of freedom," 21–2

Richard, Nelly: on aesthetic production, 36, 72; on allegory as resistance, 5, 7; cultural critique in, 72–3; on disidentity, 73–4; on the liberal "cathartic" effect, 32; on *testimonio*, 200–201n38; transnational paradigm and, xii; violence/trauma in, 26, 65

Richardson, Brian, 207n20

Riley, Denise, 13–4, 16–8, 20

Rilke, Rainer Maria, 161

Roman, David, 190

Romero, Lora, 53–4, 204n11

Roof, Judith, 51

Rousseau, Jean-Jacques, 105

Sánchez, Rosaura, 204n11

Sánchez-Eppler, Benigno, 165

Santiago, Esmeralda, 30

Sarduy, Severo, 159–60

scenarios, ix, 9, 196n9

Schein, Louisa, 166, 188

sexual identity: community identity and, 39, 44, 52, 61; cross-racial desire, 45–7, 49–50; diasporic sexuality, 151–2, 155–6, 166; exclusionary identity and, 47–8; exilic melancholy and, 156–9; homosexual fetishes in *Almanac*, 84–5; *La Malinche* paradigmatic sexuality, 17–18, 40, 64; Latina sexual stereotype, 17–8, 142, 214n14; outsider sexuality, 54, 164–5; political vs. sexual (mis)alliance, 42; reading as intimate intersubjectivity, 147–8, 152, 155; residual desires and, 182; sexuality of displacement, 179–80; transgressive sexual identity, 41, 44, 51–2, 61, 166, 208n27. *See also* Chicana lesbian identity

shame, 56, 58–9

Shih, Shu-Mei, 3, 4, 6–7, 21, 30–1, 35, 41, 45, 202n50

Sia, Beau, 1, 8–9, 15, 21, 35

Silko, Leslie Marmon, vii, xi–xii, 125, 132, 207n20–21. *See also Almanac of the Dead*

Simmons, Russell, 10

social order/social formations: Chicana/o status in, 27; contingency vs. complicity in, 200n34; control of affect by, 197n14; discipline vs. control in, 198n16; hegemonic

social order/social formations (*cont.*)
    capacity of genres, 108–9; hegemonic
    colonial discourses, 83; melancholy
    and, 22–6; neoliberal power
    regimes, 72; scapegoating by,
    201n39; tropicalization discourse
    and, 83. *See also* whiteness
Sommer, Doris, 3, 115, 148
Sommers, Joseph, 111, 118
specular epistemology, 199n24
Spenser, Edmund, 206n14
Spivak, Gayatri, xiii, 35
stereotype: abstract other and, 105,
    198n19, 204–5n2, 211n17; as
    allegorical representation, 3–4, 17,
    78–9, 88; colonialism and, 199n24;
    as cross-cultural communication,
    14; disidentification and, 22, 42,
    196n8, 215n6; irony and, 7–8, 14–5;
    "Latino as excess" stereotype, 196n4;
    novelistic destabilizing of, 117–8;
    predetermined signifieds and, 30–2;
    subjectivation and, 201n39;
    tolerance discourse and, 19. *See also*
    identification; identity
Stoler, Ann Laura, 196n5, 199n28
structures of feeling, 3–4, 20, 22, 37,
    195n3 (Chap. 1), 200n32. *See also*
    affect
subjectivity: celebratory readings of,
    25; exilic subjectivity, 21, 137,
    139–41, 160–1, 175–6;
    instrumentalization of life, 73;
    postsubject technologies and, 13, 19;
    subjectivation, 27, 201n39. *See also*
    identification; identity
Sulieman, Susan, 51
suspension: ambivalence as, 24;
    apocalyptic suspension, 96; in
    autobiographical narration, 141,
    157; as device of irony, 12–4;
    evacuation of identity and, 197n11;
    identity politics and, 2;
    interdependence of psychic and
    political structures, 28–9; as
    oscillation, 26–9, 54–5; parodic

suspension, 193; "suspended selves"
    paradox, 1–2, 8. *See also*
    identification; identity; oscillation

Taylor, Diana, ix, xiii–xiv, 9, 196n9
technologies of selfhood, xv, 4, 13, 17,
    19, 21, 196n5
testimonio, 200–201n38, 202n50
textual accounting, 137
Think Again!, 10
Third World allegory, 6, 31, 45
transculturation, 107, 109–10, 112–3,
    118. *See also* assimilation
translation, 103
transnationalism: in *Almanac*, 72;
    American imaginary and, xi–xii, 2;
    in *Milk of Amnesia*, 191–2;
    Transamerica, 5, 29; transamerican
    dead zones, 73–4, 154; transmission
    of narratives and, vii–viii;
    transnational *latinidad*, 142, 185,
    215n8
trauma, 22–6, 65, 168, 173–4, 202n50,
    215n3–4. *See also* melancholia;
    memory; mourning
tribal community, 60, 67–8
tropicalization, 83
Tropicana, Carmelita (Alina Troyano),
    164–6, 175, 189–91, 216n10,
    216n12. *See also Milk of Amnesia*
Troyano, Alina (Carmelita Tropicana).
    See Tropicana, Carmelita
Turner, Frederick Jackson, 82

Valdés, Zoé, xii, 36, 135–8, 146, 172,
    185, 212n1, 213n8. *See also Café
    Nostalgia*
Vargas Llosa, Mario, 114, 210n7,
    211n15
Vasquez, Alexandra, 142, 214n14
ventriloquism, 102
Villarejo, Amy, xiv, 10, 197n14

Ween, Lori, 201n46
whiteness: Chicana lesbian
    oppositional identity and, 44–6;

Chicana/o critique of, 203n5; Chicana/o tradition and, 52–3; cross-racial desire and, 45–7, 49–50; *gavacho* cultural type, 53, 54, 58; lesbian sexuality and, 54; melancholia and, 23, 201n39; "national affect" of whiteness, 196n4; shame in whiteness, 58–9, 63; white feminist hegemony, 41–4, 204n11. *See also* social order/social formations

Williams, Raymond, 3–4, 20, 195n3 (Chap. 1), 200n32

witnessing, 99–100, 133, 164, 167–8, 171–2

Wittgenstein, Ludwig, 18

wounding: exile and, 144, 173; historical wounding, 27; *La Malinche* and, 40; nostalgia and, 138; wounded attachments, 20–1, 25, 34, 59; wounded narcissism, 127–8, 144

writing: authority of, 125, 130–1; female-writing figure in *Oficio*, 126–7, 129; oral culture and, 106, 124, 125; self vs. collective and, 137; sent and unsent letters, 129, 149–52. *See also* literature; narrative; reading; representation

Yaegar, Patricia, 208n32

Yarbro-Bejarano, Yvonne, 190, 216n10

¡Yo! (Alvarez), 176, 180

Zamora, Hilly Nelly, 94–5, 141, 209n35

Zamora, Lois Parkinson, xii, 94, 207n21, 212n26

Zapatista movement, viii, 67–8, 209n3

Zebadúa-Yañez, Véronica, 73–4, 82

Zizek, Slavov, 21–2